Metals

and

How to Weld Them

SECOND EDITION

By

T. B. Jefferson

Publisher, WELDING ENGINEER
PUBLICATIONS, INC.

Editor, THE WELDING ENCYCLOPEDIA

and

Gorham Woods

Metallurgist

This book may be ordered directly from

THE JAMES F. LINCOLN ARC WELDING FOUNDATION

CLEVELAND 17, OHIO

Published by

THE JAMES F. LINCOLN ARC WELDING FOUNDATION

First Printing 10,000, February, 1954
Second Printing 20,000, March, 1955

SECOND EDITION

First Printing 10,000, January, 1962
Second Printing 10,000, December, 1962
Third Printing 10,000, December, 1963
Fourth Printing 10,000, February, 1965
Fifth Printing 10,000, February, 1966
Sixth Printing 20,000, January, 1967
Seventh Printing 20,000, January, 1969
Eighth Printing 8,500, June, 1970
Ninth Printing 15,000, June, 1971
Tenth Printing 15,000, September, 1972
Eleventh Printing 20,000, October, 1973
Twelfth Printing 10,000, December, 1974
Thirteenth Printing 10,000, December, 1975
Fourteenth Printing 15,000, June, 1976
Fifteenth Printing 10,000, June, 1977
Sixteenth Printing 5,000, January, 1978
Seventeenth Printing 10,000, June, 1978
Eighteenth Printing-December 1978
Nineteenth Printing 15,000, December, 1979

Other Books published by The Lincoln Arc Welding Foundation

"Design of Weldments," this complete design manual relates both theoretical and practical information through formula review, load analysis and problem solving using practical application examples, 432 pages, 8½ x 11 inch page size, over 1200 illustrations, charts, drawings and nomographs, $5.00.

"Design Ideas for Weldments," Volume 1—Weldment design ideas abstracted from 56 outstanding design entries in the Foundation-sponsored professional award program. Hundreds of tested answers for design problems related to cost, vibration, impact, appearance, machining, strength and rigidity, 156 pages, over 190 illustrations and tables, 8½ x 11 inch page size, $2.00.

"Design of Welded Structures," an 832 page reference handbook containing theoretical analysis and practical solutions for all types of design problems in arc welded structures. 8½ x 11 inch page size, over 1500 illustrations, charts, drawings and nomographs. $7.00

"Modern Welded Structures," Volume II—A series of reports reviewing current design approaches to buildings, bridges and other structures. These structural ideas were abstracted from the design entries of recognized structural design authorities in the Foundation-sponsored professional award program, 280 pages, 8½ x 11 inch page size, over 150 illustrations and tables, $2.50.

"Arc Welding Instructions for the Beginner" by H. A. Sosnin. This text contains a series of 21 basic skill instruction lessons for industrial vocational, apprentice and in-plant training. Discussions concentrate on describing the manipulative skills, 160 pages, $2.00.

LFB-2

Library of Congress Catalog Card Number: 54-2508

Printed in U.S.A.

The James F. Lincoln Arc Welding Foundation
Purposes, Activities, Organization

The James F. Lincoln Arc Welding Foundation is a non-profit educational organization established in 1936 by The Lincoln Electric Company through a deed of trust, "to encourage and stimulate scientific interest in, and scientific study, research, and education in respect of, the development of the arc welding industry through the advance in the knowledge of design and practical application of the arc welding process."

The Foundation's activities consist of both fostering the development of knowledge of arc welding and making this knowledge generally available at minimum cost. Its fields of activity are in schools, colleges, industry, business and agriculture.

In its award programs, the Foundation has made awards and provided scholarship funds for papers describing improvements and developments in arc welding and its application. Programs have been conducted covering all phases of manufacturing, design and research. Programs have been conducted to encourage design of welding highway bridges. A program for textbook manuscripts has produced three college texts. Other books have been published to present the information gathered in the various award programs.

Two award programs have been conducted to encourage farmers, agricultural leaders and educators to investigate how welding may contribute to improved farming methods. Two books were the direct results of this program, and two supplemental teaching manuals for farm welding were also developed. Strip film, manuals and project sheets have also been prepared for vocational agricultural training.

An annual design competition is conducted for college engineering undergraduates. An annual program for high school students is also sponsored. Engineering libraries have been established in over 250 accredited engineering schools in the United States.

TRUSTEES AND OFFICERS OF THE FOUNDATION

Inquiries about the Foundation and its work are welcomed and communications may be directed to:

THE JAMES F. LINCOLN
ARC WELDING FOUNDATION
CLEVELAND 17, OHIO

PREFACE TO FIRST EDITION

The authors prepared this volume to fill a need for those who are curious as to what happens when working with metals. Metals have become a most important part of our everyday life, yet few people know much about them. It is the feeling of the authors that a basic knowledge of metals will enable those working with metals to do a better job while using the materials to a better advantage.

No matter what type of work is being done on metals eventually there arises the problem of joining them. Since the only logical way to join metals for permanence is to weld them, the subjects of "Metals and How to Weld Them" seem to make a perfect combination for the better use of modern materials and methods.

"Metals and How to Weld Them" has been written for all who are interested in welding who want a better understanding of what takes place when welds are made. This volume has been designed as a text for classroom or home study use. It is equally well suited to serve as a reference book for the student, the craftsman or the engineer who must deal with welding, metals and their related problems.

All of the welding processes and their uses are discussed but the greatest emphasis has been placed on the basic fundamentals of metallurgy and the various metals that might be welded. Though metallurgy is generally considered a highly technical subject, the authors simplified the discussion of this subject to make it readily understandable, even though the reader may not have had prior knowledge of metallurgy. It has been the authors' desire to present this material in such a manner as to be understood by high school students should this book be used to supplement their study. By the same token, however, even a graduate engineer may obtain a better understanding of metals and metallurgy from this presentation.

The welding of various metals is discussed in separate chapters. The problems that may be encountered in welding any commercial metal, from aluminum to tool and die steels, are covered completely. There is a special chapter devoted to hardsurfacing and an extremely important chapter on how to make good welds. The Appendix, in addition to a weldor's dictionary, include a number of tables of useful information pertaining to welding.

No special credit has been given for the illustrations appearing in "Metals and How to Weld Them" because many of the photos used came from the unidentified photo files of THE WELDING ENGINEER. It is known however, that many of these were contributed by companies serving the welding industry. To these companies and other organizations serving the welding field the authors are deeply indebted for pictures and other data presented in this book.

CHICAGO, ILLINOIS

CLEVELAND, OHIO

JANUARY, 1954

T. B. JEFFERSON

GORHAM WOODS

PREFACE TO SECOND EDITION

The rapid advance of welding since the first edition of METALS AND HOW TO WELD THEM has produced new knowledge and understanding of welding techniques and procedures as they relate to specific metals. These developments dictated a complete review of the entire text to determine the need for and requirements of a second edition.

The first edition of METALS AND HOW TO WELD THEM sold 30,000 copies. Its unqualified acceptance readily justified the decision to print a completely revised second edition and make the changes and improvements necessary to maintain the text's reputation of being one of the foremost in its field.

Many sections have been completely rewritten. Editorial clarifications in language and sentence structure have been made on every page. Where appropriate, the text has been modified to reflect industry's trend toward welding mechanization. Almost all illustrations and data have been replaced or improved. An entirely new chapter on the exotic metals has been added. The book has been completely reset in a new, easier-to-read type face, and the headings have been restyled and rearranged to aid the reader by supplying an outline of subject matter coverage to quickly acquaint him with the chapter and serve as a guide for future reference. All of these changes have been made in the interest of easier reading and better understanding.

This major revision has not altered the book's basic purpose. Its objective remains unchanged: namely, to equip the average reader with a practical knowledge of the structure and properties of metals and how these metals adapt to welding. It is intended as a reference book for students, weldors, plant managers and engineers. To accomplish this, technical explanations and descriptions have been simplified for easier understanding.

The officers and trustees of The James F. Lincoln Arc Welding Foundation are grateful to Mr. T. B. Jefferson for his suggestions, editorial review and willingness to make available, for illustrations, the photo file of THE WELDING ENGINEER. Special acknowledgement is also made to the skill with which Mr. Watson Nordquist executed the major portion of the reorganization, restyling and writing of this second edition.

Charles G. Herbruck, Secretary

THE JAMES F. LINCOLN

ARC WELDING FOUNDATION

CLEVELAND, OHIO

NOVEMBER, 1961

TABLE OF CONTENTS

CHAPTER 1

WHAT'S THIS ALL ABOUT?

The progress of man really started at the time he began to use metals. Until man became the master of metals life was hard, cruel and difficult. Many people seem to think these conditions of life have not changed very much. But do you realize how much easier life is because of metals? Without metals many products we know as common necessities would be impossible, while other items would be very unsatisfactory substitutes by presentday standards.

Without metals our activities would depend on our ability to use wood and stone. Stone axes and hammers may have served the caveman, but they would not meet the needs of skilled craftsmen of today. With only stone and wood available as materials, practically all our modern conveniences would be non-existent. We would not have modern means of transportation—the automobile, ocean liner, train or airplane. Likewise, we would not have modern means of communication—the radio, telephone or television. In fact, we now depend so much on metals it is difficult to think of how we could live without them.

Early man probably discovered metals as a result of building his campfires on the sands of a desert or lake shore. These sands contained copper, and possibly tin or aluminum. The heat of the fire caused them to melt, and the hot molten metal flowed out over the sand. As the metal cooled, it hardened into a solid piece. It was then that early man realized he had a new material with which to work—a material we now know as metal. This metal was not in a very usable shape, just an icicle in the sand, but man soon learned that he could cast this metal in usable shapes by making small molds in the sand. Metal then became valuable.

We call the period of history when man was limited to the use of stone and wood, the Stone Age. His first experiences with metals led him into the Bronze Age. Bronze is a metallic material made up of copper and one or more other metals, like tin or zinc or aluminum, that melt at a relatively low temperature. And then, about 1400 years before Christ, people in Egypt and the countries of Asia Minor along the Mediterranean Sea began to use iron in making tools, weapons and other products. This was the beginning of the Iron Age of civilization.

In those early days, our ancestors could not always make castings in the exact shape desired. The small-village craftsman was unable to create enough heat to melt some metals for casting. Iron, for instance, requires much higher temperature to melt it than bronze does. So the ancient craftsman frequently hammered the rough casting into a more

1

useful shape. The use of heat made his job easier. This was man's first attempt at forging, and even today we have blacksmiths who still shape metal by hammering. It wasn't until about 200 years ago that man first developed machines with which he could make castings and forgings repeatedly, to the same exact shape desired.

When man first attempted to join pieces of metal together, he faced more problems. In the beginning he limited himself to joining metal in the same manner by which he had joined pieces of wood.

Fig. 1-1. Forging is one of our oldest crafts. From this shaping of metal by heat and hammering came the idea of forcing metal together by forge welding, a process which has become obsolete for most purposes.

Later, man learned that he could heat two pieces of metal and then force them together by hammering. For centuries, craftsmen used this practice of *forge welding** to join metals. (Fig. 1-1). Unfortunately, the heat and pressures applied in this process were not great enough for complete fusion of the two pieces being joined. In *fusion* the metal would be melted sufficiently for a thorough blending of the material in

*Definitions of italicized words are listed at end of chapter, and in the "Dictionary of Metallurgical and Welding Terms" at back of this book.

both pieces . . . hardening, as they cool, into a single, continuous solid mass. In forge welding, however, the effect was more a mechanical locking-in of the two surfaces in contact, and any fusion was limited to the thin outer "skin" of the two surfaces. With these conditions, a relatively low force when applied in certain ways could break the joint and separate the pieces.

The discovery and invention of modern welding processes, starting about 70 years ago, provided man with the ideal means of joining metal plates or shapes, castings to castings, forgings to forgings, or forgings to castings. This is how metals should be joined—by fusion, resulting in a complete, permanent union of the two pieces with the weld area being stronger than either of the pieces joined. With the proper welding materials and techniques, man now can join together almost any two pieces of metal so as to become a single unit. Overlapping of pieces to be joined is not necessary, and thickness at the weld area can be held to the thickness of the member to either side.

Arc welding today is widely accepted as the best, the most economical, the most natural and the most practical way to join metals.

All metals are weldable provided the proper process and techniques are used. Occasionally an attempt to weld metal ends in failure because one of these two factors—the proper process or the proper technique—has been overlooked. If, however, the engineer and the weldor understand the composition, structure and properties of a metal, they will be able to design and make better welds. This creates a close relationship between the metallurgy of a metal and its weldability.

What Is Metallurgy?

Metallurgy is the science and technology of extracting metals from their ores, refining them, and preparing them for use. It includes the study of metals—their composition, structure and properties—and how they behave when exposed to different conditions of use. Let's look at this definition more closely. It contains words that may be new to you.

Ore is the rock or other natural form in which we find a metal. Most of the metals used commercially are not found in a pure state. By this we mean you probably wouldn't find iron, for example, all by itself buried in a mountainside. It and other metals are usually combined by Nature with other elements, which often are undesirable in the finished product.

You probably know what an *element* is. It is Nature's building block. We have 26 letters in the alphabet, and each is different from all the others. If a child has a block for each letter, he can build an almost endless number of words. Similarly, each element is a substance different from all others, and these can be mixed or joined together by Nature or by man to build an almost endless number of materials. There are only 103 elements, and everything on Earth and possibly in all the Universe is an arrangement of some of these elements.

An element can never be broken down into two other substances; however, the smallest unit of an element is the atom—a particle that has all the characteristics of the element but is so tiny we can't see it even under the microscope. We need millions of an element's atoms all locked together before we have enough to do anything useful.

Many of these elements are metals. Most of us know what a metal is. Technically, a *metal* is an element that has all or most of the following characteristics: it is solid at room temperature; it is opaque (you can't see through it); it conducts heat and electricity; it reflects light when polished; when viewed under a microscope, it is seen to be made up of tiny crystals; it expands when heated and contracts (shrinks) when cooled.

There are still other characteristics of all metal elements, but these do not directly concern us and don't mean much except to the laboratory man. The word metal also is used for a material which has strong metallic characteristics, even though it has more than one element. Bronze is a good example, since it contains some combination of tin, zinc, aluminum, lead, silver, phosphorus, silica or other elements, in addition to copper, its main ingredient. Metallurgists call this type of material an *alloy* to indicate it is not a pure metal element.

Metallurgy is a big subject. Most metallurgists (scientists or engineers working in this field) are specialists, just like some people in the building industry are carpenters, while others are masons, plumbers, electricians or painters. There are two main divisions of metallurgy—process and physical.

Process metallurgy deals with the first operations—getting metal from a mine into the form of basic mill products, such as structural plate or bar stock.

The processing of metals requires many steps, which may be grouped as follows: (1) extracting metals from the ore, that is, separating the metals from the unwanted materials of the earth and rock in which they are found in Nature; (2) refining them, that is, separating the various metals extracted from the ore, in order to have a relatively pure metal for further processing; and finally (3) the conversion of relatively pure metals into usable combinations (alloys) and basic forms such as castings, sheets, structural shapes and plates for use by other industries.

Physical metallurgy relates to the composition of metals and what happens to their structure and properties during shaping, fabricating, heat treating, and so on.

Briefly, *composition* refers to what elements are present in the alloy and in what amount. For example, a common low-carbon steel (SAE 1020) is made up mostly of iron but also has from 0.18 to 0.23% carbon, 0.60 to 0.90% manganese, not more than 0.04% phosphorus, and not more than 0.05% silica. Note that in this material none of these elements, other than iron, amounts to even 1% of the total weight. Yet, these elements greatly influence the strength of the alloy and its weldability.

The *structure* refers to how these elements arrange themselves within the alloy. Further on in the book, we'll learn about the formation of crystals and how these affect the way metals behave under various conditions. *Properties* of a metal are those characteristics by which we can tell how good it will be for a particular use. Hardness is one important property.

A study of physical metallurgy may require testing the metals before, after, and often even during the process of converting them into useful products. People with special training perform most of these tests, especially those requiring laboratory equipment. However, an understanding of what these people do is extremely helpful in making good welded joints.

Tests may be made in a variety of ways: by pulling a metal apart to determine its strength, by denting the metal to determine its hardness, by bending the metal repeatedly to determine when it will fail from fatigue, or by some other test to find out how satisfactory the metal will be for a particular purpose. The quality of a welded joint is often determined by these same tests.

There are many ways to examine a piece of metal. One is to merely "look it over" to see if it is standing up under service; or, an x-ray examination might be made to see if there are any hidden defects. Regardless of how the testing or examining is done, it is a part of physical metallurgy.

Why Metallurgy Is Important

Although the term itself is mysterious to some people, metallurgy is of wide interest and importance. Many thousands of people are employed in the casting, rolling, drawing, and extrusion of metals. Hundreds of thousands of people are engaged in the manufacture of finished consumer products from these basic mill shapes.

Everyone is dependent to some degree on metals. Most of us have daily contact with metals. After thinking about it for a few moments, most of us know we could not get along without metals. But few people realize that man used metals for many centuries without ever knowing very much about them or the reasons for their varied and often strange behavior.

Why is it that some metals are brittle at room temperature, while others are brittle only when extremely cold or when extremely hot? Why will some metals stretch while others won't? What makes some metals stronger than others?

For a long time man did not know enough about metals and their properties to answer questions like these. However, metallurgical research during the past 100 years has given us such knowledge. As a result, we now do much better in using the right metal in the right place for a specific purpose.

Metallurgists have developed new ways to obtain metals from their ores. As a result, industry has metals of higher quality with which to work. Metallurgists have learned to combine various metals to produce new alloys possessing better properties for a particular type of application.

Improved methods of producing metal now provide us with a wide range of useful mill products of necessary shape, size, accuracy, composition, and so on . . . to meet the needs of specific applications. We use machinable metals, formable metals, and weldable metals. Nearly all metals can be welded, but some more readily than others.

As a result of research, we know what happens when metals are suddenly heated and cooled as in welding. Metallurgical research is also of great help in the constant improvement of welding equipment, materials and practices.

Where Does Metallurgy Fit Into Welding?

Study of the arc welding process involves both process metallurgy and physical metallurgy. What happens first in the welding operation, the heating and melting of the metal, is a subject for process metallurgy. Further study of the operation as it continues through the cooling of the metal into a solid state, and the subsequent shaping or machining, is an application of physical metallurgy.

Let's review what takes place when you make a weld.

Intense heat is needed to melt the metal, causing it to be fluid in the immediate weld area. This heat comes from the arc which forms as electric current jumps across a gap in an electrical circuit (Fig. 1-2). The gap exists between the welding electrode (a metal wire or rod to

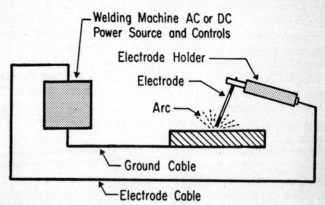

Fig. 1-2. In arc welding, current flows through the welding electrode, jumps the gap to the workpiece, and then returns to the source. The arc that occurs in the gap creates the heat for melting the metal.

which electrical current is fed from a power source) and the *base metal* or workpiece.

A common practice, when joining two plates of metal, is to first cut a groove along the line where the plates meet. This provides room for penetration by the heat to the full thickness of the metal. The space between the workpieces must be filled up with metal as strong or stronger than the base metal. This filler metal comes from the electrode, which it gradually consumes (uses up) as it welds.

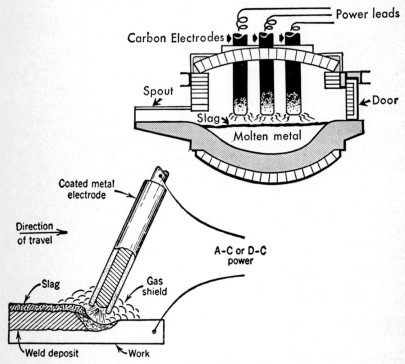

Fig. 1-3. (Above) In electric furnace production of steel, the arc from huge carbon electrodes keeps the metal bath in a molten condition. (Below) Similarly, the metal in the joint directly under the welding electrode is kept molten by the arc. The intense heat and boiling effect provides a high quality weld metal comparable to the fine "electric steels".

The heat from the arc not only melts the base metal, it also melts the electrode; and the molten metal drops from the electrode into the joint.

Welding is very much like steelmaking (Fig. 1-3). As the intense heat from the electric arc melts base metal and electrode filler, a small amount of molten metal collects within the joint. This weld puddle is like the molten contents of an electric arc furnace used in

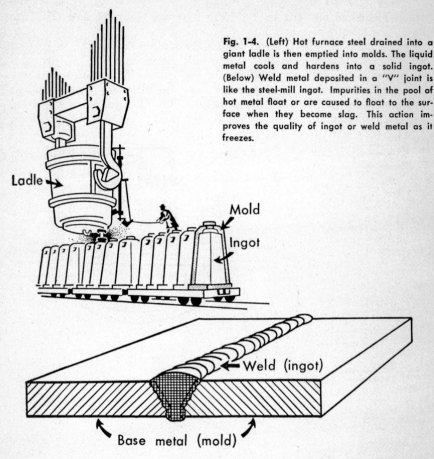

Fig. 1-4. (Left) Hot furnace steel drained into a giant ladle is then emptied into molds. The liquid metal cools and hardens into a solid ingot. (Below) Weld metal deposited in a "V" joint is like the steel-mill ingot. Impurities in the pool of hot metal float or are caused to float to the surface when they become slag. This action improves the quality of ingot or weld metal as it freezes.

Ladle

Mold

Ingot

Weld (ingot)

Base metal (mold)

steelmaking. In both welding and furnace operation, the formation of a non-metallic blanket called slag, over the molten metal, helps to control the temperature and cooling rate, and assists in preventing and removing impurities from the metal.

Since the molten puddle in the weld joint is confined within a limited area, it might further be compared with molten steel when poured into the ingot mold, after first having been tapped or drained from the furnace into a big ladle (Fig. 1-4). In the welding operation the base or parent metal is often preheated, just as the ingot mold is preheated, to prevent the molten metal from cooling too rapidly.

As the weld metal cools, it solidifies or "freezes." The same thing happens to the steel in an ingot mold. Very often a completed weld is placed in service "as welded." At other times, it is further processed by heat treatment, which will be discussed in a later chapter. Or, it may be shaped, machined, or the weld flattened by rolling. As in the case of steel mill products, this hot or cold working is for the purpose of meeting the particular requirements of the application.

By these comparisons it may be seen that both process (metal producing) metallurgy and physical (metal working) metallurgy have an important place in all welding operations.

Welding Metallurgy

Fortunately, a weldor needs know only "how to make a weld" and not all the engineering behind welding . . . for, in addition to metallurgy, welding involves electrical, mechanical and ceramic engineering.

Many welds are made without any knowledge of metallurgy. However, the average weldor who develops an understanding of some basic principles of the subject can greatly improve the quality of his work. He can successfully weld metals that would be very troublesome to other weldors, and he can in general simplify his own job.

Correct application of welding metallurgy principles helps to avoid mistakes that could weaken a weld. It assists in developing techniques which reduce stresses and strains associated with the expansion and contraction of metals during heating and cooling. A knowledge of welding metallurgy explains what happens as a result of welding heat and helps the weldor to avoid the undesirable effects of improper welding practices.

Welding metallurgy may seem like a difficult subject, but it need not be if taken in easy stages and in sequence. In this way, the basic fundamentals become known and these will provide easy solution of many annoying welding problems. With a knowledge of the tie-in between welding and metallurgy, the weldor can turn out a welded product that will meet the engineering objectives: lighter in weight, stronger, more pleasing in appearance, and less costly.

Definitions of New Words

Alloy. A material having metallic characteristics and made up of two or more elements, one of which is a metal.

Base metal. Often called *parent metal,* the metal used in workpieces being joined together.

Composition. The contents of an alloy, in terms of what elements are present and in what amount (by percentage of weight).

Element. A substance which can't be broken down into two other substances. Everything on Earth is a combination of such elements, of which there are only 103.

Forge welding. A process of joining metals by pressure, usually with the assistance of heat but at temperatures below that at which there would be true fusion.

Fusion. Melting of metal to the liquid state, permitting two contacting or neighboring surfaces to partially exchange their contents with the result that there is a thorough blending of the compositions after cooling.

Metal. An element that has all or most of these characteristics: solid at room temperature; opaque; conductor of heat and electricity; reflective when polished; expands when heated and contracts when cooled. For all practical purposes, we also use the word *metal* in speaking of many *alloys*—materials having metallic characteristics, even though they may contain more than one element including non-metals.

Metallurgy. The science and technology of extracting metals from their ores, refining them, and preparing them for use.

Ore. The rock or earth in which we find metals in their natural form.

Physical metallurgy. That division of metallurgy applying to the changes in structure and properties of metals as a result of shaping, fabricating and treating.

Process metallurgy. That division of metallurgy applying to the extracting, refining, and primary shaping of metals into a usable form.

Properties. Those features or characteristics of a metal that make it useful and distinctive from all others.

Structure. The way in which the elements of an alloy, or the atoms of one element, are arranged.

Review Questions

1. How did man first discover metals?
2. Why is welding so ideally suited for joining of metals?
3. What are the three major activities covered by process metallurgy?
4. Why are metals tested?
5. How can welding be compared to the making of steel in an electric furnace?
6. What happens in the welding process?
7. What is slag?
8. How does slag help in the welding process?
9. Is a knowledge of metallurgy necessary for welding?
10. How can metallurgical knowledge be applied to improved welds?

CHAPTER 2

MECHANICAL PROPERTIES OF METALS

When you look at a piece of copper and then look at a piece of lead, you know they are two different metals. Why? Because of the difference in color and weight and other external characteristics.

If you take a slug of copper and another of lead (both of small diameter but quite thick), position them in a bench vise so pressure can be applied against flat ends of both pieces simultaneously, and then squeeze them with enough force, you will find that one cracks and then begins to crumble before the other does. This difference between the two metals we call compressive strength.

Compressive strength is only one of numerous *mechanical properties*. These are characteristics of a material that tell us how well the material stands up to some kind of force applied against it. In addition to compressive strength, the mechanical properties include tensile strength, hardness, ductility and others. These will all be explained in this chapter or the following one. The strength of a metal can be determined only by mechanical test. This is true for all mechanical properties.

All that we know about properties, we have learned by comparing one thing with another. In order to describe and classify our knowledge so that it will be most useful, standards have been established by various technical societies, industry associations, and government agencies. These groups have standardized many of the tests by which we measure properties. A few of the more common and important tests are described in this book.

Some properties of a metal do not relate to an applied force of some kind. These are called *physical properties*. Among them are density, resistance to corrosion, electrical and thermal conductivity, and thermal expansion. Some handbooks and manufacturers' literature do not separate physical and mechanical properties but list them all together.

How Properties Are Important to Us

The properties of a metal or other material are the characteristics by which we can: (1) accurately identify it, or (2) determine its unique range of usefulness. If we are trying to select the right metal to do some particular job, we should first learn what the properties of each available metal are. Without such knowledge, many products and structures would be doomed to failure.

Metals can be broken, bent, twisted, dented, scratched or otherwise damaged. Most of us have seen examples of metals that have been

11

stretched, and even, in some cases, pulled to pieces. All metals have all properties but not to the same degree. One metal might have high compressive strength but low tensile strength, while another metal has low compressive strength but high tensile strength. By knowing to what extent each property exists in a metal, we can use the metal wisely and with assurance that it will meet the requirements of a specific job.

For example, if a manufacturer is making razor blades, he needs a material that is hard, is resistant to corrosion, and can bend without breaking. Some hardened steels meet these requirements. For a watch spring, the material must likewise be hard and resistant to corrosion, but it also must be non-magnetic and able to withstand repeated bending without becoming permanently deformed or breaking. Special spring steel alloys meet these requirements. For a bridge cable, steel wire of high tensile strength and elasticity is used because it is strong even after bending and can withstand the varying loads on the bridge.

All metals are important, just as all people are important. It's essential, though, to match up a man's personality and other qualifications with the needs of a specific job. Likewise, it's essential to match up a metal's properties or qualifications with the needs of a specific job.

The properties of the *parent metal* (that is, the material being welded) constitute the reason why the design engineer specified that particular metal. In welding, it is essential that metal in the welded

The right ELECTRODE for the right JOB

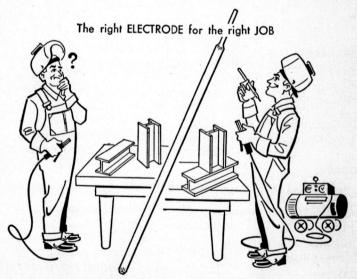

Fig. 2-1. Properties of a base metal must match properties required by the application. Similarly, the weld metal's properties must equal or exceed the base metal's. Each type electrode provides filler metal having a unique combination of properties.

joint area have properties equal to or better than the properties of the parent metal. This is a natural quality of a well-made weld tailored to meet the specific requirements of a job.

Some welding consists of repairing machinery parts or members that were never welded originally, or at least weren't welded at the point of failure. A part often fails as the result of a local or temporary application of force greater than what the metal could stand. Perhaps there is some operating condition that is not continually repetitive, and the engineer was unable to predict the situation. Obviously then, the weldor who makes the repair must not be concerned just with filling a crack or joining two pieces of a broken part. He also must strengthen the structure at that point so that it can withstand any repeat of the force that caused it to fail.

Kinds of Strength

Knowledge of the strength of a metal is most important to the weldor. When he knows the strength property of a metal, he can build a structure that is strong enough to carry the maximum load expected without wasting material. Likewise, when the weldor knows the strength of his weld metal as compared with the parent metal, he will neither underweld nor overweld the product. Overwelding will prove to be costly, while underwelding may result in a product not strong enough to do the job for which it has been designed.

Strength is the ability of a metal to withstand some kind of force without breaking down. For example, a metal can resist failure from pulling, hitting, pressure, repeated bending, twisting or shearing. These strength properties are called, respectively, tensile strength, impact strength, compressive strength, fatigue strength, torsional strength, and shear strength. A metal will eventually fail under any of these forces if the *load* (amount of applied force) is increased sufficiently.

If we can figure the maximum load that a structural member will be exposed to, we can select a metal that will withstand a higher load. Or, we can obtain the necessary strength by increasing the cross-section dimensions of the critical member.

Any force that is applied against a metal or structural part can be measured in terms of pounds. We often say the metal or part *supports* this load, even when the load is a force applied by pulling or twisting.

What Is Tensile Strength?

Tensile strength is the resistance of a material to a force that is acting to pull it apart. It is generally the most important property in evaluating metals. Metallurgists measure the tensile strength of a metal by determining the maximum load in pounds per square inch (abbreviated *psi*) it will withstand. This maximum load is also known as *ultimate tensile strength* because any additional load, no matter how small, will cause failure, like the last straw that broke the camel's back.

Tensile strength data of most commercially available materials are provided by the company that produces the material. These values for tensile strength and other properties of the more commonly used metals are also included in various technical handbooks. However, the values listed in the handbooks usually are minimum values which the metal must have in order to meet industry standard specifications. A specific manufacturer's SAE 4640 steel, for example, may have strengths in excess of the handbook values.

The pulling load a specific product part can support without failure depends on the cross-sectional area of the part. (The length of the bar does not materially affect its strength). A bar 2 inches square will support in tension four times the load that a bar 1 inch square will support, because the larger bar has four times the cross-sectional area. (A bar that is 1 inch square = 1 in. x 1 in. = 1 sq in., while a bar that is 2 inches square = 2 in. x 2 in. = 4 sq in.).

To calculate the load (in pounds) a given part can support, the material's tensile strength (in psi) is multiplied by the cross-sectional area (in sq in.). For example, if the tensile strength of a particular kind of steel is 60,000 psi, a bar of that material 2 in. square (4 sq in.) will support a load of 60,000 x 4, or 240,000 lb.

This total load is the maximum strength of the specific part; for example, a chain, a rope or a steel rod. An important point to remember is that when we talk about the strength of a part, or structural member, we express the value (amount) of load in pounds (not psi). There are times when we don't know the tensile strength of the metal and it is convenient to test an actual part made from the metal. The tensile strength of the metal (in psi) can be calculated by dividing the maximum load (in pounds) by the cross-sectional area (in sq in.).

This can be written as a formula:

$$\text{Tensile strength (psi)} = \frac{\text{maximum load (lb.)}}{\text{cross-sectional area (sq. in.)}}$$

Testing for Tensile Strength

In making a test for tensile strength, an extremely important requirement is to apply the load gradually and at a uniform rate of speed. In fact, it is impossible to determine the tensile strength if the load is applied suddenly or in jerks. You have experienced many times the relative weakness of a material when given a sudden hard jerk. The most common experience is that of breaking a string. Even when the string is strong enough that a steady pull will not break it, it does break when suddenly jerked.

Metallurgists determine the tensile strength of metals by using a tensile testing machine, Fig. 2-2. This machine has two heads (one above the other) equipped with grips or jaws. Ends of a sample of the metal to be tested are fastened in the grips, and the movable head is slowly and steadily moved away from the stationary head, stretching the sample, thereby putting a tensile (pulling) load on the test piece. This is called a pull test. The total load is indicated (in pounds) on a dial indicating gage. The testing machine shown in Fig. 2-2 is equipped with a motor-driven strip chart that automatically provides a continuous record of the test. On some machines the number of pounds is read directly from the dial gage and recorded at regular, frequent time intervals while the test is in process.

Fig. 2-2. A tensile testing machine applies a pulling force on the test piece. The maximum load applied before failure of the piece is the tensile strength.

The highest reading of the gage is the maximum load the test piece can support. If the cross-section of the test piece is 1 square inch in area, the maximum load in pounds will be the tensile strength of the metal expressed as pounds per square inch.

It is not always practical to test a metal sample exactly 1 square inch in cross-sectional area. Fortunately, we can determine the tensile strength of a metal by using samples having any cross-sectional area (within maximum size or force limits established for the particular machine). Samples less than 1 square inch are usually less expensive to make and do not require as high loads to cause them to fail. The test, therefore, can be made more quickly.

The most common specimen size for tensile testing metal is called a 505 specimen. This is a cylindrical sample of the metal, to be tested, which has been machined and ground to standard specifications including a diameter of 0.505 inch (Fig. 2-3). This diameter greatly simplifies calculations since its cross-sectional area is $\frac{1}{5}$ of one square inch.

Using the formula presented a few paragraphs earlier, we can calculate the tensile strength. If a 505 steel specimen fails at a load of 10,000 lb, the steel's

$$\text{Tensile strength} = \frac{10,000}{\frac{1}{5}} = 10,000 \times 5 = 50,000 \text{ psi}$$

So, all you have to do to find the tensile strength of a 505 test specimen is multiply the maximum load by 5. What could be simpler?

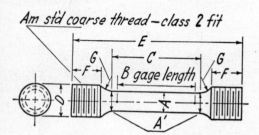

Fig. 2-3. Standard test specimens are made to rigid specifications. The commonly used 505 specimen, left, is identified in the table below as Specimen C-1, and is made to those dimensions shown in the row to the right of C-1.

Test Specimen Dimensions							
SPECI-IMEN	A[(2)] in.	AREA[(1)] sq. in.	B	C[(3)] in.	D in.	E[(4)] in.	F[(4)] in.	G[(4)] in.
C-1	0.505	0.200	2	2¼	¾	4¼	¾	5/8
C-2	0.437	0.150	1¾	2	5/8	4	¾	3/8
C-3	0.357	0.100	1.4	0.165	½	3¼	5/8	¼
C-4	0.252	0.050	1	1¼	3/8	2½	½	3/16
C-5	0.126	0.0125	½	¾	¼	1 5/8	3/8	3/32

A' = A min.
(1) Cross-sectional area = 0.785 x A²
(2) Tolerance, ± 1%
(3) Approximate
(4) Minimum
NOTE: Dimensions A, B, C and G shall be as shown, but the ends may be of any shape to fit the holders of the testing machine in such a way that the load shall be axial.

Sometimes it is desirable to test for the tensile strength of a welded steel plate. See Fig. 2-4. The sample cut from the plate will be larger than the standard 505 specimen and will be of full plate thickness. Calculations will be as follows:

A maximum load of 50,000 lb is required to break a welded steel sample (Fig. 2-5), which is ½ in. x 1½ in. at the weld. The tensile strength of the steel is figured by dividing the load by the cross-sectional area. The area (½ x 1½) is ¾ sq in. Therefore:

$$\text{Tensile strength} = \frac{50,000}{\frac{3}{4}} = 50,000 \times \frac{4}{3} = 66,666 \text{ psi}$$

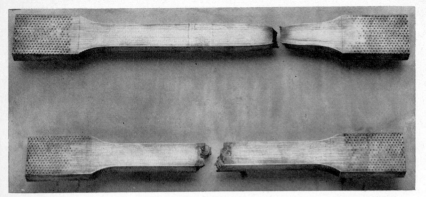

Fig. 2-4. A good weld is stronger than the plate (upper), but a poor weld (lower) fails under a tensile test.

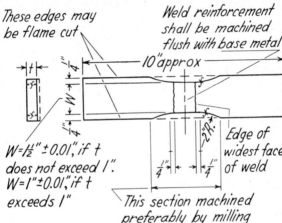

Fig. 2-5. A test sample for the welded-plate test (Fig. 2-4) is made to these standard specifications.

These edges may be flame cut

Weld reinforcement shall be machined flush with base metal

10"approx

$W=1\frac{1}{2}"\pm 0.01"$, if t does not exceed $1"$.
$W=1"\pm 0.01"$, if t exceeds $1"$

Edge of widest face of weld

This section machined preferably by milling

Stress and Strain

Much of the laboratory testing of metals and of welding and other joining processes is critical. In order that metallurgists can talk to one another, and to other engineers and shop people, a number of technical terms have come into being. These are quite specific in meaning. The weldor doesn't have to know all of these, but an understanding of the terms in most general use will help clear away much of the mystery as to what engineers are striving for in the design and fabrication of a welded member or structure.

Two such terms that you will hear very often are stress and strain. *Stress* is the load (amount) of a force applied against a material. This force may be any of numerous types, such as tensile or compressive. *Strain* is the physical effect of the stress. In the case of tensile stress, the resulting strain in the material is measured by the amount of stretching or elongation that takes place.

Yield Point

The maximum stress or maximum load, indicated on the gage of the tensile testing machine, is not always the actual breaking load. Many metals will continue to stretch after this maximum load is reached, and from this point on the stretch will occur mostly within a very short section of the test piece. The result is a narrowing of this section, with complete failure taking place within this "necked-down" section.

The testing machine (Fig. 2-2) pulls the test at a <u>constant</u> rate, permitting the load on the test piece to either increase or decrease. In Fig. 2-6, a crude test setup calls for loading the test piece with heavy weights. The tensile load increases as more weights are added, one at a time, and finally the addition of one more weight causes

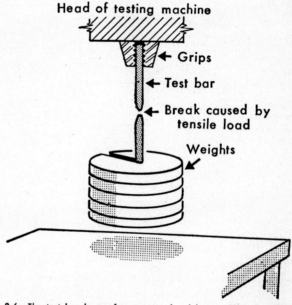

Head of testing machine

← Grips

← Test bar

← Break caused by tensile load

Weights

Fig. 2-6. The test bar hangs from an overhead beam. Slotted weights are added, one at a time, onto a support plate secured to the lower free end of the bar. The maximum load the bar will carry cannot be determined, because the point where the bar began to weaken is unknown. We don't know whether a greater or lesser load would cause continued stretching from here to the point of failure.

instant failure of the test piece. With this type of loading, the actual strength at failure cannot be measured since the loads cannot be reduced after the test piece begins to weaken.

When a sample of low- or medium-carbon steel is tested, a stress point is reached beyond which the metal stretches <u>without</u> an increase in load. This is the *yield point*. Other steels and non-ferrous metals do not have a yield point.

During a tensile test of a low or medium-carbon steel, the yield point can be seen on the dial gage of the machine. The gage pointer will stop advancing, or even drop back a little, when the yield point is reached. A drop-back indicates that the load is decreasing as the stretching continues.

You can often feel the yield point in a soft steel wire when you pull it by hand. First, the wire tightens and stretches a little. Then, as the pulling force is increased, the wire suddenly yields and stretches with ease.

Yield Strength

For low- and medium-carbon steels the yield point is considered to be the *yield strength*. For other metals, the yield strength is the stress required to strain the test piece by a specified small amount beyond the elastic limit. The *elastic limit* is the maximum stress the metal will support without permanent deformation. Any stress below this point will stretch the metal, but when the force is removed the material will return to its original dimensions . . . like a new rubber band.

For ordinary commercial purposes, the yield strength is considered to be identical with the elastic limit. A metal with a high yield point or high elastic limit is needed for parts that must hold their exact shape and size.

Weld metals of high yield strength are used in surfacing punch press dies that must hold their shape accurately. However, a low yield strength is an advantage when a part is to be cold bent or formed. Less force is required to form metals that have a low yield strength.

Stress-Strain Relationship

Figure 2-7 shows what happens when a metal is moderately loaded. A sample bar of the metal is arranged in suspension from an overhead beam, with a light platform secured to the bar's free lower end. A dial indicator gage is attached to the test piece so as to show the amount of stretching or elongation that takes place. Weights of 100 lb each are added, one at a time, and the reading of the gage is taken as each weight is added. After three weights have been added, they are then removed. Removal of all the weights causes the indicator to return to zero, showing that the metal has returned to original size. This test demonstrates that the amount of stretch, between clamps holding the indicator, is directly proportional to the amount of pull. (The gage pointer had advanced the same distance each time a weight was added.)

If the values of the load and the elongation are plotted on a graph, they will fall along a straight line, Fig. 2-8.

The test performed according to Fig. 2-7 and Fig. 2-8 is simple, but has limited value. It provides no values that can be used for comparison of the elastic behavior of one metal with another. Neither the cross-sectional size of the test piece nor the distance over which the elongation was measured is known.

The standard tensile testing machine (Fig. 2-2) and similar machines for evaluating strength provide much more information. The variations in load (stress) and elongation (strain) are indicated continuously. One advantage is that we can obtain a much better picture of what happens as the metal begins to fail. When these values for stress and strain are plotted on a graph, the stress is expressed as pounds per square inch (psi), and strain is expressed as deformation

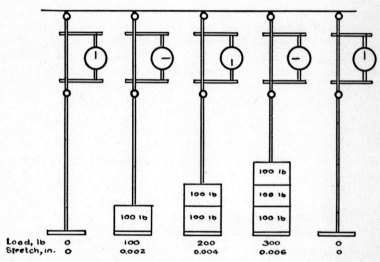

Fig. 2-7. Under moderate loading, the stretch of metal is proportional to the load.

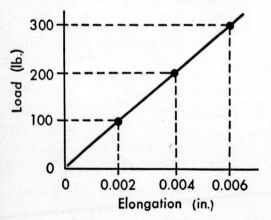

Fig. 2-8. A simple stress-strain diagram of the test shown in Fig. 2-7. (If the load is 100 lb and the amount of stretch is 0.001 in., a "point" is plotted at the intersection of these two lines). When all test points have been plotted, a line drawn through them is the "curve" of the diagram, even though here it is a straight line.

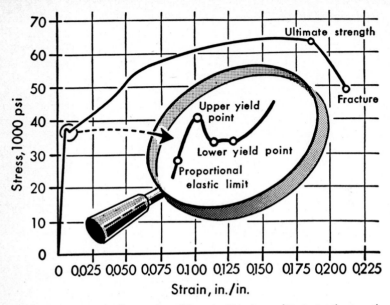

Fig. 2-9. A stress-strain diagram for mild steel which shows ultimate tensile strength, proportional elastic limit, upper yield point and lower yield point. Here, the most critical portion of the curve is magnified for more detailed study.

in inches per inch of test piece length. (In a tensile test, the strain or deformation occurs as an elongation of the metal.) A line drawn through points plotted on a graph is a curve showing the relation between stress and strain (Fig. 2-9).

To summarize some of our terminology:

$$\text{Stress (load per unit area)} = \frac{\text{Load, in pounds}}{\text{Cross-section area, in sq in.}}$$

$$\text{Stress} = \text{pounds per sq in. (psi)}$$

$$\text{Strain (deformation per unit area)} = \frac{\text{Elongation, in inches}}{\text{Original gage length, in inches}}$$

$$\text{Strain} = \text{in./in.}$$

Modulus of Elasticity

Some materials require higher stresses to stretch than others do. We may restate this idea by saying that some materials are stiffer than others. To compare the stiffness of one metal with that of another, we must determine what is known as the modulus of elasticity for each of them. The *modulus of elasticity* is the ratio of the stress to the strain.

$$\frac{\text{Stress}}{\text{Strain}} = \text{Modulus of elasticity}$$

On a stress-strain diagram (Fig. 2-9) the modulus of elasticity is represented visually by the slope of the straight portion of the curve, where the stress is directly proportional to the strain. The steeper the curve (closer to being vertical), the higher the modulus of elasticity. The stiff material has the steep curve.

In Fig. 2-10, stress-strain curves are given for tungsten, steel, and approximate curves for cast iron and rubber. From the curves we can see that a load of 30,000 psi will stretch a steel sample (having a cross-section of 1 sq in.) 0.001 in. for each inch of length. It would require 50,000 psi to stretch a piece of tungsten of the same size the same amount. Practically no stress at all is needed to stretch rubber.

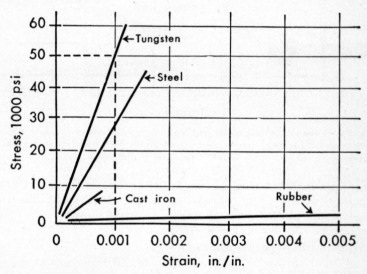

Fig. 2-10. Partial stress-strain curves for different materials (using only that portion of the curve which shows a proportional or straight-line relationship between stress and strain) show their relative elasticity.

From the curve for steel, we determine that the modulus of elasticity, expressed by the ratio of stress to strain, is:

$$\frac{30,000 \text{ psi}}{0.001 \text{ in./in.}} = 30,000,000 \text{ psi}$$

This figure of 30,000,000 psi is the modulus of elasticity for all steels: low-carbon, high-carbon, alloy, hard and soft steels. Tungsten has a modulus of 50,000,000 psi. Cast iron has a modulus of 10,000,000 to 25,000,000 psi, depending on the type of cast iron.

A material that stretches easily has a low modulus (curve is closer to being horizontal). A low stress divided by a high strain results in a low modulus. And, where a high stress produces a small strain, the modulus is a high figure.

As the comparison of their respective moduli shows, steel is two to three times stiffer than cast iron. Let's take two bars of equal size, one cast iron and one steel, and weight them each on one end while the other end remains fixed. The cast iron bar will deflect twice as far as the steel bar. If two steel bars are thus compared—even though one may be hard tool steel and the other soft mild steel—they will deflect the same amount.

Although steel is stiffer than cast iron, it is more ductile. The cast iron bar will break with a brittle fracture as the stress is increased, while the steel will bend and deform.

The modulus of elasticity is not a measure of the amount of stretch a particular metal can take before breaking or deforming. It simply tells us how much stress is required to make the metal stretch a given amount. The modulus of elasticity is used in formulas to calculate the amount of deflection a given piece of metal will have under a certain load. It must not be confused with the elastic limit.

Ductility: The Ability to Stretch

When making a tensile test, we can determine still another property of metals. This is *ductility*, the ability of a metal to stretch and become permanently deformed without breaking or cracking. Ductility is measured by the percentage reduction in cross-sectional area and the percentage elongation of the test bar. Ductile steels are necessary for formed and drawn steel parts such as automobile body panels and fenders.

A metal with high ductility will fail or break gradually. Because a ductile metal stretches, the total load is not concentrated on one small

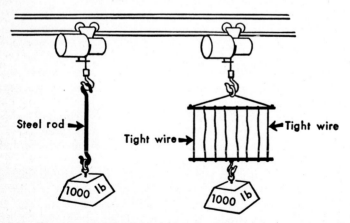

Fig. 2-11. The wires supporting the weight at the right total the same cross-sectional area as the rod supporting the weight at the left. Ductility of the metal used in the wires will permit the shorter outer wires to stretch, so that almost immediately all wires carry an equal share of the 1,000-lb load.

area but is distributed throughout the piece. A metal with low ductility fails suddenly with a brittle fracture. Because the metal will not stretch, the load is concentrated on a small area, which leads to early failure. Sometimes this failure causes the load to be transferred to other parts of the structure so suddenly that even other more ductile parts will fail.

Figure 2-11 illustrates the important effect that ductility has on metals. At left, a 1,000-lb weight is suspended by one steel rod, in the form of a double-ended hook. Here, the only important property of the rod is its tensile strength. This must be high enough for the rod to hold the weight without failure. To the right, a 1,000-lb weight is shown suspended by a number of steel wires of small diameter. The wires have the same total cross-sectional area as the steel rod to the left. If the wires all are of the same length and each carries its portion of the load, they will be pulled in tension equally and the load will be supported. If, however, the wires are not all the same length, ductility becomes an important property. If the two outer wires are shorter, they will be tight while the others are loose as the load is first applied. If the wires are sufficiently ductile, the two outer wires will stretch until they are the same length as the others. At this point each wire assumes its share of the load. But if the wires are not ductile, the two shorter wires will be overloaded and will fail. As the load transfers onto the other wires, they too will fail progressively.

This is a good explanation of what is called progressive failure. In the design of structures, engineers take great care to secure uniform distribution of the load. They avoid designs that will give off-center or unbalanced loads. They avoid designs that throw a large load on a very small section or on a single structural member.

As a practical example, steel wires forming the cables for a suspension bridge are tightened individually so that each wire can carry its share of the load. Since the amount of tightening required for each wire cannot be calculated with great precision, the wires must be made of a ductile material. When the bridge is loaded, the wires that are momentarily carrying more than their share of the load simply stretch, thereby allowing the other wires to do their share.

For many applications, ductility is one of the principal properties required in the welded joint. This is particularly true where the weldment is to be later formed into a slightly different shape, but it is equally important in many other applications.

Ductility is measured on the standard tensile-strength testing machine by checking the deformation which results in the test specimen during the pulling. Two punch marks (also called gage marks), spaced exactly 2 in. apart, are made on a standard 505 specimen before it is placed in the testing machine. During the test, the specimen elongates uniformly along its entire length until the metal's ultimate strength is reached. Then the load begins to fall, and the specimen elongates

Fig. 2-12. An arc-welded test specimen made to standard 505 specifications, and shown here after tensile testing. It had tested to a tensile strength of 76,100 psi, with 25.8% elongation in 2 in., and 48% reduction in cross-section area.

primarily in a small local area. First, the diameter of the piece necks down and becomes appreciably smaller, after which the load continues to fall until the specimen breaks, Fig. 2-12.

The final diameter of the small necked-down portion at the break is measured and its area is calculated. Dividing this by the initial cross-sectional area (0.200 sq in.) gives us the percentage of reduction in area, which is one measure of ductility. For example, if the cross-sectional area at the point of breakage is 0.100 sq in., the reduction in area is 50%.

Another measure of ductility is the percentage of elongation. The fractured ends of the specimen are held together so that the distance between the gage marks can be measured. Dividing the distance in excess over 2 in. by the initial length of 2 in. gives us the percentage of elongation. Let us say, for example, that the final distance is 2.40 in. The elongation in 2 in. is 2.40 - 2.00 = 0.40 in. Thus, 0.40 in. ÷ 2 gives an elongation of 20%. The percent reduction in area and the percent elongation are both measures of ductility and are used together as standards for comparison.

Brittleness

Brittleness is very nearly the opposite of ductility. Brittle materials show practically no permanent distortion before failure. Such materials fail suddenly without warning. Glass is an excellent example of this. Glass is also elastic because it will bend a little and return to its original shape. If bent a little further, however, the glass will break readily. Cast iron is an example of a brittle metal; especially the extremely hard, white cast iron.

More on Elasticity

If a tensile load is released before it becomes too large, the metal test piece or product part will spring back to its original length. The metal behaves very much like a stiff spring. This behavior is known as *elasticity*.

A simple spring balance scale operates on this principle. If a 1-lb force moves the scale's pointer ½ in., a 2-lb force will move it twice as far, or 1 in. The spring stretches and moves the pointer in proportion to the amount of weight on the scale.

When a material is elongated by loading and then returns to its original length when the loading is removed, we say it has been deformed elastically. Practically all materials have some elasticity.

Ductility and elasticity must not be confused. Ductility is the ability to permanently elongate, when stretched, without breaking. Elasticity is the ability to elongate and return to original size. All ductile metals have considerable elasticity because they will return to the original length if they are not stretched beyond a certain point. A metal may be elastic, however, without being ductile. It stretches up to a certain point at which it suddenly breaks, instead of stretching further as a ductile metal would do.

The Elastic Limit

The *elastic limit* of a metal is the maximum stress that it will withstand without permanently bending or breaking. We have seen that in the case of cast iron the modulus is lower than that of steel, and the metal stretches more easily. However, the cast iron does not stretch very far since it has a low elastic limit. The elastic limit for cast iron is close to its ultimate or tensile strength. It breaks as the load reaches the elastic limit. That is why cast iron is considered to be a brittle, non-ductile material.

Steel is not only harder to bend than cast iron, but it also will withstand higher stresses and still return to its original shape. If, however, we bend a steel wire too far, it will only spring back part way. The wire has been permanently deformed because the bending in this case exceeded the elastic limit.

Metallurgists determine the elastic limit of a metal during the tensile pull test. The elastic limit of a steel test specimen is shown on a stress-strain curve. In Fig. 2-9, you can find a point on the curve where the increase in strain (elongation) and the increase in stress (load) are no longer proportionate. At this point, the curve ceases to be a straight line (Fig. 2-9).

If we wanted to be real technical, we would call this the *proportional limit*. Use of very sensitive instruments shows that this point (where increase in stress is no longer proportionate to increase in strain) is somewhat below the actual elastic limit (where elasticity is lost). The difference is so small, however, that for commercial purposes we can assume these two limits are at the same point on our stress-strain diagram. Because of this assumption, metallurgists often call this value the *proportional elastic limit*. As mentioned earlier, the term yield strength also refers to the same value as elastic limit.

If the specimen is taken out of the testing machine before the stress reaches the value on the curve just cited, the distance between the 2 in. punch marks on the specimen is still 2 in. If the test specimen is placed back in the machine and stressed beyond that point (the elastic limit), it is found when measured to be permanently elongated.

Summary of Properties Measured by Tensile Test

By pulling the test specimen until it breaks, we learn the ultimate or tensile strength of the material, which is the maximum load the material will support in tension. This value must be expressed in pounds per square inch to be usable as a standard for comparison.

The tensile test also tells us how much of a load (stress) in pounds per square inch must be applied to make the material stretch a given amount (strain). The ratio of the stress to the strain is the modulus of elasticity, which is used to compare the elasticity of materials.

The tensile test also shows the maximum load that can be put on a material without its becoming permanently deformed or breaking. This is called the elastic limit. For commercial purposes, it may be referred to as the yield strength.

Compressive Strength

The *compressive strength* of the material indicates its ability to resist crushing. Rubber, for example, has a comparatively low compressive strength, while steel which can carry extremely high loads without deformation, is certain to have high compressive strength. The relation of compressive strength to tensile strength varies according to the material group. In the case of most steels and the aluminum and magnesium alloys, these values are approximately equal. Low-strength cast irons may have a compressive strength several times the tensile strength. It is important to know the relative compressive strengths of materials so that we can stay within limits which will prevent failure from compressive stress.

Fatigue Strength

A knowledge of the tensile strength properties makes possible the design and fabrication of a structure that will support a steady load pulling or pushing in one direction. These properties, however, do not indicate the strength a metal will have if used in a structure where the load is applied first from one direction then another. When the load alternates like this in a cycle, at one moment the force is tension and at another compression.

The piston rod on a locomotive cylinder undergoes a complete reversal of stress from tension to compression and back again to tension. The rods used for oil well pumps are in tension at all times, but the tension is higher on the up stroke and lower on the down stroke. A railroad car axle is stressed in tension at the top and in compression at the bottom. At any point on the axle, each revolution produces a change from tension to compression. Structural members of a bridge floor go through a cycle of stresses every time a car goes over them.

Metals will fail under a changing load at a lower stress than if the load were steady. Failure under a changing load is called *fatigue failure.* To see what we mean by fatigue failure, let us look at a piece of steel wire. It will support a heavy load; you cannot break it by pulling on it with your hands. However, you can break it rather easily by bending it back and forth a dozen times or so. Since the wire is ductile it does not break with a brittle fracture when first bent. Ductile or not, however, the wire can stand only so many bends. Eventually, it gets tired, becomes fatigued, as engineers say, and there is a fatigue failure. The fatigue failure usually starts with a small crack, which progressively becomes larger under the repeated stress cycle until the wire is completely broken.

If the metal of which the wire is made has a tensile strength of 100,000 psi, the wire could support a steady hanging load of 95,000 psi indefinitely. It would, however, fail from fatigue if a load of only 75,000 psi were hung on it, removed and replaced several thousand times.

Fatigue strength is the ability to resist fracture when the stresses are variable and alternate through a cycle. Fatigue tests are made by subjecting a test specimen to variable loads. Some tests bend the piece alternately in one direction, then in the other. Others apply and remove tensile loads. Still others make a cycle of tension and compression by rotating a loaded specimen.

By making such tests, it is possible to determine the maximum stress that a metal will support indefinitely under conditions where that stress comes in a variable load. This is called the *endurance limit,* also the *fatigue limit.* Any stress above the endurance limit will eventually cause a crack that will progress to a fatigue failure.

For practical purpose in testing steels, 10,000,000 cycles is taken as the number of reversals which a specimen must withstand to establish the endurance limit. It is considered that a metal able to withstand a given stress for this number of cycles will continue to do so indefinitely.

For steel, the endurance limit varies between 40 and 60% of the ultimate strength of the material in tension. The exact limit depends both on the nature of the material and on the surface condition.

The surface condition of a metal is important to its fatigue strength. If the test specimen is rough, or if the test is made in a corrosive liquid or corrosive atmosphere, the fatigue strength will be very much lower. Surface treatments such as polishing, hardening and shot peening will raise the endurance limit.

Fatigue failures start at the surface as tiny cracks, which spread into the metal until failure occurs. Scratches, tool marks, threads and other surface irregularities act as places for the cracks to start. The fatigue strength of a specimen with lathe tool marks may be half that of one with a smooth polished surface. Changes in the cross-sectional area of a piece of metal such as a shaft shoulder or a keyway also reduce the fatigue strength.

The making of welds on metals that must have a high fatigue strength is an exacting job. Besides matching the strength of the parent metal, the weld must not be the source of any undue hardening or softening of the parent metal. Repair of a part that has failed from fatigue is especially critical. Any obvious imperfection in the weld—undercutting, cracks, or excessive build-up—may create a change in the cross-sectional area that can start a fatigue crack.

Definitions of New Words

Brittleness. The tendency of a material to fail suddenly by breaking, without any permanent deformation of the material before failure.

Compressive strength. The resistance of a material to a force which is tending to deform or fail it by crushing.

Ductility. The ability of a material to become permanently deformed without failure.

Elastic limit. The maximum stress to which a material can be subjected without permanent deformation or failure by breaking.

Elasticity. The ability of a material to return to original shape and dimensions after a deforming load has been removed.

Elongation. The stretching of a material, by which any straight-line dimension increases.

Endurance limit. The maximum stress that a material will support indefinitely under variable and repetitive load conditions.

Fatigue failure. The cracking, breaking or other failure of a material as the result of repeated or alternating stressing below the material's ultimate tensile strength.

Fatigue limit. The maximum stress that a material will support indefinitely under variable and repetitive load conditions.

Fatigue strength. The resistance of a material to repeated or alternating stressing, without failure.

Load. The amount of a force applied to a material or structure.

Mechanical property. A material's ability to resist or withstand a particular kind of physical force applied against the material. This ability is measurable by mechanical means.

Modulus of elasticity. The ratio of tensile stress to the strain it causes, within that range of elasticity where there is a straight-line relationship between stress and strain. The higher the modulus, the lower the degree of elasticity.

Parent metal. The metal to be welded or otherwise worked upon; also called the base metal.

Physical property. An inherent physical characteristic of a material which is not directly an ability to withstand a physical force of any kind.

Proportional elastic limit. The stress point beyond which (1) an increase in stress is no longer proportionate to the increase in strain, and (2) an increase in stress results in permanent deformation.

Proportional limit. The stress point beyond which an increase in stress is no longer proportionate to an increase in strain.

Strain. The physical effect of stress, usually evidenced by stretching or other deformation of the material.

Stress. The load, or amount of a force, applied to a material, tending to deform or break it.

Support. The act of carrying or holding up under the load of any applied force.

Tensile strength. The resistance of a material to a force which is acting to pull it apart.

Ultimate tensile strength. The maximum pulling force to which the material can be subjected without failure.

Yield point. The amount of stress at which point the material will continue to elongate without increase in the force applied.

Yield strength. The stress point at which permanent deformation results.

Review Questions

1. A steel rod ¼ in. square is pulled in the testing machine, and it breaks at a load of 4,000 lb. What was the ultimate strength— 10,0000 psi? 64,000 psi? 100,000 psi?

2. Suspension bridge cables are made up of thousands of steel wires. Which of the two types of steel wires do you think would make the stronger cable?

	Yield Strength	Tensile Strength
Steel A	90,000 psi	180,000 psi
Steel B	140,000 psi	180,000 psi

3. Draw a stress-strain diagram for a low carbon steel and show the yield strength, the tensile strength, and how the modulus of elasticity can be calculated. Use handbook data if available.

4. If the modulus of elasticity of steel is 30,000,000 psi, how many pounds will be required to stretch a bar of steel 10 in. long and 1 in. square .01 inch?

5. If the elastic limit of a stainless steel is 140,000 psi, what is its yield strength?

6. If a load of 60,000 lb is applied to a test piece having a cross-section ¾ in x ¼ in., what is the stress?

CHAPTER 3

TOUGHNESS AND OTHER PROPERTIES

In Chapter 2 we learned about mechanical properties, how they differ from physical properties, and why knowledge of them is important in becoming a better weldor.

Hardness, which we haven't discussed in detail, is one of the most important properties. This is especially important to the weldor and other craftsmen because we can determine the hardness of a metal with relative ease and low cost. Some of the tests for other properties can be made only in a laboratory and at considerable cost. If we know how hard a metal is, we can estimate some of the other properties. The tensile strength of steel, for example, increases in direct ratio with the increase in Brinell hardness.

High tensile strength is sometimes, but not always, associated with toughness—the ability of a metal to withstand the sudden shock of a rapidly applied force. The combination of high tensile strength and toughness is highly important in many welded structures. Toughness is more a quality of a metal than a single property.

Weldability, like toughness, is difficult to evaluate. We can weld most metals, but some more easily than others. However, we cannot measure the weldability of a metal very precisely. Factors that subtract from a metal's weldability are tendency to crack, excessive hardening, formation of gas pockets, and high melting point of the metal or of alloying elements contained in it.

The weldor frequently faces the problem of thermal expansion in working with weldable metals. Rapid expansion of a metal under high heat tends to cause misalignment in the final welded product, and requires the weldor to carefully follow the proper welding procedure in order to control it.

The Meaning of Toughness

The term "toughness" is used rather loosely by many people. In many instances, it relates to the combination of properties that enables a metal to stand up against certain stresses experienced in a specific type of application. On one application of the metal, toughness means one thing; on another application, it means something different.

Even so, we can look at all of these uses of the word and make some general statements that will be true most of the time. Part of the problem stems from the fact that no one test has been devised to measure toughness in a way that will meet all requirements.

Usually, *toughness* means the general ability of a metal to withstand the shock of a rapidly applied load. Here, toughness is primarily the result of combined yield strength, ultimate strength and ductility, although elasticity also is important. This suggests one popular method of estimating the relative toughness of metals, which is to study the stress-strain diagrams for each of the metals, Fig. 3-1. The larger the area under the curve, the more toughness that metal will have.

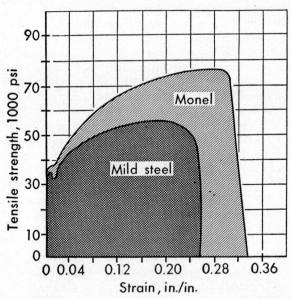

Fig. 3-1. From this comparison of stress-strain curves, it appears that monel not only has a higher tensile strength than mild steel, but the greater ductility (indicated by the elongation beyond the straight-line portion of the curve) increases the area and thus the toughness.

The area under the stress-strain curve represents the amount of energy absorbed by the metal before failure. Using a tensile stress-strain curve is directly applicable only where the metal's toughness is to be demonstrated against a tensile load.

Table 3-1 lists some common metals according to their relative toughness, with copper being the toughest.

Table 3-1. Order of Toughness of Metals

1. Copper	4. Magnesium	7. Lead
2. Nickel	5. Zinc	8. Tin
3. Iron	6. Aluminum	9. Cobalt

Unfortunately, the stress-strain curves normally result from tests in which the load conditions are static (without motion). Tensile tests call for increasing the load slowly and steadily. However, when evaluating toughness the speed with which the load is increased and the velocity with which the load is applied are both important. So is the speed with which the energy can be absorbed and distributed through the metal. Some metals are ductile; yet, under a rapidly increasing load they fail to absorb the energy fast enough and thus they fracture quickly.

A good indicator of how quickly the metal can absorb energy is the rate at which it conducts heat (thermal conductivity). Various technical handbooks and supplier literature list this rate for the more commonly used metals. If a metal is a good conductor of heat in addition to having good ductility, it usually has considerable toughness.

Impact and vibration are the two most common types of loading that require toughness in the metal. Rapidly applied loads also occur in the form of a rolling action—as in axles, gears, chain sprockets, and others. Or, the loading can be a pulsating force.

Notch Toughness

Certain conditions and defects of a metal or the product part tend to reduce considerably the toughness of metals by what we call the *notch effect.* Such conditions include deep V-grooves, cracks, tool marks, and sharp inside corners or other sudden change in the part's cross-section. See Fig. 3-2.

Some steels, like high alloy tool steels, are especially sensitive to notch effect. Others have a high degree of *notch toughness:* their

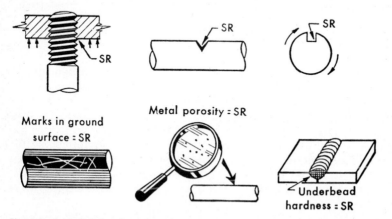

Fig. 3-2. Typical design features and metal defects and injuries that create a notch effect, thereby lowering the metal's toughness. Conditions like these are known as *stress raisers* (SR), since they result in a localized concentration of stress as a load is applied.

toughness is not affected much by the presence of notches or similar conditions. Notch-sensitive metals fail more readily than others under impact or repetitive loading. The notch sensitivity of a metal usually increases as the hardness of the metal increases and as the operating temperature decreases.

Probably because any lack of toughness is most dramatically revealed under an impact load, many people have come to rely greatly on a metal's strength under impact as a measure of the metal's toughness under other types of loading. This may be a costly practice.

Tests for impact strength are usually based on the use of a notched specimen and therefore can't be depended upon completely for every application that requires a high degree of toughness. Many metals and product parts are free of stress raisers, and the service conditions may be unlikely to duplicate the test conditions.

In general, a metal that shows extreme strength under impact as a notched specimen will demonstrate great toughness under most service conditions. Unfortunately, a metal or product part that shows up poorly under a notch-type impact test may have more than enough toughness under certain types of service conditions.

The notch effect is also a great factor in fatigue strength. Since fatigue tests are dynamic (moving loads) and not static (stationary loads), they too tell us much about a metal's toughness. A product is often used under conditions where vibration is present, even though not always visible to the naked eye. Although the stresses are not very great, as a rule, they occur at such high speed that the total effect can mean disaster to a metal that has relatively low toughness. Stress raisers in the metal or product substantially reduce the fatigue life.

Toughness vs. Brittleness

Toughness and brittleness are often thought of as direct opposites. This is true to a great extent, and is helpful in the study of failures under actual service conditions.

A *tough fracture* looks like the two pieces of a broken metal part were torn apart. The broken surfaces are very irregular and, in many instances, show up the fiber-like nature of the metal's internal structure. These surfaces are usually dull in appearance. A tough fracture occurs slowly. It may take minutes, hours, days or even longer for the break to travel completely across the metal part. A tough fracture is often called a *ductile fracture*. The latter term is especially well used when the metal has high ductility and there is considerable reduction in the cross-section and a corresponding elongation in the area of fracture.

In contrast, a *brittle fracture* frequently looks almost like the two pieces were sheared apart. In some cases the metal is actually shattered and there are more than two pieces or even many small fragments. The broken surfaces are clean, sometimes smooth, but often with jagged edges. The surfaces usually show up the crystal structure of the metal rather than a fibrous-like quality. The surfaces generally are bright in appearance. A brittle fracture travels across the part very quickly, often within a fraction of a second.

The Effect of Temperature

While metals may be identified as tough or brittle on the basis of their normal appearance when fractured, some caution is needed. A metal that appears to have great toughness and produces a tough or ductile fracture at usual working temperatures, may fail under lighter loads and produce a brittle fracture at a lower temperature. The presence of stress raisers in a metal that tends to lose its toughness rapidly at low temperatures will cause it to fail under a much lighter load.

We call this point—at which the change from ductile fracture to brittle fracture happens—the *transition temperature*. When evaluating tests made to determine such temperature levels, we must consider very carefully the size and nature of the load under which this change occurs and then make certain it corresponds with what the metal will face in service.

Testing for Impact Strength

Impact strength is the ability of a metal to withstand a sharp, high-velocity blow. Thus, it is a particular kind of toughness. A metal may show good tensile strength and good ductility in a standard pull test, and yet break if subjected to a sharp, high-velocity blow. Fur-

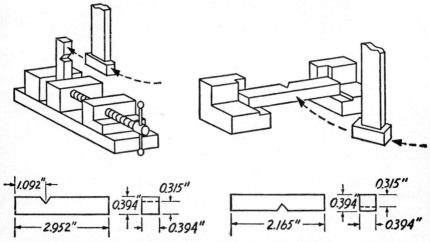

Fig. 3-3. Typical Izod (left) and Charpy (right) impact test specimens, methods of holding and of applying the test load. The V-notch specimens (shown) have an included angle of 45 degrees and a bottom radius of 0.010 in. in the notch.

thermore, the break may be in the nature of a brittle fracture. This is a characteristic of low impact strength.

Nearly all testing for impact strength is done with notched specimens, in which case it is more accurately the testing for notch toughness.

Impact strength is measured in foot-pounds, which is a unit of energy or work. The two standard methods for determining impact strength are the Izod and the Charpy tests. The two types of specimens used for these tests and the method of applying the load are shown in Fig. 3-3. Both tests can be made in the universal impact testing machine shown in Fig. 3-4.

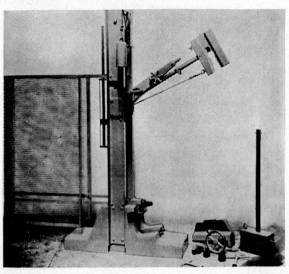

Fig. 3-4. This universal impact testing machine may be used for Izod, Charpy or other impact tests.

In making the test for impact strength, the specimen is placed in the machine near the floor. The operator then releases a heavy pendulum which swings from a standard height to strike the specimen. If the sample is broken by the blow, the strength of the specimen is determined by calculating the amount of energy needed to break it.

The amount of energy in the falling pendulum is known. The distance through which the pendulum swings after breaking the specimen indicates how much of the total energy was used in breaking it. With no specimen in the machine, the pendulum swings to the zero reading on the scale. The tougher the metal specimen which is broken by the swing, the shorter the distance travelled by the pendulum beyond the point of impact. The shorter the distance, the higher the reading on the indicating scale.

Steels or welds are commonly tested for notch toughness or impact strength right in the shop without such elaborate testing equipment. The weldor or inspector first saws a notch in a small specimen of the metal to be tested and places it in a bench vise, Fig. 3-5. He then hits the piece on the notch side with a sledge or other heavy hammer, attempting to break it with a single blow. This is the *nick-break test.* The force required to break the sample, the amount of bending at the break, and the appearance of the fractured surfaces all indicate the relative impact strength of the metals being tested.

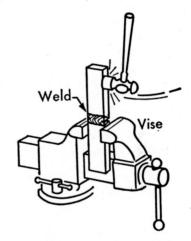

Fig. 3-5. Although considerable experience and sound judgment are necessary, the nick-break test is simple to make and quickly provides much useful information.

Hardness Testing

Hardness is a property with which the weldor must be thoroughly familiar. The heat of welding may change the hardness of the metals being welded, or the end result may be a difference in hardness between the deposited weld metal and the parent metal. A difference in hardness usually indicates a difference in strength and other properties. Through the study of welding metallurgy, we can learn more about the causes of such change in hardness and how to control the hardness. However, in many cases no change or difference in hardness accompanies the welding process, in which case there is no concern over hardness control.

We commonly test a material for hardness by trying to scratch it with a fingernail. We might find that we can scratch a harder material with a knife but not with a fingernail. Further up the scale, only a diamond makes an impression.

What you think hardness means depends a great deal on what you are. The metallurgist thinks of *hardness* as the ability of a material to resist indentation or penetration. The mineralogist thinks of hardness as the ability of a material to resist abrasion or scratching. A machinist, on the other hand, considers hardness as an index of machinability.

From a metallurgical point of view, the chief reason for making a hardness test is for what it will tell us about other properties. For example, the tensile strength of a material is directly related to the hardness. Generally, the tensile strength can satisfactorily be estimated from the hardness value obtained in the measurement. A conversion table is included as an appendix at the end of this book.

Hardness tests are both inexpensive to make and non-destructive. A hardness test, therefore, may be substituted for the harder-to-make and destructive tensile test.

In general, the harder of two metals of similar composition has a higher tensile strength, lower ductility and more resistance to abrasive wear. High hardness also indicates low impact strength, although some steels when properly treated have both high hardness and good impact strength.

Hardness tests are widely used to check the uniformity of metal parts as they are being made. Any non-uniformity in the material is

Fig. 3-6. A Brinell Hardness Tester.   Fig. 3-7. A Rockwell Hardness Tester.

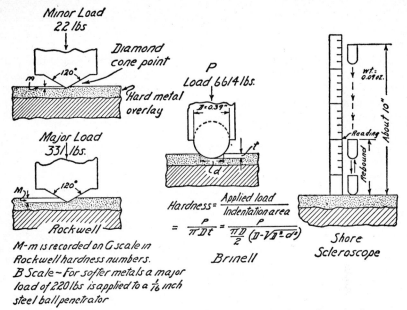

Fig. 3-8. The three most common methods of testing for hardness of metals; they are Brinell, Rockwell and Shore Scleroscope.

quickly revealed by its being either too hard or too soft.

The Brinell test is the oldest commercial method of determining indentation hardness. A steel ball of 10 millimeters (about ⅜ in.) diameter is pressed into the surface of the metal with a load of 3,000 kilograms (6,614 lb). Then the diameter of the impression is measured with a special microscope, and the reading is converted to the Brinell hardness number by consulting a table. Soft iron is about 100 Brinell, and file-hard steel about 600. A Brinell test machine is pictured in Fig. 3-6. Physical property tables in catalogs and handbooks often abbreviate—BHN or Bhn, for Brinell hardness number.

The Rockwell hardness test is widely used in production inspection. This test is also of the indentation type, but the penetrator is smaller and the loads are lighter than those used for the Brinell test. With a sample of the work positioned on the anvil of the machine, a diamond cone is pressed into the metal with a load of 150 kilograms (around 330 lb), Fig. 3-7. The depth of the impression is indicated on a dial, and the reading that is obtained is called the Rockwell C hardness. A typical reading might appear on specifications as 52 Rc.

To determine the hardness of the softer metals, the hardest metals and for very thin metals, other loads are used on the diamond cone. For soft metals, the diamond may be replaced by steel balls of ¼₆ in. diameter. A load of 100 kilograms is used, and the reading is given on the B scale.

The Shore Scleroscope hardness test measures the height of rebound of a diamond pointed hammer. Hard metals cause a higher rebound than soft metals.

The file and scratch test is a quick procedure for checking hardness. Shopmen frequently use this method to predict the machinability of a metal. It consists of simply trying to scratch or cut the surface of a metal with a file or pointed object of known hardness. All scratch tests reveal only a superficial or outer skin hardness. They tell us nothing about the hardness $1/8$ in. below the surface.

Table 3-2 gives a relation between Brinell hardness and the hardness as estimated with a machinist's new hand file.

Table 3-2. File Hardness Test Data

BRINELL HARDNESS	FILE ACTION
100	File bites into surface very easily
200	File removes metal with slightly more pressure
300	Metal exhibits its first real resistance to the file
400	File removes metal with difficulty
500	File just barely removes metal
600	File slides over surface without removing metal. File teeth are dulled.

Simple Hardness Tester

Weldors sometimes make their own set of hardness testers, by heat treating $1/4$-in. high carbon steel electrodes to give a graduated series of hardnesses. The rods are labeled with their respective Rockwell C hardnesses. A sharp point is then ground on the end of each rod, taking care not to soften the steel by overheating.

By drawing these scratch testers, one at a time, over a smooth metal surface, the weldor can determine which rod has a hardness about the same as the metal being scratched. If the sharp point of the scratch tester digs in and leaves a scratch, its hardness is greater than that of the metal being tested. If the point only slides over the surface without scratching, the scratch tester is softer than the metal tested.

The hardness set is inexpensive and is convenient to use in hard-to-reach places, where a conventional test would be impossible.

Corrosion Resistance

Corrosion is the wasting away of metals by slow gradual combination with other elements and chemical compounds. *Corrosion resistance* is the ability of a metal to resist such attack. The chemical attack may be made by a gas or a liquid, either hot or cold. Such a common gas as air and such a common liquid as water may cause metals to corrode. The effects of corrosion are generally enhanced by heat, though for most purposes corrosion is considered to be an attack at room temperature.

The danger of loss of metal through corrosion is ever present and must be guarded against in making anything of metal. The stainless steels and other alloys have been especially developed to resist corrosion.

The rates at which particular metals corrode and the tests used to determine their rates do not constitute useful knowledge to the weldor and so will not be described. The weldor should know, however, which metals are more resistant to corrosion than others.

The rate of corrosion of a metal may be changed when in the presence of another metal. If one metal is brought into contact with another metal that is lower on the list, the higher metal will be protected from corrosion. The technique of galvanizing or plating is sometimes used in protection of a metal against corrosion. In this way, a base metal of low cost but high strength can often be used effectively.

The form of corrosion with which we are most familiar occurs when metals react with the oxygen in the air to form oxides. Rust, for example, is iron oxide. If the attack continues, eventually all of the iron will be turned into iron oxide. Bridges and other structures must be repainted periodically to protect them against rusting since the loss of metal may seriously weaken the structure.

This chemical attack by oxygen on metals is called oxidation. Rusting is a form of oxidation. In the case of some metals, the rate of oxidation is so fast that heat is given off by the chemical reaction, and the heat is sufficient to maintain the reaction until the metal is completely burned up. This effect is especially noticeable at high temperatures.

Aluminum oxidizes very quickly at room temperature, but the effects are not the same as those of rust. The aluminum oxide forms an invisible film over the surface of the metal that protects the metal below against further reaction. Because of the use of nickel and chromium as alloying elements, stainless steels do not react with oxygen in the air even at high temperatures.

The rate of oxidation of metals and the properties of the oxides that are formed have considerable effect on welding procedures.

Electrical Resistance

Electrical resistance is the "friction" that an electric current encounters when it flows through a material. As the resistance offered by a material increases, a higher voltage is required to force a given current (number of amperes) through the material.

When an electric current flows through a metal, some of the electrical energy is converted into heat. The amount that the metal is heated is proportionate to the resistance of the material and to the square of the current flowing.

As the resistance to electrical flow decreases, less energy is lost and less heat is created in the conductor.

The ability to conduct electrical current is the opposite quality from resistance and is called *electrical conductivity*. Conductivity is the measure of the relative efficiency of a material in conducting electricity.

Of the metals, silver and copper offer the least resistance to electricity and hence have the greatest conductivity. For purposes of comparison, the conductivity of silver is taken as 100%.

Fusibility: The Ease of Melting

Fusibility is a measure of the ease of melting. Mercury (the metal with the lowest melting point) melts at -38 degrees Fahrenheit, while tungsten, which has the highest melting point, melts at 6,100 F.

A pure metal has a definite melting point, which is the same temperature as its freezing point. Alloys and mixtures of metals, however, have a temperature at which melting starts and a higher temperature at which the melting is complete.

Figure 3-9 gives the melting point of a few metals and other temperatures of interest. Centigrade (C) temperatures are shown to the

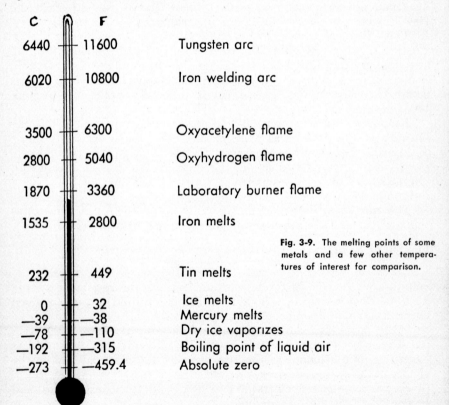

C	F	
6440	11600	Tungsten arc
6020	10800	Iron welding arc
3500	6300	Oxyacetylene flame
2800	5040	Oxyhydrogen flame
1870	3360	Laboratory burner flame
1535	2800	Iron melts
232	449	Tin melts
0	32	Ice melts
—39	—38	Mercury melts
—78	—110	Dry ice vaporizes
—192	—315	Boiling point of liquid air
—273	—459.4	Absolute zero

Fig. 3-9. The melting points of some metals and a few other temperatures of interest for comparison.

left of the thermometer and Fahrenheit (F) temperatures are to the right. The melting points of many metal elements are also listed in an Appendix at the back of this book. A chart for rapid conversion of temperature readings from Centigrade to Fahrenheit or from Fahrenheit to Centigrade, is also located in the Appendix.

Heat of Fusion

The *heat of fusion* is the quantity of heat necessary to change one pound of a solid material to a liquid without temperature change.

The British thermal unit (Btu) is used to measure the quantity of heat; for all practical purposes, it is the amount of heat required to raise the temperature of 1 pound of water 1 degree Fahrenheit.

The heat of fusion of ice is 144 Btu per lb. In comparison, here are the heats of fusion of a few metals:

Table 3-3. Heat of Fusion of Metals

Aluminum	170 Btu per lb	Tungsten	79 Btu per lb
Magnesium	160 " " "	Silver	45 " " "
Chromium	136 " " "	Zinc	43 " " "
Nickel	133 " " "	Gold	29 " " "
Molybdenum	126 " " "	Tin	26 " " "
Iron	117 " " "	Lead	11 " " "
Manganese	115 " " "	Mercury	5 " " "
Copper	91 " " "		

More heat is required to melt a pound of ice than is needed to melt a pound of iron (provided of course that both materials are at their melting point). The figures are 144 Btu for water and 117 Btu for iron. It takes more heat, however, to melt a pound of aluminum than a pound of ice—170 Btu as against 144 Btu.

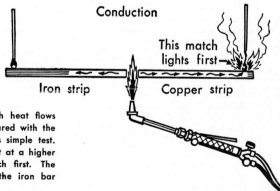

Conduction

This match lights first→

Iron strip   Copper strip

Fig. 3-10. The rate at which heat flows through copper can be compared with the same property in iron by this simple test. The metal which conducts heat at a higher rate (copper) lights the match first. The match at the outer end of the iron bar will burst into flame later.

Thermal Conductivity

Thermal conductivity is a measure of the rate at which heat will flow through a material. The difference in thermal conductivity between iron and copper is easily demonstrated, Fig. 3-10. The copper conducts heat much faster than does the iron.

If one end of a copper bar is kept in boiling water (212 F) and the other end in chipped ice, heat will flow into the bar from the water, then through the bar and to the ice, causing it to melt. The rate at which the ice melts indicates the rate heat is flowing through the bar.

The amount of ice that melts depends upon:

1. Time	The longer the time, the more ice will melt.
2. Size of the bar	The larger the cross-sectional area of the bar, the more heat will flow.
3. Length of the bar	The shorter the bar, the faster the ice will melt.
4. The temperature to which the bar is heated	The higher the temperature of the hot end of the bar, the faster the ice will melt.
5. Thermal conductivity	The higher the thermal conductivity of the bar, the more heat will flow.

The amount of heat flow, therefore, depends upon time, area, length, temperature difference and thermal conductivity.

Table 3-4. Thermal Conductivity of Metals

Metal	Chemical Symbol	Btu/sq ft/in./ hr/°F	Relative Conductivity Based on Silver as 100%
Aluminum	Al	1428	49.7%
Copper	Cu	2664	92.7
Gold	Au	2037	70.9
Iron-Pure	Fe	467	16
Iron-Steel		313	10.9
Iron-Cast		316	11
Lead	Pb	241	8
Mercury	Hg	476	17
Molybdenum	Mo	1004	34.9
Nickel	Ni	412	14.3
Platinum	Pt	483	16.8
Silver	Ag	2873	100
Tin	Sn	450	15.6
Tungsten	W	1381	48
Zinc	Zn	770	27

The thermal conductivity, or the heat-conducting capacity, of a material is frequently expressed in Btu's per sq ft of area per in. of length (or thickness) per hour per °F. The thermal conductivities of a few of the metals are given in Table 3-4.

Thermal Expansion

Thermal expansion is the increase in dimensions of a body due to a change in its temperature. See Fig. 3-11 for thermal expansion of selected materials.

The coefficient of linear expansion is the ratio of the change in length of a material, caused by heating it one degree, divided by the original length.

The coefficient of linear expansion of iron at room temperature is 0.0000065 per degree F. ($6.5 \times 10^{-6}/°F$).

The total increase in length of an iron bar 100 feet long which is heated from 10 F to 110 F will be:

0.0000065 x (110-10) x 100 = 0.065 ft or 0.78 in.

The coefficient of cubical expansion equals approximately three times the coefficient of linear expansion.

Note that the curve in Fig. 3-12 shows the volume expansion; the linear expansion of iron is ⅓ of the values given.

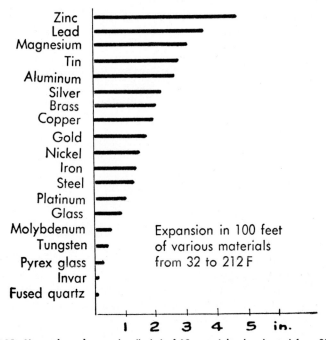

Fig. 3-11. Linear thermal expansion (in in.) of 19 materials when heated from 32 F to 212 F.

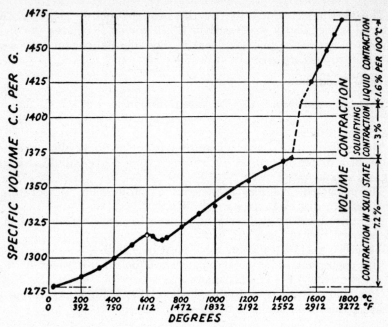

Fig. 3-12. The change in volume of a pound of cast iron as it is heated to and above its melting point.

Definitions of New Words

Brittle fracture. A metal fracture or break, in which the crystalline nature of the metal is revealed and where there is little or no evidence of bending, elongation or cross-section reduction before fracture. Fracture occurs quickly.

Corrosion resistance. The ability of a metal to resist the chemical attack by other elements and chemical compounds.

Ductile fracture. A metal fracture or break, in which the fiber-like nature of the metal is revealed and where there is considerable reduction in the cross-section and a corresponding elongation in the area of fracture (or evidence of other deformation prior to fracture). Fracture occurs slowly.

Electrical conductivity. The rate at which electric current will flow through the metal.

Electrical resistance. The resistance of the metal to the flow of an electrical current through it.

Fusibility. The relative ease with which a metal melts.

Hardness. The ability of a material to resist indentation, penetration, abrasion, and/or scratching.

Impact strength. The ability of a metal to withstand a sharp, high-velocity blow without fracture.

Nick-break test. Made in the shop to give a fast evaluation of relative impact strength. It consists merely of nicking a sample of the metal and striking it a heavy blow on the nick side, sufficient to break it.

Notch effect. The influence of an irregularity within a metal or in the surface or geometry of a product part, tending to cause a concentration of stresses and thereby weakening the metal.

Notch toughness. The resistance of a metal to adverse effects from the presence of notches or similar irregularities.

Stress raisers. Irregularities within a metal or in the surface or geometry of a product part, tending to cause a concentration of stresses as the load is applied.

Thermal conductivity. The rate at which heat will flow through the metal.

Thermal expansion. The extent of increase in physical dimension due to a change in the metal's temperature.

Tough fracture. See ductile fracture.

Toughness. The ability of a metal to withstand the shock of a rapidly applied load.

Transition temperature. The point below which the metal fails with a brittle fracture, and above which the failure is in the form of a ductile fracture.

Review Questions

1. Is magnesium tougher than aluminum? Than copper?
2. What is the purpose of a stress-strain curve?
3. Name the following methods of hardness testing: (1) A scratch method. (2) The rebound test. (3) Depth of impression made with a diamond with a conical point. (4) Diameter of impression made with a 10 mm. diam. steel ball.
4. Which commonly used commercial metal has the greatest resistance to corrosion? The least?
5. If the specific heat of water is 1.00 and of iron is 0.11 Btu/lb/F, will it take more heat to raise the temperature of one pound of water or one pound of iron from room temperature to 200 F?
6. When a file removes metal with difficulty, what is the approximate Brinell hardness of the metal?
7. Is oxidizing of aluminum the same as rusting of iron?
8. How does tensile strength and ductility affect the toughness of a material?
9. What is the Brinell method of testing hardness?
10. Is there an advantage of using a steel ball over a diamond cone in testing hardness?

CHAPTER 4

THE METALS WE USE

Any metal may be welded if the proper welding process and techniques are used. Much of the difficulty a weldor experiences is due to using a wrong process or technique when welding a specific metal. Fortunately, weldors are required to weld only a few of the metals known to man. Most welding activity is confined to metals of construction. The most common of these are steel, iron, aluminum, copper, magnesium and alloys of these.

In this chapter we'll study some of the more important facts about the *ferrous* materials—those in which iron is the main ingredient. In the following chapter we'll study the *non-ferrous* materials—such as aluminum and brass.

The purpose of these two chapters is to gain quickly a bird's-eye view of the various metals, how they differ from one another and why. Later chapters will take up each main metal group in turn and discuss it in greater detail, especially its relationship to welding requirements.

What Steels Are Like

Rolled carbon steels are the simplest of steels and consist mainly of iron, carbon and manganese (see Table 4-1). In addition, these steels contain such elements as phosphorus, sulphur and silicon. These are usually present as impurities. The effects of these elements when present in larger quantities are discussed under alloy steels and again in detail in Chapter 7.

Table 4-1 shows that the strength of steel increases as the carbon content increases, but the ductility decreases. The strengths listed in this table are for general comparison only and should not be taken as a positive statement of a particular steel's strength. Under actual conditions of use, the physical properties of steels having the same carbon content vary widely, depending upon the heat treatment they receive.

Carbon steels are grouped according to their carbon content; that is, low, medium, high and very high carbon. For typical uses, see Table 4-2. The groupings by percentage of carbon content, as listed below, reflect the weldability of various steels within each group. Suppliers of steels for a specific industry may show a slightly different medium-carbon range—0.20 or 0.25 to 0.50%, for example; but such a grouping would reflect possession of properties related to a range of application for the metal, not its weldability.

Low-carbon steels—have a carbon range between 0.05 and 0.30%. Steels in this range are commonly referred to as mild steel. In addition to these, there is a special high purity iron with a carbon range of 0.01

Table 4-1. Typical Ferrous Materials

MATERIAL	SPEC.	CHEMICAL ANALYSIS		MECHANICAL PROPERTIES			
		CARBON	OTHERS	YIELD STRENGTH	TENSILE STRENGTH	ELONGATION % IN 2 IN.	BRINELL HARDNESS
Cast Iron, Gray, Grade 20	ASTM A48-56	3.00-4.00		.....	20,000	...	163
" Gray, Grade 30	ASTM A48-56	3.00-4.00		.....	30,000	...	180
" Nickel		2.00-3.50	Ni 0.25-0.50	.....	40,000	...	310
" Chrome-Nickel		2.00-3.50	Ni 1.00-3.00 Cr 0.50-1.00	.....	53,000	...	510
" White		2.00-4.00	Si 0.80-1.50	.....	46,000	...	420
" Malleable	ASTM A47-52	1.75-2.30	Si 0.85-1.20	35,000	53,000	18	140
Iron, Wrought, Plates	ASTM A42-55	0.08	Si 0.15 Fe 99.45-99.80 Slag 1.20	26,000	46,000	35	105
" Forgings	ASTM A75-55	0.01-0.05		25,000	44,000	30	100
Steel, Cast, Low Carbon		0.11	Mn 0.60 Si 0.40	35,000	60,000	22	120
" " Medium Carbon		0.25	Mn 0.68 Si 0.32	44,000	72,000	18	140
" " High Carbon		0.50		40,000	80,000	17	182
Steel, Rolled, Carbon	SAE 1010	0.05-0.15		28,000	56,000	35	110
" Carbon	SAE 1015	0.15-0.25		30,000	60,000	26	120
" Carbon	SAE 1025	0.20-0.30		33,000	67,000	25	135
" Carbon	SAE 1035	0.30-0.40		52,000	87,000	24	175
" Carbon	SAE 1045	0.40-0.50		58,000	97,000	22	200
" Carbon	SAE 1050	0.45-0.55		60,000	102,000	20	207
" Carbon	SAE 1095	0.90-1.05		100,000	150,000	15	300
" Nickel	SAE 2315	0.10-0.20	Ni 3.25-3.75	90,000	125,000	21	230
" Ni.-Cr.	SAE 3240	0.35-0.45	Ni 1.50-2.00 Cr 0.90-1.25	113,000	136,000	21	280
" Moly.	SAE 4130	0.25-0.35	Cr 0.50-0.80 Mo 0.15-0.25	115,000	139,000	18	280
" Cr.	SAE 5140	0.35-0.45	Cr 0.80-1.10	128,000	150,000	19	300
" Cr.-Va.	SAE 6130	0.25-0.35	Cr 0.80-1.10 Va 0.15-0.18	125,000	150,000	18	310
" Si.-Mn.	SAE 9260	0.55-0.65	Mn 0.60-0.90 Si 1.80-2.20	180,000	200,000	12	390

to 0.05% and a total of all elements other than iron of less than 0.20%. This material is known as ingot iron rather than low-carbon steel. Ingot iron has good corrosion resisting qualities but is quite expensive and is produced only on a very small scale.

Steels in the low-carbon group are generally tough, ductile and easily formed, machined and welded. Although low-carbon steels are not especially hard, some grades respond to heat treatment and are readily case-hardened by carburizing, cyaniding, flame-hardening, etc.

Table 4-2. Uses for Steel by Carbon Content

CARBON CLASS	CARBON RANGE %	TYPICAL USES
Low	0.05 - 0.15	Chain, nails, pipe, rivets, screws, sheets for pressing and stamping, wire.
	0.15 - 0.30	Bars, plates, structural shapes.
Medium	0.30 - 0.45	Axles, connecting rods, shafting.
High	0.45 - 0.60	Crankshafts, scraper blades.
	0.60 - 0.75	Automobile springs, anvils, bandsaws, drop hammer dies.
Very High	0.75 - 0.90	Chisels, punches, sand tools.
	0.90 - 1.00	Knives, shear blades, springs.
	1.00 - 1.10	Milling cutters, dies, taps.
	1.10 - 1.20	Lathe tools, woodworking tools.
	1.20 - 1.30	Files, reamers.
	1.30 - 1.40	Dies for wire drawing.
	1.40 - 1.50	Metal cutting saws.

Medium-carbon steels—have a carbon range of 0.30 to 0.45%. They are strong, hard and not so easily forged or welded as low-carbon steels. If extensive welding is to be done on medium-carbon steels, it is desirable to use those steels at the lower end of the carbon range—between 0.30 and 0.35% carbon. As the carbon content increases above 0.35%, the steel becomes increasingly difficult to weld since there is a greater tendency toward brittleness of the weld. Special electrodes and procedures are often necessary to prevent weld cracking.

High-carbon (0.45 to 0.75%) and **very-high-carbon** (0.75 to 1.5%) steels—are very strong and hard. Both properties increase with an increased carbon content.

While carbon has an important influence on the characteristics of steel, the degree to which impurities are not removed by refining is also important. A slight increase in the percentage of phosphorus or sulphur will materially lower the ductility, malleability, fatigue and shock resistance and welding qualities of a steel.

High- and very-high-carbon steels respond well to heat treating. Nearly any degree of hardness, temper or strength may be obtained. In the annealed state, most of these materials may be readily machined. They also may be hot-worked for forming.

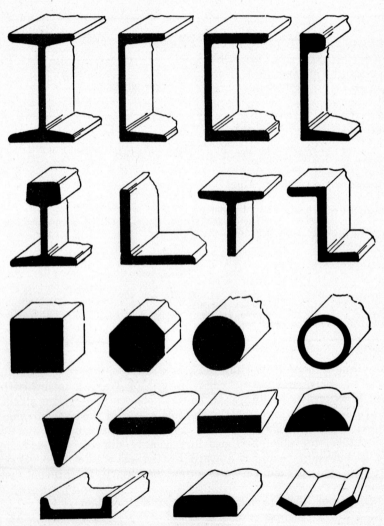

Fig. 4-1. A great many different shapes of rolled carbon and low-alloy steels are available from steel warehouses.

Steels from 0.45 up to about 0.75% carbon are sometimes welded, although special electrodes, preheating, special welding techniques and post-welding stress relief are usually required. Steels in the very-high-carbon range are seldom production welded, because their properties set over-all manufacturing restrictions on their application. These steels are used primarily for small tools, and welding is hardly ever required or desirable except for repair work. Welding of these steels is possible by using low-hydrogen or alloy steel electrodes, as well as special heat treatment before, during and after welding.

Alloy steels—have special physical and mechanical properties that depend on the presence of certain metal elements such as nickel, chromium, molybdenum, vanadium, tungsten, silicon or manganese, or on a considerable increase in silicon and manganese over that found in carbon steel. The effects of various elements in steel are discussed in Chapter 7.

Each of these elements gives certain qualities to the steel in which they are present. Some of the alloying elements combine with the carbon to form compounds that are present as hard constituents; other elements do not form compounds but remain in *solution* in the *ferrite* (pure iron) at ordinary temperatures. A simplified explanation of "in solution" is that the element remains uncombined with other elements, although its atoms are held suspended in crystals of the basic metal. This is like small pebbles being held in concrete. Those elements that on slow cooling combine with carbon to form *carbides* are manganese, chromium, molybdenum, tungsten and vanadium. Copper, nickel and silicon remain in solution in the ferrite after slow cooling.

One large group of alloy steels comes under standards set up by the Society of Automotive Engineers (SAE). This organization has developed a simple means of identifying the chemical composition of various grades of steel in common use by means of a numbering system. For most steels, the SAE numbers are the same as those established by the American Iron and Steel Institute (AISI). In an SAE number, the first digit indicates the general type of steel; the second digit indicates the approximate percentage of the alloying element that dominates the composition; while the last two digits indicate the average carbon content in hundredths of 1%. The basic numerals for various types of SAE steel are given in Table 4-3.

The tool and die steels, another large group of alloy steels, have as their outstanding characteristic the ability to retain their hardness at high temperatures. This property is known as *red hardness*. The welding of tool steels, which is discussed in detail in Chapter 19, presents a special problem—that of retaining the hardness of the steel without a reduction of its shock resistant qualities. These steels are also used as construction materials for their heat and corrosion resistance.

The principal advantage of alloy steels is their ability to respond to heat treatment. Small sections of carbon steel can be heat treated so as to obtain a tensile strength and hardness only slightly inferior to those obtained with alloy steels, but large sections of carbon steels cannot be hardened thoroughly by a quenching treatment.

Practically all of the alloying elements, when dissolved at quenching temperature, slow up the *transformation rate* and thereby contribute to the deep hardening of steels. (This will be explained in Chapters 7 and 8). Large sections of alloy steels, therefore, can be hardened to a much greater depth than corresponding sections of carbon steels. Some of the alloying elements slow up the *growth of grains* in steel at temperatures above the critical range. This permits a wider range of quenching temperatures and a more uniform structure as a result of heat treatment.

Most alloy steels may be welded provided the carbon content is not above the desirable welding range. Special welding electrodes and techniques are usually required. As a rule, these steels require heating before, during and after welding. This eliminates internal stresses from developing because of the heat of welding.

Table 4-3. SAE Steel Numbering System

TYPE OF STEEL	NUMERALS (AND DIGITS)
Carbon Steels	1xxx
Plain Carbon	10xx
Free Cutting (Screw Stock)	11xx
Free Cutting, Manganese	X13xx
High-Manganese Steels	T13xx
Nickel Steels	2xxx
0.50% Nickel	20xx
1.50% Nickel	21xx
3.50% Nickel	23xx
5.00% Nickel	25xx
Nickel-Chromium Steels	3xxx
1.25% Nickel, 0.60% Chromium	31xx
1.75% Nickel, 1.00% Chromium	32xx
3.50% Nickel, 1.50% Chromium	33xx
3.00% Nickel, 0.80% Chromium	34xx
Corrosion and Heat Resisting Steels	30xxx
Molybdenum Steels	4xxx
Chromium	41xx
Chromium-Nickel	43xx
Nickel	46xx and 48xx
Chromium Steels	5xxx
Low-Chromium	51xx
Medium-Chromium	52xxx
Corrosion and Heat Resisting	51xxx
Chromium-Vanadium Steels	6xxx
Tungsten Steels	7xxx and 7xxxx
Silicon-Manganese Steels	9xxx

Low-alloy, high-tensile steels—feature a low carbon content, a proportionately small content of alloying elements, and a very advantageous combination of yield strength and ductility. The chemical analysis of the various low-alloy, high-tensile steels indicates a wide variation in the alloying elements and their relative proportions.

These steels are somewhat higher priced than ordinary carbon steels, but their all-around excellence has led to their adoption in many important applications. These steels are used for bridges, boats, ore handling equipment, tanks and other large structures. It is possible to use thinner sections because of high physical properties and resistance to corrosion. The resulting saving in weight often gives a lower over-all materials cost.

The yield strength is often 90,000 psi or higher, as compared to 33,000 psi for typical low-carbon steels. Because of the thinner sections, structures are designed to provide maximum rigidity.

The low alloys, in addition to high yield strength, high ductility, high impact and endurance values, offer ease of forming, good corrosion resistance and good weldability.

Precipitation-hardened low-alloy, high-tensile steels—contain from 0.6 up to about 4.0% copper. These steels are susceptible to *precipitation hardening* due to the low solubility of copper in ferrite. This condition tends to increase tensile strength, yield strength and Brinell hardness. Elongation and cross-sectional reduction of area under stress decrease after hardening. The effects, however, diminish as the carbon content of the steel is increased. The presence of copper in this class of steels increases, somewhat, the corrosion resistant qualities of the material.

Like the other low alloys, precipitation-hardening low-alloy, high-tensile steels may be readily worked and welded.

The Main Classes of Cast Iron

Gray cast iron—is the most common type of cast iron used in machinery frames, beds and housings, as well as in numerous other applications. It is essentially an alloy of iron, carbon and silicon; yet, not all gray cast irons are alike. The name "gray" comes from the broken surfaces of this type iron, which have the characteristic gray color of graphite, Fig. 4-2.

This graphitic condition results from the slow cooling of molten iron. The chemically combined iron and carbon has time to partially disintegrate, and much of the carbon separates out as tiny flakes of graphite uniformly distributed throughout the metal. This free or *graphitic carbon* is distinct from the carbon that remains chemically combined with the iron as iron carbide.

Alloy cast iron—is a term specifically applied to gray cast iron that has a more uniform structure, greater strength and other improved properties due to the addition of nickel, chromium, molybdenum and other elements. Because of these alloying agents, the alloy cast irons are higher priced than conventional gray cast iron.

The most common alloys are those to which nickel has been added, usually in amounts from 0.25 to 5.0%. Up to about 4%, the nickel addition promotes uniformity of grain, hardness and strength throughout sections of considerable or uneven thickness. Nickel is often added in combination with other alloying elements such as chromium and molybdenum. The addition influences machinability, texture, hardness, density, heat and corrosion resistant properties and resistance to wear.

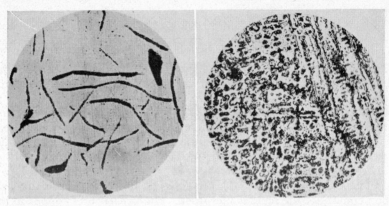

Fig. 4-2. Note the graphite flakes in gray cast iron when magnified to 100 times its original size (100x).

Fig. 4-3. Note that the carbon formation of white cast iron (100x), above, is much different than that of gray cast iron.

In general, nickel cast iron alloys are harder, stronger and of better structure with equal machinability in comparison with plain iron castings.

From 0.40 to 1.0% chromium is added to cast iron for additional hardness or increased wear resistance. In heavy sections, the use of chromium helps to give a more uniform structure and tends to eliminate porosity. Chromium cast irons have better tensile strength at elevated temperatures and minimum tendency toward grain growth.

Nickel-chromium cast irons are used on many applications. The usual ratio of nickel to chromium is 2½ to 1. As a rule, the chromium content is not over 3%. Nickel and chromium are used together primarily to refine the structure and to harden and strengthen the gray iron casting without lowering its machinability.

A combination of 4.5% nickel and 1.5% chromium is sometimes used in chilled or white cast iron to produce extreme hardness as well as toughness and strength.

Molybdenum is often added to gray cast iron in quantities from

0.25 to 1.25% for the purpose of increasing tensile strength, transverse strength and hardness.

Each of these alloying elements may be added separately or in combination with other elements. The particular alloy cast iron takes its name from that element which has the dominant effect.

Other elements added to cast iron to produce various effects include copper, aluminum, titanium and zirconium. All of these influence the material's strength, for example. Use of aluminum in cast iron has one disadvantage in that an aluminum oxide forms on the surface, tending to produce a lack of soundness in the casting.

In recent years a family of patented cast irons known as Meehanite has come into use in the machine tool field. These irons contain silicon, manganese, phosphorus, sulphur and carbon, and are treated in the molten state with calcium silicide. The exact composition and structure of Meehanite depends on the mixture of elements and the process, both of which vary to meet specific service requirements. There are many different grades available, each having a separate and distinct combination of properties. Some of the grades may be heat-treated and flame-hardened. The Meehanite cast irons are supplied by numerous licensed foundries.

White cast iron—contains carbon in the combined form. It is produced, usually, by cooling molten metal so rapidly that the carbon does not separate from the iron carbide compound, Fig. 4-3 and Fig. 4-4. White cast iron is readily distinguished from other forms of cast iron because of its extreme hardness. When fractured, sidewalls of the break appear silvery and white.

White cast iron in its original state has comparatively few applications. White cast iron surfaces on gray iron cores, however, are used extensively. This condition is produced by casting against chilled surfaces (often water-cooled) of the cast iron mold. The hot metal

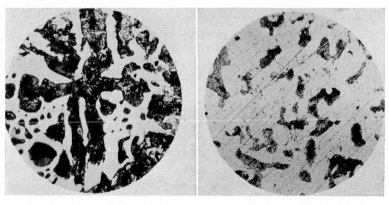

Fig. 4-4. White cast iron at 500 diameters (500x).

Fig. 4-5. Malleable cast iron has an even distribution of carbon.

coming into contact with the mold is cooled quickly to produce a file-hard chilled surface to a depth of ¼ to ½ in. Such cast iron is known as chilled iron.

Malleable cast iron—is produced by subjecting white iron castings to an annealing process for several days at a temperature ranging from 1500 to 1650 F. This treatment transforms a portion of the carbon into the free and refined state of low temper carbon. Carbon in this form assumes the shape of rounded particles, which are more evenly distributed than the flaky graphitic carbon of gray cast iron, Fig. 4-5. Because of this, the properties of malleable cast iron depend largely on the amount of carbon present.

The carbon content varies from 2 to 3%. The greater the amount of carbon, the greater the tendency toward a weaker and less ductile (though more sound and better appearing) casting. A high carbon content generally increases machinability.

Malleable cast iron bends or otherwise deforms plastically before it breaks and, therefore, stands shock better than gray cast iron. In addition to better ductility, malleable iron is stronger and tougher that gray cast iron.

Nodular irons—make up a newer group of premium-priced cast irons. These are tougher than gray cast iron, as the result of a relatively simple change in the material's internal structure. Figures 4-6 and 4-7 show why very clearly. The dark areas are graphite (similar to the "lead" in pencils you write with), which is always present in gray cast iron.

If the graphite is long, snaky or flaky and is connected together in the form of stringers (Fig. 4-6), the iron is weaker than when the graphite is present in rounded masses—"spheroids" or "nodules" (Fig. 4-7). The presence of spheroidal instead of flake graphite is largely

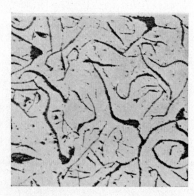

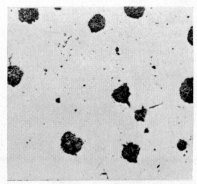

Fig. 4-6. Gray cast iron's strength is limited due to the stringer arrangement of its graphitic carbon content, 100x.

Fig. 4-7. Ductile iron has a stronger character because of the nodular formation of its carbon as melted, cast and processed, 100x.

responsible for the excellent ductility that results after annealing. Nodular iron (also known as **spheroidal** or **ductile** iron) has high tensile strength, good casting qualities and also retains the excellent corrosion resistance of gray iron.

The unique grain structure of ductile iron is the result of adding small amounts of magnesium to the iron at the time of melting.

Typical mechanical properties of four important types of commercially available nodular irons are as follows:

Type A. Tensile strength, 95,000 to 105,000 psi; yield strength, 70,000 to 75,000 psi; elongation, 2.5 to 5.5%; Brinell hardness, 225 to 265; usual condition, as cast; structure, pearlitic; mechanical wear resistance, good.

Type B. Tensile strength, 85,000 to 95,000 psi; yield strength, 65,000 to 70,000 psi; elongation, 5.5 to 10%; Brinell hardness, 195 to 225; usual condition, as cast; structure, pearlitic-ferritic. Provides good strength and toughness combined.

Type C. Tensile strength, 65,000 to 75,000 psi; yield strength, 50,000 to 60,000 psi; elongation, 17.0 to 23%, Brinell hardness, 140 to 180; usual condition, annealed; structure, fully ferritic usually the result of short anneal of either Type A or Type B. Provides optimum machinability and maximum toughness.

Type D. Tensile strength, 85,000 to 95,000 psi; yield strength, 65,000 to 75,000 psi; elongation, 1.0 to 3.0%; Brinell hardness, 230 to 290; usual condition, as cast. Has higher phosphorus content than preceding grades, also higher manganese content. Provides high strength and stiffness, but only moderate impact strength.

Wrought Iron

Wrought iron is a ductile, tough, fibrous, ferrous material composed of relatively pure iron and iron silicate. This iron silicate, a member of the glass family, is commonly referred to as *slag*. The slag is distributed throughout the pure iron in the form of threads or

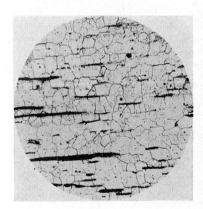

Fig. 4-8. A longitudinal section of a wrought iron rail showing slag stringers, 100x.

Fig. 4-9. Wrought iron is characterized by its tough, fibrous structure.

Fig. 4-10. Compare the crystalline or granular appearance of the fractured steel above with that of the wrought iron in Fig. 4-9.

fibres that extend in the direction of rolling, Fig. 4-8. In the finished product, the slag content varies in amount up to 3% by weight.

Wrought iron was used very extensively as a structural material in years past. It has now been replaced by less expensive and usually superior steel. Wrought iron, however, is still superior to steel where corrosion and severe fatigue conditions exist. The difference between wrought iron and other materials is most apparent when fractured samples of each are compared. In structure, the fracture of a piece of wrought iron resembles a broken piece of hickory wood (Fig. 4-9), while the fracture of a piece of steel, pure iron or cast iron has a crystalline or granular appearance very similar to the break of a lump of sugar (Fig. 4-10).

Generally speaking, there is only one kind of wrought iron, although the quality varies considerably because of the range of carbon, manganese, phosphorus, sulphur and silicon. Since wrought iron consists of high purity iron and iron silicate and since the constituents are distributed between the metal and the slag, the desirable analysis is one that discloses such distribution. A typical analysis of wrought iron is given in Table 4-4.

Table 4-4. Wrought Iron (3% Slag, by Weight)

CONSTITUENT	COMBINED ANALYSIS	SEPARATE ANALYSIS SHOWING DISTRIBUTION OF ALLOYING ELEMENTS	
		Base Metal	Slag
Carbon	.02%	.02%	....
Manganese	.03	.01	.02%
Phosporous	.12	.10	.02
Sulphur	.02	.02	....
Silicon	.15	.01	.14
Total Alloying Content		.16	.18

A shortcoming of wrought iron results from its high percentages of phosphorus and sulphur. Sulphur tends to develop *hot shortness,* a condition that makes a material brittle at elevated temperatures. On the other hand, excessive phosphorus leads to *cold shortness,* a brittle characteristic at room temperatures or lower.

Nickel wrought iron—is alloyed with nickel, occasionally as much as 5%. For most purposes, however, a 1½% to 3% nickel content is satisfactory. Table 4-5 indicates how properties of unalloyed and 3% nickel wrought iron compare in the same class of product.

This tabulation reveals that the addition of a nickel alloy has a more marked effect on the yield strength than on the ultimate strength. These properties of the alloy material may be enhanced further by proper heat treatment.

Years ago the strength of wrought iron varied between the longitudinal and transverse rolling directions. Cross-rolling has eliminated this variance so that the ultimate strength of wrought iron is now approximately the same in either direction.

Table 4-5. Effect of Nickel on Wrought Iron Properties

PROPERTY	UNALLOYED WROUGHT IRON	3% NICKEL WROUGHT IRON
Tensile Strength, psi	48,000	60,000
Yield Point, psi	30,000	45,000
Elongation in 8", per cent	25	22
Reduction of Area, per cent	45	40

The Cast Steels

This term is applied to metal that, when leaving the steel-making furnace, is cast directly into the shape in which it is finally to be used. Steel castings are classified according to their chemical composition and generally fall into one of four groups: carbon steel, low alloy steel, alloy steel, or stainless steel. Table 4-1 lists the typical analysis of different types of cast carbon steel.

Carbon steel castings—are usually specified as low-, medium- or high-carbon cast steel. Low-carbon castings have less than 0.20% carbon. Tensile strength is around 60,000 psi, and the material is relatively soft. Medium-carbon steels have a range between 0.20 and 0.50% carbon and their tensile strength is around 75,000 psi. They are somewhat harder than low-carbon cast steel but have better machining qualities. High-carbon castings have more than 0.50% carbon content and their tensile strength extends to above 125,000 psi.

Low-alloy steel castings—have a carbon range from 0.15 to 0.60% and a total alloy content of less than 5%. At least 75 different alloy combinations fall within this classification. Some have but one special alloying agent while others have as many as four.

Alloy steel castings—have about the same carbon range as the low alloys; however, their total alloy content ranges higher than 5%. Alloy steel castings are usually simple alloys, in that only one alloying agent is employed. Vanadium, manganese and molybdenum are commonly used. Castings of this type are especially desired because of their high tensile strengths and their ready response to heat-treating applications. Generally these castings can be machined readily and often are machined prior to heat treating so that the finished surface will have the desired properties imparted by such heat treatment.

Manganese steel castings—are used widely in construction machinery and where severe abrasion is to be encountered. It possesses the unusual characteristic of work hardening; that is, its surface becomes increasingly hard as it is subjected to impact blows or friction in service. Because of this quality, manganese steel is exceptionally desirable for machines such as rock crushers, that are subjected to abrasion and impact.

Manganese steel is a non-magnetic steel containing 10 to 14% manganese. The carbon range is usually from 1 to 1.4%. This material is extremely hard and brittle when cast, but this difficulty is overcome by placing the manganese castings in a furnace and slowly heating them to a temperature of from 1850 to 1950 F. They are suddenly quenched at this temperature, the result being an extremely tough high strength material. While this material is not very hard, it has a tensile strength ranging from 120,000 to 136,000 psi.

Manganese steel is usually used in "as cast" and heat treated condition. Its machinability is very poor, although it may be finished by grinding. It can be readily welded using a chromium-nickel, nickel-manganese or copper-manganese welding rod or electrode. Arc welding is generally preferred in the welding of manganese steel, because it is difficult to do a good job of oxyacetylene welding without getting the casting too hot. When overheated, the casting changes its characteristics and tends to again become a hard, brittle material.

Stainless steel castings—have a high chromium or chromium-nickel content. These castings are usually used where extreme corrosive conditions are to be overcome, and especially where their excellent heat-resisting will be an additional advantage.

The Stainless Steels

The most outstanding characteristic of stainless steels is their ability to resist corrosion. Because of this, corrosion resistant steels are normally classified into three groups.

Group 1. Chromium-nickel steels—contain 0.25% or less carbon, 16 to 25% chromium, and 6 to 22% nickel. The most prominent member of the group is the 18-8, meaning 18% chromium and 8% nickel. The 18-8 steel is usually an AISI 302 or 304. The same basic composition with the addition of 2% molybdenum is AISI 316, and with 4% molybdenum is AISI 317. Each of these alloys has progressively higher resistance to corrosion and temperature. A distinctive characteristic of a chromium-nickel steel is that its strength cannot be increased by heat treatment, although it may be increased by cold working. The latter property is called *work hardening*. These steels are termed **austenitic** stainless steels.

Group 2. Hardenable chromium steels—contain 12 to 18% chromium with carbon ranging all the way from 0.15 up to 1.20%. As indicated by their name, they are hardenable by heat treatment. These steels are termed **martensitic** stainless steels and are commonly used in the manufacture of cutlery.

Group 3. Non-hardenable steels—contain from 12 to 27% chromium and 0.08 to 0.20% carbon. They are not hardenable by heat treatment. Their use is primarily in refinery and other equipment subjected to high temperatures and pressures. These are **ferritic** stainless steels.

Most of the stainless steels in these three groups are readily welded, although special techniques may be required. If gas welding is used, care must be exercised to avoid an excess of oxygen, as the metal will bubble and a porous weld will result. In inert gas or shielded-arc welding, proper procedures can produce welds that, after being ground and polished, cannot be distinguished from the base metal. Stainless steels of all thicknesses can be welded with most of the existing processes.

ELC stainless steels—have the same analyses as the regular austenitic alloys of corresponding type number, except for an extra-low carbon (ELC) content. The more common types are 304 ELC and 316 ELC. (These are also referred to as 304L and 316L.) Whereas 304 and 316 steels have a maximum carbon content of 0.08%, their ELC counterparts each have 0.03% maximum carbon.

The corrosion resistance of austenitic stainless steels depends on a uniform distribution of chromium throughout the metal. This in turn depends on the stability of the basic austenite structure. In the initial mill cooling of the metal and any subsequent heat treatment, a carefully controlled cooling rate is required. Of specific interest in welding is the tendency for the uniform chromium distribution to be upset by the welding heat. This is because the austenite breaks down partially, and chromium carbide *precipitates* (separates and gathers) along edges of the crystals. When this happens, the welded assembly has to be annealed in order to restore the full austenite structure.

The ELC stainless steels resist this tendency toward carbide precipitation, because there is less carbon to unite with the chromium.

Other types of austenitic stainless steels—called *stabilized stainless steels*—have been developed to provide a similar advantage through the addition of columbium, titanium, or columbium tantalum. These elements have a greater attraction for carbon than does the chromium. As temperature changes during the welding operation, any formation of carbides does not disturb the distribution of chromium.

Both ELC and stabilized stainless steels retain their corrosion resistance at higher temperatures than do ordinary austenitic types. The ELC types are used primarily where service temperatures will not exceed 800 F. The stabilized types are used where service temperatures range above this figure.

Clad Steels

In some instances, designers use a composite steel, one that has been protected on one or both sides with a dense homogeneous layer of pure nickel, stainless steel or silver, Fig. 4-11. Such material provides a surface that will adequately resist corrosive action but at a much lower cost than would be necessary were an entire plate of corrosion resistant material of sufficient strength used.

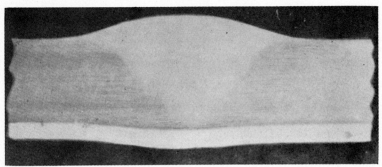

Fig. 4-11. An etched cross-section of a welded silver-clad plate.

The desired strength may be obtained through a carbon steel backing. The corrosion resisting layer need be only 5 to 20% of the total plate thickness. Clad steel manufactured in this manner possesses the same chemical and physical properties as the hot rolled or hot forged cladding material. It is firmly and permanently bonded to the steel base and does not separate from it as a result of changes in temperature, pressure or vacuum or because of deformation during forming. Clad steels are usually used for pressure vessels or containers that might be exposed to weathering, or corrosive vapors or liquids.

Like other stainless steels, clad steels may be welded. Care must be exercised because of the special problem presented by the two different materials to be welded. To obtain the full benefits of the clad material, welding procedures must be the same as those for welding a solid plate of this material. Thus, in nickel-clad steel, the nickel cladding is welded in the same manner as a pure nickel plate.

Definitions of New Words

Carbide. The chemical combination of carbon with some other element. A metallic carbide takes the form of very hard crystals.

Cold shortness. The characteristic tendency of a metal toward brittleness at room temperature or lower.

Ferrite. Pure iron crystal structure.

Ferrous. Dominated by iron in its chemical composition.

Grain growth. The increase in size of individual crystals as the result of absorption within a crystal of atoms at the grain boundaries, or of the wedding of adjacent similarly-oriented crystals.

Graphitic carbon. Free, uncombined carbon existing, in a metallic material, in the form of flakes.

Hot shortness. The characteristic tendency of a material toward brittleness at elevated temperatures.

Non-ferrous. Lacking iron in sufficient percentage to have any dominating influence on properties of the material.

Precipitates. A result of a solid solution decomposing, usually into another solid solution and the precipitate—one or more elements, atoms of which tend to group together.

Precipitation hardening. The process of heating to a temperature at which certain elements precipitate forming a harder constituent, and usually then cooling at a rate to prevent return to the original structure.

Red hardness. The property of a metallic material to retain its hardness at high temperatures.

Slag. The non-metallic layer that forms on top of molten metal. It is usually a complex of chemicals (oxides, silicates, etc.) that float to the top of the hot molten metal. When a bead of weld metal cools, the slag "cap" on the bead can be readily chipped or ground away. In wrought iron, slag is the iron silicate constituent which is distributed throughout the pure iron in the form of threads, fibres or stringers extending in the direction of rolling.

Solution. The state in which atoms of one element are dissolved (uncombined, but held suspended) by crystals of another element.

Stabilized stainless steel. A high-chromium steel that does not lose its chromium from solid solution by precipitation, because of the addition of elements that have a greater attraction for carbon than does chromium.

Transformation rate. The rate of speed at which a metallic material changes from one state (type of physical structure) to another, as temperature of the material increases or decreases. Unless otherwise identified, it applies to the transformation of a heated material into that crystal structure which exists permanently at room temperature.

Work hardening. The capacity of a material to harden as the result of cold rolling or other cold working involving deformation of the metal.

Review Questions

1. How can the amount of carbon in a ferrous material be used to help determine whether a material is steel or a cast iron?
2. Name the four basic types of carbon steel.
3. When does an added metal element become an alloying element rather than an impurity in steel?
4. What are SAE steels? What is the significance of SAE steel numbers?
5. How do low-alloy, high-tensile steels differ from low-carbon steels?

CHAPTER 5

NON-FERROUS MATERIALS

While much of our presentday metal fabrication involves only steel, many non-ferrous materials are used extensively and all weldors should be acquainted with these. Non-ferrous metals are those that do not contain an appreciable amount of iron, although very small percentages of iron may be present in some of the alloys. The most common non-ferrous materials are copper, aluminum, magnesium, nickel, zinc and lead. All of these are weldable, though some require special precautions as well as special techniques.

Copper and Copper Alloys

These are the most common of the non-ferrous materials available to man. Copper enters freely into alloy with at least 30 of the 102 known chemical elements. Of these elements, 17 are used in making commercial copper alloys. The more common copper alloys fall into two general classifications: brasses and bronzes.

Copper that is to be welded should be thoroughly deoxidized. Spot or seam welding of high conductivity copper is not done commercially unless the surfaces are first tin plated. Copper, however, is easily butt welded, silver brazed or soldered, these being the most common methods of joining this material.

Brass—is the most common class of copper alloys, in which zinc is the alloying element. The amount of zinc ranges from 1 to 50% in making at least 15 individual commercial brasses. The low-zinc brasses are ductile and quite suitable for cold working, but are difficult to machine. Gilding brass and commercial brass are used for bullet jackets and articles exposed to weather. Red brass finds extensive use for imitation gold jewelry, but is also used extensively for piping, radiator cases and condenser shields.

Those brasses containing 20 to 40% zinc have a variety of uses. Brazing brass, which may be spun or cold drawn with ease, is used extensively for musical instruments and ornamental architectural work. Cartridge brass, which is tough and ductile, is quite suited to deep drawing or spinning and is used extensively in the manufacture of cartridge cases. Yellow brass is the cheapest of all brasses, and may be cold drawn. It is used extensively in the manufacture of screws and rivets. When used in parts that are cold formed, it should be annealed after final forming to prevent cracking. Muntz metal (60% copper, 40% zinc) is not malleable when cooled, and should be worked only at a red heat. Brasses containing over 40% zinc are not widely used.

Practically no straight copper-zinc alloys are used for casting.

Castings are usually complex brasses that have had manganese or some other alloying element added to them. Scrap brass is often used in castings where accurate control of the properties is unnecessary.

In addition, brasses to serve specific purposes have alloy additions of tin, lead and aluminum. Aluminum brass, for example, is used extensively for condenser tubing. Naval brass and admiralty metal are used to resist salt water corrosion. Forging brass, containing 2% lead, may be readily hot worked while brasses containing up to 3% lead are often cold formed. The addition of the lead greatly improves their machining qualities.

Bronzes—are copper alloys that have principal alloying elements other than zinc. Tin, silicon, aluminum and beryllium are the most common additions. Some of these alloys are capable of being hardened by heat treatment. As a result, extremely high tensile strengths may be developed.

All of the bronzes, like the copper-zinc alloys, may be hardened by cold working. Since some of them may also be hardened by heat treatment, they are generally divided into two classes—heat treatable alloys and the non-heat treatable alloys.

Of the heat-treatable bronzes, some are hardened like steel, while others are hardened by solution heat treatment and precipitation hardening. The most common of those that are hardened like steel is aluminum bronze. The amount of aluminum in this alloy varies up to 12%. Up to 4% iron is sometimes added to increase the alloy's endurance limit and shock resistance.

Aluminum bronze is a rather versatile alloy. Its properties can be controlled over a wide range either by varying the alloying elements or by heat treatment. Aluminum bronze is used for gears, cams, rollers, dies, sliding machine members, etc. In most instances, it may be substituted for brass because of its superior strength and corrosion resistant qualities. It also resists abrasive wear and has good impact values.

The most common of the nonheat-treatable alloys are the copper-tin alloys deoxidized with phosphorus. These are generally known as phosphor bronze or tin bronze. The range of tin in these bronzes may be from 1 to 11%, while the phosphorus content may range up to 0.5%. Occasionally up to 4% lead is added to improve the machinability of this alloy. The strength and hardness of phosphor bronzes increase as the percentage of tin is increased. This material is known for its high strength, resiliency, and resistance to wear and fatigue. It is highly recommended for springs; however, it is not as good for this purpose as beryllium bronze. Phosphor bronze is also used for shafts and bushings, these items usually being made from the leaded type.

Silicon bronze is another of the nonheat-treatable bronzes. Its average composition is 3% silicon, 1% manganese or zinc and the remainder copper. It is used quite extensively for tanks, boilers and other pressure vessels where high strength and good corrosion resistance are required.

There are other copper alloys in this nonheat-treatable group, primarily those with nickel which are used extensively on corrosion resistant applications. The most common of these is cupronickel, which is 70% copper, 30% nickel alloy. This material is used extensively for tubing in condensers. Nickel-silver, a copper alloy containing 64% copper, 18% zinc has the appearance of silver and possesses good corrosion resistance and fairly high electrical resistivity. This material is used widely in food handling equipment and in jewelry.

There are many bronzes other than those mentioned here. Many of these carry specific trade names, being produced by only one manufacturer. Others are less commonly used, an example being gun metal, which is a copper alloy containing 8 to 11% tin. Another material, manganese bronze, is in reality a brass consisting of copper and zinc with manganese as a deoxidizer.

Weldability—most of the bronzes may be welded. Those having high zinc content present difficulties where soldering or brazing is concerned. Flux-coated electrodes are used advantageously in arc welding these materials. In the welding of many bronzes, the use of an inert-gas arc process may be advantageous. Oxyacetylene welding may be used in some instances; however, care must be taken not to oxidize the materials. Resistance welding may be used at times, but because of the high electrical conductivity of copper alloys, some difficulty is generally experienced.

Aluminum and Its Alloys

These materials are used primarily on applications that demand good strength, light weight, high thermal and electrical conductivity or corrosion resistance. Commercially pure aluminum in the annealed or cast state has a tensile strength about ⅕ that of structural steel. Cold working increases the strength considerably, as does alloying the aluminum with other metals. Alloying with copper, silicon or zinc permits heat treating to increase strength. In some cases, the strength is increased to a point where it is comparable with steel.

Although some steels have comparable weight-strength ratio, structural aluminum alloys have proved themselves superior in some applications.

The melting point of pure aluminum is 1215 F. Alloys usually melt at lower temperatures. It is important to remember that aluminum has a coefficient of thermal expansion at least 50% greater than copper and twice that of steel and cast iron. Commercially pure aluminum, known as 1100, is often used for such shapes as sheet, tubing and rod where good corrosion resistance is required.

When commercially pure (1100) aluminum is not satisfactory from a strength standpoint, an alloy (3003) with approximately equal corrosion resistance is frequently substituted. This alloy, which contains

1.25% manganese, is somewhat stronger.

Wrought aluminum alloys—contain relatively low percentages of alloying elements. Aluminum is frequently alloyed with silicon and manganese for corrosion resistance; however, zinc, iron, copper and tin are only slightly less corrosion resistant. Some of the aluminum alloys may be hardened by cold working.

Of the wrought aluminum alloys that can be precipitation hardened, an alloy containing 1.25% manganese (3003) is the most important. It is not only stronger but is harder than pure aluminum. Unlike the other alloys, its corrosion resistant properties are almost as good as those of pure aluminum. This alloy is used extensively in the making of cooking utensils, as well as in conduit and pipe.

The aluminum-copper-magnesium-manganese alloys such as 2014, 2017 and 2024 are heat treatable. For a long time 2017 was the most popular of these alloys and was used extensively in making a variety of lightweight commodities. The alloy 2024, quite similar to 2017, is often used where extra high strength is required.

These high strength, heat-treatable alloys are available in either plain or clad form. For example, clad 2024 is an aluminum alloy having a core of 2024 and a thin coating of high purity aluminum (1230) on one or both sides. As a rule the clad materials can be formed satisfactorily, although they cannot be welded without the possibility of damaging the pure corrosion resistant surface. Incidentally, the heat of fusion welding may lower the mechanical properties of these heat treatable alloys considerably unless proper precautions are taken.

Among the aluminum alloys of higher tensile strength is 5052, an aluminum-magnesium-chromium alloy. This alloy has a moderately high tensile and yield strength—about double that of 1100 and 3003 in corresponding tempers, but only half that of the higher strength alloys like 2024. Within the same group, the aluminum-magnesium-manganese alloys (5083 and 5456) are extensively used in welded construction, because of their high tensile strength after softening by the heat of welding.

Alloys such as 6053, an aluminum-magnesium-silicon-chromium alloy, and 6061, an aluminum-magnesium-silicon-copper-chromium alloy, can be *solution heat treated*. These materials possess high strength characteristics together with workability qualities. They may be welded, although care is required with 6053. The 6061 alloy is the strongest of the more weldable aluminum alloys. It is used extensively in architectural and furniture designs where applications call for high strength. Such designs require that the aluminum sections be placed so as to carry the load and be simply joined by welding, since welding may reduce the alloy up to about ⅓ its normal strength along the heat-affected margins. Some applications permit partial or full restoration of this strength by heat treatment after welding.

Cast aluminum alloys—generally contain a higher percentage of alloying elements than the wrought alloys. The additions greatly improve casting qualities, but make machining and subsequent working more difficult. Copper, the principal added element, increases the hardness of the aluminum. A 5% silicon alloy (43) is generally used for permanent mold castings or sand castings because of its good resistance to corrosion, high fluidity when poured, and freedom from hot shortness. A 12% silicon alloy (13) is used principally for die casting. It has good casting qualities also, and corrosion resistance.

An aluminum alloy that is widely used for general purpose castings is 212. This has 8% copper, 1.2% silicon and 1% iron. All of the alloys that contain silicon as a hardener have excellent casting qualities and can be used in the production of large, thin section castings of intricate design. They also cast satisfactorily where there are adjacent light and heavy sections, or where they must withstand fluid pressures without leading. Aluminum castings, as a rule, may be satisfactorily welded.

Magnesium and Its Alloys

Magnesium is a silvery white metal with a density about $\frac{2}{3}$ that of aluminum and $\frac{1}{4}$ that of steel, making it the lightest of the commercial metals. Pure magnesium is of little structural value because of its low strength. The alloys, however, are stronger and many of them can be hardened by precipitation heat treatment. Magnesium and its alloys have good corrosion resistance in most atmospheres.

Magnesium alloys—usually contain aluminum, manganese, and often zinc. The most popular alloys contain approximately 6% aluminum and 3% zinc. These may be precipitation hardened to give high strength and hardness. Another alloy having about 9% aluminum and 2% zinc is used extensively where castings must withstand great pressure, because of its relative freedom from *microshrinkage*.

Weldability—of magnesium alloys is quite similar, in many respects, to that of aluminum alloys. Both groups of metals have the following in common: high heat conductivity, low melting point and high thermal expansion.

Magnesium alloys may be joined by gas welding or inert-gas, shielded-arc welding as well as by the more common resistance welding methods.

Magnesium alloys are not welded to other metals because of brittle inner-metallic compounds that tend to form, and often because the combination of metals will likely contribute to corrosion. This latter hazard exists even when joining two magnesium alloys that differ only slightly in composition. Soldering is sometimes used to join magnesium alloys, but the resultant joint is subject to even greater corrosion than is experienced with welded magnesium joints. Solder should not be used to join parts that must withstand stress.

Magnesium alloys, especially as castings, are rarely subjected to heat treatment, nor can any of the magnesium alloys be flame cut.

Zinc and Its Alloys

Zinc, while used extensively for die-casting and galvanizing, is probably more widely used as an alloy with copper in brass, as previously discussed. It is a fairly heavy, bluish white metal that has excellent corrosion resistance and alloying properties, coupled with low cost. Its density is slightly less than that of copper.

Nickel and Nickel Alloys

Nickel is a tough silvery metal of about the same density as copper. It has excellent resistance to corrosion and oxidation even at high temperatures. Nickel readily alloys with many materials and is a basis for a number of steel and copper alloys.

Most important of the nickel-copper alloys is Monel, which is 67% nickel, 28% copper and 5% manganese and silicon combined. Monel is used extensively where parts are subject to wear and corrosion. Since the coefficients of thermal expansion of Monel and steel are approximately equal, the two metals are often used together.

K Monel has 2 to 4% aluminum in addition to the straight Monel composition. H and S Monels are made by adding 3 to 4% silicon to the material. These latter Monels have excellent characteristics and may be hardened by heat treatment. R Monel, with about 0.35% sulphur, is a free machining type. N Monel is a nickel-iron alloy that possesses extremely good resistance to oxidation and corrosion, and impact strength superior to that of any of the steels.

Inconel is a nickel-chromium alloy. It has a high corrosion resistance to acids and alkaline compounds. It is especially resistant to oxidation and scaling at elevated temperatures and in corrosive atmospheres.

Welding procedures similar to those used on steel are used on nickel and nickel alloys, and all of the common welding methods may be employed.

Lead

Lead is one of the oldest metals known to man. It is commonly available in four grades: (1) Antimonial lead, which averages about 6% antimony, is used extensively in the manufacture of storage batteries. (2) Corroding lead is a high purity lead used principally in the manufacture of high quality paint pigments such as white lead. (3) Common lead is somewhat lower in purity than corroding lead and is used where high purity is not necessary, such as for cable covering, roofing and similar applications. (4) Chemical lead, containing 0.04 to 0.08% copper which improves lead's resistance to corrosion, is used extensively in the chemical industry.

Lead may be welded either by oxyacetylene, air-acetylene, or carbon-arc processes and also may be soldered.

Definitions of New Words

Microshrinkage. Shrinkage of individual crystals or crystal "trees," that tend to pull away from each other. Such shrinkage is microscopic, as opposed to shrinkage that tends to change the over-all dimensions of the entire body.

Solution heat treatment. Heating an alloy to a suitable temperature for a sufficient period of time for one or more alloying constituents to enter into solid solution (to be dissolved by the principal grains), and then cooling rapidly in order to retain the solution at room temperature.

Review Questions

1. Name the one particular characteristic that makes copper difficult to weld.
2. What are the alloying elements in brass?
3. How do bronzes differ from the brasses?
4. How does the tensile strength of steel and aluminum compare?
5. What is the melting point of pure aluminum? Does the addition of alloys raise or lower the melting point?
6. How does the coefficient of thermal expansion of aluminum compare with that of copper? Of steel? Of cast iron?
7. What effect does a high silicon content have on the brazing or soldering of bronze?
8. What is meant by clad aluminum?
9. Is it possible to weld magnesium to other metals?
10. How does the welding of nickel alloys differ from the welding of steel?

CHAPTER 6

METHODS OF WELDING

Metals can be successfully joined in many ways. Excluding such methods as use rivets, pins, threaded fasteners or adhesives, we still have the many welding processes on which to concentrate. More than 45 different methods are used to join metals by fusion, with or without the help of added metal. A Master Chart of these welding processes is included in the Appendix at the back of this book. This chapter you are now reading describes the most important welding processes and the differences between them. Later chapters will provide more information on how to select and use these processes for various metals.

Before discussing specific processes, a few terms should be reviewed. The metal in the pieces being joined are referred to as the base metal or parent metal. The material frequently added to complete the welded joint is called *filler metal*. This is supplied from an electrode or welding rod depending on the process being used.

Arc Welding Processes

The arc welding processes are the most widely used of all the 45 methods. In arc welding, the arc supplies the heat needed to melt the base metal surfaces being joined and the filler metal which then fuse together (Fig. 6-1). What makes this arc? It is produced by a low-voltage, high-amperage electric current jumping an air gap between a metal or carbon electrode and the base metal being welded.

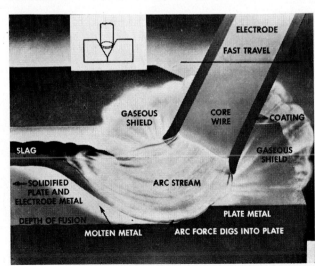

Fig. 6-1. Representation of the action that occurs in shielded-arc welding, using a coated consumable metal electrode.

The arc may be as hot as 7,000 F, although it is usually less than this. The extreme heat melts the base metal in an extremely small area, and also melts the filler metal in the electrode or welding rod when used. The arc is either unshielded or shielded, the purpose of *shielding* being to protect the molten metal from oxidizing or otherwise reacting with elements in the surrounding air. Shielding may be accomplished in several ways: by the melting of a coating on the electrode, by a blanket of powdered *flux,* or by a surrounding atmosphere of inert gas or vacuum. Properties of metal deposited by shielded arc are much superior to those of metal deposited by an unshielded arc.

The electrode may be one of two types: consumable or non-consumable. A *consumable electrode* establishes the arc and gradually melts away, being carried across the arc (deposited) to provide filler metal to the joint. A *non-consumable electrode* simply establishes and maintains the arc but does not melt. Non-consumable electrodes are used for producing both fusion welds or fill welds. When using a non-consumable electrode for fill welds, a metal *welding rod* is introduced into the arc where it is melted by the intense heat and thereby contributes the filler metal needed to complete the weld. Both carbon and tungsten electrodes are non-consumable.

In a *fusion weld,* the base metal along two mating surfaces is melted and fusion occurs without the addition of other metal. In a *fill weld,* there is also fusion of metal but the two members being joined do not fuse together directly; an intermediary or filler metal is added to the joint and fuses with the base metal on each side. Fill welds serve many purposes. One of these is to provide a ductile cushion joining two dissimilar metals (Fig. 6-2).

Most arc welding processes can be automatic, semi-automatic or manual. In an *automatic welding* process, the electrode or welding rod supplying filler metal is fed automatically into the arc to compensate for its melt off, thus maintaining the correct length of arc. The electrode held by a mechanically supported and mechanized welding head is caused to travel automatically along the joint, either by mechanized movement of the work below it or movement of the welding head along the joint. In *semi-automatic welding,* the electrode or welding rod is fed automatically but the welding head or gun is held in the hand and moved manually along the joint. In *manual welding,* the electrode is in fixed position in a holder held by the weldor, who guides it along the joint while maintaining the proper arc gap. If granular flux or inert gas is needed for shielding the arc, this is applied automatically in both automatic and semi-automatic welding.

The entire family of arc welding processes is commonly divided into two subgroups: metal-arc and carbon-arc. Of these, the metal-arc processes are the most important.

Coated electrode shielded metal-arc welding and **bare electrode unshielded metal-arc welding**—incorporate the consumable electrode

Fig. 6-2. Metal-arc welding of stainless steel to mild steel. Using a high-alloy filler metal, the alloy content of the stainless steel is maintained and stresses due to differences of base metals are minimized.

principle. The vast majority of electrodes used today are of the coated type (see the section on Arc Welding Electrodes later in this chapter), and this process is usually referred to simply as shielded-arc welding. A *coated electrode* is preferred to a bare electrode for many reasons. A properly coated electrode has a more stable arc, gives increased speed of welding, smoother weld beads, and substantially improves the mechanical properties of the deposited filler metal by direct effect on the metallurgical characteristics of the weld, as will be brought out later in this chapter. In fact, it was the development of coated electrodes that gave welding the great impetus it has received during the past 20 years.

Shielded-arc welding is used extensively in joining most classes of ferrous metals.

Carbon-arc welding—is a small group of processes in which the arc is established between a carbon electrode and the base metal, or between two (twin) carbon electrodes in an "arc torch." This arc provides the heat for fusing the base metal but does not deposit any filler metal. If filler metal is needed, it is supplied in the form of a welding rod, the analysis of which usually corresponds to the analysis of the parent metal being welded. The welding rod can be coated but is usually bare since the carbon arc provides its own shield.

Inert-gas-shielded arc welding—is a highly important joining process in which the arc is shielded from the air by a chemically *inert gas,* such as argon or helium. This process is often called inert-gas welding for short. There are two major subdivisions: TIG and MIG.

The first method of inert-gas welding obtains the necessary heat for welding from a very intense arc established between a virtually non-consumable tungsten electrode and the parent metal (Fig. 6-3). This is called tungsten-inert-gas or TIG welding. This method can be used for fusion welds or fill welds. In the latter case, where the joint requires filler metal, a welding rod is fed into the arc.

In the second type of inert-gas welding, a consumable metal electrode replaces the non-consumable tungsten electrode. The electrode is fed mechanically into the arc. This method is called metal-inert-gas or MIG welding (Fig. 6-4).

Both methods of inert-gas welding, TIG and MIG, have been adapted for full- or semi-automatic use. Since inert-gas arc welding finds its greatest use in joining non-ferrous metals, the (usually bare) filler metal electrode or welding rod is also non-ferrous and capable of producing *weld metal* having properties comparable to those of the material being welded.

Inert-gas welding is used advantageously in joining aluminum (Fig. 6-5), magnesium, copper, stainless steel and cast iron. The process can successfully weld plain carbon steel, but in most instances this has proved uneconomical when compared with other processes.

Inert-gas spot welding is a modification of the basic TIG and MIG

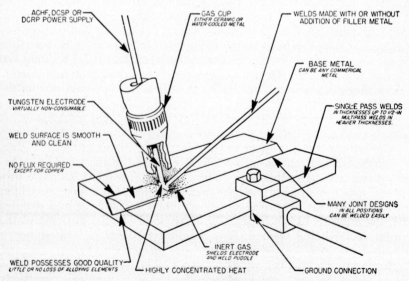

Fig. 6-3. Representation of a typical TIG (tungsten inert-gas shielded-arc) welding setup.

Fig. 6-4. (Above) In this semi-automatic MIG (metal inert-gas shielded-arc) welding operation, the continuous consumable electrode is fed mechanically but the gun is held and guided manually.

Fig. 6-5. (Right) With the TIG process, a contoured nipple is welded to an aluminum 3003 pipe header. The welding rod is held in the operator's left hand. Two passes completed this joint.

welding methods. Two lapped pieces of metal are spot welded together by applying heat from an electric arc to the top surface of the joint. Welding action is controlled by the current input to the arc and the time the arc dwells on the material being welded. Shielding of the arc, electrode (consumable metal or non-consumable tungsten) and fluid weld puddle is similar to that of conventional inert-gas shielded-arc welding. The resulting spot weld parallels that produced by resistance welding techniques; however, no electrode pressure is required and welding is done from one side of the plate without requiring any weld back-up. Both TIG spot welding and MIG spot welding are experiencing widespread industrial use.

CO_2 MIG welding—is similar to the inert-gas process, but in this case the arc is shielded by a blanketing of the arc area with a continuous flow of carbon dioxide gas (Fig. 6-6).

Two variations of the process exist. The first uses an electrode containing suitable *deoxidizers* that produce a sound weld under the CO_2 shield. The second uses a flux-cored or coated electrode that produces the deoxidizing and scavenging action in the molten weld crater.

In the flux-cored electrode, the flux is wrapped within an outer

Fig. 6-6. Steel being joined by CO_2 MIG welding. In this process, carbon dioxide gas shields the arc.

steel sheath. The flux-coated electrode is accomplished by feeding a magnetic flux material into the arc area where it magnetically attaches to the bare electrode being mechanically fed into the arc.

This arc welding process is used for production welding some of the ferrous metals. CO_2 MIG welding also has been adapted for spot welding.

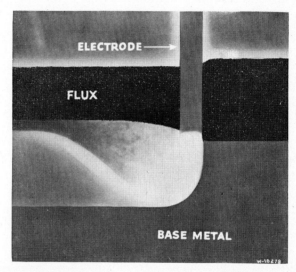

Fig. 6-7. Representation of the action that takes place in submerged-arc welding. Granulated flux completely blankets the weld area and effectively shields the arc action and molten metal from the atmosphere.

Submerged-arc welding—employs a granular flux that is fed around a consumable electrode as the latter is mechanically and continuously fed into the joint being welded (Fig. 6-7). The flux blankets the arc, the molten weld metal and the base metal during welding, thereby preventing contamination from the surrounding atmosphere and helping to control the cooling rate. The flux also supplies deoxidizers and scavengers, which improve the quality of the weld metal as it takes form. The process is extensively used with either semi- or full-automatic welding equipment (Fig. 6-8).

In either automatic or semi-automatic welding, the bare electrode is mechanically fed through an electrical contacting jaw or nozzle. The welding current passes through the electrode, and an arc is maintained between the base metal and the electrode. The arc is invisible under the granular flux, thus the name submerged-arc welding. The heat of the arc causes a local melting of the base metal, electrode and flux to accomplish *penetration*, filling and fusion of the joint.

This process usually employs higher amperage than the previously described processes, in order to increase the filler-metal *deposition rate* and welding speed. The higher currents and welding speed also reduce weld shrinkage and hold any subsequent distortion of the welded structure to a minimum.

On some full-automatic applications of submerged-arc welding, two or more electrodes are fed simultaneously into the same joint while the weld crater is still molten. This adaptation provides maximum deposition rate and welding speed, and is known as twinarc or tandem-arc welding depending on the method used.

For semi-automatic welding, the welding gun—essentially a flux dispenser and welding nozzle—is manually supported and guided along the joint by the welding operator (Fig. 6-9). Adaptations of semi-automatic submerged-arc welding include the use of mechanical accessories that can be attached to the welding gun so that it can be mechanically travelled and even completely supported. This effectively converts semi-automatic equipment to full-automatic use. The operator thus retains the advantage of the portability and adaptability of semi-automatic equipment while gaining the increased welding speed performance of full automation.

The submerged-arc process lends itself to the production welding of most ferrous metals, and the depositing of alloy surfaces. The nature

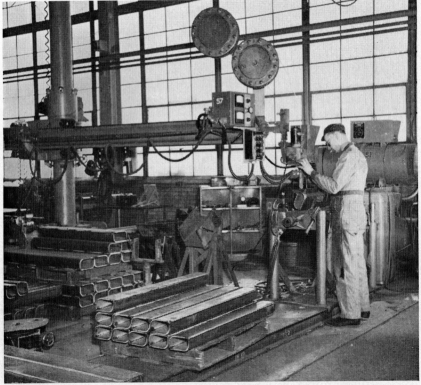

Fig. 6-8. Full-automatic welding with the submerged-arc process is capable of high production rates on a wide variety of ferrous and nickel alloys.

Fig. 6-9. Portability of the submerged-arc process, without loss of flux control, is provided by this manual semi-automatic equipment. The weldor here is working on a massive all-welded 40-ton frame for a hot-steel billet shear.

of the process permits a relatively small number of standard electrodes to take care of a very wide range of applications, with the flux often incorporating alloying elements needed for weld metal of specific properties. Consequently, this process is usually preferred for production welding of the alloy steels.

Vapor-shielded metal-arc welding—incorporates a vapor shield as opposed to the gas or flux shielding principles of the other metal-arc welding processes. This vapor shields the arc and weld metal from atmospheric contamination (Fig. 6-10). A tubular electrode, mechanically fed into the arc, contains all the ingredients (deoxidizers and metallic salts) necessary to generate the vapor shield and to refine the molten metal. As this electrode is consumed in the arc, the shielding ingredients vaporize, expanding outward into the cooler surrounding atmosphere where condensation forms the dense vapor blanket.

Both semi- and full-automatic welding equipment have been developed for production applications. The process is basically versatile. In its semi-automatic form, it offers the opportunity to increase the speed of production welding ferrous metals (Fig. 6-11). Full-automatic adaptation of the process on light-gage mild steel applications gives double and triple the production performance of the previously used processes. A major advantage is the elimination of pressurized gas tanks and hose and all external shielding materials.

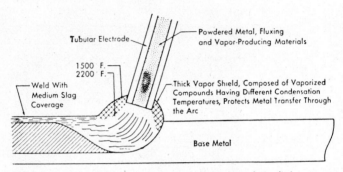

Fig. 6-10. Representation of the action that takes place during vapor-shielded welding. Shielding provided by ingredients in the tubular metal electrode produces high quality welds at high deposition rates.

Electroslag welding—is another metal-arc welding process. It is a further development in application of the submerged-arc principles. This process involves fusion of the base metal and continuously fed filler wire under a substantial layer of high-temperature, electrically conductive molten flux. By feeding one or a combination of two or three electrodes simultaneously into the arc, plates ranging from 1 to 14 in. thick can be joined in a single pass.

The weld is deposited upward along a vertical path, the joint to be welded being in a vertical position. The plates being joined are spaced from 1 to 1-5/16 in. apart, with flame-cut edges being adequate joint preparation. On materials of considerable thickness, electrodes are mechanically oscillated across the face of the molten weld crater as the welding progresses. Water-cooled copper shoes, located to each side of the joint, travel vertically with the welding head. These shoes bridge the gap and effectively form a mold for the molten weld metal during solidification.

Advantages of the process include minimum plate preparation, single pass welding procedure on any plate thickness within the range mentioned, no problem with slag removal or flux recovery, and the ability to minimize distortion and reduce residual stresses.

Metal-arc stud welding—is the end welding of a stud, ordinarily a machine screw, at a particular spot by fusion resulting from an arc struck between the stud serving as the electrode and the base plate. A compact portable unit, called a stud welder, is employed and the arc is shielded or unshielded.

Impregnated-tape metal-arc welding—parallels coated (shielded) electrode arc welding, but the arc shield is obtained from decomposition of the tape that is wrapped around the electrode.

Plasma-arc welding—exists in several forms. The basic principle is that of an arc or jet created by heating electrically a plasma-forming gas (such as nitrogen or hydrogen) to such a high temperature that its molecules become ionized atoms possessing extremely high energy. When properly controlled, this process results in very high melting temperatures. Plasma-arc welding holds the potential solution to the easier joining of many hard-to-weld materials.

When modified for metal cutting, this process achieves unusually high cutting speeds. Another application is the depositing of materials having high melting temperatures to produce surfaces of high resistance to extreme wear, corrosion or temperature.

Fig. 6-11. Semi-automatic vapor-shielded welding doubles or triples previous production rates. In outdoor applications, there's no problem with wind blowing shield away from weld. Continuous electrode fed mechanically through the lightweight gun enables weldor to follow any joint easily.

Fig. 6-12. The most common of the gas welding processes is oxyacetylene welding, using a hand-held torch and welding rod.

Gas Welding Processes

An inflammable gas can be burned with either air or oxygen to produce sufficient heat for welding. When air is used as the combustion supporting medium, the heat is not high enough to weld any ferrous or non-ferrous metal with the exception of lead. The flame is far hotter, however, when the flammable gas is burned in an atmosphere of pure oxygen.

The fuel gas is usually acetylene (oxyacetylene welding). However, hydrogen (oxyhydrogen welding), natural gas, manufactured gas, propane or butane can also be used. The last four fuel gases are used principally for welding metals and alloys having a low melting point.

Flame temperatures in oxyacetylene welding range from 5,800 to 6,300 F, depending on the ratio of oxygen to acetylene. The oxyhydrogen flame is around 5,000 F. Natural gas, propane or butane combined with oxygen produce a flame temperature of approximately 5,300 F. The temperature of a flame of acetylene in compressed air is around 3,400 F—too cold to melt steel for satisfactory welding.

The flame of the torch (Fig. 6-12) produces the desired welding heat and shields the weld joint and filler metal from the surrounding atmosphere while the metal is molten. Usually, a welding rod is used in this process, having the same, or nearly the same, analysis as the base metal. Steel, aluminum, brass, copper and braze-welded joints are commonly made by gas welding. When materials other than steel are gas welded, a flux is usually needed. The flux may be applied to the welding rod or to the surface of the joint to be welded to facilitate cleaning the base metal, retarding oxidation and aiding fusion.

Resistance Welding Processes

A number of welding processes are based on the principle that a current passing through a resistance generates heat. In this case, the parts are clamped between copper conductors (electrodes), and a low-voltage high-amperage current is passed through the conductors and the work. The difference in the conductivity of the work and the poor surface contact between the unjoined parts creates the needed resistance and enough heat is generated to raise the metal to fusion temperature. At this point, pressure is applied to force the parts together so that they are solidly but locally welded.

Much of the success of any type of resistance welding depends on accurate control of the welding current. This calls for the proper interruption of the current flow at split-second intervals, made possible by the extensive use of electronic contactors and timers.

Spot welding—is the most common resistance welding process. It is usually employed in the welding of thin metal sheets and is accomplished by placing the sheets between movable electrodes of a copper alloy. The electrodes carry the welding current and can be actuated to apply the proper pressure during the welding cycle (Fig. 6-13). Carbon steels, nickel alloys and stainless steels are easily spot welded. Aluminum presents a special problem because of its high electrical conductivity. So does copper, which has practically the same conductivity as the electrode material.

Although most spot welding is done on thin sections to be welded, steel plates slightly over 1 in. thick have been successfully welded by this process.

Fig. 6-13. Spot welding is the most widely used of the resistance welding processes. Here, mounting clips are spot welded to stainless steel letters for a large sign.

Seam welding—is fundamentally a spot welding process. One or two electrode wheels running along a straight line at a fast rate of travel, make a series of closely-spaced spot welds. When the welded spots are so close that they actually overlap, they form a gas-tight or water-tight seam, as required for a pressure vessel. In other cases, the series of spots may be spaced so that the process becomes a mere tack welding operation in the assembly of the unit. This is called roll-spot welding and is used to speed up standard spot welding.

Typical welding speeds range from 10 to 60 in. per minute, depending primarily on the spacing of the spots. The more welds you have to make, the slower you travel. The spacing of the spots, the welding current and time cycle are adjustable by setting the control equipment.

Projection welding—is another method of resistance welding. It differs from those previously described, since it uses projections or embossments to localize the current flow and welding heat at predetermined points. These projections that will serve as points of contact are designed into one or both of the parts to be joined. The parts are supported and pressed together by special dies during welding.

Flash welding—is a resistance welding process in which fusion is produced by the high localized heat obtained from the electrical resistance existing between two touching surfaces. This type of resistance is evidenced by a flashing or shower of sparks, which is the arcing of the current at the adjoining surfaces. This is unlike the previously discussed processes in which the resistance was that to a flow of current within the base metal. The most common application of flash welding is in making butt welds.

For butt welds, the two pieces are brought together end-to-end, with surfaces in light contact with each other, and constitute part of an electrical circuit which is completed only by current flowing across the joint. Surface irregularities provide an interrupted gap effect between the two contact surfaces. Current introduced into the circuit results in an arcing (flashing) in the joint. When the temperature of the metal has increased to where the adjoining surfaces have plasticized, the parts are forced together under pressure to make the weld. A portion of the metal squeezes out (upsets) to form a "flash." This must be trimmed off and the joint then ground or otherwise finished to the section desired.

Upset welding—is a process in which fusion is produced by the heat obtained from electrical resistance through the area of contact of two surfaces held together under pressure. In this case, the force is applied prior to introduction of the electrical current and is continued until heating is complete. The continued force produces an upsetting as in flash welding. The force may be limited at the start, in order to raise the initial contact resistance, and then increased as the contact resistance becomes zero and the resistance is entirely the resistance within the base metal. Since the surfaces are in solid contact with one another, there is no arcing or flashing effect.

The most common application of upset welding is in making butt welds. Round bars up to at least 6 in. diameter have been upset butt welded.

Percussion welding—is a process in which fusion temperature results from an arc created across a gap between two surfaces to be joined, the arc being caused by a rapid discharge of electrical energy, with percussive (impact) force applied during or immediately following the electrical discharge. Since the total depth of the heat-affected zone is only about 0.010 in., the process is especially helpful in butt welding small sections of hardened, high-alloyed steels.

Electron Beam Welding

This process directs a bombardment of electrons at the workpiece placed in a vacuum. The electrons are emitted from a filament, acting as a type of non-consumable electrode, and are highly accelerated by a high-voltage potential between the electrode and the work. The high-velocity energy of the electrons converts to heat when they strike the work. The electron flow is electrically concentrated into a beam by means of an electron gun.

The parts to be welded are moved at a suitable speed under the electron gun, the joint directly in line with the electron beam. Since the operation is carried on in a vacuum, the process can be used to weld highly reactive metals without contamination. Material thicknesses range from foil to ⅛ in.

Thermit Welding

This process is based on the chemical reaction between aluminum and iron oxide. The members to be welded are prepared and aligned in proper relation, and a mold is built around the ends to be joined. A pouring gate in the top of the mold receives the molten steel. The thermit charge is placed in a crucible having a pouring hole in its bottom. The charge is a mixture of iron oxide and granulated aluminum together with small quantities of alloying elements in the iron oxide. Ignition of this mixture produces a reaction between the iron oxide and aluminum, liberating a large amount of heat. The aluminum combines with the oxygen in the iron oxide and releases free molten steel, which flows into the mold producing the weld.

The high temperature (5,000 F) steel in the crucible may be produced, if desired, in large volumes. For this reason, thermit welding is suited to the joining of large elements of very heavy cross-section such as railroad rails or large castings.

Forge Welding

Although forge welding was commonly employed by the blacksmith of yesteryear, it holds very little interest today with two exceptions:

Friction welding—is based on the fact that a rapidly moving part in pressure contact with a stationary part generates heat at the contacting surfaces. When the fusion temperature is reached, movement is stopped and pressure maintained or increased until the weld is completed.

The process is economically suited to high production circumferential butt welding of small round or tubular parts.

Pressure welding—is a process in which two pieces of ductile metal are butt welded or lap welded by the application of pressure only, without any of the metal reaching the melting point. Heat, if applied, is sufficient only to facilitate plastic flow of the metal under pressure. Bonding depends upon the ability to bring a large number of atoms on the two surfaces being joined into intimate contact. This requires perfect cleanliness of the surfaces, good alignment and application of high pressures. The pressure is a squeezing action rather than impact.

This process is used primarily in joining alloys of aluminum and of copper, and is of little importance except on thin-gage sheets, foil and wire and particularly in making electrical connections.

Brazing and Braze Welding

The processes of brazing and braze welding are used to join similar or dissimilar metals by using a metal or alloy of lower melting point than either of the components to be joined. The most commonly used brazing alloys are copper, copper alloys (bronze for instance) or silver alloys.

Brazing is accomplished by heating the pieces to be joined to a temperature higher than the melting point of the brazing metal or alloy. The melted alloy wets the surfaces between the parts to be joined. It flows between the parts by surface action, and actually diffuses into the base metal surface so that a strong joint is produced when the alloy solidifies. Brazed joints are often stronger than the brazing material itself, if the parts are closely fitted.

If a large gap must be filled, there is no capillary action, and the process is known as **braze welding**. The more commonly used brazing processes are listed below. Flux must be used with all brazing and braze welding applications.

Torch brazing—is a method by which the parts to be joined are usually positioned in correct relationship with each other, and the brazing alloy placed in the joint prior to heating or added as brazing progresses. The brazing is accomplished by heating the base metal with a gas heating torch or flame until it reaches a suitable temperature, when the filler metal melts and distributes between the closely fitted parts by capillary action.

Furnace brazing—calls for the parts to be joined to first be aligned, with brazing material—in the form of wire, strip, powder or paste—placed in the joint. This assembly is then placed in the furnace, which usually has a controlled atmosphere to prevent oxidation during brazing. Furnace temperature is then raised to a point where the brazing material melts to accomplish the brazing.

Dip brazing—has a molten metal or chemical bath in which the parts to be brazed are submerged. The molten bath makes it possible to heat the parts to brazing temperature more quickly than in the controlled-atmosphere furnace because of the greater heat conductivity of a liquid medium. Since the work is submerged, the molten bath also provides a shield to prevent oxidation.

Induction brazing—employs high-frequency electric current to heat the brazed parts to the melting point of the brazing material in much the same manner that they are heated in the furnace. This process is rapid and effective, and it is becoming increasingly popular for production applications.

Soldering

Although soldering is not included in the Master Chart of welding processes, it is an important method of joining metals. Soldering differs from brazing in that lower temperatures are involved. Most solders are made of varying proportions of tin, lead, bismuth and other metals having low melting points. Soldering temperatures range from 300 to 500 F. In comparison with welded or brazed joints, a soldered joint has considerably less strength and is used primarily for liquid or air tightness.

Other Welding Processes

Other processes worthy of mention but which will not be discussed in detail include:

Flow welding—a process wherein fusion is produced by heating with molten filler metal poured over the joint until the welding temperature is attained and the required filler metal has fully penetrated the joint.

Explosive welding—wherein a surface-to-surface bond is achieved by the compressive force of a controlled explosion.

Ultrasonic welding—a process using high intensity vibrational energy to weld aluminum, magnesium and their alloys as well as some dissimilar metals. This principle has also been found capable of improving conventional welding processes.

Induction welding—similar to induction brazing but involving higher temperatures. Heat for fusion is obtained from the resistance of the work to the flow of an induced electric current. In both induction welding and induction brazing, the pieces to be joined are placed within a radio-frequency field, usually developed to the inside of a radiating coil that has been designed to approximate the shape of the intended assembly. Thus, these processes are primarily for production joining. Filler metal having a low melting temperature is distributed through the heated joint by capillary action.

Filler Metals for Welding

Arc and gas welding processes usually require filler metal in order that welds have the most desirable properties. The American Welding Society (AWS) has developed specifications for these filler metals (as consumable electrodes or welding rods) to cover the arc welding of carbon steels, alloy steels, stainless and corrosion-resisting steels, copper and copper-based alloys and aluminum alloys. The AWS has also developed specifications for filler metals used in the gas welding of carbon steels. Through these specifications and their classification, the user is informed that a certain electrode or welding rod can produce a weld metal having specific mechanical properties. At the same time, the system classifies electrodes for various positions of welding, for their ability to penetrate adequately into the root of a joint, and for power supply (alternating or direct current).

The importance of this AWS classification system in helping the user select the right electrode or welding rod for each specific job, is obvious. A particular type of filler metal may deposit a high strength, ductile weld for example.

Arc Welding Electrodes

As indicated earlier, arc welding has become the most widely used welding process. This resulted from the development of flux-coated electrodes capable of making welds having physical properties that equal or exceed those of the parent metal.

Prior to development of the coated electrode, the gases of the atmosphere in the high-temperature welding zone formed oxides and nitrides with the weld metal. In general, oxides are low in tensile strength and ductility and tend to reduce the normal properties of the base metals. The coating materials on the electrode provide an automatic cleansing and deoxidizing action in the molten crater. As the coating burns in the arc, it releases a gaseous inert atmosphere that protects the molten end of the electrode as well as the molten weld pool. This atmosphere excludes harmful oxygen and nitrogen from the molten weld area, while the burning residue of coating forms a slag to cover the deposited weld metal. This slag also serves to exclude oxygen and nitrogen from the weld until it has cooled to such a point that oxides or nitrides will no longer form. In addition, the slag slows the cooling thereby producing a more ductile weld.

Besides these benefits, other advantages are gained by coating electrodes. The coating improves weld appearance, provides easier arc striking, helps maintain the arc, regulates the depth of penetration, reduces spatter, improves x-ray quality of the weld, and sometimes adds alloying agents to the weld metal or restores lost elements. The slag from the coating not only protects the weld bead but assists in shaping it.

In addition, powdered iron has been added to the coating of many of the basic electrode types. In the intense heat of the arc, the iron powder is converted to steel and contributes metal to the weld deposit. When added in relatively large amounts, the speed of welding is appreciably increased and weld appearance improved.

The coating also serves as an insulator for the core wire of the electrode. It affects arc length, welding voltage, and controls the position of welding in which the electrode can be used.

Obviously, the composition of an electrode coating is extremely important. The blending of the proper ingredients is an art. Besides having the previously listed performance characteristics correctly balanced, the coating should have a melting point somewhat lower than that of the core wire or the base metal. The resultant slag must have a lower density in order to be quickly and thoroughly expelled from the freezing weld metal. Where the electrode is to be used for overhead or vertical welding, the slag formed from the melted coating must solidify quickly.

The differences in the operational characteristics of electrodes may be attributed to the coating. The core wire is generally from the same wire stock. For the common E-60xx series of electrodes, the core wire is SAE 1010 carbon steel, having a carbon range of 0.05 to 0.15%.

AWS Classification of Carbon-Steel Electrodes

In setting up its classification for carbon-steel electrodes, the American Welding Society adopted a series of four- or five-digit numbers prefixed with the letter "E." The "E" indicates electric welding use. The numerals to the left of the last two digits times 1,000 indicate minimum tensile strength of the (stress relieved) deposited metal; the next to the last digit indicates the position of welding; and the last digit tells the power supply, type of slag, type of arc, penetration, and presence of iron powder. For data regarding further interpretation of these classification numbers, see Tables 6-1 and 6-2.

Some of these electrodes are for direct current (DC) and some for alternating current (AC). Some DC electrodes are for *straight polarity* (electrode holder connected to the negative pole), Fig. 6-14, and some for *reverse polarity* (electrode holder attached to the positive pole), Fig. 6-15.

Carbon-Steel Electrodes

The carbon-steel electrodes for welding low- and medium-carbon steels carry AWS classification numbers E-4510 and E-6010-11-12-13-14-15-16-18-20-24-27 and 28. E-4510 is a bare electrode; the others, all in the E-6000 series, are coated electrodes. Very few welding applications employ bare steel electrodes today, so our principal concern is with the E-6000 series.

AWS E-45XX electrodes have a tensile strength of 45,000 psi in the

Table 6-1. AWS Electrode Classification System

DIGIT	SIGNIFICANCE	EXAMPLE
1st two or 1st three	Min. tensile strength (stress relieved)	E-60xx = 60,000 psi (min) E-110xx = 110,000 psi (min)
2nd last	Welding position	E-xx1x = all positions E-xx2x = horizontal and flat E-xx3x = flat
Last	Power supply, type of slag, type of arc, amount of penetration, presence of iron powder in coating	See Table 6-2

Note: Prefix "E" (to left of a 4 or 5-digit number) signifies arc welding electrode

stress-relieved condition. The E-4510 is for use in all positions and operates on reverse-polarity DC.

AWS E-6010 electrodes are designed for all-position welding with reverse-polarity DC. They are best suited for vertical and overhead welding and some sheet metal applications.

The thickness of the coating is held at a minimum to facilitate welding in the vertical and overhead position, but is sufficient to develop the shielding necessary for a high-quality deposit. Some coatings have a small amount (less than 10% by coating weight) of iron powder to improve arc characteristics. The arc has a digging characteristic to produce deep penetration. This calls for skillful manipulation of the electrode by the operator to minimize spatter and the tendency to undercut. The slag formed is light and easily removed. The profile of fillet welds is relatively convex on horizontal and vertical deposits. Beads deposited by E-6010 electrodes have a rather coarse ripple.

Table 6-2. Interpretation of Last Digit in AWS Electrode Classification

LAST DIGIT	0	1	2	3	4	5	6	7	8
Power supply	(a)	AC or DC rev polarity	AC or DC	AC or DC	AC or DC	DC rev polarity	AC or DC rev. polarity	AC or DC	AC or DC rev. polarity
Type of slag	(b)	Organic	Rutile	Rutile	Rutile	Low Hydrogen	Low Hydrogen	Mineral	Low Hydrogen
Type of arc	Digging	Digging	Medium	Soft	Soft	Medium	Medium	Soft	Medium
Penetration	(c)	Deep	Medium	Light	Light	Medium	Medium	Medium	Medium
Iron Powder in Coating	0-10%	None	0-10%	0-10%	30-50%	None	None	50%	30-50%

Notes: (a) E-6010 is DC reverse polarity; E-6020 is AC or DC
     (b) E-6010 is organic; E-6020 is mineral
     (c) E-6010 is deep penetration; E-6020 is medium penetration

The E-6010 electrode is excellent for temporary tacking because of ductility and deep-penetration qualities. Its physical properties are excellent and, when properly applied, its deposits will meet the most exacting inspection standards.

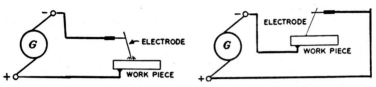

Fig. 6-14. Straight polarity DC welding circuit.   **Fig. 6-15.** Reverse polarity DC welding circuit.

AWS E-6011 electrodes are sometimes described as the AC counterpart of the E-6010 type. Performance characteristics of the two electrodes are quite similar; however, the E-6011 electrodes perform equally as well with either an AC or DC power supply. These electrodes have a forceful digging arc, resulting in deep penetration. While the coating is slightly heavier on E-6011 electrodes, the resultant slag and weld profiles are similar.

AWS E-6012 electrodes are designed for general-purpose welding in all positions, either DC or AC being used. They are specifically recommended for horizontal and most downhill welding applications. An E-6012 electrode has a rather quiet type of arc, with medium penetration and no spatter. Good build-up and no excess penetration make this electrode excellent for welding under poor fit-up conditions. Since the arc is highly stabilizing, the welds have good appearance and are relatively free from undercut. Fillet welds usually have a convex profile of a smooth even ripple in the horizontal or the vertical down position. The slag coverage is complete, and the slag may easily be removed.

When used with a DC power supply, straight polarity is preferred. It is used extensively where appearance and high rates of deposition are more important than maximum ductility. For example, this electrode is particularly suited to making highly satisfactory welds on sheet metal, where single-pass welds will pass radiographic inspection.

Here, as with E-6010 type, some designs have a small amount of iron powder in the coating to improve arc characteristics.

AWS E-6013 electrodes have been designed for welding in all positions, AC or DC. While they are similar to the E-6012 electrodes, they possess some notable differences. They have minimum spatter and minimum tendency to undercut. The beads are fine rippled and are superior in appearance.

Slag removal is easier with the E-6013, and the arc is very stable. This facilitates striking and maintaining the arc, even with extremely small ($\frac{1}{16}$ and $\frac{5}{64}$ in.) electrodes. Hence the E-6013 is ideally suited to welding thin metals. The arc is soft and the penetration very light. The mechanical properties of the E-6013 are slightly better than the E-6012. The same may be said for its *radiographic quality*.

Changing from one manufacturer's E-6013 electrode to another's may result in the nature of the molten metal transfer in the arc stream being changed. Some manufacturers compound their coating so that a globular transfer is obtained, while others produce a fine spray transfer. Ordinarily the spray transfer is preferred for vertical or over-head deposits. The amount of spatter from this electrode varies with different brands, too. Some manufacturers have also introduced small amounts of iron powder into the E-6013 electrode coatings.

AWS E-6014 electrodes have a coating similar to that of the E-6012 and E-6013 types. However, the coating of this electrode type is considerably thicker since it contains substantial iron powder (30% of coating weight). The presence of powdered iron permits higher welding currents, which means higher deposition rates and welding speeds. The thicker coating does not make it as ideally suited to out-of-position production welding on thin-gage material; however, it will perform adequately when the occasional job demands it. Its performance characteristics do make this electrode particularly suited to production welding of irregular-shaped products where some out-of-position welding is encountered.

Mechanical properties of E-6014 weld metal compare favorably with those of the E-6012 and E-6013 types. Fillet weld contour ranges from flat to slightly convex. Slag removal is very easy and sometimes self-cleaning. Shallow penetration and rapid solidification are characteristics that make this electrode type well suited to handling poor fit-up conditions.

AWS E-6015 was the first DC reverse-polarity, all-position electrode designed for the welding of high-sulphur and high-carbon steels that tend to develop weld porosity and crack under the weld bead. Metallurgists found that the presence of hydrogen in molten metal aggravates the tendency to porosity being formed during solidification and to underbead cracking. The E-6015 electrode's coating was designed to have a very low moisture content, thereby preventing the introduction of hydrogen into the weld. The successful performance of this electrode led to the later development of the E-6016 and E-6018 types which also have a very low moisture content coating. These electrodes are commonly known as *low-hydrogen electrodes*.

AWS E-6016 electrodes contain potassium silicate or other potassium salts added to the coating which make the electrode suitable for use with AC as well as DC reverse-polarity.

AWS E-6018 electrodes are of low-hydrogen design, having a 30% powdered iron coating. Like the E-6016 electrodes, this type operates on either AC or DC reverse polarity. It has all the desirable low-hydrogen characteristics for producing sound welds on troublesome steels such as high-sulphur, high-carbon and low alloy grades. Its slightly thicker coating and the presence of powdered iron make it generally easier to use than the other low-hydrogen types. For these reasons, it is the most widely used.

The minerals of the low hydrogen electrodes' coating are limited to inorganic compounds such as calcium fluoride, calcium carbonate, magnesium-aluminum-silicate, ferro alloys, and such binding agents as sodium and potassium silicate. These electrodes are referred to as lime-ferritic because of the general use of lime-type coatings. (Lime is a decomposition product of such compounds as calcium carbonate.)

Since the coating of these electrodes is heavier than normal, vertical and overhead welding is usually limited to the small-diameter electrodes. The current used is somewhat higher than for E-6010 electrodes of corresponding size.

Mechanical properties (including impact strength) of low hydrogen electrodes are superior to those of E-6010 electrodes that deposit weld metal of similar composition. Use of low-hydrogen electrodes reduces the preheat and postheat of welds, thus making for better welding conditions and lowering or eliminating preheating cost.

AWS E-6020 electrodes are designed to produce high quality horizontal fillet welds at high welding speeds, using either AC or DC straight polarity. In the flat position, these electrodes can be used with AC or DC of either polarity. The E-6020 electrodes are characterized by a forceful spray-type of arc and a heavy slag, which completely covers the deposit but is quite easily removed. Penetration is medium at normal welding currents, but high currents and high travel speeds will result in deep penetration. The deposits of this electrode are usually flat or even slightly concave in profile and have a smooth, even ripple. The radiographic qualities are excellent, and the weld beads show medium spatter and a tendency to undercut.

AWS E-6024 electrodes are ideally suited for production fillet welding. Their 50% powdered iron coating assists in producing a deposition rate and welding speed that are considerably higher than that of the E-6012, E-6013 and E-6014 types which have similar performance characteristics. Operating characteristics include a soft quiet arc which produces practically no spatter. The ability to drag the electrode coating on the parent metal while welding produces a very smooth bead appearance. Physical properties of the weld deposit compare favorably with the E-6012-13 and 14 types. As in the case of the E-6020, welding position is limited to flat and horizontal.

AWS E-6027 electrodes are of 50% powdered iron design, for either AC or DC operation. The arc characteristics of this type electrode closely duplicate the E-6020 type. Having a very high deposition rate and a slag that crumbles for easy removal, the E-6027 electrode is particularly suited to multiple-pass, deep-groove welding.

The E-6027 electrodes produce high quality weld metal having physical properties that closely duplicate those of E-6010 electrodes. Operating characteristics make this electrode slightly harder to handle than the E-6024 type; however, properly-deposited weld beads can have smoother appearance.

AWS E-6028 electrodes have a low-hydrogen coating containing 50% powdered iron. Designed for AC or DC reverse-polarity operation, the heavy coating gives this electrode a very high deposition rate. Although capable of producing the physical properties and weld quality typical of low-hydrogen designs, these electrodes are suitable for only flat and horizontal position welding.

Alloy Steel Electrodes

The expanding use of high-strength alloy steels has initiated the development of coated electrodes capable of producing weld deposits having tensile strength exceeding 100,000 psi. Mechanical properties of this magnitude are achieved through the use of alloy steel in the core wire of the electrode. In most electrode designs, the electrode coating is of a lime-ferritic nature typical of the low-hydrogen designs and frequently contains powdered iron. For this reason, these high tensile electrodes usually have an E-xx15-16 or 18 classification. Operation characteristics parallel those of typical 60,000 psi low-hydrogen designs.

The flexible system of electrode identification established by AWS readily catalogs these electrodes in groups established for the E-60xx series. For example, the E-11018 electrode has 110,000 psi tensile strength, and like the E-6018 type will weld all position, uses AC or DC reverse-polarity power, has a low-hydrogen type slag, has medium arc force and penetration, and has 30% iron powder in its coating. Table 6-3 lists the AWS standard suffixes that indicate specific additions of alloying elements. In a complete electrode designation, these letter symbols appear after the four- or five-digit basic number.

Stainless-Steel Electrodes

A variety of stainless-steel electrodes are being manufactured that can produce weld metal similar to the composition of most base metals. The analysis of the core wire may differ from the base metal, however, in order to improve corrosion resistance of the weld deposit, eliminate underbead cracking, or minimize carbon precipitation. In the transfer of metal through the arc, very little nickel is lost from nickel-bearing stainless electrodes. There is a slight loss of chromium and a greater loss of the other elements.

Manganese and silicon are included in the electrode coating to reduce oxidation; titanium to promote arc stability, to produce an easily removable slag, and to prevent carbon precipitation; and columbium, in some designs, to prevent carbide precipitation. Lime has been an extremely important ingredient in the coating since it tends to eliminate hydrogen, the formation of which leads to underbead cracking. Any material that is high in carbon is excluded because of the affinity of chromium for carbon, especially at welding temperatures. The low-hydrogen type of coating used on stainless electrodes is similar to that employed on certain carbon-steel welding electrodes: E-6015 and E-6016.

Special Electrodes

The large volume of electrodes used in present welding practice are: (1) the mild-steel electrodes, (2) the alloy-steel electrodes that are manufactured in comparable classifications but for higher tensile strength, and (3) the stainless-steel electrodes.

In addition to the above, there are many special-purpose electrodes covering specific fields. These include electrodes for hardsurfacing, and for welding copper and copper alloys, aluminum, cast iron, manganese and nickel-manganese steels, and nickel alloys. These various types of electrodes differ widely in their composition and are usually designed to match the base metals on which they are to be used. Hardsurfacing electrodes, however, are designed to produce a weld deposit that resists abrasion, impact or other abusive action that tends to wear away metals.

In some instances, these special electrodes may be used to weld metals other than those matching their composition. Examples are found where nickel or bronze electrodes are used for welding cast iron, austenitic stainless steel, manganese or high-carbon tensile steels, etc. Composition of the coating on these special-purpose electrodes depends entirely on the purpose for which they are to be used.

Table 6-3. AWS Designation of Major Alloying Elements in Arc Welding Electrodes

SUFFIX TO AWS ELECTRODE NO.	ALLOY ELEMENT, %				
	Mo (Molybdenum)	Cr (Chromium)	Ni (Nickel)	Mn (Manganese)	Va (Vanadium)
A_1	0.5				
B_1	0.5	0.5			
B_2	0.5	1.25			
B_3	1.0	2.25			
B_4	0.5	2.0			
C_1			2.5		
C_2			3.5		
C_3			1.0		
D_1	0.3			1.5	
D_2	0.3			1.75	
G*	0.2	0.3	0.5	1.0	0.1

*Need have minimum content of one element only.

Submerged-Arc Welding Electrodes and Fluxes

The electrodes and granular fluxes used in conjunction with submerged-arc welding are not classified. It is necessary to seek the manufacturer's recommendations for a suitable combination for a specific application. Low- and medium-carbon steels can be readily welded with a mild-steel electrode and a neutral flux since the deposit produced by this combination is low hydrogen in nature and will have suitable physical properties. See Fig. 6-16. Variations in neutral flux designs affect their freezing and deoxidizing characteristics. These variations make certain fluxes particularly suited to specific joint designs and welding conditions.

Special alloy *agglomerated* fluxes and alloy electrodes exist that adapt submerged-arc welding to the production of sound welds on high-strength, alloy steels, stainless steels, austenitic manganese steels, and the depositing of hardsurfacing overlays with specific abrasion or impact resisting properties.

Gas Welding Rods

Welding rods for supplying filler metal needed in the oxyacetylene or other gas welding of steel conform to specifications set up by the American Welding Society. These rods are usually high-grade, low-carbon steel, similar in characteristics and composition to the core wires used in the E-60xx series electrodes. They are not coated since control of the oxyacetylene flame makes it possible to determine whether the weld will be of the oxidizing or carburizing nature. The tensile strength requirements of gas welding rods are obtained by variation in the carbon and alloy contents of the rods.

Similar welding rods are available for the gas welding of nonferrous metals and their alloys.

Factors Affecting Weld Metal Properties

The mechanical properties of the weld depend on the analysis (chemical composition) of the weld deposit. Since the base metal and the filler metal are both brought to the molten state and mix within the weld crater, it is apparent the final analysis of the weld is related to the analysis of the base metal, the analysis of the filler metal, and their mixing ratio.

In shielded-arc welding, the chemical analysis of the deposited metal depends on the analysis of the core wire and also the analysis and action of the electrode coating. The composite design can be arranged to deposit practically any carbon or alloy steel. Electrode coatings can be made to add carbon to the deposit, to add alloying metals and also to burn out objectionable ingredients from the weld.

One class of electrode coatings reacts with the sulphur in the core wire to give a deposit that is appreciably lower (20 to 30%) in sulphur than the original electrode.

Some shielded-arc electrodes deposit metal as very fine droplets or as a spray, and these particles must be heated to a very high temperature when they are in the arc; in fact, some of the iron may be vaporized. The intense heating and the cleaning action of the slag results in a purified weld metal.

Penetration controls the mixing ratio of filler and parent metal. It may be increased or decreased by manipulation of the electrode. In gas, carbon-arc and submerged-arc welding, the penetration may be changed by altering the welding procedure. Inclining the work and welding downhill decreases the penetration, whereas welding uphill ensures deep penetration.

In metal-arc welding, an E-6010 electrode, used with DC straight polarity (electrode negative), gives a spray-type of arc that will deposit only a little metal, most of it flying off into the air as fine droplets. This type of arc is useful to fuse together the flanged edges of sheet steel (vertical edge welds).

The effects of travel speed on penetration are illustrated by Figs. 6-17 and 6-18.

By using a slow travel speed and keeping the arc stream directed on the deposited metal, the penetration may be kept to a minimum. The penetration may even be reduced to zero, resulting in no weld. In contrast, fast travel and the arc stream directed on the base metal ahead of the deposited metal results in more penetration.

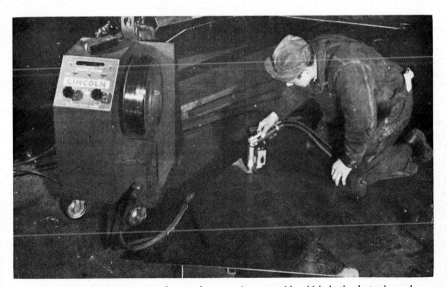

Fig. 6-16. Semi-automatic submerged arc equipment, with which both electrode and granulated flux are fed mechanically, permits greatly speeded production on applications previously requiring manual welding. Here, parts of a power plant flue system are being assembled at double the former welding speeds.

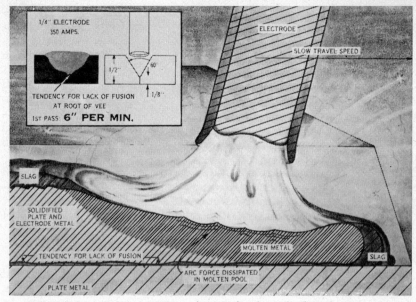

Fig. 6-17. On a 60-degree V-groove, slow travel and upright electrode position lead to low penetration. In extreme cases, penetration is too shallow and poor fusion results. Some high alloys demand light but not excessively-low penetration.

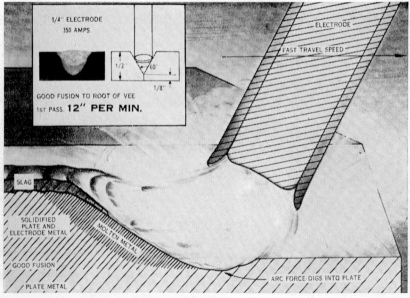

Fig. 6-18. High travel speed and inclined electrode enable the arc force to dig into the plate. On most applications of coated electrodes, the deeper penetration ensures better fusion and a more desirable weld.

The percentages in Fig. 6-19 give the approximate amount of base metal that is melted and mixed with the deposited metal in the weld. The first figure shows the typical percentage of base metal contained in the final weld metal under normal welding conditions. The lower figure shows the percentage range that is possible under extreme welding conditions. View A applies when filler metal is deposited from a welding rod, the electrode being non-consumable. View B applies

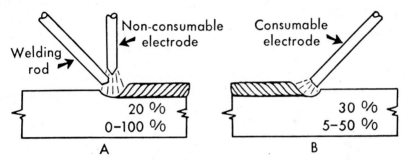

Fig. 6-19. When welding, arc penetration of the base metal causes it to melt and mix with the deposited metal. The upper figure in each view shows the typical percentage of base metal in the final weld metal. The lower figures show the possible range of base metal content.

when filler metal is deposited directly from a consumable electrode. Although each process is different in application, the figures given are characteristic for oxyacetylene, carbon-arc, metal-arc or submerged-arc welding. In submerged-arc welding, for example, 1 lb of deposited metal can be made to melt 2 lb of base metal, so that the final weld bead is $\frac{2}{3}$ base metal and $\frac{1}{3}$ electrode metal.

Definitions of New Words

Agglomerated flux. A granulated flux for submerged-arc welding to which any alloying elements can be added without loss of individual and physical identity. Thus, during welding no complex chemical compounds in the flux need be broken down before the alloying element is free to enrich the weld metal as intended.

Automatic welding. Welding with equipment that automatically controls the entire welding operation (including feed, speed, etc.). In arc welding, the electrode or welding rod supplying filler metal is fed automatically into the arc to compensate for its melt-off and thus maintain the correct length of arc. Granulated flux or shielding gas, when called for by the specific process, is also fed automatically through the welding head.

Coated electrode. A consumable metal arc-welding electrode having a relatively thick covering around the core of filler metal. As the covering melts off, it stabilizes the arc and provides the chemicals needed for removing impurities from the weld metal.

Consumable electrode. A metal electrode that establishes the arc and gradually melts away, being carried across the arc (deposited) to provide filler metal into the joint.

Deoxidizing. The removal of oxygen from the molten weld metal, usually by chemical combination with other elements forming inorganic compounds that float to the surface of the molten metal to form slag when cooled.

Deposition rate. The speed with which filler metal is added to a weld joint, usually stated in terms of volume of metal deposited per minute.

Fill welds. Welds in which a filler metal is deposited into the joint from an electrode or welding rod, fusing with the base metal on each side.

Filler metal. The metal which is deposited into the joint from an electrode or welding rod in order to achieve a weld of desired properties.

Flux. A fusible non-metallic material that dissolves and prevents further formation of metallic oxides, nitrides or other undesirable inclusions within the weld.

Fusion welds. Welds in which the two metal members to be joined are fused directly to each other, without the addition of filler metal from consumable electrode or welding rod.

Inert gas. A gas, such as helium or argon, which does not chemically combine with other elements. Such a gas serves as an effective shield of the welding arc and protects the molten weld metal against contamination from the atmosphere until it freezes.

Manual welding. Welding in which the electrode is in fixed position in a holder held by the weldor, who guides it along the joint while maintaining the proper arc gap.

Non-consumable electrode. A carbon or tungsten welding electrode that merely establishes the arc and maintains it, without being melted.

Penetration. The depth below the surface of the base metal to which welding heat is sufficient for the metal to melt and become liquid or semi-liquid. Also called the depth of fusion. The word "penetration" is also applied to the ability of arc or electrode to reach into the root of the groove between two members being welded.

Radiographic quality. Soundness of a weld that shows no internal or underbead cracks, voids or inclusions when inspected by x-ray or gamma ray techniques.

Reverse polarity. An arrangement of the leads from a direct current power source whereby the electrode is the positive pole and the workpiece is the negative pole of the arc.

Root. The narrowest point in the gap between two members to be welded, or the point in the gap furthest removed from the electrode. Usually these points are one and the same.

Semi-automatic welding. Welding in which the electrode, welding rod and/or flux is fed automatically but the welding head or gun is held in the hand and guided manually along the joint.

Shielding. Primarily the protection of metal molten by the arc from oxidizing or otherwise reacting with elements in the surrounding air. Usually, the shielding also stabilizes the arc.

Straight polarity. An arrangement of the leads from a direct current power source whereby the workpiece is the positive pole and the electrode is the negative pole of the arc.

Weld metal. A product of fusion, the metal that was fully melted by the heat of welding.

X-ray quality. See "radiographic quality."

Review Questions

1. How many different welding processes are in use?

2. Connect the following terms that are associated, and cross out the term that has no equivalent stated:
   AC current
   DC electrode positive
   DC electrode negative
   Reverse polarity
   Straight polarity

3. Which of the following methods of welding is most likely to result in a weld contaminated with carbon?—— Oxygen?—— Nitrogen?——
   (a) Metal-arc with coated electrode
   (b) Metal-arc with bare electrode
   (c) Carbon-arc, electrode positive
   (d) Oxyacetylene with oxidizing flame
   (e) Oxyacetylene with carburizing flame

4. What advantages does welding have over riveting, bolting and other forms of mechanical fastening?

5. What are some advantages of metal-arc welding over gas welding?

6. List a number of welding procedures according to their similarity to metal casting, starting with the welding method that uses a mold and finishing with a process for welding steel involving no melting of metal.

7. The metal-arc welding process consists of adding molten steel in small amounts to a pool of molten base metal and allowing

the metal to solidify. In what ways and why is the "cast" weld metal superior in properties to cast steel of the same analysis?

8. The E-6018 electrodes are better than other electrodes for welding some of the following materials. Which ones? Mild steel, high-carbon steel, wrought iron, high-sulphur steel, and aluminum.

9. What welding process should give best results on mild steel when available weldors have little experience?

10. If welding procedure does not give sufficient penetration, what three changes might be made to effect better fusion?

CHAPTER 7

FUNDAMENTALS OF METALLURGY

A knowledge of metallurgy is not essential for the design of a welded product or for doing a welding job, but it will help make both of these tasks easier and more understandable. A complete discussion of ferrous metallurgy would fill many books and is far beyond the requirements of most people engaged in any phase of welding. For this reason only the barest fundamentals of the subject will be presented in the next few chapters. The mastering of these fundamentals, however, will enable the weldor to understand a great many things that happen during a welding operation.

The metallurgical interest of those engaged in welding centers around the effects of heat. It was shown in Chapters 2 and 3 that the changing of the amounts of alloying elements in a metal changes its physical and mechanical properties. It is also known that these properties may be changed by heating and cooling. In welding there is heating and cooling; so will the properties of the metal be changed? Can these changes be avoided? Controlled? Limited?

The answers to these questions and many others on metals and their behavior during heating and cooling are found in the basic fundamentals of metallurgy. A study of metallurgy likewise reveals how metals are put together and what makes them stay together. It tells about the structure of metals.

Microscopic Study of Metals

The surface of a metal gives no indication of its makeup; but, if the metal is broken, the fracture will show a granular appearance. The *grains* may be large enough to be seen readily, or they may be so small that a magnifying glass is needed to show their presence.

A high-magnification examination of a fracture will show little, for the rough surface cannot be brought into focus. Some parts will be too near and other parts too far. Animal and plant tissues are examined by preparing thin slices and allowing light to shine through the sample into the microscope. Metal samples are examined by light that is reflected from a polished surface. The metal specimen is prepared by grinding a flat surface. This is polished with finer and finer abrasives until a scratch-free mirror surface is obtained.

In the polished condition, the grains can be seen when the sample is examined through a high-powered metallurgical microscope. At a magnification of 100 diameters (0.01 in. magnified to 1.0 in.), designated as 100x, a sample of fine-grained steel may show little more than a smooth, structureless field unless the sample contains foreign

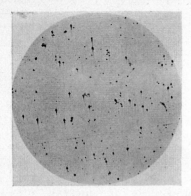

Fig. 7-1. A photomicrograph of steel having dirty inclusions (black spots). Magnification 100x.

matter or holes. Higher magnification is usually required to provide much detailed information about the internal structure of higher-alloyed steels.

Fig. 7-1 is a *photomicrograph* (photograph taken through a microscope) of a sample of dirty metal at a magnification of 100x. The black spots are holes or pits left after the non-metallic material fell or was pulled out during the polishing (modern polishing techniques will not pull out the non-metallic inclusions). No grains are seen because

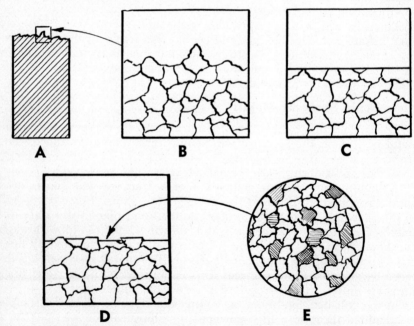

Fig. 7-2. Steps in preparing a photomicrograph. (A) Fractured edge of metal. (B) Enlarged section of edge, 100x. (C) Section of edge after polishing, 100x. (D) Section of polished edge after etching, 100x. (E) Surface of polished and etched edge, 100x.

the polishing has smeared over the surface a thin film of metal that covers the grain boundaries and other surface details. To see the grains, it is necessary to treat the sample with a suitable etching reagent that will dissolve this film. A solution of 5% nitric acid in alcohol (called nital) is an etchant frequently used for carbon steel.

Fig. 7-2 E is drawn from a photomicrograph of low-carbon steel. Grain boundaries are seen as black lines and some of the grains are darkened. By changing the angle at which light falls on the specimen, it can be shown that the darkening is caused by differences in the depth of the etching. Each grain is a *crystal* of metal, and the etching rate and depth depend on the angle at which the grain is turned or oriented. Grains cut parallel to a face etch smooth, while those cut at an angle may etch to give a rough and darker looking surface.

A magnification of 100x is usually enough to show the grains in pure metals; higher magnifications will not reveal any further subdivisions of the metal grains or crystals. Magnifications up to 50,000x are possible with the electron microscope. For most metallurgical examinations, however, a magnification of 100x to 500x is sufficient, depending upon grain size in the specific material.

Nature has formed nearly all of the solids in the earth by crystallization, either from the liquid state or from a water solution. The rounded, dull pebbles found in a handful of gravel are made up of crystals—either single crystals like feldspar or quartz, or many small crystals like granite.

A microscopic examination of some alloys will show nearly perfect crystals surrounded by the metal alloy. When the alloy first started to cool, some metal compounds separated out of solution, forming tiny crystals. These crystals grew in size as more and more of the compound became available with the lowering temperature. Finally, the remaining metal alloy, called the *matrix,* solidified around the crystals.

Fig. 7-3. This tungsten carbide alloy is 82% tungsten, 12% cobalt and 4% carbon. At 250x magnification the tungsten carbide crystals appear as triangular prisms.

Figure 7-3 is a section of a tungsten-carbon-cobalt alloy. Crystals of tungsten carbide have formed in the tungsten-cobalt matrix and there was enough room so that many could grow without interference. If the carbon content had been lower, there would be less tungsten carbide formed and the crystals would have had even more room to grow without interference.

Tungsten carbide crystals are triangular prisms, and it is interesting to note that the triangles, squares, rectangles and five-sided figures can all be formed by sections of a triangular prism.

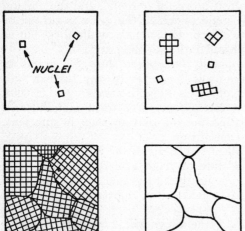

Fig. 7-4. A diagrammatic representation of the formation of seed crystals, their growth and the final grains each with its individual orientation.

Single crystals (unit cells) have been prepared by tedious laboratory procedures. It is difficult to produce them because when iron and other metals solidify, the crystals grow so rapidly that they interfere with each other, resulting in crystals, or grains, of irregular shape. Fig. 7-4 is a diagrammatic representation of the formation of the *seed crystals*, their growth, and the final grains each with its individual orientation.

Ferrous Metals and Their Alloying Elements

Since 95% of today's welding is done with ferrous alloys, this discussion will center about ferrous materials.

Ferrous alloys are so called because their major constituent is "ferrum" which is the Latin name for iron. The most common of ferrous alloys are the cast irons and steels. These are alloys of iron and carbon and other chemical elements which may be present to impart definite properties or as an impurity.

Plain carbon steels, or carbon steels as they are generally called, are alloys of iron and carbon containing these two elements and only traces of others.

As other chemical elements such as aluminum, chromium and cobalt are added to the simple carbon-iron alloys, these steels become more complex. The addition of alloying elements often influences the grain structure and structural characteristics of a metal. Some of the elements, such as phosphorus and sulphur, are found in nearly all steels. Other elements may appear in a limited group of special-alloy steels. The alloying elements, listed alphabetically rather than in the order of their importance, are:

Aluminum—is extensively used as a deoxidizer in steel production. As such, it is an effective purifier. Aluminum also lessens grain growth by forming dispersed oxides or nitrides.

Carbon—is the principal hardening agent in steel. In most cases, alloy steels containing carbon up to about 0.20% are hardened by carburization. Alloy steels containing over 0.20% carbon are generally considered heat-treatable steels, and they are heat treated by quenching and drawing to obtain increased strength. In some cases, these steels are used in their as-rolled condition. In most alloy steels, carbon has about the same effect upon hardness as it does in the plain-carbon steels.

Chromium—has many functions as an ingredient in alloy steels. It is a hardening element, and it also tends to increase the strength of the steel. In higher percentages, say from 12 to 30%, chromium tends to increase the corrosion resistance and oxidation resistance of the steel. This holds true at both high and low temperatures. Because of this vauable property, chromium is one of the basic ingredients in the stainless steels. It is also one of the basic ingredients of steels that are to be used at high temperatures where resistance to oxidation is desired. There is little loss of strength in chromium steels at temperatures up to 900 F.

Cobalt—is added to steel for which high strength and/or high hardness at high temperatures are desired. It imparts the quality known as red hardness; i.e., the ability to remain hard when red-hot.

Copper—as an alloying agent in steel tends to improve its atmospheric corrosion-resisting qualities. It also increases strength.

Columbium—improves the high-strength properties of heat-resisting steel alloys. Its major service, however, is as a carbide stabilizer in the austenitic grades of stainless steels. This will be discussed in the chapter on stainless-steel welding.

Manganese—is indispensable to all steelmaking. In percentages up to about 0.80%, manganese is generally intended to combine with sulphur to offset embrittlement and hot shortness. In higher percentages, 1 to 15%, manganese increases the toughness and also the hardening ability of the metal.

Molybdenum—tends to increase the hardness and the endurance limits of steel. It likewise contributes to deep hardening. It decreases the tendency toward high-temperature *creep,* which is the slow stretching of a steel under stress at high temperatures. Molybdenum also increases the corrosion-resistant qualities of stainless types of alloy steel and prevents temper embrittlement of low-chrome alloys. Generally, it is used in comparatively small quantities, ranging from about 0.10 to 4.00%.

Nickel—increases the strength and toughness of a steel at low temperatures. It is generally added in quantities from 1 to 4%, although in some nickel-steels the nickel content will run as high as 36% or more. No matter what the percentage, the addition of nickel will increase the strength without decreasing the toughness of the steel; there are, however, instances where the addition of nickel promotes embrittlement when heated.

Steels with 24% or more nickel are non-magnetic.

A steel with 36% nickel has a very small coefficient of expansion when heated up to 900 F. In the lower range of nickel—up to about 4%—it is usually estimated that the tensile strength is increased about 6,000 psi for each additional 1% of nickel.

Nitrogen—is generally found combined with other elements as a nitride. Nitrides usually have a detrimental effect. Nitrogen is useful, however, for the stabilization of austenite and for the lessening of grain growth in some stainless steels.

Oxygen—forms iron oxide (rust), which is not desirable and makes welding difficult. In steelmaking, it is used to burn out excess carbon and to shorten melting time. Oxygen is essential in oxyacetylene welding and cutting.

Phosphorus—is one of the elements found in all steels. In high percentages, it is considered an impurity. In low percentages, however, it improves the machinability of a steel, whether high carbon or low carbon. The phosphorus content is usually restricted to about 0.05%, particularly so in steels in the higher carbon ranges. Phosphorus slightly improves the strength and corrosion resistance of low-carbon steel.

Sulphur—like phosphorus, is always present in steels, generally as an impurity. The sulphur content of steel may range up to 0.3%, but it is usually held below 0.06%. A sulphur content of 0.1 to 0.15% materially improves machining qualities. A high sulphur content may produce poor weldability due to hot short cracking and severe porosity. The tendency to cracking and porosity may be overcome by using a low-hydrogen electrode.

Silicon—is added to the molten steel bath to control the oxygen content of the steel. This function is known as deoxidizing. In high percentages, silicon is used to produce certain magnetic characteristics in steel used for electrical magnetic applications. Its addition tends to improve oxidation resistance and increases the hardenability of steels carrying non-graphitizing elements. Silicon also contributes to the strength of low-alloy steels.

Tantalum—is sometimes added to steel to increase its hardness by the formation of carbides.

Titanium—is another deoxidizer. It is also useful in restricting the effects of nitrogen and carbon since it readily combines with these elements. Titanium will lessen grain growth and may be used to prevent steel from hardening. Like columbium, titanium is used to stabilize austenitic stainless steels.

Tungsten—has a very important job to do in tool steels, which must retain hardness at high temperatures. When used in amounts of from 17 to 20% (and in combination with other alloys), tungsten produces a steel having the quality of red-hardness. Tungsten is also used in certain heat-resistant steels where the retention of strength at high temperatures is important. Tungsten is usually used in combination with chromium or other alloying agents. Used in relatively small quantities, it tends to produce a fine, dense grain structure.

Vanadium—tends to produce a fine grain structure during the heat-treating process. Because of this, vanadium often eliminates the bad effects of overheating. Vanadium also tends to promote hardenability; it causes a marked secondary hardness that resists tempering.

Zirconium—is a powerful deoxidizer but is not used for this purpose in steel unless combined with other deoxidizing elements. Its principal use in steel is to prevent age hardening and blue brittleness.

Structure of Metals

Though the alloying elements may change the structure of metals, their characteristics are due to two structural factors: (1) the *atoms* making up the metal and (2) the manner in which the atoms are arranged. An examination of metals, however, even under the most powerful microscope will not reveal atoms. All that can be seen are grains or crystals.

The smallest grain that we can see under the microscope is, of course, made up of a very large number of atoms. If the biggest atoms known to scientists were arranged side-by-side in a straight line, it would take about 25,000,000 of them to make an inch. Anything so small as an arrangement of 9 or 14 atoms must remain forever invisible, even under the electron microscope. How, then, do we know that such patterns exist? From the shape of the crystals that we can see, it is logical to assume that their shape must be due to the arrangement of atoms that make up the ultimate units of the grain. The accuracy of this assumption has been proved by the application of x-ray analysis to crystalline structure. However, we are getting beyond the scope of this book.

While the addition of alloying elements forms a complex steel, the study of metallurgy is complex enough when confined to simple carbon steel; so, the alloys discussed will be those of iron and carbon only. An idea of the structure of an 0.83% C (carbon) steel may be obtained from Fig. 7-5. This sketch is a schematic magnification up to 35 million times larger than when viewed by the eye. Such a magnification of the crystalline structure may be obtained only by x-ray diffraction, though powerful microscopes can produce 1000 times (1000x) and 2500x magnifications using ordinary light.

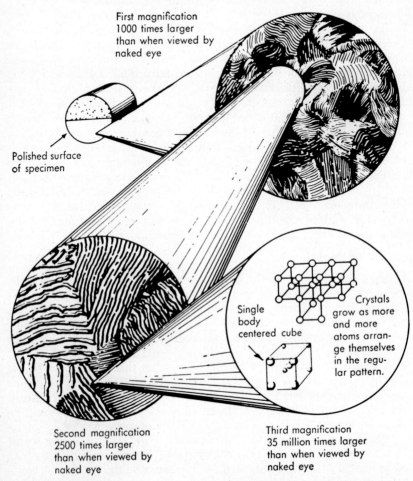

First magnification 1000 times larger than when viewed by naked eye

Polished surface of specimen

Single body centered cube

Crystals grow as more and more atoms arrange themselves in the regular pattern.

Second magnification 2500 times larger than when viewed by naked eye

Third magnification 35 million times larger than when viewed by naked eye

Fig. 7-5. Schematic magnification of a steel containing about 0.83% carbon to give an idea of manner in which the constituents arrange themselves. The third magnification is incomplete but shows how iron atoms are arranged as a crystal forms. The lines joining atoms are merely to help in visualizing the arrangement.

What Are Grains?

What are grains, and why do they grow? Grains, or the crystals of a metal, have almost any external shape. Like salt or snow, a metal is a crystalline substance, but the *crystals* of commercial metals and alloys are commonly referred to as *grains*. Grains are in general regular in shape and, though they may vary in size, the grains of a particular metal are always similar in angular pattern to each other.

A grain's internal atomic structure, however, is based upon the *space-lattice* of the particular metal.

All grains or crystals are composed of atoms bound together in a definite pattern or structure. This atomic structure is called the space-lattice. The space-lattice arrangement of atoms determines the shape of the crystalline structure, just as the arrangement of bricks determines the shape of a building. The atoms in a grain are spaced a definite distance from one another, and this spacing cannot be changed. Hence, metallurgists often think of these atoms as being held together by imaginary lines. These lines do not actually exist, but they help us to more easily visualize the arrangement of atoms.

Space-Lattice Types

It has been found that there are 14 possible space-lattice types. However, we need know only three: (1) body-centered cubic, Fig. 7-6; (2) hexagonal close packed, diagrammed in Fig. 7-7; and (3) face-centered cubic, Fig. 7-8. Most metals crystallize into one of these three types. Some metals (iron is one) have two space-lattice structures.

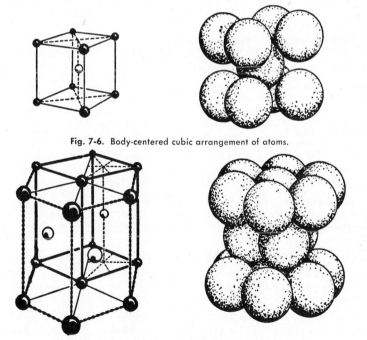

Fig. 7-6. Body-centered cubic arrangement of atoms.

Fig. 7-7. Hexagonal close packaged atom arrangement.

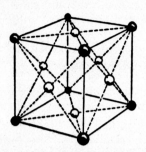 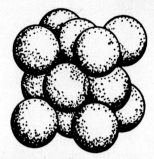

Fig. 7-8. Face-centered cubic atom arrangement.

The body-centered cubic lattice takes 9 atoms—one at each corner of the cube and one in the center of the cube. The face-centered cubic lattice requires 14 atoms—one at each corner of the cube and one in the center of each of the six square faces. The hexagonal close-packed lattice takes 17 atoms—one at each of six corners on each of the two end faces, one in the center of each of the two end faces, and three equally spaced between the two end faces.

The body-centered cubic form is generally assumed by iron, chromium, columbium, molybdenum, tungsten and vanadium. The face-centered cubic form is assembled by aluminum, copper, gold, lead, nickel, platinum and silver. Among the metals having a close-packed hexagonal form are cadmium, cobalt, magnesium, titanium and zinc.

The atoms in an 0.83% C steel are in a body-centered cubic form at temperatures below 1333 F, Fig. 7-5. Above that temperature, the *critical temperature*, the grains assume a face-centered cubic form, Fig. 7-9. In pure iron, the atoms are arranged in body-centered cubic form at room temperature. Above about 1670 F, iron has a face-centered cubic structure. Some high-alloy steels have a face-centered cubic form at all temperatures. This change from one type of space-lattice to another takes place while the metal is in a solid state and does not change density or volume. Since there are nine atoms in the body-centered cubic unit and 14 in the face-centered cubic unit, there is rearrangement of atoms within the grain. This shifting of atoms is referred to as an *allotropic change*.

Metals with body-centered cubic grains are higher in yield strength and lower in cold working properties than metals with the face-centered cubic pattern.

By comparing the grain structures of the two schematic sketches, Fig. 7-5 and Fig. 7-9, it will be seen that they are different. The bar of Fig. 7-5 is at a temperature below 1333 F and as a consequence is composed of *ferrite* (pure iron) and *cementite (iron carbide)*. This grain structure is called pearlite and is best shown in the 2500x magnification. In Fig. 7-9 the structure is austenite, a condition existing in an 0.83% C steel above 1333 F.

Pearlitic Structure

Pearlite grains are composed of alternate plates of soft, ductile, pure iron and hard, brittle iron carbide. In steel, all the carbon is in the form of iron carbide, unless other elements are present. If there are other elements, there may be carbides of these elements as well. When a steel has about 0.83% carbon, all the grains are pearlite (body-centered cubic) and it is known as a *eutectoid* mixture. If less than 0.83% carbon, the structure will be composed of ferrite (pure

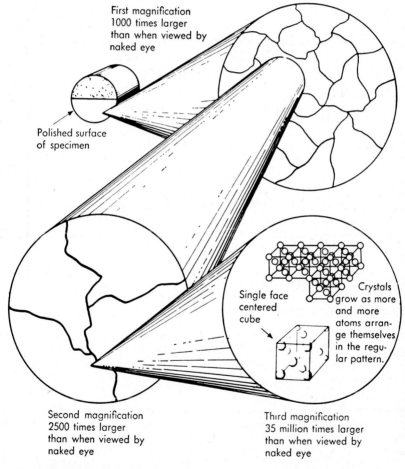

First magnification
1000 times larger
than when viewed by
naked eye

Polished surface
of specimen

Single face
centered
cube

Crystals
grow as more
and more
atoms arran-
ge themselves
in the regu-
lar pattern.

Second magnification
2500 times larger
than when viewed by
naked eye

Third magnification
35 million times larger
than when viewed by
naked eye

Fig. 7-9. Steels heated above the critical temperature are, of course, too hot to be polished, etched or viewed through a microscope. Some alloys, however, retain their austenitic (face-centered cubic) arrangement after cooling to room temperature. Any work, such as forging, on austenitic steel would change the shape of the grain.

iron) and pearlite grains, Fig. 7-10. If above 0.83% carbon, there would be a structure of pearlite grains surrounded by iron carbide, Fig. 7-11.

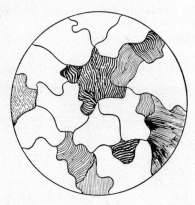 

Fig. 7-10. Steel having less than 0.83% carbon has a structure composed of ferrite and pearlite.

Fig. 7-11. Steel having more than 0.83% carbon has a structure of pearlite surrounded by iron carbide.

Austenitic Structure

As this eutectoidal mixture (0.83% C) steel is heated above 1333 F, the grains of pearlite change from a body-centered cubic (9 atoms) arrangement to a face-centered (14 atoms) cubic structure to form grains of *austenite*. As the steel passes through the critical temperature (1333 F), and the above mentioned rearrangement takes place, the iron carbide separates into iron and carbon. The carbon then goes into solution in the iron to become evenly distributed throughout the alloy. This action takes place while the metal is in the solid state and is referred to as a *solid solution*.

How Do Grains Grow?

A few paragraphs back, we discussed seed crystals—each of which is a single or unit cell. As molten metal cools in a mold, a large number of these seed crystals will first form at scattered locations in those areas of the mass where the temperature is falling most quickly. Almost immediately, additional cells of the crystal will begin to form on the seed. If the crystal structure is body-centered cubic, the seed cell will share four atoms on one face with the second cell. See Figs. 7-5 and 7-9. Simultaneously, molten metal closer to the center of the mass is cooling sufficiently for new seed crystals to form.

This growth of the crystal continues along three-dimensional lines from the original seed, thereby forming the space-lattice. In the case of a metal, the crystals are often called grains. Their growth tends to extend principally in a direction perpendicular to a chilled surface;

however, there are other forces that prevent all of the grains from being so oriented.

Each grain grows until it meets another growing grain. If the two are oriented along parallel lines, they usually join together as one larger grain. If the grains are not oriented similarly, there can be no perfect wedding of the two. The intersection of two such grains is therefore irregular in outline and is called the *grain boundary*.

When austenite is first formed, the grains are small. If the steel is held at a high temperature, however, these grains will become larger. The higher the temperature (below the melting point), the faster the grains will grow.

The rate at which the austenite grains become larger at a given temperature depends on the chemical content of the steel, and on the melting, casting and rolling practice used in its manufacture. Steels may be ordered to grain-size specifications, according to the numbers: -3, -2, -1, 0, 1 and on up to 12. The grain-size number tells us the number of grains per sq in. the steel will have after it has been given a specified heat treatment to cause grain growth, Fig. 7-12. A steel of No. 1 grain size, for example, will have only about one grain per sq in. at a magnification of 100 diameters, while a steel of No. 8 grain size will have about 100 grains per sq in. at the same magnification.

Coarse-grained steels are desired for some uses, and fine-grained steels for others. However, a coarse-grained steel can be heat treated to secure a fine-grained product, and a fine-grained steel can be heat treated to produce coarse grains.

Why Metals Stretch

The surface of a metal can be observed while the metal is stretched. Looking through a microscope at a polished and etched sample, we see that as the metal is stretched a slipping or shearing takes place between the grains. The grains elongate parallel to each grain, but the lines in different grains are at various angles to each other. These lines are called *slip lines*. When two or more parallel lines are near together in the same grain, they are called *slip bands*. They appear because, during the stressing, a part of a grain slid upon another part. This forms a step, which appears in the microscope as a line across the grain. The surfaces that slid or slipped are called *slip planes*.

The angle of the slip planes depends upon the way the grain is turned. The grains do not seem to be weakened by the slipping. As the stressing is continued, additional slip lines form instead of more slip taking place where the slip or sliding first started, as you might expect. Failure finally occurs by the slip continuing until some of the grains slide off of each other and by actual fracture through the other grains. Failure in pure metals is not likely to occur at the grain boundaries.

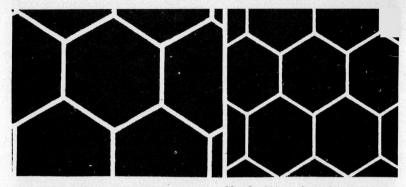

Grain Size No. 1; Up to 1½ per sq.in.   No. 2; 1½ to 3 grains per sq.in.

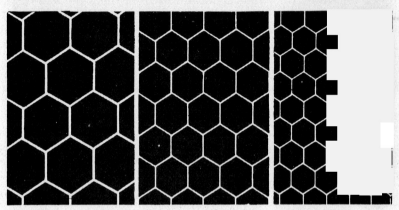

No. 3; 3 to 6 grains   No. 4; 6 to 12 grains   No. 5; 12 to 24 grains
per sq.in.   per sq.in.   per sq.in.

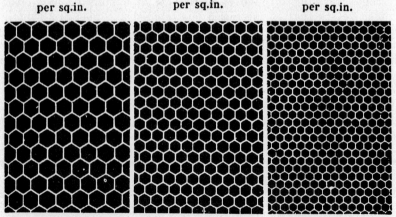

No. 6; 24 to 48 grains   No. 7; 48 to 96 grains   No. 8; More than 96
per sq.in.   per sq.in.   grains per sq.in.

Fig. 7-12. Grain size is determined by the number of grains per sq in. after steel has received a standard heat treatment.

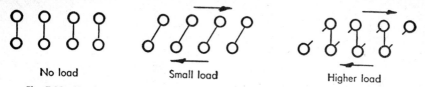

No load   Small load   Higher load

Fig. 7-13. Metal atoms in a grain. When stressed, a small amount of the atoms move out of position but will return when the stress is removed. Higher stress will cause the atoms to slide over and assume a new position with new partners.

In Chapter 2 on mechanical properties, it is stated that all metals have elastic properties; that is, they will return to their original dimensions after a small load is removed. The small load causes the atoms to move a little from their perfect cubic arrangement, but they will drop back to their original positions when the load is removed. When the load is high enough to cause permanent deformation, a layer of atoms will move past their partners and then drop into new positions with new partners, Fig. 7-13.

Making Metals Strong

Physicists, who have calculated the forces that hold atoms together, tell us that metals should be many times as strong as we find them to be by tensile testing. We know that small wires have a higher strength than larger test pieces because they are more uniformly loaded, and we also know that the strength of a metal increases as the grains are made smaller. If all the grains of a metal could be made to line up in the ideal direction, and if we could load them all uniformly, then indeed we might have metals of super strength.

This is not possible—as yet. We can, however, greatly increase the strength of a metal or alloy by cold working. As an example, cold-worked pure copper has a tensile strength of over 50,000 psi; before cold working the tensile strength is only 30,000 psi. Since the metal's hardness also is increased by cold working, the material is often said to be work-hardened.

Cold stressing of a metal causes the grains to yield by internal slippage. Once slippage has taken place, the atoms seem to adhere more strongly at the new plane than ever. We know this is so because a greater force is required to cause more slippage at the new plane. In some manner, the grains have been strengthened by the stressing. One way of accounting for it is to assume that each grain has some planes that will slide easily, making the metal soft and easily stretched. Stretching the metal "takes up the slack," and the grains become more resistant to deformation.

On the practical side, metals may be made both stronger and harder by stretching, pounding or otherwise subjecting them to a form of cold working. Sometimes the cold working is done deliberately, as when wire is cold drawn to make it stronger. Sometimes it is accidental and its effects are unwanted. A part being formed into shape, for example, may be so hardened by cold working that it must be softened by *annealing* in order to complete the processing.

The effects of cold working can always be completely removed by heat. Heating first results in a realignment that relieves the unequal stresses in the cold-worked metal. Higher heating causes *recrystallization*: the distorted and elongated crystals disappear and are replaced by small and uniform but irregularly shaped crystals. Heating at a higher temperature or heating for a longer time allows these small crystals to combine and become larger.

When cold-worked pure copper is heated to 300 F, it recrystallizes and is softened; whereupon the tensile strength drops from 50,000 to 30,000 psi. Iron that has been cold worked will recrystallize at temperatures above 1000 F.

The recrystallization of metals that have been cold worked is not to be confused with the transformation of iron when it is heated above 1670 F. When iron recrystallizes below the transformation temperature, there is only a gradual growth of new crystals. At the *transformation temperature* a total rearrangement of the atoms takes place quickly, resulting in an absorption of heat, change in volume and an entirely new (austenitic) grain structure.

Iron is the only common metal that transforms in this manner.

Effect of Hot Working on Grain Size

Rolling, forging or any kind of hot working breaks up the austenite grains and makes them smaller. Cold working such as drawing, forming or peening will make the ferrite and pearlite grains smaller by elongating or distorting them; however, the steels tend to become hardened and embrittled by the cold working before there has been much grain refinement.

A steel forging will have a fine grain as the result of being heated to forging temperature (2000 to 2200 F) and then forged while the steel cools until the austenite starts to transform. If the hot working is stopped appreciably above the transformation temperature, the grains of austenite will grow while the steel cools to the critical range; then, when the steel has returned to room temperature, the grains will still be large.

A fine-grained steel has a much higher impact strength than a coarse-grained steel. Quenching of austenite shortly after it has formed on heating gives a fine-grained product. Heating steel for a long time in the austenite range or overheating steel allows the austenite grains to grow. Then both the quenched product and the slowly cooled steel will be coarse-grained. However, coarse-grained structures are desired for some uses because they will harden to a greater depth than fine-grain steels.

Definitions of New Words

Allotropic change. The shifting of atoms relative to one another, resulting in a change in the state or structure of a material. Certain metals are allotropic in that their atoms can rearrange from one crystal structure to another at certain critical temperatures, each structure having distinct properties and stable within definite limits of temperature and pressure.

Austenite. A solid solution of carbon or iron-carbide in face-centered cubic iron.

Cementite. Iron-carbide (Fe_3C) constituent of steel and cast iron. It is hard and brittle.

Creep. The slow deformation (for example, elongation) of a metal under prolonged stress. Not to be confused with that deformation which results immediately upon application of a stress.

Critical temperature. See "transformation temperature."

Eutectoid mixture. A mixture of two or more constituents, formed on cooling from a solid solution, to which state it can return again when heated.

Ferrite. Body-centered cubic iron, which is soft and ductile.

Grain boundaries. The irregular separations of adjacent crystals that are oriented in different directions and therefore cannot join in a continuation of the basic lattice pattern.

Matrix. The principal, physically continuous metallic constituent in which crystals or free atoms of other constituents are embedded. It serves as a binder, holding the entire mass together.

Orientation. The principal direction in which a crystal has developed, relative to a polished surface or some other reference plane.

Pearlite. A continuous granular mixture composed of alternate plates or layers of (pure iron) ferrite and (iron-carbide) cementite.

Photomicrograph. A photograph taken through a microscope, showing a greatly enlarged area and revealing structural details not visible to the naked eye.

Seed crystals. Solitary crystal units, or unit cells (often a single cube), which are formed first as metals cool and which are repetitive in three dimensions. The growth of the crystal extends outward from this original seed crystal.

Slip bands. Bands, visible under a microscope, stretching across a deformed polished surface and caused by numerous closely spaced parallel slip lines.

Slip lines. The parallel lines, visible under a microscope, on a specimen that has been polished and then deformed. Lines show the strain along slip planes which permitted the deformation to take place.

Slip plane. The plane within a crystal along which one layer of atoms slip, under stress, relative to another layer of atoms.

Solid solution. A continuous crystal in which one metal remains dissolved within another, without interruption of the atomic structure of that metal.

Space lattice. The definite geometric pattern or structure in which atoms arrange themselves, and in which a basic cell is repeated along three-dimensional lines. Each solid crystal (or "grain," if atoms are of a metal element) develops around such a space lattice.

Transformation temperature. The temperature at which a metal changes from one type of structure to another. This is usually different when heat is being added than when heat is being taken away. And usually, the transformation starts at one temperature and is completed at a slightly higher or lower point.

Review Questions

1. Why does a highly polished sample of iron fail to show the grain structure when examined microscopically?

2. How many iron atoms are there per unit cube in the body-centered crystals? Face-centered crystals? Hint—Note the number of unit cubes shared by each iron atom.

3. Why are the grains (crystals) in iron irregular in shape instead of being cubic?

4. Metals are made stronger by cold working. Can metals be made weaker by cold working?

5. Explain by sketches how a grain of metal can:
   a. Stretch elastically by slipping through the grains.
   b. Yield elastically by slipping through the grains.
   c. Fail elastically by slipping through the grains.

6. Define or describe: (a) Austenite (b) Pearlite (c) Ferrite (d) Cementite

7. Which of the above will be found in a slowly cooled sample of low carbon steel? 0.83% carbon steel? 1.0% carbon steel?

8. How does carbon in steel affect the tensile strength? Yield strength? Ductility?

9. At what temperature does iron transform from one crystal structure to another? How about 0.83% carbon steel?

10. Name an alloying element that is often used in steels to restrict grain growth. Name another one used to provide high strength at high temperatures.

CHAPTER 8

METALLURGY AND HEAT TREATING

Heat is conducted through metals much more rapidly than it is through air or water. Even so it has been found that steel does not change its temperature uniformly when heated or cooled. Because certain changes take place in steel at various temperatures, there are times when its temperature will remain constant, even though heat is added or taken away at a uniform rate.

When a pan of cold water is placed over a gas flame, the temperature increases uniformly. If temperature readings of the water are taken every minute and the values of both temperature and time are plotted on a graph, we get a sloped curve, Fig. 8-1. But when the water reaches the boiling point, the temperature remains constant as long as any water remains. This appears in Fig. 8-1 as a flattening out of the curve.

Figure 8-2 is a graph of the change in temperature of water as it is cooled slowly. The solid line shows that ice starts to form as soon as the freezing temperature was reached. Sometimes water can be cooled below 32 F without freezing; such water is said to be *super-cooled*. Stirring supercooled water or adding a grain of sand may start the crystallization (freezing). The addition of a particle of ice will be sure to cause the water to begin to freeze. This bit of added ice is known as a *seed crystal*.

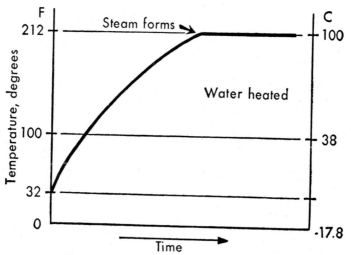

Fig. 8-1. A time-temperature curve of water heating.

The temperature of the supercooled water (broken line in Fig. 8-2) actually increases from a few degrees below freezing to 32 F when the ice crystals begin to form. This is because heat is given off when water changes from the liquid to the solid state. When supercooled water starts to freeze, the ice crystals that form give off enough heat to warm the remaining water to 32 F; freezing then proceeds as it did with the water that started to freeze at 32 F.

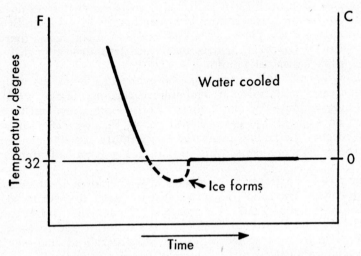

Fig. 8-2. A time-temperature curve of water cooling.

Having observed the cooling of water, let us now see how iron cools. Molten pure iron is cooled slowly in a well-insulated crucible. During this process, temperature readings are taken at closely-spaced time intervals. At the same time, the condition of the iron is noted. The first unusual condition is noted at 2780 F, Fig. 8-3. At this point, the molten iron has cooled enough for crystals to begin to form. The *freezing* action proceeds rapidly; and, as soon as the iron has become completely solid, the temperature again falls.

At 2550 F, a slight lag in the falling temperature indicates another change is taking place in the solid iron—a change from delta iron to gamma iron. In delta iron the atoms are arranged in a body-centered cubic structure (Fig. 7-6), and in gamma iron the same atoms have rearranged themselves into face-centered cubic crystals (Fig. 7-7).

The temperature again falls and as it reaches 1670 F, it once more remains constant for a short time. At this point, atoms of the gamma iron shift back into the form of body-centered cubic crystals, which are characteristic of alpha iron.

The temperature at which a change in the crystalline structure takes place is called the critical or transformation temperature. While

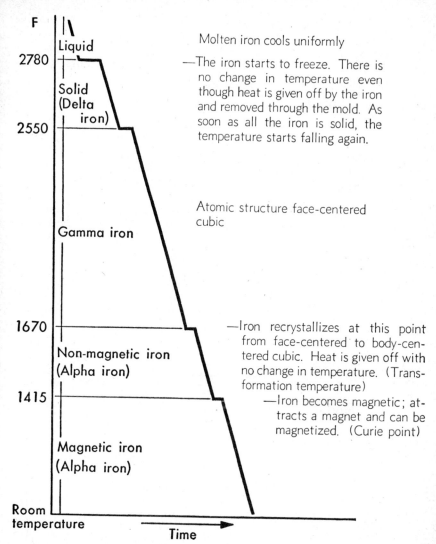

Fig. 8-3. What happens to the temperature of molten iron as it is uniformly cooled.

this change takes place, the movement of atoms gives off energy in the form of heat which tends to offset the normal fall in temperature and keep it constant until the transformation is about completed.

In heating iron the transformation takes place in a reverse manner. As the crystalline structure is rearranged, however, heat is absorbed instead of given off. Hence the transformation point on heating iron is higher than the transformation point when iron is cooled.

At 1415 F there is another change in the cooling iron. It is at this point that the magnetic properties return. Above 1415 F, iron is not attracted by a magnet; below this temperature it is attracted. The *Curie point* is the temperature at which the change occurs in iron, cobalt and nickel, the only *magnetic* metals.

How Steels Solidify

We have now learned that pure molten iron solidifies or freezes at 2780 F to form a solid mass of grains (crystals) and that additional changes take place in the atomic arrangement and in the shape and size of the grains as the iron continues to cool. Do the same changes take place when the iron is alloyed with carbon to form a plain-carbon steel?

Similar changes do take place when carbon is alloyed with the iron. The changes on cooling or heating, however, are more complicated. Following the cooling process of steel, step by step, will make these changes easier to understand.

Step No. 1—Freezing Point. As previously explained, the main constituents of a carbon steel are carbon and iron. The carbon is uniformly dissolved in the molten steel in the same manner that salt is dissolved in a salt solution. When salt is put into solution in water, the temperature at which the water freezes is lowered. Salt water does

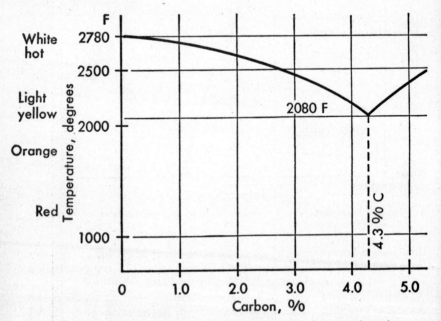

Fig. 8-4. The freezing temperature of iron-carbon combinations lowers as the carbon content increases up to 4.3% carbon.

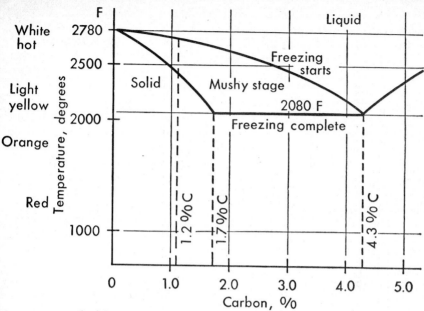

Fig. 8-5. Iron-carbon alloys and their solidification temperatures.

not freeze at 32 F, the freezing point of pure water. Similarly, when carbon is in solution in molten iron, the effect is to lower the temperature at which the solution freezes. For this reason, carbon steel solidifies at a lower temperature than pure iron. The more carbon there is in solution, the lower will be the temperature at which freezing starts (except for alloys with more than 4.3% carbon). Figure 8-4 shows the temperatures at which various alloys of carbon and iron start to freeze.

Step No. 2—Mushy Stage. Pure iron freezes at 2780 F, and the temperature of the freezing iron remains constant until all of the iron is solidified. When carbon is present, however, the alloy continues to get colder as the freezing or solidification process continues.

Figure 8-5 repeats the Fig. 8-4 curve representing the temperatures at which the steel begins to freeze. In addition, it shows a curve representing the temperatures at which freezing is completed. This also is in relation to the percentage of carbon content.

From the curves, we see that steel with a carbon content of 1.0% starts to freeze at 2640 F. A few crystals form and, as the temperature is lowered, these grow and others form. Then, at 2450 F the last of the molten steel becomes solid.

Between temperatures of 2640 and 2450 F, the steel is in a condition that is part solid and part liquid; that is, tiny grains or crystals of steel are floating in the molten steel. This condition is called the *mushy stage.*

As an example: Plumber's wiping solder (a combination of 40% tin and 60% lead) starts to form solid crystals in the liquid at about 460 F and is wholly solid at about 360 F. While in this 100-degree range of the mushy stage, the plastic mixture of solder can be formed and wiped around a lead pipe or lead cable to produce a leakproof joint. Steel is in a similar condition in the mushy stage and can be fused in this temperature range.

Step No. 3—White-Hot Stage. When in the white-hot and light yellow range of temperature (from solidification down to about 2000 F), iron will dissolve an appreciable amount of carbon. It is easy to picture carbon dissolved in liquid iron because we are all familiar with such liquid solutions as brine or salt dissolved in water. However, we have no everyday example of a solid dissolved in another solid. You do not get such a solid solution when brine freezes; when freezing of brine occurs, the water separates out of the solution to freeze in the form of salt-free ice. However, there is such a thing as a solid solution, and it is extremely important to ferrous metallurgy. Because iron is able to hold dissolved carbon when in the solid stage, iron-carbon alloys can be heat treated to give a wide variety of properties.

The solid solution of carbon in iron is known as austenite, named after the English metallurgist Sir W. Austen. Under the microscope, austenite looks like a pure metal rather than an alloy.

A strip of white-hot carbon steel when examined at high magnification* reveals only one constituent—the grains of austenite (remember Fig. 7-9). If the carbon were not in solution, the steel would be a mixture and we could distinguish the grains of iron from the grains of carbon and from grains of an iron-carbon compound.

A clear understanding of the metallurgy of welding steel depends upon a clear understanding of the solid solution, austenite.

We have seen that at a temperature above 1670 F, iron atoms are arranged in a face-centered (14 atoms) cubic structure. When the atoms are arranged in this form, there is space between them for some carbon atoms. This is not true, however, with the body-centered (9 atoms) cubic structure, the usual iron arrangement at room temperature. Then there is not enough space between the iron atoms for the carbon atoms. Now we can see why carbon is soluble in hot iron but is not soluble in cold iron. The carbon atoms can readily move about in the austenite; the higher the temperature the more readily the carbon can move.

If a low-carbon steel bar is packed in charcoal or other material containing carbon, and heated to about 2000 F, the surface of the bar will absorb carbon which will migrate toward the center of the bar. After 24 hours of heating, an appreciable amount of carbon will have penetrated to a depth of ½ in. into the bar. Refer to Fig. 8-6.

---

*Special equipment and technique are required to examine a metal at a high temperature.

Step No. 4—White-Hot to Room Temperature. The changes that take place as carbon steel cools from white-hot to room temperature will depend upon the amount of carbon in the steel. The cooling of a steel with 0.83% carbon, one with less than 0.83% carbon and one with more than 0.83% carbon will be discussed in detail. There is a significant reason for the figure of 0.83% carbon as was shown in Chapter 7.

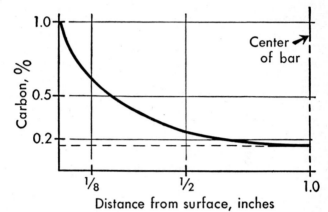

Fig. 8-6. The carbon distribution in a bar of steel that has absorbed carbon.

When Steel Is Cooled Slowly

0.83% Carbon content results in a steel's existing in the liquid state above 2670 F. As the molten steel cools, solidification starts at 2670 F. At 2500 F, solidification is complete, with all of the carbon dissolved in the iron. (If the cooling is excessively slow, carbon-rich areas develop at the grain boundaries where the final freezing occurs.) Between 2500 and 1333 F, the face-centered cubic arrangement allows the carbon atoms to remain tucked away between the iron atoms.

When this solid solution (austenite) has cooled to 1333 F, the iron atoms begin to shift to form a new arrangement (body-centered cubic) that has no room for carbon atoms. The growing crystals of ferrite (pure iron) squeeze the carbon out of solution to the grain boundaries. Each of these freed carbon atoms then unites with three iron atoms to produce the chemical compound: iron carbide, Fe_3C. This compound is called cementite.

The cementite crystals arrange themselves in thin parallel plates sandwiched between layers of ferrite crystals. The resulting structure of cementite and ferrite is called pearlite. The name pearlite was chosen because the structure when magnified resembles the mother-of-pearl found in a shell, which also has a multiple-layer structure.

This entire transformation from austenite to pearlite occurs during a very narrow temperature range at about 1333 F. The levelling of temperature at this point until transformation is complete is due to the release of heat by the shifting of the atoms. Another change occurring at 1333 F is that of the metal becoming magnetic.

Less than 0.83% Carbon. A steel containing 0.30% carbon will be taken as an example for the cooling of steel with less than 0.83% carbon.

The 0.30% carbon steel starts to freeze at a higher temperature than does 0.83% carbon steel, and solidification is complete at a higher temperature. The austenite starts to transform at 1500 F, changing into body-centered cubic crystals of ferrite. As carbon is squeezed out of solution, it is redissolved by the austenite that has not yet transformed, for this austenite is not saturated with carbon and can readily take more carbon into solution. As the temperature falls lower, and more austenite transforms, the ferrite crystals become larger and more numerous. The rejected carbon continues to enrich the untransformed austenite. Finally, the remaining austenite has its carbon content increased to 0.83%. At about 1333 F, this last austenite changes to pearlite, just like the 0.83% carbon steel already discussed.

The microstructure of slowly cooled low-carbon steel (Fig. 8-7) shows the ferrite appearing white, and the pearlite dark or black. Since the 0.83% carbon steel has a microstructure made up of 100% pearlite, you no doubt have realized that pearlite always contains 0.83% carbon. Even the small amount of pearlite found in 0.10% carbon steel thus has 0.83% carbon.

More than 0.83% Carbon. As an example, we will take a steel with 1.2% carbon. By following down the 1.2% carbon line on Fig. 8-5, we find that this steel starts freezing at 2600 F and that the freezing is complete at 2400 F. The austenite grains in steel are very small at first, but they combine with each other to become larger as the temperature drops. When the temperature has fallen to 1550 F, the solu-

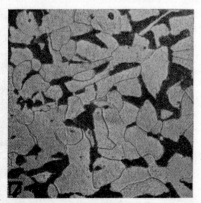 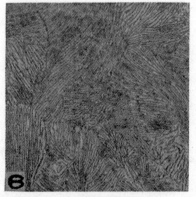

Fig. 8-7. Slowly-cooled steel has ferrite (white) and pearlite (black), as shown in the photomicrograph at left. A close-up of the pearlite, at right, reveals its "laminated" structure: alternating plates of ferrite and cementite.

bility of carbon in austenite has been lowered to where the austenite cannot hold all the carbon in solution. Some of the carbon is rejected, and it combines with iron to form cementite (iron carbide). With continued lowering of the temperature, more cementite is formed. At about 1333 F, the remaining austenite has a carbon content of 0.83% and transforms to pearlite, Fig. 8-8.

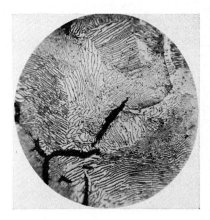

Fig. 8-8. Pearlite formed from austenite at about 1333 F.

To summarize (Fig. 8-9):

In cooling, steel of exactly 0.83% carbon transforms entirely to pearlite.

In cooling, steel of less than 0.83% carbon transforms to ferrite and pearlite. The pearlite has exactly 0.83% carbon; the ferrite is pure iron.

In cooling, steel of more than 0.83% carbon transforms to cementite and pearlite. As before, the pearlite has exactly 0.83% carbon; the cementite is an iron-carbide compound.

The more detailed iron-carbon diagram (Fig. 8-10) shows the temperatures at which austenite starts to decompose, forming ferrite or cementite, plotted against the carbon content of the steel. The temperature at which this transformation begins is called the *upper critical temperature.*

The diagram also shows the temperature at which all of the austenite is transformed. The last austenite, in both low-carbon and high-carbon steel, transforms into pearlite at about 1333 F. This last austenite contains exactly 0.83% carbon. The temperature at which transformation ends is called the *lower critical temperature.* Temperatures between the upper and lower limits cover the *transformation range.*

Within the transformation range, the low-carbon steel has been forming ferrite, using up iron and thereby increasing the carbon content of the untransformed austenite. The high-carbon steel has been forming cementite, using up carbon and thus lowering the carbon

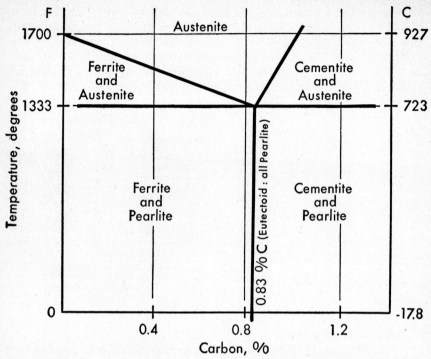

Fig. 8-9. Steel of 0.83% carbon transforms to pearlite at about 1333 F. The lower the carbon content below 0.83%, the greater the amount of ferrite will be. The higher the carbon content above 0.83%, the greater the amount of cementite will be.

content of the remaining austenite. The result of both types of change is that the austenite finally reaches a carbon content of 0.83% carbon and transforms into pearlite at 1333 F.

These curves and transformation temperatures apply to carbon steel that is being slowly *cooled*. When the steel is *heated* slowly, the changes take place in the reverse order, as you would expect, but not at the same points. The transformation or critical temperatures are somewhat higher upon heating than the temperatures when the steel is cooling.

When the rate of cooling is increased, the transformation temperatures are lowered. These temperatures are also lowered by some of the alloying elements used in steel.

What Happens When Steel Is Quenched

The opposite of slow cooling is *quenching*—rapid cooling from a high temperature. We have just discussed the structures of carbon steels as they are cooled at slow rates from the molten condition. These are equilibrium conditions, for enough time is allowed for the changes that take place to proceed uniformly and without interference.

If a hot, concentrated sugar solution is cooled slowly, large sugar crystals (rock candy) result. What happens if the solution is cooled quickly? The crystals will be much smaller, and they will start forming at a lower temperature than when the solution is cooled slowly.

Now let a piece of carbon steel be cooled at a fast rate. The usual changes are delayed, and the resulting structures and properties of these structures are entirely different than when the metal is slowly cooled.

When freezing slowly, steel produces large crystals of austenite. After solidification, the crystals become still larger, and the carbon shifts from the higher carbon areas to those of lower carbon content. Rapidly cooled steel does not have time to form large austenite crystals or time for the carbon and other elements to segregate. As a result, the metal at a temperature above 2000 F is a mass of very small austenite grains with carbon uniformly distributed.

In order to produce ferrite, pearlite and cementite, when austenite is cooled, the carbon must physically move through the austenite. To make pearlite with fine laminations, the carbon has to migrate only a

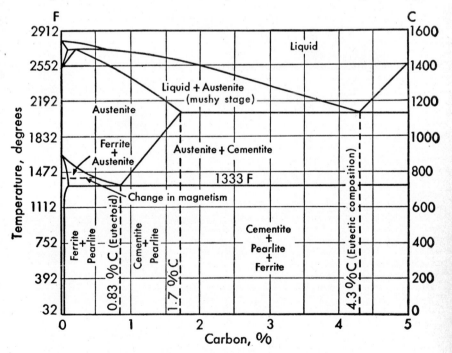

Fig. 8-10. By combining data on solidification temperatures and critical ranges (Fig. 8-5) and phase changes (Fig. 8-9), the iron-carbon diagram is obtained.

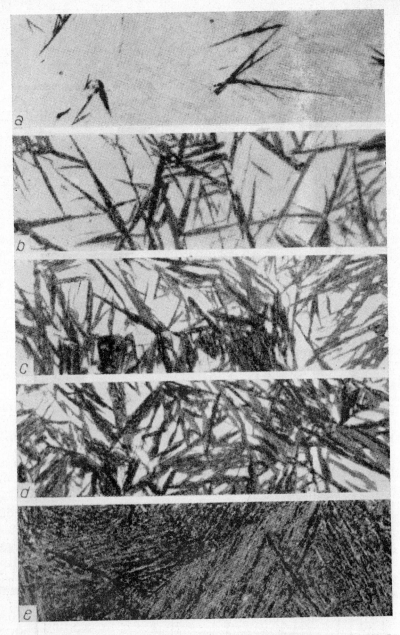

Fig. 8-11. Examples of transformation in eutectoid steel (0.83% carbon) at 500 F, 1500x. (A) 400 seconds, transformation begins. (B) 500 seconds, 25% transformed. (C) 850 seconds, 50% transformed. (D) 900 seconds, 75% transformed. (E) 2500 seconds, 100% transformed to martensite.

few millionths of an inch, but when coarse-grained ferrite is formed, the carbon really has to move.

When carbon steel is quickly cooled from the 100% austenitic state, the carbon simply does not have time to go where it ought to go. It is, literally, "frozen" in or near its original position in the austenite, preventing the segregation that is required to make ferrite, cementite and pearlite.

The structure that is formed when carbon steel is rapidly cooled is named *martensite*. (Fig. 8-11). Under the microscope, martensite shows needlelike crystals in a darker and not well defined matrix. Martensite is the constituent that gives quenched steel its high strength and high hardness.

Martensite is usually produced by quenching high-carbon steel in water. It may, however, be produced from 0.20% carbon steel (a low-carbon steel) by very rapid cooling, such as by quenching in iced brine.

Quick cooling of a carbon steel results in no changes in the austenite until at about 300 F, when the iron changes from the face-centered atomic structure to the body-centered structure. The iron (ferrite) does not have room now for the carbon. When steel is slowly cooled, the ferrite gradually pushes out the carbon and it accumulates to form pearlite or cementite. When the transformation takes place at 300 F, however, the carbon cannot move between the iron atoms. The expelled carbon atoms stay where they were pushed out. Such action must result in a distortion or bulging of the normal crystalline structure of the iron. The distorted or strained condition is thought to produce the higher strength and hardness of the martensite.

How is this possible? Without going into technical details, let us think of a deck of cards being shuffled. Clean cards slide over each other easily. If, however, there is a grain of sharp sand on each one of the cards, the deck has a high resistance to slipping. Like the grains of sand, the carbon atoms (pushed out between the iron atoms) act as keys to prevent one plane of iron atoms from slipping over the adjacent plane.

The curve in Fig. 8-12 gives the maximum hardness obtained by cooling steels of various carbon contents very fast. Tests with alloy steels give much the same hardness as the carbon steels. This shows it is the carbon content that determines maximum hardness to be obtained by quenching steel. The high-carbon steels and the alloy steels did not require the extreme cooling rates that were needed to secure maximum hardness with the low-carbon steels.

Carbon steels are softest when they are cooled very slowly. As the cooling rate is increased, the steel becomes harder due to the finer grain structure. The ferrite and the pearlite grains are smaller, and the laminations in the pearlite are closer together. At a rate of cooling that is almost fast enough to form martensite, the pearlite laminations

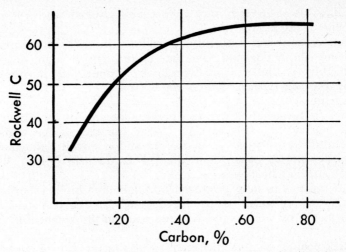

Fig. 8-12. Effect of the carbon content on the maximum hardness obtained by water quenching.

may be so fine that they cannot be seen with an ordinary microscope. This structure, however, has been identified as pearlite by the use of the electron microscope, Fig. 8-13.

With further increase in the rate of cooling, martensite is produced in increasing percentages. When the cooling is fast enough to give 100% martensite (this is called the *critical cooling rate*), we obtain the steel's maximum hardness.

We have now discussed the formation of ferrite, cementite, pearlite and martensite. It may be interesting to see how these compare in mechanical properties, Table 8-1.

Heat-Treating Processes

We have talked a great deal about heat treatment without explaining just what we mean by the term. The truth is that heat treatment is not a simple process but a whole group of procedures, some more or less complicated.

Table 8-1. Properties of Ferrous Crystal Structures

	HARDNESS	BRINELL HARDNESS	TENSILE STRENGTH PSI	REMARKS
Ferrite	Soft	90	40,000	Slowly cooled steel of less than 0.83% C
Cementite	Very hard	600-700	Too brittle to determine	Slowly cooled steel of over 0.83% C
Pearlite	Medium	250-300	125,000 to 150,000	Slowly cooled steel of 0.83% C
Martensite	Hard	400-700	200,000	Quickly cooled steels

Stress relieving—is a form of heat treatment well known to every weldor who has to work with high-carbon, medium-carbon or alloy steels. It consists of the uniform heating of the welded structure to a temperature sufficient to relieve the major portion of the stresses created by the welding heat. This treatment is also used to relieve stresses caused by machining or cold working. The stress-relieving temperature is always below the critical range, and stress relieving is followed by a uniform cooling. Stress relieving must not be confused with other forms of heat treatment such as annealing and normalizing.

Annealing—is used to soften steel so that it can be more readily machined and cold worked, to refine the grain, and to remove stresses. The steel is heated to about 100 F above the transformation range and held there long enough for the carbon to distribute itself uniformly throughout the austenite. This may require a number of hours for some steels. The steel is cooled in the furnace or buried in ashes, cinders, lime, or some other insulating material that will insure a

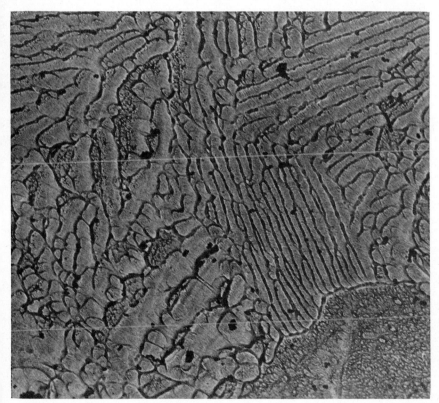

Fig. 8-13. Pearlite in steel, magnification 10,000 diameters, photographed by an electron microscope.

sufficiently slow rate of cooling. The structure of annealed steel is made up of grains of pearlite with grains of ferrite if the carbon is less than 0.83%.

Normalizing—is faster than annealing. In this process, the steel is heated to about 100 F above the transformation range, held there only briefly, and then cooled in air. This process also refines the grain and is frequently used before quench hardening. Many steels are used in the normalized condition. Annealing may make low-carbon steels too soft and gummy for fast machining, while normalizing makes the steel just hard enough to machine freely, leaving a surface free from tears.

Spheroidizing—renders high-carbon steels even softer and more readily machinable than annealing. The steel is heated to just below the transformation range for a number of hours and slow cooled throughout the upper part of the cooling range. The cementite collects into tiny globular or spherical-shaped particles, leaving a matrix of ferrite. There are other methods of producing spherical cementite, but they all involve heating of the steel just below or just in the transformation range. After the part is machined, the steel is reheated to put the carbides into solution in the austenite. It may then be hardened by quenching.

Quenching—is the rapid cooling of a metallic object from an elevated temperature by immersion in or blanketing with a liquid, gas or solid medium that absorbs the heat or conducts it away. The speed with which the object is transferred from its heat source to the quenching medium and the efficiency of the quenching medium in removing heat, both affect the cooling rate. The cooling rate and the length of time the object is in the quenching medium control the depth of hardness.

Quench hardening—is a process in which the steel is first heated at about 100 F above the transformation range and held there long enough for the center to be fully transformed to austenite. *Overheating* and prolonged heating should be avoided because they cause grain growth. Quench hardening is then accomplished by quickly cooling the steel by immersing it in water, oil or some other medium. Other cooling methods may be used; for example, a liquid jet or spray; or thin steel can be quickly cooled by pressing it between two copper plates. In full hardening, the rate of cooling and duration of time in the quenching medium converts the austenite to martensite all the way through to the center.

It is customary to follow the quenching with a tempering treatment to reduce the possibility of stress cracks. For this, the work is taken from the quench and put immediately into the tempering furnace.

Tempering—is a process in which a hardened steel is reheated to some point below the transformation range and cooled either in air or water. This relieves internal stress and toughens the metal, but also somewhat reduces the hardness. The degree of hardness desired governs the temperature to which the steel is reheated.

Martempering—is a process for obtaining exceptional mechanical properties in small high-carbon steel parts. The steel is heated as for quench hardening to produce a uniform austenite structure, and is then immersed in a liquid bath of salt or metal held at a constant temperature at the upper limit of the martensitic transformation range. The part is kept in the bath long enough for the temperature to become uniform throughout the workpiece. It is then removed from the bath and air-cooled. The product is a form of martensite with a hardness of about 50 Rockwell C but very much more ductile than the martensite formed by ordinary quenching and tempering to the same hardness. Warpage and distortion are minimized by this process.

Case hardening—is any process of hardening a metallic object so that the surface layer or *case* is made substantially harder than the interior or *core*. Typical processes employed for case hardening are carburizing and quenching, cyaniding, nitriding, induction hardening and flame hardening.

Carburizing—is a process of adding carbon to a solid ferrous alloy. This is done by heating the object in contact with a carbon material— solid, liquid or gas—to a temperature above the transformation range and holding it at that temperature. Carburizing is generally followed by quenching to produce a hardened case. *Soaking* the object in the carbon material under heat allows the carbon atoms to migrate toward the center of the piece, permitting a more uniform distribution of properties.

Cyaniding—is a process of case hardening a ferrous alloy object by heating in molten cyanide, thus causing the alloy to absorb carbon and nitrogen simultaneously. This is usually followed by quenching to produce a harder, deeper case.

Nitriding—is a process of case hardening a ferrous alloy of suitable composition by absorption of nitrogen. This is done by heating in an atmosphere of ammonia, or in contact with other material containing nitrogen.

Induction hardening—is a process of hardening (case or full) a metallic object by heating it within an alternating magnetic field to a temperature within or above the transformation range, and then quenching.

Flame hardening—is a process of local hardening or case hardening by exposure to a continuously moving oxyacetylene or other flame, followed immediately by a quenching jet of water, air or nitrogen.

Partially Hardened Steels

Carbon steel is rarely used in the fully hardened condition; that is, quenched in a manner to make it all martensite. In this state, the steel is too brittle and may be harder than is required. There are three ways to treat carbon steel so that it will be partially hardened.

The first method is to heat the steel for an appreciable time just below the upper critical temperature, where it is a mixture of both ferrite and austenite. After this heating, the part is quickly cooled. The ferrite remains as ferrite, and only the austenite transforms to martensite. Hence, the steel has soft grains of ferrite embedded in a hard and brittle network of martensite. Hardness tests show medium hardness values, but the steel has neither high ductility nor high impact strength. If the hard martensitic grains were in a network of the softer ferrite, the ductility would be greatly increased without impairing the hardness.

The second method of partially hardening a steel is to heat it properly above the critical temperature, but to cool it less rapidly than the critical cooling rate (the rate that is fast enough to give 100% martensite). This procedure results in a steel with a hardness depending on the cooling rate. A medium cooling speed gives a fine-grained structure of pearlite and some martensite. Faster cooling results in more martensite with a structure that appears as a dark background when examined through a microscope. The resulting steel has good mechanical properties, but the properties are not uniform because the surface of the part will have a higher hardness and lower ductility than the center of the part. To finish with the desired hardness, the cooling rate must be accurately controlled. This rate must be adjusted when there are changes in the carbon content of the metal treated.

The third, and more widely used, technique is to temper the carbon steel after it has been quenched to yield 100% martensite. This procedure is less expensive and gives more reliable results. The tempering is accomplished by reheating to a temperature below the transformation temperature (usually below 1000 F). This reheating is called tempering or sometimes drawing (not to be confused with the drawing of steel wire through dies). It results in the best possible compromise for tensile strength, elongation, reduction of area, and impact strength.

Steel that has been quenched to be 100% martensitic is at its maximum hardness and tensile strength but is low in ductility and may be stressed internally. The tempering lowers the hardness and the strength of the steel but at the same time raises the ductility and lowers the internal stresses.

Heating in boiling water will appreciably toughen hardened carbon tool steel, but higher tempering temperatures are commonly employed. This is commonly 300-400 F. These relatively low temperatures do not change the martensite structure, but they do reduce the internal stresses and also may allow a little readjustment of the atomic structure. Higher temperatures result in the disappearance of the needlelike martensite structure and the formation of another structure that, for simplicity, is called *tempered martensite.*

Carbon steels may be cooled slowly from the tempering temperature, or they may be quickly cooled by water quenching. Either method will result in the same final mechanical properties and structure. However, parts with both thin and heavy sections should be cooled slowly to eliminate the possibility of new stresses that may cause distortion or cracking.

Heat Treatment of a Cold Chisel

The common cold chisel can serve as a simple example of an actual heat-treat problem. A properly heat-treated cold chisel has an edge that is hard and strong enough to cut and chip mild steel without the edge bending or upsetting. The edge, however, is also ductile enough to resist chipping or nicking. The head of the chisel should be soft enough so that it will not chip when hit with a hammer. It must not be so soft that it will mushroom when hit.

When a cold chisel is made of high-carbon steel, 0.80 to 0.90% carbon for example, here is the proper procedure for heat treating it:

1. Heat the tapered portion of the chisel (the cutting end), to about 1425 F, a cherry red. Check the temperature by a magnet; an 0.83% high-carbon steel is not attracted by a magnet when it is heated above 1333 F.
2. Quench the cutting end of the chisel in cold water. Hold the chisel vertically and about an inch deep in the water. Move it up and down slightly so that there will be a gradual change from the quenched end to the non-quenched body.
3. When the color has gone and the violent steaming has ceased, remove the chisel from the water and clean off the oxide from the cutting end with a file. As the heat retained in the shank of the chisel transfers to the cutting end, the cleaned bright edge will show the temper colors that indicate its temperature.
4. When the color tint is purple, put all of the chisel under water and swish it around until it is cold. The purple color forms at about 550 F. If a tougher edge is needed (of course at the sacrifice of some hardness), the final cooling should be delayed until the edge has reheated past the purple to the bright blue (about 600 F).

The Effect of Quenching on Hardness

The Rockwell hardness is roughly proportional to the strength of the steel, but the hardness will not indicate the ductility, brittleness, impact strength or the resistance to cracking or shattering.

There is not much change in hardness between a quenched (hardened) steel as tempered at 200 F, and one tempered at 400 F, but the 400 F temper appreciably increases the impact strength.

Steel can be heat treated to a hardness of 40 Rockwell C (380 Brinell) in two ways: (1) by tempering the quenched steel at about 600 F, or (2) by quenching the steel from just the right temperature, somewhere around 1300 F. In the first case, the structure will be made up of hard, tough tempered martensite; in the second case, we will have a mixture of hard and brittle martensite and the softer and weaker pearlite. All mechanical properties except hardness will be much lower when the second method is followed.

We can obtain maximum hardness either by quenching from 1450 F or by quenching from 2200 F. As explained before, the steel quenched from the higher temperature will have a coarser grain and less resistance to chipping or cracking (even after tempering) than the steel that was quenched from the lower temperature.

A carbon-steel rod over ½ in. in diameter will not be completely hardened at the center when it is water quenched. The fact that carbon steel does not harden all the way through a thick section makes it a highly desirable material for tools such as axes and hammers that must have a hard edge or surface and a softer, more ductile body.

Definitions of New Words

Case. A thin layer of metal below the surface having composition, structure or properties distinctly different from the main body, or core, of the part.

Core. The innermost mass of metal having composition, structure or properties distinctly different from the outer or surface metal, known as the case.

Critical cooling rate. A rate of cooling that is fast enough to transform austenite into 100% martensite.

Curie point. The temperature at which a cooling metal (iron, nickel or cobalt or an alloy of these) becomes magnetic. At temperatures above this point, the normally magnetic material is nonmagnetic.

Freezing. The solidification of a hot liquid metal. In the case of pure iron, this starts and ends at the same temperature. With the addition of carbon, freezing starts at one temperature and ends at a lower temperature.

Lower critical temperature. The temperature at which an alloy completes its transformation from one solid structure to another, as it cools.

Martensite. A structure resulting from transformation of austenite at a temperature considerably below the usual range, achieved by rapid cooling. It is made up of ultra-hard, needle-like crystals that are a supersaturated solid solution of carbon in iron.

Mushy stage. The elevated temperature range during which a metal or alloy is essentially a liquid with a varying content of solid crystals.

Overheating. Sufficient exposure of a metal to an extremely high temperature for an undesirable coarse grain structure to develop. The structure often can be corrected by suitable heat treatment, cold working, or a combination of these.

Soaking. Prolonged heating of a metal at a selected temperature.

Supercooled. The condition of a material that has been cooled at such a rate that it is still liquid at a temperature below its normal freezing point. In the case of a metallic material, this effect may also be the result of certain alloying elements.

Transformation range. Unless otherwise specified, the temperature range during which a metal when cooled is changing from one type of crystal structure to the structure it will have permanently at room temperature.

Upper critical temperature. The temperature at which an alloy begins to transform from one solid structure to another, as it cools.

Review Questions

1. What simple method can be used to check the temperature of a piece of iron at about 1415 F?

2. The melting temperature of low carbon steel is about—
   2250 F?   2550 F?   2780 F?   3005 F?

3. A steel with 0.83% carbon transforms completely within a very narrow range at 1333 F. Does a steel with 0.40% carbon start to transform at a higher or lower temperature? How about a steel with 0.90% carbon content?

4. When a 0.40% carbon steel is slowly cooled to room temperature, what is the nature of its crystal structure: austenite, ferrite, pearlite, cementite, or martensite?

5. If annealed SAE 1040 steel is heated to 1000 F and quenched in water, will it become harder, softer, or will there be no appreciable change in hardness?

6. When quenching a heated steel, what controls the depth of hardness?

7. When steel is cooled so that the austenite changes to martensite, during the transition is there expansion, contraction, or no appreciable change?

8. What undesirable properties would a steel casting have if it were taken out of the sand mold a short time after pouring while it was at 1600 F and quenched in water?

9. Some hatchets have a hard edge and surface with softer steel in the body. What grain size and what heat treatment should be used to give this harder surface and softer interior?

CHAPTER 9

METALLURGY AND WELDING

By this time, you have probably come to agree that we can better understand the problems encountered in welding if we know something about metallurgy. In previous chapters, we studied the effects of heat on the ferrous or iron-based metals. The metallurgical effects of welding are the effects of heat. Whether the welds are made by a gas flame, a metal arc, or electrical resistance, the effects on the parent metal are due to heat.

Every fusion welding operation involves a logical sequence of thermal or heat events. These include: (1) heating of the metal; (2) manipulation of the electrode or torch flame to deposit weld metal; (3) cooling of the weld deposit as well as the base metal; and (4), in some instances, reheating of the entire structure for stress-relieving purposes.

In every weld, the metal immediately under the flame or arc is in a molten state; the welded section is in the process of cooling off; and the section to be welded has not yet been heated and so is comparatively cool. These various conditions are encountered at the very same instant, Fig. 9-1.

As a result of welding, the structure of the welded ferrous metal may become martensitic, pearlitic or even austenitic in nature. The weldor who knows metallurgy can predict which structure will be found when the weld has cooled. It is most important to know this because the final condition of the structure after welding is the one that determines the strength, hardness, ductility, resistance to impact, resistance to corrosion and similar mechanical and physical properties of the metal. All these properties may be affected by conditions that exist during the welding operation, so it is well to become acquainted with possible difficulties and see how they may be avoided.

To avoid confusion, this discussion will be confined to steel. The effects of heating and cooling will not necessarily be the same for the non-ferrous metals and alloys. In some cases, a considerable difference in temperature ranges and other characteristics exist.

The arc welding of steel involves very high temperatures. The resultant weld is essentially cast steel. Since the base metal very close to the weld is comparatively cool, a considerable variation in the grain structure develops within the weld area. The iron-carbon diagram, Fig. 8-10, shows how the rate at which the weld cools will alter the grain structure in both the weld itself and the immediately adjacent base metal, known technically as the *heat-affected zone.*

147

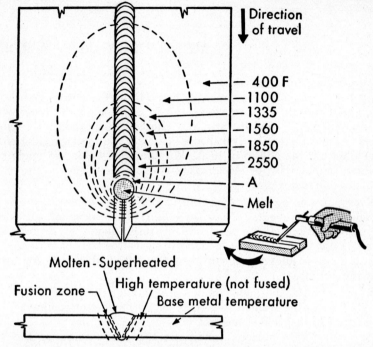

Fig. 9-1. There is a great variation in the temperature of base metal during metal arc welding. The shaded area "Melt" is the molten weld pool. Area A is metal heated to mushy stage.

Danger from the Air

Unless extreme care to shield the weld metal is exercised during welding, the possibility exists that oxygen or nitrogen or both will be absorbed from the air. What either of these gases can do to weld metal is pitiful. An oxide or nitride coating will form along the grain boundaries. Oxidation along the grain boundaries greatly weakens the weld metal, and greatly reduces the impact strength and also the fatigue resistance of the welded part. Nitrogen forms iron nitrides in chemical composition with the iron, and these make the weld extremely brittle.

The extent to which oxides and nitrides penetrate a steel will depend upon the type of steel, the temperature to which it is heated and the length of time it is held at this temperature. Extreme care should be exercised to prevent the penetration of air into high-temperature welding regions. The most satisfactory way to prevent oxide or nitride contamination in metal-arc welding is to make sure that the electrode has a coating that provides adequate shielding. The arc and weld metal may also be shielded by carbon dioxide (CO_2) or vapor. In Tig or Mig welding (inert-gas-arc welding), the inert gas will provide the shielding. With submerged-arc welding, the molten flux that covers the arc does the job. Fluxes or a reducing flame provide the needed protection during gas welding.

When the oxyacetylene torch is used for cutting, it is desirable to oxidize the steel. It is rapid oxidation that makes it possible for the flame to sever steel.

Besides oxygen or nitrogen, another gas absorbed during welding may have harmful effects on some types of metals and alloys. This gas is hydrogen, and usually comes from moisture in the electrode coating or from the use of hydrogen in the welding flame. The presence of hydrogen in the weld metal will weaken the structure and lead to cracking of the weld. Hydrogen is a contributing cause of underbead cracking. To avoid this harmful weld defect, use low-hydrogen electrodes of the E-xx15, E-xx16 and E-xx18 series.

Heat-Affected Zone

Figure 9-2 shows the close relationship that exists between thermal conditions, grain structure and hardness in the arc weld. So that this relationship might be clearly established, a photomicrograph of a section through a welded 0.25% carbon steel plate has been inserted in an iron-carbon diagram. This diagram was split on the 0.25% carbon line and opened up to allow insertion of the photomicrograph.

The photomicrograph is of a single automatic weld bead. The bead as deposited on the ½ in. plate produced a heat-affected zone that extended for about ⅛ in. adjacent to the weld. This zone shows a variation in grain structure (starting at the bottom) from the normal base metal structure into a band of finer grain structure between the lower and upper critical temperature points and then to a coarse overheated grain structure adjacent to the weld.

The extent of the change in the grain structure depends upon the maximum temperature to which the metal is subjected, the length of time this temperature exists, the composition of the steel, and the rate of cooling. The cooling rate will not only affect grain size but it will also affect physical properties.

As a rule, faster cooling rates produce a slightly harder, less ductile and stronger steel. For low-carbon steels, the relatively small differences found in practice make insignificant changes in these values. However, with higher carbon content in appreciable amounts of alloying material, the effect may become serious.

The speed of welding and the rate of heat input into the joint effects change in structure and hardness. On a given mass of base metal, at a given temperature, a small bead deposited at high speed produces a greater hardening than a larger bead deposited at a higher heat input per unit length of joint. This is because small high speed beads cool more rapidly than the larger high heat beads.

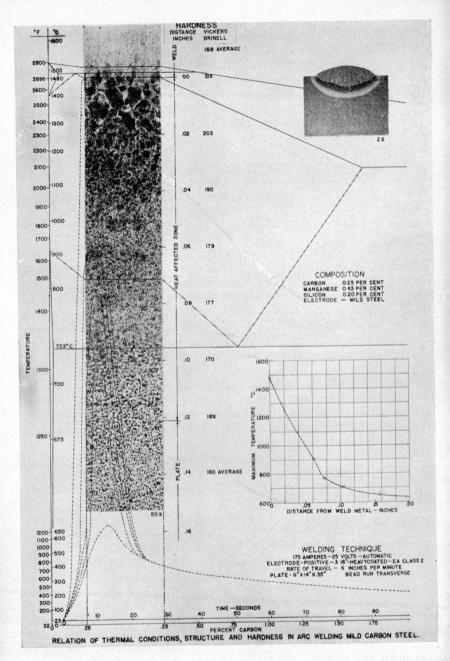

Fig. 9-2. Relation of thermal conditions, structure and hardness in arc welding mild steel.

The effect that heat from welding has on the base metal determines to a great degree the weldability of a metal and its usefulness in fabrication. A metal that is sensitive to heat conditions or heat changes, as in the case of high-carbon and some alloy steels, may require heat treatment both before and after welding.

Admixture or Pick-Up

When you weld a base metal with a filler metal of different composition, the two metals will naturally mix and blend together in the molten weld pool. Consequently, the weld metal will be a mixture of two materials. It will not necessarily be an average of them, however.

The amount of base metal picked up in the molten weld pool varies greatly relative to the amount of deposited electrode metal. Some welds are made up principally of base metal, while others are primarily deposited electrode metal. The specific process of welding, the rate of electrode travel, the current selected, the width of the joint, the base metal composition, the plate thickness—all these factors determine the volume of base metal brought to a molten temperature, and therefore the amount of base metal *pick-up* or *admixture* into the weld.

In some cases, the deposited metal and the base metal are sufficiently alike in composition that the amount of admixture is of little significance. At other times, admixture is an advantage in that the weld metal is made stronger or otherwise improved by a pick-up of carbon or other needed elements from the base metal.

Unfortunately, under some conditions alloying elements or chemical combinations of the base metal tend to concentrate—to precipitate, or to *segregate* during the heating and cooling cycle and reform into *stringers* or other arrangements that harden, embrittle, weaken or otherwise cause inferior welds. Sometimes, the stringer itself is a source of weakness. At other times, the segregation of an element or its loss into the slag or atmosphere "starves" the newly formed weld microstructure of elements needed for certain physical properties.

In general, admixture should be limited unless the metals and the processes involved justify a procedure that calls for a specific amount of pick-up. This is discussed further in later chapters on the welding of specific metal groups. To minimize the effects of pick-up, electrode coatings or fluxes are often treated with alloying elements that bring the deposited metal up to the desired composition. These alloying elements replace those that might be destroyed or lost to either parent metal or weld metal during the high-temperature welding operation.

Carbide Precipitation

Sometimes, because of rapid cooling, steels, particularly stainless steels, are not given time to go through all of the temperature changes indicated in the iron-carbon diagram. As a result, a concentration of the solid solution (austenite) is retained at a temperature where it simply has no business existing. This being against nature, so to speak, the dissolved elements will eventually recrystallize. This type of recrystallization is known as *aging*. Suppose, however, the metal is reheated before recrystallization can occur. In this event, the carbon will crystallize out of the austenite as iron carbide. This phenomena is known as carbide precipitation.

Stainless steels of the nickel-chromium variety are austenitic in nature even at room temperatures. When such steels are heated, as by welding operations, carbide precipitation is apt to occur. The carbides, or carbon compounds, are chromium as well as iron. When chromium is used up in this way, in chemical union with the precipitated carbon, the remaining austenite is deficient in the chromium element. The result is a serious reduction in the corrosion-resisting properties of the stainless steel.

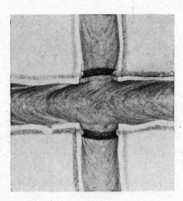

Fig. 9-3. Ordinary austenitic stainless steels are subject to excessive carbide precipitation in a readily visible zone parallel to the weld bead. Carbide precipitation is avoided by using a stabilized filler metal to weld a stabilized or ELC stainless steel.

When the carbides are precipitated in stainless steel, they appear mainly at the grain boundaries. If subjected to corrosion, the carbides along the grain boundaries will be attacked readily. Severe corrosive conditions will cause the grains to lose their coherence and the steel to fail.

In making a weld on stainless, there will always be a region some distance back from the weld where the base metal will be at the exact temperature of the precipitation range: 800-1500 F (Fig. 9-3). Consequently, the stainless qualities of the structure will be lost unless steps are taken to prevent precipitation.

Austenitic stainless steels may be stabilized against carbide precipitation by the addition of elements known as stabilizers. Such elements are columbium and titanium. These elements have a ready affinity for carbon; they will grab and hold fast the carbon that might otherwise have been attracted to the chromium. Moreover, both titanium and columbium carbide resemble stainless steel itself in having high resistance to corrosion. Stabilized stainless steels, therefore, will not fail under the combination of heat and corrosive attack. Austenitic stainless steels also are available in several grades with extra low carbon (ELC). Since there is less carbon, the possibility of chromium migration to the grain boundaries is minimized.

It is well to remember that the stabilized and ELC austenitic steels will resist carbide precipitation. If the welded stainless is to be subjected to corrosive conditions, particularly at elevated temperatures, the base metal should be a stabilized steel and it should be welded with electrodes or filler rods that have also been stabilized.

Crater Cracks

In some instances, both arc welds and gas welds develop crater cracks. These come from *hot shrinkage*. The crater cools rapidly while the remainder of the bead is cooling slowly. Since the crater solidifies from all sides toward the center, the conditions are favorable to shrinkage cracks, Fig. 9-4. Such *crater cracks* may lead to failures under stress—brittle failures since there is an inclination towards fracture without deformation. The remedy is to manipulate the electrode to fill up the craters when you are welding.

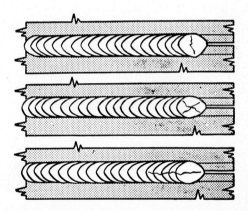

Fig. 9-4. Crater cracks are caused by hot shrinkage. At top is a radial or transverse crack; at center is a star crack; at bottom is a longitudinal crack.

Blowholes, Gas Pockets and Inclusions

Other common welding defects known as blowholes, gas pockets and inclusions involve problems of electrode manipulation rather than metallurgy. These difficulties are created because of the weldor's failure to retain the molten weld pool for sufficient time to float entrapped gas, slag and other forms of material.

A *blowhole* or gas pocket represents a bubble of gas in the liquid weld metal. A gas pocket is one that did not reach the surface before the metal began to freeze. Consequently, the gas remains entrapped in the solidified metal.

Some gases, particularly hydrogen, are absorbed by the molten metal and are then given off as the metal begins to cool. If the metal is in a molten condition, the gas bubbles make their way to the surface and disappear. If the bubbles are trapped in the growing grains of solid metal, blowholes are the result.

Blowholes are particularly prevalent in steels high in sulphur. In this case the entrapped gas is either sulphur dioxide or hydrogen sulphide, the hydrogen being supplied from moisture, the fuel gas (in gas welding), the electrode coating or the hydrogen atmosphere that surrounds the weld in atomic-hydrogen welding.

Blowholes may be minimized in the weld area by using a continuous welding technique so that the weld metal will solidify continuously. Most welding operators, through practice, learn to develop welding techniques that will produce a relatively gas-free weld. One of the secrets of such a technique is to keep the molten weld pool at the temperature necessary for the rapid release of absorbed gases. At the same time an unbroken protective atmosphere must be provided over the pool. Modern electrode coatings aid in this problem, for they contain scavenging elements that cleanse the weld pool while it is in molten condition.

Inclusions of slag and other foreign particles in the weld present a type of problem similar to gas pockets and blowholes. These inclusions tend to weaken the weld. Slag is frequently entrapped because of the operator's failure to manipulate torch, filler rod or electrode so as to maintain a molten condition long enough to float out all the

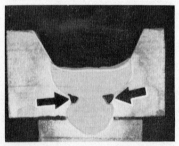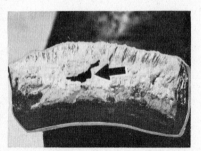

Fig. 9-5. Poor fusion and slag inclusions are usually the results of poor welding technique. Cross-section through weld, at left, shows entrapped slag. Photo at right shows a weld broken open, revealing slag inclusion.

foreign material. Ordinarily, the liquid slag freezes and forms a protective coating for the weld deposit. On some occasions, however, because of the force of the flame or arc, it is blown into the molten weld pool. The pool freezes before the slag particle or particles can float to the top, thus producing a defective weld. See Fig. 9-5.

Slag inclusions are more common in welds made in the overhead position. The lower density of the slag tends to keep it afloat on the weld pool. In overhead welding, the weld pool first forms at the narrow part of the vee, which is uppermost in the weld. Since the pool tends to drip if kept molten too long, the weldor works to have it solidify as rapidly as possible. As a result, inclusions are frequent. This problem in overhead welding can be overcome by using gaseous, non-slagging types of electrodes.

Faulty plate preparation contributes to slag inclusions. If edges of V-joints are bevelled at too steep an angle and the gap between plates is too small, the weld metal bridges the gap and leaves a pocket at the root in which slag tends to collect. If back of joint is accessible, slag can be removed by back gouging; however, if this operation is omitted, the result is a defective weld. With a J-joint or U-joint, improper arc manipulation may burn back the inside corners and form pockets that can entrap slag or gases.

In repair of a broken surface, a groove along the break line should be burned out or ground so as to provide clean surfaces properly angled and spaced. Failure to do so may leave an overhang of base metal or an unfilled crack that can entrap slag or gases.

Surfaces to be welded should be thoroughly cleaned of scale, dirt, paint, lubricants, and other chemicals that might contribute to formation of gas or dirt inclusions in the weld.

Welds that contain blowholes, gas pockets and inclusions may develop other defects upon hot work. By the action of hot working, the basic defects are exaggerated to form larger defects. For example, if a piece of weld metal containing a blowhole is rolled, the tendency is to flatten and elongate the hole. This develops a long fibrous defect running in the same direction as the piece that is rolled. Such a condition, known as a *lamination,* will reduce the strength of the metal, particularly in directions at right angles to the lamination.

Definitions of New Words

Admixture. The interchange of filler metal and base metal during welding, resulting in weld metal of composition borrowed from both. Limited admixture is necessary to complete metallurgical union across the joint.

Aging. The recrystallization that occurs over an extended period of time, resulting from austenite or other normally elevated-temperature structure being retained at a temperature and under conditions where it has no permanent stability. The result may be a change in properties or dimension. Under some circumstances, aging can be advantageous.

Blowhole. A defect in metal caused by hot metal cooling too rapidly when excessive gaseous content is present. Specifically, in welding, a gas pocket in the weld metal, resulting from the hot metal solidifying without all of the gases having escaped to the surface.

Crater cracks. Cracks across the weld bead crater, resulting from hot shrinkage.

Heat-affected zone. The portion of the base metal, adjacent to a weld, the structure or properties of which have been altered by the heat of welding.

Hot shrinkage. A condition where the thin weld crater cools rapidly while the remainder of the bead cools more slowly. Since metal contracts or shrinks as it cools, and shrinkage in the crater area is restrained by the larger bead, the weld metal at the crater is stressed excessively and may crack.

Lamination. An elongated defect in a finished metal product, resulting from the rolling of a welded or other part containing a blowhole. Actually, the blowhole is stretched out in the direction of rolling.

Pick-up. The absorption of base metal by the weld metal as the result of admixture. Usually used specifically in reference to the migration of carbon or other critical alloying elements from the base metal into the weld metal. Depending upon the materials involved, this can be an asset and not a liability.

Segregation. The tendency of alloying elements, under certain heat conditions, to separate from the main crystalline constituent during transformation and to migrate and collect at the grain boundaries. There they often combine into undesirable compounds.

Stringers. The tendency of segregated atoms of alloying elements or their compounds to attach to one another in thread-like chains.

Review Questions

1. What is the cause of pick-up? How can it be avoided? Why is pick-up undesirable?
2. What is meant when it is said a metal is aging? Is this a desirable quality?
3. Why does 18-8 stainless steel sometimes rust after being welded?
4. Is slag entrapment more likely to occur with gas welding than metal-arc welding? Explain.
5. What causes crater cracks and how can they be avoided?
6. What effect does an inclusion have on the strength of the weld?
7. How does slag become trapped in the weld?
8. What is meant by the heat-affected zone?
9. Give the sequence of thermal events occurring in every weld.
10. What dangers lurk in the atmosphere so far as welding is concerned?

CHAPTER 10

WELDING LOW-CARBON STEEL

First a word about that marvelous construction material: ferrous metal with a carbon content of less than 0.30%. This is low-carbon or mild steel. Low-carbon steel has built our great bridges and our skyscrapers, and more of it is being produced today than all other types of steel plus aluminum and magnesium.

Low-carbon steel will stand rough treatment and abuse. It can be bent double or deep drawn. We can punch holes in it or notch it and still use it safely. Furthermore, it can be heated red hot, or even white hot, and quenched in cold water without appreciable embrittlement.

Low-carbon steel can be welded by any of the welding processes. Selection of the process and welding procedure to give a balance of low cost and high weld performance should take into consideration such factors as the thickness of the metal to be welded, joint design, welding position, and production required.

In welding the high-alloy steels and some of the non-ferrous materials, there is less of a selection to be made and the applicable welding processes result in wider differences in cost and weld performance. In contrast, selection of process for welding low-carbon steel is more difficult because of the wider choice and the smaller differences that exist. Selection of the best process is usually even more important, however, because of the widespread use of low-carbon steel and the great volume of welding in this category, and because assembly cost often is an important factor in a fabricated product's remaining competitive. A few cents saving per foot of weld takes on real importance when multiplied by many thousands of feet.

When welding low-carbon steel, it is not at all difficult to duplicate or better the properties of the base metal in the weld metal.

All carbon steels are readily arc welded. Strange as it may seem, however, if the carbon content is too low, they are not suited to high speed production welding. This is generally true of those steels having less than 0.13% carbon and 0.40% manganese. They tend to develop a slight increase in internal porosity in the weld metal. Low-carbon steels, however, range up to 0.30% carbon and have ideal welding quality. These steels require only the normal welding precautions recommended for good welding practice, that is, good setup, clean surfaces, etc.

Representative mechanical properties of a low-carbon steel having about 0.20% carbon are given in Table 10-1. Steels with lower carbon content, say about 0.13%, have lower tensile strength and hardness but higher ductility and impact strength. At this lower end of the carbon

Table 10-1. Typical Properties of Cast Carbon Steel
0.20% carbon (1 in. sq. test specimens)

	AS-CAST	FULL[1] ANNEALED	NORMALIZED[2]	NORMALIZED & TEMPERED AT 1,200 F	QUENCHED IN WATER AND TEMPERED AT 1,200 F
Ult. Tensile strength, psi	65,000	68,000	70,000	69,000	75,000
Yield point, psi	35,000	36,000	38,000	37,000	45,000
Elongation in 2 in., %	30	30	30	32	32
Reduction of area, %	50	52	53	55	65
Brinell Hardness	140	140	145	140	150
Charpy Impact, ft-lb	20	25	32	37	42
Fatigue limit, psi	32,000	35,000			

[1]Full annealed. Treatment-heated to 1,650 F, held at temperature for five hours and then cooled in the furnace.

[2]Normalized treatment. Heated to 1,650 F and cooled in still air. These properties are included to show that low-carbon steel is not appreciably influenced by heat treatment.

Table 10-2. Typical Properties—Weld Metal and Base Metal
(using coated electrode)

	WELD METAL	MILD STEEL BASE METAL
Ultimate strength, psi	60-75,000	55-70,000
Yield point, psi	50-60,000	30-32,000
Elongation in 2 in., %	17.0-40.0	30.0-40.0
Elongation-free bend, %	20.0-35.0	——
Reduction of area, %	35.0-65.0	60.0-70.0
Density, grams/cm³	7.80-7.85	7.85
Endurance limit, psi	26-36,000	26-30,000
Impact (Izod), ft-lb	40-70	50-80

Table 10-3. Comparative Analyses—Filler Metal and Weld Metal
(using coated electrode)

ELEMENT, %	FILLER METAL (CORE WIRE)	TYPICAL WELD METAL
Carbon	0.10-0.15	0.08-0.15
Manganese	0.40-0.60	0.30-0.50
Silicon	0.025 max.	0.05-0.30
Sulphur	0.040 max.	0.035 max.
Phosphorus	0.04 max.	0.035 max.
Oxygen	0.06 max.	0.04-0.10
Nitrogen	0.006 max.	0.01-0.03

range, there will be still less difference between the as-cast and the heat-treated properties.

Steels within the low-carbon range (0.13 to 0.30% carbon) are recommended for use where extensive welding is required, provided the analysis will meet the other physical requirements for the intended service. A large percentage of tanks, piping, welded structural shapes, machine bases and parts are made from these steels.

Shielded Metal-Arc Welding

A major portion of the welding of low-carbon steel is done by manual arc welding. The mild-steel coated electrodes of the E-60xx series may be used. These same electrodes may be used also for medium-carbon steels where their strength and other properties meet service requirements. Table 10-2 compares the properties of typical mild steel base metal and weld metal, using a suitable coated electrode. Table 10-3 compares the chemical compositions of filler metal and weld metal, when using a mild-steel coated electrode.

Submerged-Arc Welding

Automatic and semi-automatic submerged-arc welding processes on the low-carbon steels produce welds that have mechanical properties equal to those made by the best coated electrodes. In this process, as was discussed in Chapter 6, a granular inert flux blankets the joint to be welded, as a bare electrode wire is mechanically fed through the welding head or nozzle. Extremely high welding currents are employed. The current carried in relation to the cross-sectional area of the electrode is often six times as great as in manual arc welding. Thus, the melting rate of the electrode is proportionately greater and the speed of welding faster.

The higher currents used in high-speed production welding result in considerable admixture of base metal with the deposited metal. This permits use of minimum filler metal and provides weld metal virtually identical with the plate being welded. If the base metal has any alloying element in higher than preferred percentage, the flux used in the submerged-arc process can be altered to include balancing elements.

With submerged arc, no groove preparation is needed for two-pass butt joints in steel up to ⅝ in. thick. For many applications the complete penetration of T joints is possible without groove preparation on material up to ¾ in. thick.

The quality of both the automatic and semi-automatic submerged-arc welding deposit is extremely high because it is protected from oxidation by molten flux.

Inert-Arc Welding

In the inert-gas-arc welding processes, helium or argon gas is employed as a gaseous shield to blanket the weld. Although indispensable for some applications of aluminum, magnesium, stainless steel and other materials, inert-arc welding is often less economical than another process for the welding of low-carbon steel. It is, however, practical to consider for a broad range of production welding applications.

Inert-gas shielding is used in both consumable electrode welding (MIG) and non-consumable electrode welding (TIG) of low-carbon steel. TIG welding is used with 20-gage or lighter steel, while MIG is more suited to heavier material and production welding of all fillets.

Both TIG and MIG are most economical in making joints on materials where little or no filler is needed. The use of filler slows up the welding process considerably.

CO_2 and Vapor Shielding

Carbon dioxide (CO_2) is applied as a shielding medium in the metal-arc welding of low-carbon steel where improved speed, better penetration, and improved soundness of weld are desired. The electrode wire is usually a mild steel composition. Because the arc is somewhat difficult to control, the electrode selected should incorporate deoxidizers in order to ensure a sound weld. Excellent results are obtained by using a flux-cored mild steel electrode.

Vapor-shielded arc welding is a high speed process for production of quality welds on carbon steels, and its performance often surpasses that of other automatic and semi-automatic processes. Weldors with relatively little experience can turn out sound, strong welds with good appearance, using this process. Even though the arc is shielded from atmospheric contamination, it is fully visible permitting easy follow of the joint. When cracking due to high sulphur in the base metal has been a problem, the vapor-shielded process is even more effective than

CO_2 MIG welding in producing sound welds. It is also more effective than submerged-arc welding when complete removal of surface oil is impractical.

Oxyacetylene Welding

An oxyacetylene weld in low-carbon steel is usually made with a neutral flame (neither excess acetylene nor excess oxygen) and a low-carbon steel filler rod. Solid weld metal may be deposited that has properties comparable with the parent metal. With a carburizing flame (excess acetylene), a higher speed is obtained, because the parent metal is not fused; it is only heated hot enough for the surface to begin to sweat or start to melt in the presence of the carburizing gas. The welding rod is melted and cast against this prepared surface. The added metal picks up some carbon from the excess-acetylene flame, so the resulting weld will have a slightly higher strength but a lower ductility than a weld made with the conventional neutral flame.

A third type of flame is the excess-oxygen or oxidizing flame. It has a very limited use and may be harmful to the weld metal. This type of flame is characterized by excessive foaming and sparking of metal.

Oxyacetylene and other types of gas welding are relatively slow, considering the capabilities of other processes, even in the repair welding of mild steel castings.

Resistance Welding

In flash welding, the completed weld contains no metal that was actually melted. If high pressures are used for the final upsetting, even metal heated appreciably below the melting point will be forced out into the flash, which is removed later. Flash welds put a minimum of total heat into the parent metal, have no molten metal to solidify and utilize applied energy very efficiently. The mechanical properties of flash welds closely approach the properties of the base metal. If the base metal is annealed low-carbon steel, the weld will have a little higher strength and be somewhat lower in ductility. In order to have the properties match more closely, the weld may be given another pulse of current in the welding machine for tempering or annealing (post-weld heating).

In spot welding, a small amount of metal is melted but so fast that the metal a short distance away from the weld is not appreciably heated. Seam welding may be thought of as continuous spot welding: one spot is welded immediately adjacent to and slightly overlapping another. The result is a continuous seam.

Although some portable equipment is available, resistance welding is considered as limited generally to applications where work can be brought to the machine. Its greatest range of usefulness is in the joining of light-gage sheet or strip materials. The upset and butt variations of the process are limited largely to high production on heavier stock.

Thermit Welding

In making a thermit weld in low-carbon steel, the heat causes some annealing and grain growth in the parent metal, and the slowly cooled weld metal will have large coarse grains. With low-carbon steel, this generally does not matter. Thermit is more of a casting procedure than any other welding process. The properties of low-carbon steel in the cast condition are similar to the annealed properties and nearly as high as the heat-treated properties. See Table 10-1. Hence, the joint usually gives satisfactory service.

Forge Welding

The blacksmith type of forge weld requires the steel to be heated to about 2500 F. Then the parts are progressively pounded together so that the scale and oxide will be worked out of the joint. Low-carbon steel pipe is sometimes lap or butt welded by a roll-forge welding process in the mill. These welds are strong enough for many purposes, but the mechanical properties of the weld do not equal those of the base metal because it's impossible to work all of the slag and oxide out of the joint.

Welding in Cold Weather

There is nothing difficult about welding steel with less than 0.30% carbon. This steel will take all kinds of mistreatment without experiencing any bad effects on its mechanical and physical properties.

The cooling rates after welding at room temperature allow the formation of ferrite. The ferrite is soft enough to prevent undue hardening and has enough ductility to prevent any stresses high enough to cause cracking.

If steel of 0.15 to 0.20% carbon steel is welded at zero temperature or even below freezing by the metal-arc process, the unusually quick cooling may result in excessive hardening of the parent metal near the weld and may cause cracking. Hence, if you have to make a weld outdoors when the thermometer is at zero, warm or preheat the parts to avoid trouble. Preheating is discussed in Chapter 11 on the welding of medium-carbon steels.

The arc should not be struck intentionally or accidentally on the base metal outside of the groove, even on a plate edge. These "hot spots" are especially susceptible to the start of cracks, and may cause ultimate fracture in service. Low-hydrogen electrodes should be used. The sum of these suggestions is to be extra careful to prevent cracks from starting when welding in cold weather.

Elements that Affect Weldability

Our discussion up to this point has assumed that our low-carbon steel was of good welding quality. Certain elements may alter this condition materially and necessitate the adoption of a special welding procedure. Let's see what these elements are.

Nitrogen—is found in all steel and may be as high as 0.030% in Bessemer steel. In this percentage it has no noticeable effect on weld metal properties.

Hydrogen—can cause steel to crack as it cools from the molten state. The small amount of hydrogen that might remain in cast or rolled steel has no significant effect on welding. Steel just removed from an acid pickling tank or a plating bath may give off enough hydrogen during welding to cause some porosity; after a few hours, however, not enough hydrogen is left to give difficulty.

Phosphorus—in amounts less than 0.30% has little effect on the weldability of low-carbon steel. Most low-carbon steels contain only 0.01 to 0.02 phosphorus, but as much as 0.12% phosphorus is used in low-carbon, low-alloy, high-tensile steels. The phosphorus strengthens these steels, but the same amount in higher carbon steels would make them brittle. Low welding currents and fast travel are recommended for welding the high-phosphorus, low-carbon steels to reduce the possibility of iron phosphide segregation.

Sulphur—in amounts up to 0.035% has no harmful effect on weldability. If, however, the sulphur is segregated in bands, cracked and porous welds may result. Free machining, low-carbon steels may contain as much as 0.33% sulphur, and these are satisfactorily welded with the low-hydrogen type of electrodes such as E-6018. Welds made in this relatively high-sulphur steel with other types of shielded-arc electrodes are porous and are prone to crack.

Selenium—used in a few steels to improve machinability, has the same effect on weldability as sulphur.

Silicon—in the usual amounts found in steel (0.15 to 0.35%), in conjunction with normal manganese content, usually assists in producing sound welds. On the high side (0.35%) there is a strong tendency toward surface holes, especially when using E-6010 and E-6011 electrodes.

Aluminum—may also be present as alumina (aluminum oxide) in steel. The small amount (only a few hundredths of 1%) used in aluminum-treated steels does not affect weldability. Larger amounts may form a surface film of aluminum oxide that gives difficulty when gas welding.

Oxygen—if present, is in the form of iron oxide (rust). It promotes shrinkage cracking, lowers the ductility of the steel and causes porous welds.

Other elements that may be found in carbon steel may increase the hardenability and in some instances, affect the weldability. **Chapters 7 and 13** discuss the effect of larger amounts of the alloying elements.

In most cases, the mild steel being welded is thin enough that the welding heat penetrates through the full thickness of metal. Only the cold metal to the side of the weld bead tends to draw heat from the weld metal. When welding thick sections, however, the greater mass of metal has drawn off heat at a sufficient rate to have a quenching effect. This in itself may result in cracks. When welding thick sections of a mild steel that has a high percentage of a crack-promoting element, the possible problems are increased. When welding under these conditions, low-hydrogen electrodes with iron powder coatings are desirable.

Effects of Expansion and Contraction

In the previous pages, we have discussed the effect of welding heat on the structure and mechanical properties without consideration of the stresses that are involved when steel is heated and cooled. Heat causes steel to expand; cooling allows it to contract. The heating and cooling stresses are important for all types of welding, heat-treating and other operations. Let's try to learn something about them.

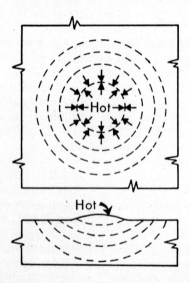

Fig. 10-1. Stresses caused by heating a spot on a steel plate are both compressive and tensile.

Heat a spot on a smooth, flat plate of metal (Fig. 10-1). The metal that is heated expands and exerts a force on the metal around it; however, the metal around the heated spot is largely unyielding and the heated metal is forced to expand upward into the air. But it is still in compression, as engineers say, and the metal around it is also in compression. Outside the metal in compression is another ring of metal that is in tension, thereby tending to balance the compressive forces.

The heated metal is stressed beyond its yield point in compression and bulges upward. As it cools, the compressive forces decrease until they reach a zero value while the metal is still hot. But shrinkage continues during the additional cooling to room temperature, and tension stresses develop around the spot. The tensile stresses acting on the surface of the unheated plate draw this area toward the heated area and produce misalignment.

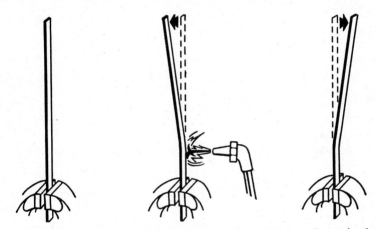

Fig. 10-2. The effects of heating on a steel bar. Left, straight bar. Center, heating causes bending as one side expands faster. Right, bend reverses on cooling.

The effect of heating the surface of steel may be readily demonstrated by placing a bar of steel in a vise (use a piece about 1 in. wide, ½ in. thick and about 2 ft long). See Fig. 10-2. The 1-in. face near the vise is heated for a few seconds with a gas torch. The free end of the bar bends away from the heat source. When the flame is removed, the bar begins to straighten out as the metal cools. It continues with further cooling until there is a reverse and permanent bend in the bar. Thus, you don't always get what you started with when you heat metal and allow it to cool.

The heated area expands in all directions. In expanding, some of its force is expended by bending the bar; some is relieved by expanding away from the surface of the metal; and some remains in the hot metal as a compressive force. The heated metal has expanded beyond its elastic limit in compression. When the metal cools, the spot shrinks and bends the bar back, but since the metal has taken a permanent set in compression, it shrinks to a shorter length than it had originally. Hence, the final result is a bent bar. Of course, if the heating is prolonged until the heat is conducted throughout the bar, the stresses will be equalized and the bar will not bend during cooling.

To straighten a bent bar by heating, we heat it on the convex side. To straighten a bar by peening, we peen it on the concave side.

In order to understand the mechanism of expansion and contraction, the following physical laws should be remembered:

1. Metals expand when heated and contract when cooled.
2. Steel is elastic when stressed to a point slightly below its yield point. An elastic body is defined as one that tends to return to its original size and shape when the distorting force is removed—the classic example, of course, being a rubber band. If steel is stressed beyond the yield point, it "yields", resulting in a plastic flow of metal and a permanent deformation.
3. If a piece of low-carbon steel is fully restricted from expanding longitudinally, an increase of only 200 F will cause it to be stressed beyond its yield point. A plastic flow of metal will take place.
4. The yield point of steel changes with the temperature, and it is quite low at the higher temperatures. As an example, the yield point may be 40,000 psi at room temperature and 5,000 to 10,000 psi at 1200 F.

Law number 3 will be further explained: In the temperature range from 32 to 500 F, steel increases in length by a fixed amount (coefficient of expansion) when it is heated one degree of Fahrenheit. Thus, if a piece of steel one inch long is heated so that it is 200 F hotter than it was, its increase in length would be $200 \times 0.000007 = 0.0014$ in.

Now in Chapter 2 it was stated that for steel

$$\frac{stress}{deformation} = 30,000,000 \text{ psi (modulus of elasticity)}$$

So, to produce a deformation of 0.0014 in., the stress must be

$$30,000,000 \times 0.0014 \text{ (deformation)} = 42,000 \text{ psi}$$

This means, simply, that it takes a force of 42,000 lb, acting on every square inch of surface, to cause a one-inch strip of steel to shorten or lengthen by 0.0014 in. If the steel is heated 200 F and held so that it cannot elongate, that is exactly the same as placing a load of 42,000 psi on it. The yield point of low-carbon steel is 30,000 to 35,000 psi, so the load of 42,000 psi will exceed the yield point and cause a permanent deformation.

Methods for Stress Control

When a bead of weld metal is deposited on a plate of metal, we have to allow for contraction of the weld metal as well as expansion and final contraction of the base metal. Any type of weld distorts the parent metal and leaves stresses in both the weld and the base metal. But the distortion and the stresses may be controlled by: (1) keeping them small or (2) having them act in a direction that will do no harm.

A few of the many ways to accomplish these results are:

• Start with the two members out of line so that they will be in line when the welding is completed.

• Prestress the parts to allow for the distortion.

• Allow the weld to expand and contract freely in two directions, which will reduce the stresses in the third direction.

• Choose the proper type of welding.

• Avoid overwelding (depositing too much weld metal).

• Use the proper speed of welding, and the best welding sequence or procedure.

• Preheat or postheat. Postheating is often called stress relieving.

Fig. 10-3. Close-up of a-c arc shows good metal transfer with an absence of arc blow.

Low-carbon steel has such a high ductility that it is not harmed by being stressed above its yield point. Hence, it is not weakened by any stresses that are left in it after welding.

The distortion and the stresses that are caused by welding have been overemphasized. Perhaps this is due to our zeal to make our welds stronger than the parent metal rather than to make them just strong enough to do the job. So, frequently after a weldment fails, we ask, "Where did it break?", when the question should be, "At what load did it fail?" In many cases, if the critical section had been machined out of solid metal, the failure would have taken place at a load lower than that which caused the welded joint to fail.

Any hot or cold-rolled metal and any cast metal unless it has been given a complete anneal contains tension and compression stresses. A large sheet of steel may have straight edges, but if it is sheared into strips, the strips will not all be straight. If an I-beam is sawed longitudinally through the web section, the two T-sections formed will be bent outward, showing that the web was formerly in tension. Annealing relieves the stresses, but the very act of stress relief results in some distortion. The quenching of steel both distorts it and leaves it stressed.

For practical means of reducing distortion during welding the reader should consult a book on welding procedure. The **Procedure Handbook of Arc Welding,** published by The Lincoln Electric Co., has a good discussion on the "Prevention and Control of Distortion."

Review Questions

1. A fine-grain fracture in steel makes us think of a hardened steel. Can a steel be fine-grain steel and be soft?
2. What part of the weld zone has the largest size grains?
3. Is there any objection to coarse grains in a weldment?
4. Why can low-carbon steel be punched without fear of breakage?
5. Why is a neutral flame desirable for the oxyacetylene welding of low-carbon steel?
6. What advantages are offered by the vapor-shielded-arc process in welding low-carbon steel?
7. Why isn't a forge weld as strong as other types of welds?
8. How does hydrogen affect a weld? Sulphur?
9. How may a welding sequence be used to control expansion and contraction?
10. List five ways to control stresses that might be set up by welding.

CHAPTER 11

WELDING MEDIUM-CARBON STEEL

"Medium-carbon" generally refers to a steel that contains 0.30 to 0.45% carbon and no other elements in amounts high enough to appreciably affect its properties. As the carbon content of a steel is increased above 0.30% it becomes more difficult to weld. This means that the carbon content of medium-carbon steels may be high enough to change the welding properties in some instances.

The basic welding recommendations, unless otherwise specified, have been established with mild steel specifically in mind. Other metals require exceptions to, or modifications of, the basic procedures. In general, the higher the carbon content over the 0.30% line, the more the welding current and deposition rate may have to be reduced relative to the basic recommendations for mild steel.

Let's be more specific and see what happens when a bead of weld metal is deposited on a plate of 0.40% carbon steel. The welding rod or electrode is about 0.10% carbon steel, and the welding may be by the oxyacetylene, the shielded-metal-arc (coated electrode), the inert-arc, the vapor-shielded-arc or the submerged-arc process.

Metal deposited by the shielded-arc process is of a higher quality than commercial steel. As the metal passes through the arc it is superheated and deposits in such a fluid state that slag and other nonmetallic particles float out of the deposit.

In all of the electric-arc processes, the deposited metal is protected from the air when it is molten. The various processes, however, differ in the amount of heat, the concentration of heat, and the rate at which the heat is supplied. The results are:

1. A difference in deposition rate (melting of the welding rod or electrode).
2. A difference in penetration (melting of the parent metal).
3. A difference in distribution of the heat in the metal plate.

Any one of the welding methods mentioned can be varied to change the deposition rate and the penetration through a wide range. The heat distribution in the plate can also be varied. The metallurgical changes involved are basically the same in all of these welding methods.

Using ordinary welding procedures, oxyacetylene welding melts less of the base metal but heats more of it. Submerged-arc welding, on the other hand, melts more of the base metal but heats less of it. How is this possible? Well, the oxyacetylene flame spreads out the heat and the submerged arc concentrates the heat. Other welding methods produce results between these two extremes.

Chemical Analysis of the Deposited Metal

By definition, the deposited metal is the metal that is melted off the welding rod or electrode; it is not the bead that is formed by the mixture of the metal from the welding rod or electrode and the melted base metal. As there is always some melting of the parent metal, it might seem impossible to get a sample of pure deposited metal for analysis. If we build up a multiple-layer weld, however, deposited metal may be obtained that will contain only a trace of the base material.

For example, let's assume the plate being welded contains 0.40% carbon and the metal deposited from the welding rod or electrode has no carbon (it does have carbon but assuming none will simplify the calculations). A typical welding procedure would result in 1 lb of plate metal being melted for each 3 lb of deposited metal. Obviously, the carbon content of the bead metal will be 0.40% × ¼ or 0.10%. A second bead will melt one-fourth of the 0.10% carbon steel, and the carbon content will be 0.10% × ¼ or 0.025%. With the same conditions, the third bead would have 0.0006% carbon, and the fourth bead would not have enough carbon to detect by ordinary analysis.

The analysis of the deposited metal is usually furnished by electrode manufacturers, and the analysis of the weld is either calculated or actually determined. In practical work, it is the mechanical properties of the weld that are important, so it is well to supplement any chemical analysis by making actual tests to see that the weld will do the job for which it is intended.

Figure 11-1 shows how a multiple-layer pad of weld metal built up with a low-carbon electrode on a medium-carbon steel plate changes in steps from the medium carbon in the plate to the low carbon in the last deposit. It is assumed that the deposited metal contains 0.10% carbon and that the admixture of parent metal is 50%; that is, for each pound of metal deposited, one pound of the base metal is melted.

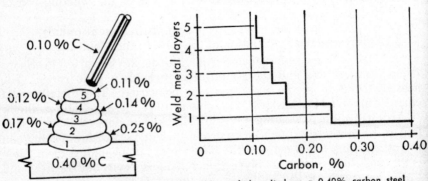

Fig. 11-1. Each additional layer of weld metal deposited on a 0.40% carbon steel plate, as shown at left, will have a progressively lower carbon content.

On medium-carbon steels, a 50% admixture of parent metal is usually within safe limits. But on high-carbon steels such as 0.60% carbon, an admixture of this degree usually results in weld metal structure that is too brittle.

Some welding codes for high-strength welding of medium-carbon steel specify that the first bead should be applied with a low-carbon steel electrode (E-60xx type) and subsequent layers with an electrode designed for higher-strength weld metal (E-80xx or E-90xx type). Figure 11-2 shows how advantage can be taken of admixture in making a weld. In this example, the first bead or root pass in a V- or U-type butt joint picks up a larger percentage of the medium-carbon base metal than do subsequent layers. Because of this pick-up, the bead will have a strength equivalent to that ordinarily obtained with a higher tensile strength electrode. Hence, the completed weld has the required strength plus a higher ductility than would be obtained by using only electrodes of the E-80xx type.

Fig. 11-2. More base metal is melted and mixed with the first layer than any of the other layers.

Steel that is deposited by the oxyacetylene, shielded-arc, vapor-shielded-arc or inert-arc processes is substantially the same in chemical analysis as the original welding rod or electrode, for the latter is just melted and allowed to drop or run into the molten puddle. The oxyacetylene flame can be adjusted to be carburizing, which will add carbon to the deposited metal; to be oxidizing (poor practice), which will slightly lower the carbon; or to be neutral (the flame generally used), which will not affect the carbon content.

Heating and Cooling Cycle

A bead of weld formed by an E-6010 electrode on a 0.40% carbon steel plate will be taken as our example for discussion. The heating and the cooling would be more gradual if the deposit were made with the oxyacetylene torch, and these thermal changes would occur at a faster rate if the weld were made by the submerged-arc process. The rate of temperature change (gradient) would be exceptionally steep if a strip of steel were spot welded to the steel plate.

If, prior to welding, our 0.40% carbon steel plate is heat treated to make it very hard (done by heating followed quickly by rapid quenching), sudden localized heating as occurs in welding may cause the cold plate to crack. In its hardened condition, it does not have enough ductility to withstand the stresses resulting from the unequal heating. Ordinarily, however, the carbon-steel plate on which a weld is to be placed is not fully hardened. The precautions taken to prevent the harm caused by fast cooling will also generally eliminate any trouble because of fast heating.

What affects the rate at which a weld cools? This can't be answered by a single statement. In estimating the cooling rate of the weld bead and the plate metal, it is necessary to take into consideration the following factors:

1. The amount of heat that is added.
2. The rate at which the heat is added.
3. The size of the area to which heat is added.
4. The size and shape of the piece or pieces to be welded.
5. The initial temperature of the base metal.
6. All factors that affect the rate at which heat leaves the welded plate—air temperature, air velocity, insulating layer of slag over the weld bead, etc.

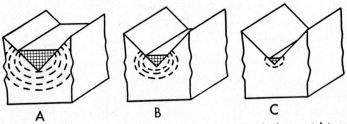

Fig. 11-3. The greater the volume of weld metal, the higher the base metal temperature.

In Fig. 11-3, we have three 1,000-lb bars (A, B and C) grooved to receive weld metal. These bars are at room temperature. Assume that molten low-carbon steel is poured quickly into the grooves and that the bars are insulated so that no heat can escape. When the bars have reached maximum temperature, the increase in temperature at the bottom of each bar is given in Table 11-1.

In each of these examples, the steel bar just below the molten steel will be heated to near the melting point. Bar A will have a considerable portion of the bar heated above the upper critical temperature for the steel, and this will cool slowly. Bar C will have only a thin zone heated above the critical temperature, and this will cool very fast; as fast as it would if cooled by water quenching.

If the steel bars are about 0.40% carbon, bar A will have a zone of coarse-grained steel right under the notch as a result of grain growth in the overheated and slowly cooled section. Progressing outward from the overheated zone, the grains become smaller until metal is reached

Table 11-1. Effect of Weld Metal Volume On Base Metal Temperature

	BAR A	BAR B	BAR C
Bar weight	1,000 lb	1,000 lb	1,000 lb
Molten steel added	100 lb	10 lb	1 lb
Amount bar is heated above initial temperature	500 F	50 F	5 F

that was heated to exactly the transformation temperature; this is the *refined zone*, in which the grains are very small. Below this is the *transition zone* where transformation had just started, and last is the metal that was only heated to a tempering temperature. If the bar had been originally annealed, there would not be much difference in the hardness from the notch to the bottom of the bar, providing it was cooled slowly. Mechanical tests would show lower ductility and impact strength for the coarse-grained portion of the bar.

Let's go back to bar C, and see what has happened. It will have a very thin overheated portion (not heated long enough to result in grain growth) which joins the thin layer that was heated just above the critical. This metal cooled so quickly that it became hardened. It is also stressed because it passed through the transformation temperature on fast cooling and expanded while the metal just below it did not transform.

Please remember from Chapter 8 that the austenite in steel transforms at a relatively low temperature when it is quickly cooled. In the case of Bar C, the austenite in the 0.40% carbon steel would transform at about 400 F to a structure containing martensite, the hardest constituent possible to obtain in carbon steel. Now at 400 F, steel is not anywhere near as ductile and yielding as it is at red heat, so a localized and partial transformation results in high stresses. When these stresses are high enough, further cooling cracks the needlelike crystals of martensite. These cracks may progress to form large underbead cracks along the *fusion line*.

You can soften the martensite by tempering and so reduce the stresses; but once cracks have formed, you'll have to heat to the melting point to rejoin the cracked crystals. Sometimes the hardened and stressed zone doesn't crack until after the metal has been at room temperature a few hours. This sort of cracking can be eliminated by an immediate tempering. When crack-susceptible steel is heat treated, it is customary to place the parts in the tempering furnace just as soon as they are taken from the quenching bath.

Figure 11-4 shows the varying grain structures for a bead of low-carbon weld metal deposited on an annealed or normalized plate of medium-carbon steel. A survey of hardness readings taken from the weld metal to the original structure (unaffected by heat) is given in Fig. 11-5.

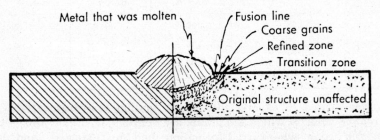

Fig. 11-4. Cross-section of a weld bead on 0.40% carbon steel.

The hardest part of the hardened zone is just below the fusion line for two reasons: First, this metal passes more quickly through the temperature (about 1300 F) where the softer constituent pearlite starts to form; and secondly, this metal has been at a higher temperature resulting in coarser grains. A coarse-grained structure tends to harden more readily than does a fine-grained portion.

If the weld is not to be machined and maximum ductility is not needed, the hardened zone may not be objectionable. In some cases, it may even be desired. It could just as well be named the strengthened zone. But this zone is in ill repute because it sometimes keeps bad company; namely, *residual stresses* and cracks. Let's see what can be done about controlling it.

If this plate had been hardened before welding, the metal just below the transition zone would be heated to a tempering temperature and

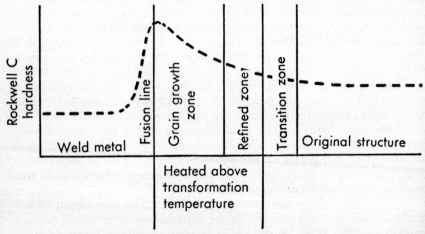

Fig. 11-5. Chart of a hardness survey across weld shown in Fig. 11-4.

thereby softened, having the structure of tempered martensite.

Heat travels through a metal like water flows into a ditch. They both flow downhill: water from a high elevation to a lower one, and heat from a high temperature to a lower one. The steeper the ditch, the faster the water will flow; and the greater the temperature difference between two steel parts, the faster the heat will flow.

Procedures to Control the Hardness

When the thin high hardness zone in the base metal at the weld does present problems, you can reduce and control it by one of three basic approaches. The first (and usually the most economical) is by controlled heating during the welding procedure. The second is by preheating the base metal in addition to controlled heating during the welding procedure. The third is by preheating the base metal, controlled heating during the welding procedure, and postheating or tempering. The second and third approaches require extra handling, additional operations, and extra equipment; these of course add up to extra cost.

Our first approach is preferred as long as satisfactory results are obtained. And they usually are when welding medium-carbon steels. The principle is to heat a large volume of the base metal during welding. This slows up the rate of cooling and prevents the formation of sharply defined zones of crystalline structure. The two chief ways to heat a large volume is by arc welding with high current at low speed or by making multiple-pass arc welds.

Let's take these one at a time. When arc welding, a larger volume of metal can be heated by using a high welding current. Also, advancing the electrode slowly heats completely through the section being welded. This practice should be weighed carefully against the additional cost of preheating but lower welding cost (because of the faster welding speed permitted by preheating). Select the most economical method to suit the application. High welding current and slow travel will give a relatively high admixture, which might be a disadvantage on some applications.

It may be advisable and possible to make a wider or U-type groove to accommodate a multiple-pass, metal-arc weld. Each pass tends to preheat the base metal that will be affected when depositing the next layer. And the heat from the next pass will temper the hardness of the base metal adjacent to the first bead. By the time the last layer is applied, a sufficient mass of the work material will probably be hot enough to prevent any appreciable hardening. This wouldn't necessarily hold true on a long joint.

Preheating and Tempering

Preheating of the work to be welded applies to various welding processes and may constitute a separate operation. For example: When metal-arc welding a 0.30% carbon steel, preheating the base metal to only 200 F and keeping it there during the welding process will slow up the cooling rate enough to practically eliminate the hardening.

After welding, you can temper the weldment (welded assembly) by heating it in a furnace; or, the heat-affected zone may be locally heated with a gas torch, in an induction coil, or by other means.

Three rules of thumb can help in determining the need for preheating carbon steel for metal-arc welding:

1. Less than 0.20% carbon—preheating is not required on plate under 1 in. thick, and only rarely on plate over 1 in. thick.
2. 0.20 to 0.40% carbon—preheating is never required on plate under ½ in. thick, and sometimes on plate over ½ in. thick.
3. Over 0.40% carbon—preheating is generally required on all plate thicknesses.

The proper welding procedure, as mentioned before, can incorporate the equivalent effect of preheating over a wide range of materials and plate thicknesses.

Frequently a welded member must be machined later across the weld, for appearance, for dimensional control, or for mating to other parts of a larger assembly. The (if uncontrolled) maximum hardness zone under the weld bead may be either too hard for the steel or cast alloy cutting tools to cut, or damaging to a finish-machining grade of sintered or cemented carbide if conditions are such that the tool enters and leaves the hardness zone at high speed. If these conditions must be met, a more shock-resistant grade of cemented carbide should be

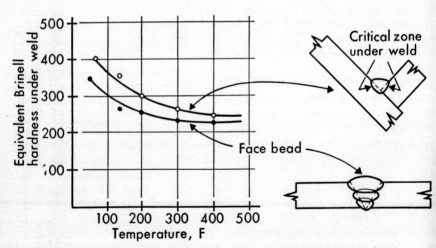

Fig. 11-6. Effects of preheat temperature on the final hardness of the critical underbead zone. The lower the hardness and the more uniform the hardness throughout the machining cut, the longer will be the tool life and the better the quality of machined surface.

selected. When the weld is to be machined, preheating prior to welding is desirable. The effects of preheating, in terms of reduced underbead hardness and better machinability, are shown by Fig. 11-6.

In addition to lowering the hardness of the parent metal, preheating has other advantages. It dries troublesome moisture from the surface and out of any joints. It burns out any grease or oil, and makes scale and other foreign matter easier to remove. Preheating also permits the welding speed to be increased.

To review the numerous factors influencing hardness, the following lists should be a guide:

Hardness is reduced by:

1. Low-carbon and/or low-alloy content of the parent metal.

2. Fine-grained base metal.

3. Thin base material (no quench effect on weld metal).

4. Work hot when weld is started and kept hot during welding.

5. Weldment allowed to cool slowly after welding.

6. Heavy bead or weld layer at slow speed.

7. High welding current; slow travel.

8. Low-temperature heat source.

9. Slow rate of heat transfer (gas welding, forge welding).

10. Single-layer deposit.

Hardness is increased by:

1. High-carbon and/or high-alloy content of parent metal.

2. Coarse-grained base metal.

3. Thick base material.

4. Work cold when welding is started, and no extra heat applied.

5. Weldment cooled quickly after welding.

6. Small weld beads (tack welds).

7. Low welding current; fast travel.

8. High-temperature heat source.

9. High rate of heat transfer (shielded-metal-arc, submerged-arc process).

10. Multiple-layer deposit.

Definitions of New Words

Fusion line. The junction between the metal that has been melted and the unmelted base metal.

Refined zone. The base metal zone of fine-grained austenitic structure below the coarse-grained zone, progressing away from the weld. Metal in the refined zone was heated to the transformation temperature just long enough to recrystallize as austenite, and then cooled before the grains had time to grow.

Residual stresses. Internal stresses that exist in a metal at room temperature as the result of (1) previous non-uniform heating and expansion, or (2) a composite structure composed of a ductile constituent and a brittle one.

Transition zone. The base metal zone of mixed structure, below the refined zone, where only some of the grains have transformed to austenite.

Review Questions

1. Explain what happens when a weld bead is deposited on a piece of 0.40% carbon steel.
2. What is the effect upon the deposited weld metal of an oxyacetylene flame that is carburizing? Oxidizing?
3. Why is it that quick local heating may cause a hardened steel plate to crack?
4. Explain what six factors determine the cooling rate of a weld.
5. In what part of the weld zone will the fine grain structure be found?
6. Does the rapidity of cooling have any effect on the temperature at which austenite transforms?
7. How may cracking in the hardened and stressed zone of a weld be eliminated?
8. Does tempering do any good once a crack has formed?
9. Describe the procedure for controlling hardness in the heat-affected zone of the weld.
10. When should base metal be preheated prior to welding?

CHAPTER 12

WELDING HIGH-CARBON STEEL

High-carbon steels (carbon 0.45% and higher) are usually called "difficult to weld." This statement is not wholly accurate. It would be more nearly correct to say that these steels are impossible to weld by mild-steel welding procedure, but are easy to weld by procedures and methods recommended for high-carbon steels.

Some of the properties of high-carbon steels that make different welding procedure necessary are these:

• High-carbon steel will not stretch as much as low-carbon steel, and a higher load is required to make the high-carbon stretch a given amount above the yield point, Fig. 12-1.

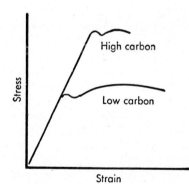

Fig. 12-1. High-carbon steel will not stretch as much as low-carbon steel.

• Extremely high cooling rates are required to cause low-carbon steel to harden. At a much slower cooling rate, high-carbon steel will harden excessively.

• The transformation range is lower for the high-carbon steels resulting in a deeper heat-affected zone.

• The high-carbon steel has enough carbon to react with other elements to form gases and has a different affinity for dissolved gases so that welding under some conditions will give porous welds. There is not enough carbon in low-carbon steel to cause this trouble.

Welding Problems

Difficulties that may be encountered when welding steels with carbon over 0.45% are listed below. These problems are not too serious when welding steel a little above 0.45%, but they become progressively more important as the carbon content is increased.

1. Cracking of the weld metal. The cracks may be across the bead (transverse), or they may be through the center of the bead (longitudinal). Longitudinal cracks are more prevalent. Sometimes they do not show on the surface of the bead, but the underportion of the bead will be cracked.

2. Porosity in the weld metal.

3. Excessive hardening of the parent metal.

4. Cracking of the parent metal. This includes both *underbead cracking*—cracks just under the fusion zone—and *radial cracks* that are at the fusion zone and extend into the parent metal.

5. Excessive softening of the parent metal.

Since hardened high-carbon steel will not stretch very much without failure, the expansion and contraction during welding are of special importance. The contraction (shrinkage) of a weld bead on steel may be compared to a cold low-carbon steel bow strung with a hot low-carbon steel wire (Fig. 12-2). As the wire cools, it contracts, and the bow and the wire must both yield in order to compensate for the contraction.

As the wire contracts, the stresses on wire and bow increase; and the deflection (bending) of the bow plus the stretching of the wire equal the difference between the length of the hot wire and the original length of the wire.

Let's assume that, after the wire has cooled to room temperature, there has been enough contraction to stress both bow and wire to the yield point. If they are now heated at 1000 or 1200 F, both will expand and yield. The tight wire causes the bow to bend a little more and the wire is stretched a little by the tension in the bow; then, when they are cooled back to room temperature, both bow and wire have the same dimensions as they did before heating, but the wire will not be as tight. The heating to 1200 F has stress relieved the assembly.

The example of the bow and wire shows what happens when a low-carbon steel is welded with a low-carbon electrode. The same illustration will be used to show the effects when high-carbon steel is welded.

In this instance, the high-carbon steel bow is strung with the hot low-carbon steel wire. The wire cools and both bow and wire are stressed. The bow bends elastically, but the stress does not reach the yield point because the wire gives first. The low-carbon wire thus takes most of the stretch, and the bow is only slightly bent. If the wire is now cut, the bow springs back to its original shape.

Rule 1 for welding high-carbon steel: Avoid excessive penetration;

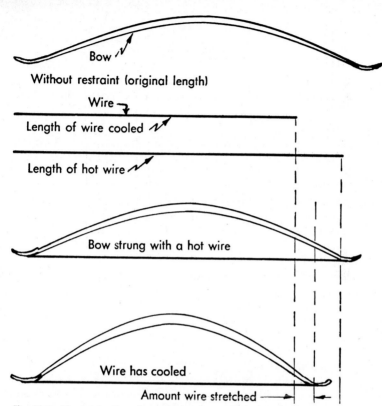

Fig. 12-2. The contraction of a weld bead on cold high-carbon steel may be compared with a steel bow strung with a hot wire.

and keep the weld metal as low in carbon content as practical. The deposit will then have maximum ductility. Otherwise, the high-carbon steel being welded would be stressed too highly. Further deflection beyond the yield point causes it to fail quickly.

From the bow and wire example, it is readily seen that a larger wire would stress the bow more. If the bow is bent enough to yield, the wire will not be stretched as greatly. Conversely, if a very small wire is used, the wire will have to carry all of the extension.

The low-hydrogen group of electrodes, which also have iron-powdered type coatings, provide sound ductile welds on high-carbon steel with minimum penetration. These electrodes also eliminate a major cause of cracking because of their low hydrogen content and their good slagging characteristics.

Of course some penetration is necessary. With some of the highest carbon steels (over 1.0%), the minimum safe penetration to produce a sound weld may raise the carbon content of the deposited metal to a

25-20 Stainless

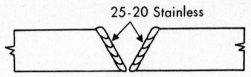

Fig. 12-3. Very high-carbon steel (1.0% C or higher) can be welded by first surfacing with stainless steel.

point too high to be sufficiently ductile to withstand contraction stresses. Under these conditions a ductile and tough weld may be obtained by welding with a 25% chromium and 20% nickel electrode. This electrode has shallow penetrating characteristics and the deposit is still ductile even after picking up some carbon from the base metal. This electrode (called 25-20 stainless and numbered E-310-15) deposits weld metal that remains in the ductile austenitic state. It is so highly alloyed that it does not transform into martensite or other hard structures even when it is very quickly cooled.

The weld may be completed with the stainless electrode. If it is a large weld, the surfaces of the parent metal may be coated or "buttered" with a layer of the stainless deposit and then the weld completed with an electrode of lower cost (Fig. 12-3).

In addition to having a high ductility, the 25-20 deposit also has a low yield point, which makes it an ideal cushioning material. It will stretch a lot without overstressing the high-carbon steel. The tensile strength is high 80,000 to 90,000 psi.

Rule 2 for welding high-carbon steel: Go slow enough to deposit a substantial bead or layer of weld metal, but on wide welds weave rather than make parallel stringer beads. Avoid thin weld cross-sections. A thin concave fillet weld between two rigid members is likely to crack (Fig. 12-4). Crater cracks, as mentioned in Chapter 9, occur in a similar way. Also known as *hot cracks*, these originate in the concave crater often left by the weldor at the end of a weld bead. The stresses concentrate in the metal that is last to freeze. If it's a crater, the thinness of the weld metal offers little resistance to the stress.

Any weld on a high-carbon steel should be well rounded (built up by using shorter arc length), and no single bead in a multi-layer weld should be finished with a crater. The crater that tends to develop at

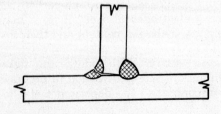

Fig. 12-4. A thin concave fillet weld between two rigid members is likely to crack.

the end of a weld should be filled in immediately, and the weld ended on top of the finished bead instead of on plate metal.

When welding in a groove or a fillet, it is the first or root bead that is most susceptible to cracking. Even though the surface of the weld is crack-free, the underportion of the bead or a lower weld layer may be cracked. Surface or *toe cracks* may be found by magnetic inspection with iron powder, while a more comprehensive check may be made by chipping out the underside, by breaking the weld, or by radiographic (gamma or x-ray) or ultrasonic inspection.

We have heard the statement, "Yes, that first bead is cracked all right, but I will burn to the bottom of the crack with the next layer." It is seldom possible to melt completely through a lower layer to eliminate a crack. It more frequently will follow up at least part way into the second bead (Fig. 12-5), and in service may lead to early failure of the weld. The only answer is to prevent *root cracks* in the first place.

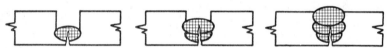

Fig. 12-5. A cracked first bead generally carries up into the second layer of weld metal.

How do root cracks happen? It is the first or root bead that picks up the most carbon from the parent metal and thus is more crack sensitive than following layers. As the weld metal cools, it shrinks. The restraint provided by the colder base metal places the weld metal under tension. Where this condition is most severe, tensile stresses at the root of the joint are biaxial (two-directional). As a result, the smaller root bead may crack and this crack may then or later propagate (grow) on up into subsequent layers of the weld metal.

Root cracks and other weld cracks are avoided by one or more of the following steps: preheating or process heating of the base metal, use of a more ductile weld metal, change of joint design, uniform gap separating plates at the groove, and leaving members being welded free to move as the weld cools.

On the higher carbon steels where even a low admixture results in considerable carbon pick-up by the first bead, stress relieving of the joint is advisable before the weldment is put into service.

Cracking of any kind in the weld metal, during welding or in later service, is more likely with higher carbon content and with appreciable gas inclusions. We'll discuss the latter under the general term of "porosity."

Porosity in the Weld Metal

Porosity is not yet fully understood by metallurgists. There are times when a fine well-distributed porosity—usually not visible to the naked eye—adds to the ductility of the base metal or the weld metal. However, any set of conditions that cause appreciably-sized, isolated or grouped gas pockets or blowholes may cause trouble in the welding of high-carbon steel, or may lower the notch toughness of the weld metal.

Molten high-carbon steel readily absorbs hydrogen, carbon monoxide, and other gases to which it is exposed. These gases are much less soluble in the solid metal crystals and so are expelled as the metal freezes. If they collect at the grain boundaries, they may be a source of weld weakness under some service conditions. The problem is increased by the presence of any high percentage of sulphur, phosphorus or silicon, which enter into combination with the gaseous elements.

Weld in such a way that the surface of the deposited metal will solidify last and so that the weld will solidify slowly. Any gas will thus be given time and an avenue of escape.

Metal-arc welding with bare electrodes allows the weld metal to absorb oxygen and nitrogen from the air. The oxygen reacts with the carbon in the steel to form carbon monoxide. These holes may be kept small and few in quantity by avoiding the excessive puddling which gives the molten metal time to absorb enough oxygen to produce porous welds.

Standard shielded-arc electrodes (organic coating) E-6010, E-6011, etc. produce an atmosphere around the arc that contains hydrogen, a notable contributor to the formation of holes in the weld metal. When using such electrodes, weld more slowly to allow the hydrogen time to escape from the solidifying weld metal.

The low-hydrogen types of electrodes E-6016 and E-6018 and the higher tensile strength grades will make solid welds on high-carbon steel without using any special precautions. The submerged-arc process will also produce solid welds in these steels. Both of these welding methods protect the weld metal by a layer of slag, and there is practically no hydrogen present to be absorbed by the weld metal.

Excessive Hardening of the Parent Metal

The factors that affect the hardness of the high-carbon base metal are the same as those discussed under the section devoted to the welding of medium-carbon steel.

Any of the welding methods will result in a hard zone near the weld if the cooling is too fast. In a brazed joint, the steel is not melted but it is heated above the transformation temperature and slow cooling is necessary to reduce the hardening.

To get the metal in the vicinity of a weld in high-carbon steel soft enough to machine readily, postheating is usually required. The degree of preheat and the slow rate of cooling that are needed to prevent hardening of the heat-affected zone may not be possible or may cost more than a tempering or annealing heat treatment after welding.

Cracking of the Parent Metal

Cracking of the parent metal is probably the most serious problem to be encountered in the welding of high-carbon steel. Cracks in the weld metal can be seen, or at least readily detected, but the cracks in the parent metal cannot be seen. If they are under a bead of weld, they may elude magnetic-particle inspection or even the vigilant x-ray.

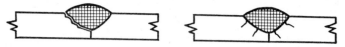

Fig. 12-6. An underbead crack and radial cracks.

Figure 12-6 shows the two kinds of cracks. The underbead crack is found following the contour of the fusion zone. The radially directed crack usually runs from the fusion zone into the base metal.

The underbead type crack (also called *hard crack*) occurs when a bead of weld metal is deposited on cold high-carbon steel. Two other conditions are necessary: hydrogen, usually originating in the coating of shielded-arc electrodes, and the formation of martensite in the base metal along the fusion line. If the work is preheated or is welded so that the weld cools slowly, the cracks do not form. If the weld is made with an electrode having a low-hydrogen or hydrogen-free coating, the zone of martensite formed on work not preheated is crack-free.

Hydrogen is very soluble in any liquid steel and is still more soluble in molten high-carbon steel. As the steel solidifies, the hydrogen is forced out of solution, diffuses through the steel, and escapes into the air. At the transformation temperature there is a sudden reduction in hydrogen solubility, resulting in an appreciable rejection of hydrogen from the iron crystals. When the steel is cooled slowly, transformation takes place slowly enough to permit the hydrogen to escape freely. When the steel is cooled quickly, however, the hydrogen does not have time to diffuse to the surface and puts an enormous stress on the metal structure.

The presence of a large percentage of sulphur makes it even less likely for the hydrogen to escape, since the hydrogen and sulphur combine as hydrogen sulphide. The ductile portions of the metal yield to the stress caused by the tiny bubbles of hydrogen and hydrogen sulphide, but the brittle martensitic crystals are likely to crack under the pressure.

The phenomenon may be compared to the experience of a deep sea diver. At high underwater pressures, his blood dissolves nitrogen; when he is raised slowly, the nitrogen slowly leaves the blood and diffuses out through the lungs. If, however, the pressure on his body is decreased quickly, by rapidly lifting him out of the water, the nitrogen will come out of the blood to form dangerous and painful bubbles. Helium mixed with oxygen has enabled divers to be taken to atmospheric pressure safely in less time, for the helium diffuses out of the body more quickly and the fatal bubbles are not formed.

Steelmakers are familiar with the cracks that are blamed on hydrogen. These cracks are called "flakes" and are found by examining a fractured surface or etching a sample of the steel in hot hydrochloric acid. One reason for the soaking treatment given to high-carbon steel ingots is to hold the ingot at a high temperature long enough to allow the excess hydrogen to diffuse out of the steel.

The low-hydrogen electrodes eliminate the underbead cracking due to hydrogen, and allow high-carbon steels to be satisfactorily welded at a much lower preheating temperature. But, we repeat, the low-hydrogen electrodes do not eliminate the hardened zone under the weld bead.

Stress cracks are usually at the toe of the weld, starting at the surface and extending down into the base metal. Sometimes they are found under the bead at right angles to the fusion line. They are also called hot cracks, and those that are open to the air can be recognized by the oxidized surface of the fracture. Stress cracks may look like underbead cracks, but they can be identified by their direction. The underbead cracks are in the hardened zone, and the stress cracks run across the heat-affected zone.

Underbead cracks are not found in oxyacetylene or atomic-hydrogen welds, but the hot cracks occur more frequently in gas welding than in metal-arc welding.

When the welded high-carbon steel plate is cooling, the stresses may be higher than the ultimate strength of the steel at the elevated temperature. A ductile low-carbon steel would yield and so reduce the stress. But high-carbon steel is not as ductile, and so we have stress cracking. Cracks of this type can occur with stainless-steel electrodes

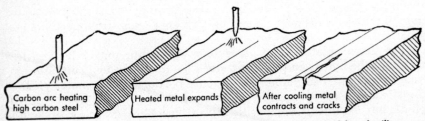

Carbon arc heating high carbon steel   Heated metal expands   After cooling metal contracts and cracks

Fig. 12-7. Cracks may be formed by heating the surface of a metal of low ductility.

and with the low-hydrogen electrodes, for they are not caused by hydrogen.

All you have to do to see a stress crack is to heat the surface of a steel plate that has low ductility (Fig. 12-7). The heating causes local expansion of the heated area. If the plate is thick, the plate will not bend enough to relieve the expansion and the metal will upset, resulting in a raised bead. When the metal cools and contracts, it is not ductile enough to stretch and a crack results.

You eliminate the stress cracks by providing means to reduce the stress on the metal as it cools and contracts. If you can, reduce the rigidity of the joint. If this is not possible, heat or stretch restraining members and allow them to return to their original length as the weld cools. Preheating may be used to reduce the localized stresses at the joint.

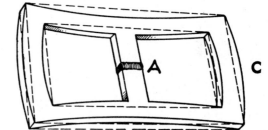

Fig. 12-8. A weld at (A) in a rigid part will probably fail in or near the weld unless the metal is ductile.

In Fig. 12-8, a weld in this rigid part of A will probably fail at or near the weld if the metal is not sufficiently ductile. We certainly do not wish to reduce the rigidity of the part by cutting the arms, B and C, but we can heat these two arms and allow them to cool and contract as the weld cools. Instead of heating B and C, a jack may be placed near the center arm and the fracture expanded and then the jack loosened after welding, to put the weld in compression thus compensating for the contraction after cooling.

If member A is preheated, it will expand and increase the tension in the weld after cooling.

When a weld like this is to be made with an oxyacetylene torch, it may be advisable to water cool the part A on each side of the weld to reduce the length of the heated area. As soon as the weld is completed, the cooling should be stopped so that the weld and base metal will not cool too quickly.

Excessive Softening of the Parent Metal

Annealed high-carbon steel will, of course, not be softened by any kind of welding. High-carbon steel is used for its superior strength and hardness, and in a finished part will be heat treated to secure these properties. If the part is to be heat treated after welding, then we do not need to consider either softening or hardening of the base metal. If the weld is to have the physical properties of the base metal, then the filler metal must be properly selected. It need not necessarily be of the same chemical analysis as the parent metal, but it must be one that will have the required properties after the heat treatment that is given the part.

Stainless steel is not a satisfactory filler metal if the weld is required to be hard. If only the surface of the weld is required to be hard, the weld may be finished with a material which will heat treat to the hardness wanted or with an alloy which has the hardness as-deposited and is not affected by heat treatment.

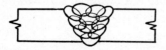

Fig. 12-9. The ability of a weld joint to bend depends on design.

It is impossible to weld a hardened high-carbon steel part without some softening or at least change in the properties of the metal near the weld. Gas welding heats the metal a considerable distance from the weld, giving a large tempered or softened area. Metal-arc welding heats less of the parent metal, but we are confronted with excessive hardening of the part that is heated. Any preheating done will increase the depth of the heat-affected and softened zone.

For best results, hardened high-carbon steel parts should be annealed, welded in this more ductile condition and then heat treated to the desired final hardness. This ideal procedure is not always possible, particularly when welding is used to repair high-carbon steel parts.

Successful welding of hardened high-carbon steel requires a knowledge of the service that is to be required and then the intelligent selection of the welding procedure and welding electrodes to make the weld just strong enough, just tough enough, and with just as much softening of the parent metal as will allow satisfactory service.

Use all the precautions practical, and preferably weld with a high-chromium, high-nickel stainless-steel electrode. A small electrode and intermittent welding will reduce the embrittling of the parent metal due to grain growth and also will make the softened area smaller. If possible, design the joint with the fusion zone at an angle to the principal stresses (Fig. 12-9).

Summary of Preventive Welding

High-carbon steel is not as ductile as low-carbon steel and must be cooled slowly. The possible welding difficulties are: (1) cracking of the weld metal; (2) holes in the weld metal; (3) excessive hardening of the base metal; (4) cracking of the base metal and (5) excessive softening of the base metal (in this case the base metal has been hardened before welding).

These welding difficulties can be eliminated or reduced by: (1) preheating, (2) using low-hydrogen electrodes or stainless-steel electrodes; (3) reducing cooling stresses on the welded joint; (4) annealing before welding and (5) hardening and tempering after welding.

The cracking of the weld metal is controlled: (1) by reducing the rigidity of the joint; (2) by reducing the penetration into the base metal thereby obtaining a lower carbon and more ductile weld and (3) by using a low-hydrogen electrode or a stainless-steel electrode which will give a deposit of higher ductility.

The holes in the weld metal may be eliminated: (1) by puddling the weld to work out the holes; (2) by reducing the penetration into the base metal and (3) by using a welding process that is less likely to give holes.

The hardening of the base metal is reduced: (1) by preheating; (2) by using higher welding current and welding more slowly and (3) by tempering after welding.

Cracking of the base metal is controlled: (1) by using low-hydrogen or stainless-steel electrodes and (2) by the reduction of cooling stresses on the welded joint.

Excessive softening of the base metal is reduced: (1) by elimination of preheating; (2) by welding faster and with small electrodes or (3) by heat treatment after welding.

The original properties of a hardened high-carbon steel cannot be duplicated by welding alone. A final complete heat treatment is necessary to get the weld and the base metal into the original condition, but in most instances the hardened steel can be welded so that it will perform its necessary functions without the final heat treatment.

Definitions of New Words

Hard crack. See "underbead crack."

Hot crack. Also known as "auto crack," resulting from stress concentration in relatively thin weld metal that is last to freeze. Both root cracks and crater cracks are forms of hot cracking.

Radial crack. A crack originating in the fusion zone and extending into the base metal, usually at right angles to the line of fusion. This type of crack is due to the high stresses involved in the cooling of a rigid structure.

Root crack. A weld crack originating in the root bead, which is usually smaller and of higher carbon content than subsequent beads. Crack is caused by shrinkage of the hot weld metal as it cools, placing the root bead under tension.

Stress crack. See "radial crack."

Toe crack. A crack originating at the junction between the face of the weld and the base metal. It may be any one of three types: (1)

radial or stress crack, (2) underbead crack extending through the hardened zone below the fusion line, or (3) the result of poor fusion between the deposited filler metal and the base metal.

Underbead crack. A crack in the hardened base metal just under the fusion line. It usually originates in the coarse-grained zone and is caused by hydrogen released from the austenite as it transforms during cooling. If cooling is rapid, the free hydrogen cannot escape to the surface and exerts tremendous pressure on the hard martensite crystals being formed. Underbead cracks occur parallel to the fusion line.

Review Questions

1. What is the cause of underbead cracking?
2. Name the difficulties encountered in welding high-carbon steels.
3. What are the three methods used to control cracking of high-carbon steel?
4. Preheating is recommended for overcoming some difficulties when welding high-carbon steel but may cause others. Can you name them?
5. What is the advantage of low-hydrogen electrodes?
6. Can welding take the place of a final heat treatment of high-carbon steel?
7. What steps should be taken to avoid porosity in a high-carbon weld?
8. Where do stress cracks usually start?
9. What are hot cracks?
10. Explain the steps necessary to obtain the best results when welding hardened high-carbon steel.

CHAPTER 13

WELDING ALLOY STEELS

Low-carbon steels may be welded without close control, but the alloy steels with their high mechanical properties are more temperamental. Some of them must be treated like prima donnas in order to bring out their outstanding properties. However, all alloy steels are weldable.

Since welding is universally used in fabricating all types of products, steelmakers have had to consider weldability in developing their steel analyses and manufacturing processes. Low-alloy steels are now available that have even better welding properties than straight medium-carbon steels as well as better mechanical properties.

The time may come when the present higher alloy steels will be replaced by steels that do not require preheating or postheating for welding. Advances are being made: molybdenum, for instance, is being substituted for some other alloying elements to improve weldability. Moreover, the low-hydrogen electrodes have lowered the preheating temperatures required and in some cases have made preheating unnecessary.

Let's briefly review some of the main principles of ferrous metallurgy. As a carbon steel is heated to a high temperature, depending upon the amount of carbon present, it changes from a mixture of ferrite (pure iron) and pearlite (an iron and iron-carbide mixture) to a solid solution of carbide in gamma iron known as austenite. A carbon steel is hardened by heating it to a point slightly above the transformation temperature, and then cooling it very quickly as by plunging it in water.

We have discussed, in Chapter 7, the effect that various alloying elements have on the hardening of steel. Some alloy steels are fully hardened when quenched in oil and others are alloyed so as to harden when cooled more slowly in air. Some, such as stainless steels of the chromium-nickel group and steels containing high manganese, remain austenitic in structure, even at room temperature. These steels do not undergo any change in the crystal structure of their iron content, and therefore they do not have a critical temperature point during cooling. They cannot be hardened by heat treatment. The austenitic stainless and high-manganese steels, however, will be discussed in later chapters.

The hardening of the parent metal under the weld may be overlooked on some jobs. If additional layers of weld metal are to be applied, the hardness will be reduced. If the whole part is given a postweld annealing heat treatment, the hard zone will be eliminated.

Excessive hardening of the parent metal is a danger sign, however, especially if the weld is made with electrodes containing hydrogen compounds in the coating, which includes all standard coated electrodes with the exception of the low-hydrogen group.

As explained in the discussion of the welding of high-carbon steel, underbead cracking can be expected if the parent metal is hardened

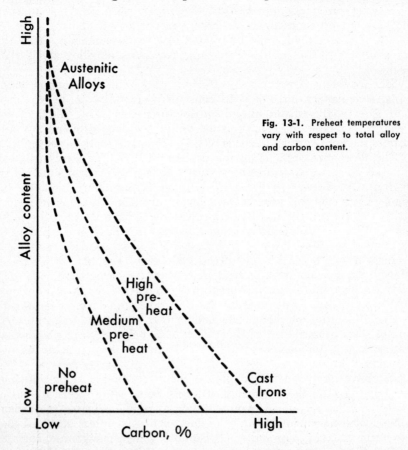

Fig. 13-1. Preheat temperatures vary with respect to total alloy and carbon content.

to 50 Rockwell C or higher. The low-hydrogen electrodes eliminate the underbead cracking but do not reduce the hardening of the parent metal.

The tendency for cracking alongside of the weld increases with the alloy and carbon content of the base metal and with the rate at which the metal cools after welding.

In order to select the proper welding method and procedure for a particular alloy steel, we need to know its chemical analysis and properties.

Low-carbon steel and low-carbon weld metal have high ductility, from solidification on down to room temperature. They have relatively low tensile strength, and hard zones and underbead cracking are absent. These qualities make low-carbon steels easy to weld.

In welding, steels of low hardenability are preferred so that hard and brittle zones will not be formed under the weld where the metal cools very quickly. When steels of high hardenability are welded, the rapid cooling and subsequent hardening may be prevented by preheating. Figure 13-1 shows how the degree of preheat necessary varies with respect to the total alloy content and the carbon content of the steel.

If the alloy content is high and the carbon is low, there is no appreciable hardening; in fact, the metal may be all alloy and may be welded without hardening. As the carbon is increased, the alloy content of the steel must be lower for welding without preheating.

Some alloys, like austenitic nickel steel, can often be welded without preheating, even though they have both high-carbon and high-alloy contents. The transformation of the austenite has been slowed up so much that it does not take place at all. The ductile and non-hardenable austenite is an ideal welding material.

In this chapter, we will divide the welding of alloy steels into three parts:

1. The surfacing of new and worn parts to combat wear, corrosion, etc. (hardsurfacing) or to build up a part to a larger size or to repair a machining error or a casting defect.
2. Welding alloy-steel parts together when the full strength or other mechanical properties of the parent metal are not required.
3. Welding alloy-steel parts together when the parent metal's mechanical properties, or even higher properties, are desired in the weld.

Hardsurfacing and Build-Up

In the first class of work, hardsurfacing with or on alloy steel, the strength of the bond between the surfacing metal and the parent metal is not of major importance. As one example, a thermocouple tube is surfaced with an alloy to prevent scaling and oxidation. The bond strength is not at all important, for a shell of the resistant alloy slipped over the tube would be adequate. A band of hardsurfacing material welded around a tool joint or drill collar is not subjected to tensile loading. The primary object is to resist abrasion, but of course the hardsurfacing must be held on tight enough so that it will not flake or chip off.

A worn shaft that is built up by welding does not require a high-strength bond. Some bearings, in fact, are built up with sprayed-on metal (metallizing), and this low-tensile-strength deposit is entirely satisfactory for this type of application.

True, high strength is sometimes necessary in built-up welds. A good example is the building up of the worn tip of an oil-well drilling bit. These bits are made of high-carbon steel. They should be preheated to about 400 F when they are built up by the shielded-arc process to prevent the formation of underbead cracks. A high-carbon steel electrode or an alloy-steel electrode is used to shape the edge and gage of the bit. This is then built up to the finished size with a hardsurfacing electrode.

When building up a high-carbon or an alloy steel, the required preheating temperature may be reduced or even eliminated by using a low-hydrogen or a stainless 18-8 or higher alloy electrode. The deposits from these electrodes do not cause underbead cracks in the high-carbon base metal. After the first layer is applied, and while the work is still hot, the build-up is finished with any desired electrode. The base metal under the first layer of weld will harden as the weld cools, but the heat from the subsequent layers will temper the hardened metal to give a strong and ductile structure.

When high-carbon steel is built up with the oxyacetylene process, the steel will probably be preheated enough in welding to eliminate underbead cracking or any undue hardening of the parent metal. But on many jobs gas welding softens the parent metal too much, and the longer the metal is held at a high temperature, the greater will be the loss in impact strength because of grain growth. In such cases the work should be heat treated after welding to reduce the grain size and to obtain the specific mechanical properties needed.

In hardsurfacing, even though preheating is not always necessary to avoid underbead cracking, the combination of surface material and base metal may require preheating to prevent excessive shrinkage stresses. Such stresses may cause cracks, spalling or peeling.

Automatic and semi-automatic submerged-arc welding is being used for production hardsurfacing and in rebuilding extensive surface areas. Various combinations of hardsurfacing fluxes and low- or medium-carbon electrode wire give a wider range of surface properties.

The building up of wear-resistant surface layers by manual and automatic methods will be more fully covered in a later chapter on hardsurfacing (Chapter 18).

When Highest Strength Is Not Needed

Our second major class of work is the joining of alloy-steel parts when the high mechanical properties of the parent metal need not be duplicated or exceeded in the joint itself. There are many reasons why joints should not be made any stronger than is required. For instance:

1. Excessive strength is usually more expensive.
2. Excessive strength at one section of a member may result in stress concentrations and overloading of other portions.

Some joints are intentionally made weaker as a safety factor so that, if overloading takes place, they will fail before more expensive parts of the assembly can be damaged—just like the fuses in your electric light circuit.

Soldering and brazing are metal-joining methods that are often useful when full-strength properties are not required. Neither involves melting of the base metal. Soft solder, which melts at a comparatively low temperature (between 250 and 500 F), is adequate for sealing joints in thin steel and for low-strength joints. Going up the temperature scale, the silver solders (silver-brazing alloys) melt between 1200 and 1600 F and can be used for joining hardened alloy steels with only local effect on the heat-treated properties. The tensile strength of the silver-soldered joint is rather high when it is properly made. The abutting surfaces must be finished to fit closely together and must be held in position until the brazing alloy solidifies.

Copper brazing of the alloy steels is commonly performed in a furnace filled with an atmosphere of hydrogen or of hydrogen and other suitable gases. This process is especially suitable for small parts that can be assembled with snugly fitting joints. Let's say that a steel sleeve is to be copper brazed on a steel pipe. The parts are machined so that the pipe makes a good tight fit in the sleeve, and a copper wire is placed around the pipe at or near the sleeve. Heating in the controlled atmosphere of the furnace to about 2000 F melts the copper. The copper spreads over the surface of the steel and is "sucked" by capillary attraction into the minute spaces between the sleeve and the pipe.

Copper furnace brazing is satisfactory for joining alloy steel to carbon steel, high-carbon steel to cast iron, or for any combination of steels. Brazed parts can not be further heat treated without appreciably weakening the strength of the joint. The copper braze has a high shear strength and fairly high tensile strength when the conditions are ideal, but it should not be used for butt joints when good tensile properties are required.

Braze-welding and brazing will produce butt joints in carbon and alloy steels with a tensile strength of 55,000 psi or more. It is necessary to distinguish between these two terms. When the parts are tightly fitted together, so that the alloy flows through the joint by capillary attraction, the process is known as brazing. If the parts are not closely fitted, so that a relatively large amount of filler metal is used, the process is called braze-welding.

The most popular braze-welding alloy is a high-zinc brass welding rod applied by the oxyacetylene welding process. It melts at about 1650 F and is used on parts that are not to be heat treated. Braze-welding is also done with the carbon-arc and the tungsten-inert-arc welding processes. The inert-arc process is particularly suited to joining thin metals where it is rapidly replacing the carbon-arc method.

Steel may be braze-welded with coated bronze electrodes that conform to AWS Class E-CuSn-C. These electrodes, however, are usually used for surfacing or for building up pads on steel, for braze-welding cast iron, and for joining non-ferrous alloys. Copper-silicon rods may be used to braze-weld thin steel.

In all of the soldering and brazing methods, there is practically no melting of the steel, no penetration into the steel. The solders and brazing materials form a thin alloy which "tins" the surface of the steel. Since a surface adhesion is involved, it is necessary to have clean bright metal for soldering and brazing.

Soldering and brazing methods of joining alloy steels are recommended only when they will give all the required physical properties.

Fusion welding, also, can be used in joining alloy-steel parts when the full strengths of the parent metal are not required. One such method is resistance spot welding. This is not recommended, however, when a high strength joint is needed. Spot welding will compete with riveting and bolting but not with the various arc welding processes or resistance butt welding for a continuously strong structural or machine member.

When high-carbon or hardenable-alloy steels are spot-welded, the welds are tempered by passing a second shot of current through the joint to delay the cooling. The tempering current is not as high as the current used for the welding, and it is left on long enough to heat the weld and the surrounding metal to a good tempering temperature, but not long enough to bring the metal again to the transformation point.

When the full tensile strength of the parent metal is not required in the weld, alloy steels may be arc welded with low-carbon metal electrodes normally used for welding mild steel. The resultant weld has higher ductility in the as-welded condition than alloy-steel weld metal would have. If the weld is completed in one pass, the pick-up of alloying elements from the parent metal serves to somewhat increase the tensile strength of the weld metal. However, the last layer of a multipass weld does not pick up enough base metal to be appreciably strengthened.

Additional strength can often be obtained by increasing the weld cross-section. This would be true in the case of fillet welds but not of butt welds.

Welds of Highest Mechanical Properties

Carbon or alloy steel deposited by shielded-arc welding has higher mechanical properties than steel of the same analysis in a casting, even after the casting has been heat treated. Properties of the weld metal compare favorably with those of rolled steel tested in the direction of rolling (properties are lower in the transverse direction).

To obtain these superior properties of the weld metal, the proper welding method and technique must be used.

The welding of an oil-well casing is one of the outstanding examples where high-quality welds meet very rigid requirements. These joints are made under adverse conditions. The casing is welded end to end and lowered into the ground to line the hole that may be an oil well. As one welding contractor puts it, "We are required to join together, by welding, two vertical pieces of pipe having diameters of from 5¾ to 18⅝ in. or even larger; to carry the tensile stresses developed by a vertical string of a mile or more of such pipe, the compressive stresses developed by an equal depth of heavy mud, and the impact of a drill stem within the pipe weighing 22 lbs per foot and revolving at 250 rpm; to remain perfectly water- and gas-tight under these stresses and pressures; to be smooth on the inside within ⅟₃₂ in.; and to hold the outside diameter at the weld as close as possible to that of the pipe. In addition, we are expected to match up the ends of the pipe perfectly and to align a piece of pipe sticking 40 ft. up in the derrick, weighing perhaps a ton, with the casing already in the hole. Bear in mind that all this must be done with the maximum possible speed."

Before the weld is cold, the slips are removed and the full length of the welded casing in the hole is suspended by the weld as the string of pipe is lowered preparatory to making the next weld. This procedure gives each weld an immediate tensile test.

Most of the discussion in the following sections of this chapter relate to the making of strength welds in the alloy steels. Some of the recommendations, of course, apply to all welds.

Fig. 13-2. The root bead can often be made with a low-hydrogen or stainless steel electrode. Staggering subsequent layers assures good slagging.

Preparing for Welding

Make sure that the surfaces to be welded are free from scale, rust, oxidized metal, grease, oil, water, etc. Check the base metal for cracks existing at the joint; alloy steel may be cracked by incorrect grinding, torch cutting, or shearing.

The U-type joint, single or double, is preferred as it gives enough room to apply and clean the first layer. It will permit use of a larger electrode on the root bead. A U-type joint, however, may be more costly to prepare and may require more weld metal. In the V-type joint, the root pass is a very narrow layer and is more subject to weld cracks as a result of shrinkage stresses. If workpieces can't be preheated, the root bead might preferably be deposited from a low-hydrogen electrode or a stainless steel electrode, which gives an even more ductile deposit (Fig. 13-2). Naturally, the wider the area filled by the first pass, the greater will be the preheating effect.

Care must normally be taken with alloy steels to control distortion. The parts may be clamped to restrain warping. This can frequently be done without taking away the ability of the plates to be pulled closer together by the weld metal as it contracts during cooling. Or, the parts may be misaligned when set up for welding, just enough to warp straight as the weld cools; or, weld metal may be applied in a sequence that will keep the work from distorting. Adopt a procedure by which the completed weld will not exceed the maximum distortion allowed.

When welds are to be made in a rigid structure, adequate provision must be made for the inevitable contraction of the weld metal and the heated parent metal as the assembly cools. The weld may not be strong enough or ductile enough to resist the shrinkage until the weldment can be stress relieved; so, expansion or contraction of a portion of the member may be necessary. On a repair job, the weld may be so located that the best procedure will be to cut a restraining member that will be simple to weld, repair the original failure, and then weld the piece which was cut.

Preheating: When and How Much

Alloy steels harden when they are heated to a high temperature and are then cooled rapidly. When these steels are welded, hardening and enbrittlement occur in the heat-affected zone parallel to the line of fusion. Unless precautions are taken, such localized hardening can be especially serious in the case of alloy steels because of the formation of multiple constituents that differ greatly in the volume change as transformation takes place. Preheating delays the cooling rate so that the parent metal near a weld will not harden excessively. Other conditions that affect the cooling rate will be discussed under the heading of "Welding Variables".

From these remarks, someone might think that preheating for the purpose of reducing the cooling rate is of value only when welding alloy steel in the soft or annealed condition. This is not so. Slowing down the cooling rate by preheating is also an important factor in preventing weld cracks caused by shrinkage stresses. Such cracks occur more frequently when welding steels in the hardened condition. A slower cooling rate permits stresses to be better distributed throughout the weld and to be partially relieved by a stretching of the weld metal while it is still hot.

Many weld failures have resulted from welding alloy steels without preheating. It is dangerous to think that the first layer of weld does the preheating for subsequent passes, and that any cracks occurring in the first layer or bead can be burned out during the second pass. It is impossible for the arc on a second pass to penetrate deep enough to melt out any cracks in the root bead.

The amount of preheating required increases with the alloying content of the base metal. Each element's influence is somewhat

Fig. 13-3. The Lincoln Welding Preheat Calculator permits weldor to quickly find the required preheat and interpass temperature.

different; 0.15% phosphorus, for example, demands as much of an increase in preheat temperature as does 1.25% copper. However, this is just about the maximum content of phosphorus you might expect to find in an alloy steel, while copper might be present in even greater ratio. Certain elements increase the hardenability of the steel; that is, the cooling rate has to be slower in order for hardening not to take place. In general, the alloying elements affect the preheating required in the following order: manganese, chromium, molybdenum, nickel, carbon, copper, silicon, vanadium, and phosphorus. The effect of these elements is cumulative.

The presence of sulphur is not considered in calculating the preheating required. Although the presence of more than 0.045% sulphur may cause "hot short" cracks, preheating does nothing to prevent this.

The "Welding Preheat Calculator," available from The Lincoln Electric Co., provides an easy, fast way to calculate the approximate preheat temperature required (Fig. 13-3). This assumes the weldor's knowing the chemical composition of the alloy he is welding.

Unless otherwise specified, the preheating temperatures recommended by the Welding Preheat Calculator and in this book and other literature apply to welds made manually with E-xx10, E-xx11,

E-xx12, E-xx13, E-xx14, E-xx20, E-xx24 and E-xx27 electrodes. The last four of these have iron-powder coatings and permit faster deposition rates. Since hardening of the parent metal is a function of time as well as temperature, a faster weld speed helps prevent excessive hardening. The benefit isn't appreciable, however, until the operation is further improved by semi-automatic or automatic method.

Submerged-arc welding combines fast travel with slower cooling under a blanket of flux and better protection against contamination that would participate in crack formation. These advantages permit preheat temperatures to be reduced by 200 to 300 degrees.

The low-hydrogen electrodes—E-xx15, E-xx16 and E-xx18—also substantially reduce the preheating required. Dry low-hydrogen electrodes are effective in preventing contamination of base and weld metal, and thus safeguard against underbead cracking. Also, they reduce the possibility of root bead cracks. These electrodes do not restrict the hardening of the parent metal unless in combination with iron-powder coatings, in which case the faster deposition rate gives less heat effect.

Tungsten-inert-gas-shielded welding also offers fast deposition and protection against underbead and weld cracking. In some cases the use of low-hydrogen electrodes, TIG welding or submerged-arc welding entirely eliminates the need for preheating.

Stainless steel electrodes of 18-8 or higher alloy content offer excellent ductility and will make crack-free welds at low preheating temperatures. However, their use may not be possible if the weld metal is required to equal the parent metal in strength.

Preheating requirements for austenitic manganese steels, the stainless steels, and tool and die steels demand special consideration. These materials are discussed separately in later chapters.

Preheating is always required when welding hardened alloy steel, but the preheat temperature must never exceed that at which the metal was previously tempered unless further heat treatment is possible. Minimum preheat temperatures are called for when use of low-hydrogen electrodes, TIG welding, or submerged-arc welding would seem to eliminate the need for preheating. The minimum preheat temperature is governed partly by atmospheric temperature and plate thickness. In general, the minimum temperature at which any hardened metal should be welded is 70 F. On plate ¾-in. thick, the minimum is 150 F. On plate 1½-in. thick, it is 300 F.

Heavier plate thicknesses always require more preheat than thin plates. Restrained welds and confined welds, such as fillets, always require more preheat than butt welds where plate ends are free to move.

It is not enough to heat the steel to the proper preheating temperature; the steel must be kept at this temperature until the weld is completed. The interpass temperature—that at any point in the joint as the arc reaches it—must be held at the same level as the preheat temperature. If the joint is a very long one and the process has relatively low heat input (as it should be when welding alloy steel), additional heating between passes may be necessary. If the joint is short or the heat input is relatively high (as with manual welding), allowing the work to cool may be necessary before making another pass.

The welding shop should be equipped for fast and economical preheating. Schedule the work so that the jobs requiring preheating can be heated by oven or hot plate while other things are being done. The oxyacetylene torch, the carbon-arc torch, or the single-carbon arc will heat metal more quickly, but these methods are more expensive and require an operator's full attention. Also, work cannot be slowly and uniformly heated by torch and, with some alloys, may damage the metal. Hardened alloys, especially, should not be preheated by torch. With good heating equipment, the "difficult-to-weld" steels are easy to weld.

For a large weldment, where local preheating would not be satisfactory, a furnace can be built around it—using fire bricks, boiler plate and sheet asbestos over the plates to keep the heat from escaping.

The exact preheat and interpass temperature required for a particular job necessarily depends on modifying the basic recommendations according to other conditions. These will be discussed under "Welding Variables".

Method for Quickly Testing for Preheat

There are occasions when it will be desirable to test a weld to make certain the preheat applied is correct. At other times, it may be necessary to establish whether any preheating is required. Or, the chemical composition of the alloy may be unknown.

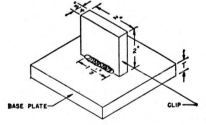

Fig. 13-4. A welded clip test specimen for determining preheat temperature required.

BASE PLATE   CLIP

There are many laboratory tests to determine the preheating temperature needed. For quick testing in the field or shop, the clip test is most satisfactory. This test was effectively used in the oil fields to show weldors the importance of preheating SAE 3140 and

SAE 4140 tool joints when welding them to the drill pipe. Sheeham of the Portsmouth Navy Yard further developed the test to provide a "spot check" suitable for use in a steel mill or a shipyard for determining the weldability of steel plate. It is described as follows: *

"The clip test will be found very useful when an unknown steel must be welded, and neither the time nor equipment are available to make a complete investigation. The test is not adaptable for thin

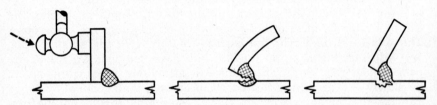

Fig. 13-5. How the clip test is made (at left). If no underbead cracks are present, failure will occur through the weld (center). The presence of underbead cracks will cause failure by "pull-out" of parent metal (right).

steel, but it can be readily used on heavy sections down to ⅜ in. thickness. Thick steel most frequently requires preheating.

"The clips or lugs to be welded onto the steel under test are low-carbon steel plates 2 or 3 in. square and ½ in. thick. The clip is fillet welded to the unknown steel as shown in Fig. 13-4. The weld is made with the size and type of electrode and the welding current and speed that will be used for the welding job. With a large electrode and slow speed, it may be in order to use a thicker clip—¾ to 1 in. thick. Allow the weld to cool for five minutes, and then break the lug off by pounding it, as in Fig. 13-5. If the lug bends and after a number of blows finally fails through the weld, the test indicates that the analysis of the steel, the temperature of the steel before welding and the welding procedure are such that serious underbead cracking is absent.

"To investigate further, the steel in question may be cooled below room temperature, say to 30-40 F and the test repeated. A failure in the weld again without pull-outs or visible cracks in the base metal will give double assurance that the steel is weldable at room temperature."

A steel that requires preheating will fail on the clip test by "pull-out" of some of the parent metal, provided a sound weld has been made. Usually the pulled-out metal is bright, showing that the crack did not extend to the surface or had not formed until after the metal had cooled below the temperature at which temper colors form.

Increase the temperature of the steel by about 200 F (if it was

*From Luther, Jackson and Hartbower. "A Review and Summary of Weldability Testing of Carbon and Low Alloy Steels". The Welding Journal, July, 1946, Supplement. See also Naval Research Laboratory Report No. M-2566 (May 1945).

at 70 F, heat it to about 270 F), and repeat the test. If the test made at 270 F pulls out the base metal, try a still higher preheat temperature.

Precautions: A fillet weld made with a concave contour is not satisfactory for this clip test, for the weld will fail too easily; the weld may fail even when underbead cracks are present.

We have recommended only a five-minute wait after welding before the lug is knocked off. A 24-hour wait will give more consistent results since five minutes is not long enough for the steel structure to change completely or for all of the cracking to take place. However, when a quick test is needed the five-minute wait is sufficiently reliable. As a safety factor, use a little higher preheat than indicated by the test.

Should the tests indicate need for a preheat temperature that is too high to be practicable for the particular welding job, use of a low-hydrogen electrode (E-6015, E-6016 or E-6018) is suggested. Make the test with the low-hydrogen electrode at a lower preheat. This electrode will produce crack-free welds at about 300 F lower preheat than is found necessary with electrodes that are not hydrogen-free.

Measuring Preheat and Interpass Temperatures

Instruments are available for measuring surface temperatures. One such instrument has a wire coil, which is placed on the work; within a few seconds the temperature may be read on the dial at the handle end of the pyrometer. Preheat temperatures, however, can be satisfactorily estimated without expensive instruments.

Several suppliers* offer materials that melt over comparatively narrow ranges of temperatures. These indicators are furnished in sticks, liquids or pellets. If a preheat temperature of, say, 400 F, is wanted, the 400 F stick is scratched over the surface of the metal; if it leaves a white line, the metal is not at 400 F. If a transparent liquid line is formed, the metal is at or above the temperature printed on the stick.

Some common items used as rough temperature indicators are listed here:

1. Blue chalk: A mark made with carpenter's blue chalk on hot metal will turn whitish gray when the metal is above 625 F.
2. Red lumber-marking crayon: Its mark melts at about 615 F. The red mark turns pink at about 635 F and turns a dirty gray at about 650 F.
3. Solder: 50-50 solder (50% lead and 50% tin) starts melting at 360 F and is completely molten at 420 F.
4. Pine stick: White pine stick chars at about 635 F (used to determine the proper pouring temperature for some babbitts).

*The Tempil Corporation; Markal Company; and Curtiss-Wright Corporation.

Another method for checking preheat temperatures is by temper colors: The temperature and accompanying color that appears on a freshly filed surface of carbon steel are given in Table 13-1.

Table 13-1. Temper Colors

TEMPERATURE, F	COLOR
400	Faint straw
440	Straw
475	Deep straw
520	Bronze
540	Peacock
590	Full blue
640	Light blue

It should be noted that the presence of alloying elements in the steel affects the colors formed, and some of the higher alloy steels have no temper colors.

Welding Variables

The choice of welding process and electrode or other welding material will be discussed after we first review some of the welding variables that affect the mechanical properties of the weld.

A few paragraphs earlier, attention was drawn to the necessity for slowing up the rate of cooling. Preheating was mentioned as the most important factor in controlling the cooling rate of metal in the heat-affected zone of the pieces welded. Table 13-2 lists all of the major factors involved in determining the cooling rate of welds.

Preheating must never be excessive. Although a high alloy content may substantially elevate the upper critical or transformation point, it has much less effect on the lower critical temperature at which point transformation begins. Preheating (of annealed metal) at temperatures approaching the critical range, excessive total heat input, or holding the metal at high temperature will have bad results. (Preheating of hardened metal must not exceed prior tempering range.) Low welding current combined with slow travel contributes to the heat problem. Overheating increases grain growth of parent metal near the weld, resulting in lower ductility and lower strength.

If the weldment is to be later heat treated by heating above the transformation range, any detrimental grain coarsening caused by welding will be reduced.

It is better to maintain preheat and interpass temperatures within recommended limits, and to use higher welding current and fast travel. These conditions permit the weld metal to cool through the transformation range at a faster rate, thereby resulting in a stronger joint.

Table 13-2. Factors Affecting Cooling of Welds

FACTORS THAT INCREASE THE COOLING RATE	FACTORS THAT DECREASE THE COOLING RATE
Cold parent metal	Hot parent metal
Heavy sections	Light sections
High speed welding (fast linear travel)	Slow speed welding (slow linear travel)
High welding current	Low welding current (when combined with slow travel)
Welds made without protective slag covering	Welds with a heavy layer of heat-insulating slag
Parent metal with a high thermal conductivity	Parent metal with a low thermal conductivity
Welds in a fillet or in a deep groove	Welds on a flat plate or on the edge of a plate or bar
Local preheating on a large member	Preheating the entire member or a large area

Heavy beads are less susceptible to stress cracking and lead to less distortion than do small beads. Also, multiple small beads that extend the length of the joint have a serious cumulative shrinkage effect. In a V-joint, for example, the greater shrinkage across the face of the weld will increase tension on the root bead and may cause it to crack. It should be noted, however, that very large beads

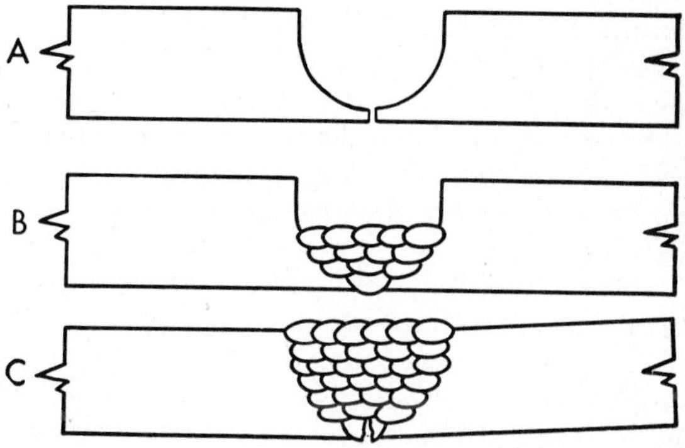

Fig. 13-6. Filling a large joint with many small beads causes accumulated shrinkage stresses, distortion, and probable cracking of the root bead.

produce a weld of lower impact strength. This effect is especially pronounced where each bead is the full width of the groove.

If the plate is heavy enough, a U-joint or a double V-joint with beads deposited alternately from both sides will help to balance the stresses and reduce the possibility of root bead cracks. Again, avoid a multiplicity of small beads that will cause high stresses to accumulate (Fig. 13-6).

Selection of Welding Process

Thin alloy steel sheets and small-diameter aircraft tubing can be welded by the oxyacetylene process, using a low-carbon steel or low-alloy steel filler rod. Making the weld thicker than the section welded increases its over-all strength relative to that of the base metal. Oxyacetylene welding, however, is usually too slow and overheats the parent metal.

High-quality joints are made economically in thin-gage alloy steel by tungsten-inert-gas (TIG) arc welding, with or without the use of filler metal. This process permits excellent concentration and control of heat. It limits total heat input, holds distortion to a minimum, and gives high-quality weld metal. When butt welding without filler metal, there should be no root opening and copper back-up bars should be used.

On heavier-gage metal, metal-inert-gas (MIG) welding may be considered, although the total cost must be carefully evaluated. Both TIG and MIG welding are readily mechanized and permit high travel speeds. They are most applicable to production shop applications. The inert-gas shielding of the arc prevents contamination from the atmosphere and discourages loss of alloying elements in gaseous compounds formed by reaction with oxygen.

Filler metals used with TIG and MIG welding are usually deoxidized low-alloy steel. These materials must be selected for good deposition qualities. They are not necessarily of the same analysis as the parent metal, but the resulting weld metal—which is filler metal plus an admixture of parent metal—must have the properties required at that point.

CO_2 MIG welding is used with some low-alloy steels. However, the composition of the shielding gas allows oxidation with some alloying elements. To some extent, balancing deoxidizers can be introduced by the filler wire to prevent porosity. In general, this process is less flexible and changing over from welding one alloy steel to welding another may radically change the quality attained.

Joints are frequently made in alloy-steel bars and tubing by resistance flash-butt welding. After heat treatment, the weld has qualities as high as those of the original steel.

The submerged-arc process (Fig. 13-7) provides maximum flexibility in the automatic or semi-automatic welding of alloy steels. This

Fig. 13-7. Submerged-arc welding of alloy steels is fast and economical. The welds produced are strong and sound. This process effectively prevents the occurrence of stress cracks and underbead cracks.

process can be used for making strength welds, for maximum-ductility welds, or for hardsurfacing. It is used in welding light- or heavy-gage materials. Standard granulated alloy fluxes are available that, used in various combinations, cover a wide range of applications. The process is readily changed over from welding one alloy steel to welding another.

In one widely used system, the agglomerated flux for submerged-arc welding is compounded by blending primary fluxes to meet the requirements of a specific class of work. Each primary flux is high in chromium, molybdenum, vanadium, or nickel, or has no alloying element. Other alloying elements can be added to the flux, but are seldom necessary. The final compounding is usually done by the supplier, but may be done by the user. The most practical way to achieve maximum economy is to use a mild-steel electrode wire and change the flux as required. In some cases, it has been desirable to use a standard stainless steel or other high-alloy electrode. Consistent weld metal composition is achieved by controlling the ratio between flux and electrode melted, and between these and the base metal that is melted.

Some applications of alloy steel (chromium-molybdenum steels for high-temperature service, for example) require weld metal having essentially the same composition as the parent metal. This requirement is easily met by adjusting the flux composition. Usually the composition of the weld metal does not need to be the same in order to have the necessary mechanical properties. In most cases, it is advisable to keep the carbon content of the weld metal less than 0.20% to help in avoiding weld cracks. This means increasing the alloy content of the flux so as to develop the yield strength, ultimate tensile strength, or other properties needed.

Where automatic welding is impractical, excellent results are obtained by shielded-metal-arc welding with manual coated electrodes. This process accounts for most field welding of the alloy steels and much of the shop welding of heavy sections (Fig. 13-8). Other processes are often more suitable for welding thin-gage sheets. A discussion of the selection of manual electrodes will best cover the application of shielded-arc welding.

Fig. 13-8. Much of the fabicating of alloy steel weldments is done with the manual coated electrodes.

Selection of Manual Electrodes

Mild-steel shielded-arc electrodes (E-60xx) may be used for one-layer welds on chromium-molybdenum steels (SAE 4130) and will give welds that compare with the strength of the normalized steel. The weld metal picks up enough carbon and alloying elements

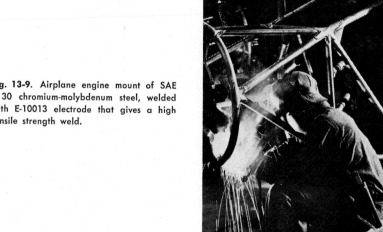

Fig. 13-9. Airplane engine mount of SAE 4130 chromium-molybdenum steel, welded with E-10013 electrode that gives a high tensile strength weld.

from the base metal to give it the better properties. After heat treatment, however, the parent metal has a higher tensile strength than the weld.

For welds that will have properties after heat treatment to compare with chromium-molybdenum steel, the higher strength E-100xx electrodes are available (Fig. 13-9). The actual tensile strength of the weld metal depends on the amount of carbon and alloy pick-up from the base metal.

In the selection of a filler material for the welding of an alloy steel, it is natural to request one that has the same chemical analysis as the metal to be welded. There are many analyses of welding rods available for oxyacetylene welding or TIG welding that can be melted to produce alloy welds that will match the base metal chemically. Shielded-metal-arc welding electrodes, however, are made in only a few alloy-steel combinations, for the following reasons:

1. It is not necessary for the filler metal to match the analysis of the parent metal in order for the weld metal to have comparable properties.
2. Satisfactory mechanical properties can be obtained with combinations of the available electrodes: using one (ductile) type for the root pass or for "buttering" and another (high strength) type for completing the fill.
3. The selected alloys result in weld metal of higher properties than can be obtained with other alloys.
4. Electrodes would be much more expensive if it were necessary to manufacture and stock an electrode to match chemically each type of alloy steel.

Fortunately, none of the alloys used in alloy steels and in the electrodes for welding them are "poison" to each other. (We are not including the austenitic stainless and high-manganese steels, which will be discussed in subsequent chapters.) An electrode that deposits a high-tensile molybdenum steel alloy may be used to weld a nickel steel alloy; that part of the weld metal that alloys with the nickel steel will have properties that compare favorably with both the parent metal and with the deposited metal that is not appreciably alloyed.

On some welded and machined parts, the weld is required to have the same color and finish as the base metal. One might think that the chemical analysis of the weld metal must be the same as the parent metal. This, however, is not always the case; if the two steels are similar in hardness, they very often will be similar in color and in surface finish.

Alloys used in high-tension welding electrodes must have superior welding properties. Molybdenum, for instance, is one of the best alloying elements for welding electrode core wire. Very little of the molybdenum combines with the slag and little is lost by oxidation. The molybdenum steels have a good combination of ductility and strength throughout the temperature range from solidification down to room temperature.

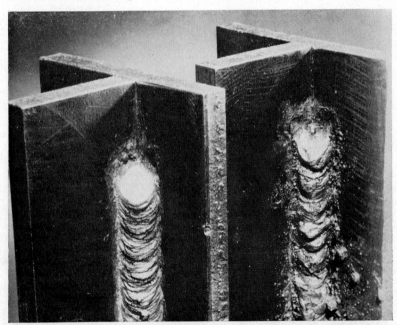

Fig. 13-10. When too high a welding current is used in vertical arc welding alloy steels, the fillet will have the appearance of the one on the right. The desired appearance of the finished fillet is on the left.

In contrast, some alloy steels when cooling from the molten state have low ductility at certain temperatures. If the steel is held in a manner that prevents free contraction in this brittle range, hot cracks develop. Certain nickel-alloy steels are unsatisfactory for use in electrodes because of a hot cracking tendency as the weld shrinks during cooling. For this reason, molybdenum-steel rods are much better for welding SAE 3140 steel (chromium-nickel) than chromium-nickel rods; this applies to both gas and shielded-arc welding.

To conclude this section on electrode selection, choose one of the low-alloy electrodes: E-70xx, E-80xx, E-90xx, E-100xx, E-110xx, or E-120xx. It is important to have as much ductility in the weld as possible. The lowest strength electrode that meets strength requirements will provide maximum ductility in the weld.

The low-hydrogen electrodes (E-xx15, E-xx16 and E-xx18) are preferred, particularly where experience with other electrodes has been unsatisfactory due to underbead or weld cracking.

Frequently, the first layer in the bottom of the "V" or "U" is deposited with a lower alloy electrode than is used for the balance of the weld. It has been mentioned before that the first layer or bead has its carbon and alloy content appreciably increased by admixture of the parent metal. This procedure will give the first layer or bead about the same strength and hardness as the rest of the weld, and also will reduce the possibility of the first bead's cracking. In this manner the weld will be more ductile than if a high-tensile type electrode had been used throughout.

In welding some of the higher-carbon, low-alloy steels it may be desirable to deposit the first layer or root bead from a lower-strength, low-hydrogen electrode or a stainless steel electrode and then complete the fill with a higher-strength electrode.

Heat-Treated High-Carbon Alloy Steels

Don't become too enthusiastic and think that any steel can be welded without heat treatment and still end up with a weld job that has all the properties of the original metal. A broken automobile leaf spring may be welded and reinforced so that it will not fail, but it will not have the flexibility of the original spring. If it is welded without reinforcement, neither the weld nor the base metal near the weld will have the same high yield strength as the original.

It is possible, but not practical, to machine or grind the weld to the thickness of the spring leaf and then heat treat it so that the welded portion has the strength and springiness of a new spring.

When a repair of this nature must be made, do not try to duplicate the original properties. Instead, weld with an austenitic stainless-steel electrode and build up the weld enough to compensate for the lower yield point of the stainless steel. Since a minimum amount of preheat will be required, the amount of tempering of the metal on each side of the weld will also be at a minimum.

Stainless-steel electrodes provide a solution to many a welding problem involving high-carbon plain or high-carbon alloy steels. When the steel to be welded is prone to crack or seems to be full of gas, a thin first bead of stainless steel may be deposited using a technique that will give low penetration. The weld can then be complete successfully with a high-tensile electrode.

Among very-high-carbon alloy steels, SAE 52100 steel (carbon 0.95-1.10%; chromium 1.20-1.50%) is often classed as being not weldable. But we can weld it, provided service conditions are not too severe. SAE 52100 to be used in leaf springs has been rolled and forged to improve its mechanical properties in the direction the steel is stressed, and has been given the ideal heat treatment for the job.

In welding this steel, we have to deposit a metal that will have properties like the parent metal. The desired properties in the fusion zone must be achieved without adversely affecting the properties of the base metal in the heat-affected zone. Can we do it by preheat? No, because the preheating necessary to prevent undue hardening and embrittling of the heat-affected metal is higher than the temperature used for tempering hardened springs. High preheating will soften the spring and destroy its original properties.

We may compromise with one of the following procedures:

1. Use a low preheat, 200-250 F, and weld with a 25-20 stainless-steel electrode. The weld metal will not be as strong as the original metal, and there will be a hardened and brittle zone at the edge of the weld, but the spring can be used for loads up to a third or perhaps half of what it could take before.

2. Use high-tensile low-hydrogen electrode E-11016 or E-11018, preheating the work to about 400 F. After welding, heat and hand forge the weld; then give the job a complete spring heat treatment. The heat-affected zone will have the original properties, but the weld will not have enough carbon to have the hardness or yield strength of the base metal.

Heat-Treated Alloy Steels

Some of the low-alloy high-strength steels are normally welded in the heat-treated condition and are placed in service without further heat treatment unless stress relieving is essential. These steels come from the mill as heat-treated materials and are not annealed except under unusual circumstances. The weldability of these materials, which have low carbon content, is far superior to that of the heat-treated high-carbon alloy steels like SAE 52100.

T-1 is one of the most widely used steels in the low-alloy, high-strength group. In many applications of T-1, the full properties of the metal are needed throughout the section. To match the physical properties of the parent metal, the weld metal must develop a minimum yield point of 90,000 psi and a minimum ultimate tensile strength of 105,000 psi without the benefit of heat treatment. Also, the weld metal must have good impact properties at low temperatures in both the as-welded and stress-relieved conditions. Filler materials are selected to produce weld metal to meet these requirements rather than duplicate the parent metal composition. It is desirable to hold the carbon content to a very low percentage, and to obtain the needed strength by increasing other alloying elements.

Manual welding of this class steel is best done with a low-hydrogen electrode of highest strength, E-11018. In automatic submerged-arc welding, a mild steel electrode is used with alloy flux that is high in chromium and molybdenum content. MIG welding is used to lesser extent, largely because of the premium-priced alloy steel electrode that is used.

Regardless of the welding process used, avoid softening of the parent metal in the heat-affected zone. Also, take care to prevent a high build-up of internal stresses. Preheating is necessary, regardless of what other measures are taken. Preheating must be high enough to assist in slowing up the cooling rate after welding, and to relieve shrinkage stresses. However, preheating must not exceed the previous tempering of the parent metal. T-1 does not lose any appreciable hardness if temperatures exceed the prior tempering point or even the critical point momentarily, but the total heat input must be restricted so as to not risk any loss of the metal's high initial property values.

Preparation of joint surfaces by oxyacetylene torch should be done carefully, to avoid overheating the metal. When possible, use a combination of groove width and electrode diameter that permits stacking one bead over another.

Beads should be deposited in a straight-line so that the full heat of the arc does not dwell at any point along the groove. Weaving the bead from side to side puts too much heat into the parent metal. It is better to use multiple stringer beads, but be sure to let the temperature between passes drop back to the preheat level. Also, remember that shrinkage stresses resulting from deposit of each bead tend to accumulate. All the previously-discussed recommendations for achieving sound welds on alloy steels should be observed.

On multiple-pass welds or when the weldment will be later stress-relieved or otherwise heat treated, do not use electrodes or alloy fluxes that contain vanadium.

Review Questions

1. What properties of alloy steels make special welding procedure necessary? Are there any alloy steels that cannot be welded?
2. How can underbead cracking be detected by inspecting a weld?
3. Name some alloy-steel welding jobs that do not require welds

as strong as the steel.

4. What procedure can be used to weld a medium-carbon alloy steel without preheating?

5. Maximum hardening of steel occurs when the steel has been heated above the transformation temperature and then quickly cooled. Through what temperature range is it necessary that the steel be quickly cooled to secure maximum hardness:

From transformation temperature to room temperature?

From 1300 to 1200 F?

From 1100 to 900 F?

6. Name some methods for measuring the preheating temperature of steel.

7. Describe the "clip test" for weldability.

8. Which of the following variables will decrease the hardening of the parent metal near a weld:

Fast travel speed or slow travel speed?

Welding with a small electrode or welding with a large electrode?

Welding in a deep groove or welding on a flat plate?

High preheat or low preheat?

9. When welding heat-treated alloy steels, what is wrong with weaving a bead?

10. Why are low-hydrogen electrodes preferred for most manual welding of alloy steels?

CHAPTER 14

WELDING CAST IRON

It is unfortunate that the name "cast iron" refers to such a wide variety of products. Some are rough, brittle and weak castings: window sash weights, for example, or counterweights for elevators and washing machines, and large housings where neither strength nor appearance is of great importance. Others are strong, high-quality castings: railroad wheels, crankshafts, cylinder blocks, fan and pulley hubs, and apparatus for use under conditions of severe heat, corrosion or fluid pressure. Many of these castings are made by precision molding processes capable of holding extremely close tolerances and with little or no surface scale.

Some of the castings are made by merely pouring the molten iron into a sand mold, depending upon gravity and the fluidity of the hot metal to carry it into all extremities of the mold. Other castings (of relatively small size) are turned over and over during the pouring of molten iron so as to eliminate internal cavities of any kind.

The characteristics for which gray cast iron is best known are especially pronounced in the lower-strength range (20,000-30,000 psi ultimate tensile strength). A typical gray iron of 20,000 psi tensile strength may have compressive strength of 80,000 psi; however, its impact properties are quite low. The modulus of elasticity in tension will be 10 to 14 million psi, only slightly more than $\frac{1}{3}$ that of any steel. Higher strength gray irons have improved rigidity, but even a grade of 60,000 psi tensile strength will only have a modulus of 20 to 24 million psi. Regardless of the grade, the yield point of gray cast iron is virtually the same as its ultimate tensile strength and elongation cannot be measured by methods that are conventional for steel. Elongation is considered to be in the neighborhood of 0.006 in./in. This nearly complete lack of ductility is one of the major reasons why gray iron is difficult to weld.

Gray cast iron is usually said to have good machinability. It is, however, a very abrasive material. In the case of sand castings, the sand inclusions at the outer surfaces of the casting are especially destructive to cutting tools. Ultra-hard chill spots are also commonly encountered. Gray cast iron can seldom be economically machined at speeds over 300 surface feet per minute. Most steels are commonly machined at substantially higher speeds, and at higher rates of metal removal.

If needed, a high-alloy cast iron with tensile strength as high as 120,000 psi can be obtained. Other quality cast irons are so distinctive they are seldom referred to as such. Malleable iron and nodular iron, for example, are not very often called cast irons by the people who use them. However, these are all premium-priced materials.

Despite the advancements made in casting processes and metallurgy, all-steel weldments are making substantial inroads in competition with iron castings. This is especially true in medium and large size products. Some advantages of all-steel weldments over cast iron are high strength-to-weight ratio, excellent rigidity, good dimensional stability without extensive aging, ease of field erection, lower shipping costs, and simplified repair. These advantages of steel usually add up to lower total cost, especially in competition with the premium-priced malleable irons, nodular irons and alloyed cast irons. Even so, cast iron is still important to design engineers and is used to advantage in many products.

What Is Cast Iron?

Cast iron is an alloy of iron, carbon and silicon. The carbon content is usually between 2.0 and 4.0%, and the silicon 0.90 to 2.80%. (Silicon content in the white irons range much lower.) All cast irons have more carbon than can be dissolved in the austenite when the alloy is heated above the transformation temperature. This excess carbon is present as graphite in gray iron, and as cementite (iron carbide) in white cast iron. When these materials are cooled to room temperature, the carbon remains in the same condition—as graphite or cementite.

Other elements commonly present in cast iron include sulphur, usually from 0.05 to 0.80%; phosphorus, from 0.07 to 0.60%; and manganese, from 0.50 to 1.00%. The elements copper, nickel, aluminum, titanium, vanadium, molybdenum, chromium and magnesium are added to provide special properties to certain grades. The addition of magnesium gives members of a major class of cast irons, the nodular or ductile irons, ductility ranging from 2-7% elongation for the high-strength grades (120,000 psi tensile) to 10-25% elongation for the lower-strength grades (60,000 psi tensile). Even these figures do not compare with steel. Hot-rolled SAE 1045 steel with an ultimate tensile strength of 120,000 psi has 10% minimum elongation, and hot-rolled SAE 1021 with an ultimate tensile strength of 61,000 psi features 24% minimum elongation.

Types of Cast Iron

Gray cast iron—contains carbon in the pearlite structure and as graphite flakes. Pearlite is a laminated arrangement of ferrite (pure iron) and cementite (iron carbide). The microstructure (Fig. 14-1) reveals areas of ferrite, pearlite, and the flakes of graphite or pure carbon. The properties of the gray iron vary with the amount, size and shape of the graphite and with the relative amounts of pearlite

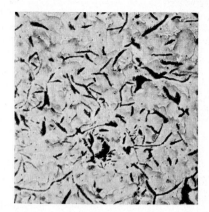

Fig. 14-1. The microstructure of gray cast iron reveals areas of ferrite, pearlite and flakes of graphite (pure carbon).

and ferrite. Slow cooling and a silicon content of from 1.0 to 3.0% cause the carbon atoms that do not form pearlite to precipitate (to separate during transformation, and gather) as flakes of graphite.

The carbon in solution, as in pearlite, is often referred to as *combined carbon*. The carbon in graphitic form is called *free carbon*. The ratio of combined carbon to free carbon greatly affects mechanical properties of the alloy. The lower the ratio, the lower the hardness.

Silicon in gray cast iron serves several purposes. Some of the silicon that is added to the charge in the casting furnace acts as a deoxidizer. Most importantly, silicon promotes a higher ratio of graphite and limits the possibility of a hard, brittle surface layer of chilled iron. Phosphorus is usually present as an impurity but also helps to remove hydrogen. Also, it is valuable in achieving fusibility and fluidity in the molten metal. It lessens the problem of shrinkage during solidification, since without it hydrogen causes a condition called *wormholing*.

Silicon and phosphorus affect the distribution of carbon and the influence of carbon content on the alloy's hardness and strength. The term *carbon equivalent** is used by ferrous metallurgists to represent this. The carbon equivalent is assumed to be the total carbon content plus about one-third of the total silicon and phosphorus content. In general, the tensile strength of cast iron increases as the carbon equivalent decreases. Thus, those cast irons with the least carbon have properties closer to those of the high-carbon steels.

In lowering the carbon equivalent in the higher-strength cast irons, the silicon and phosphorus content is lowered enough to help raise the ratio of combined carbon to free carbon. This means that the hardness is increased as well as the tensile strength. Low carbon and low silicon content are associated with a fine pearlite and fine

*The term "carbon equivalent" has another and different meaning which is more commonly used by welding engineers. See the listing of new words at end of this chapter for an explanation of the difference.

graphite structure, which contributes to the high physical properties achieved. Too slow a cooling rate causes grain growth which weakens the composition.

Since the relation between carbon, silicon and phosphorus is an extremely complex one, the most common way for engineers to specify gray cast iron is by ASTM* class number. This ranges from 20 through 60. The principal requirement is a minimum tensile strength equal to the class number multiplied by 1000. Class 20 gray cast iron is thus required to have at least 20,000 psi tensile strength.

The free carbon in the form of graphite flakes gives the gray cast irons their characteristic good machinability. All gray cast irons are hardenable by proper heat treatment, and the hardness can be more than doubled in this way.

Alloy cast irons—are numerous and have varied properties. By proper alloying, one or more of the following properties may be improved: tensile strength, strength at elevated temperatures, machinability, wear resistance, depth of hardening, fatigue resistance, corrosion resistance, and many others. Alloy combinations called *inoculants* cause the graphite to separate in shapes that give the iron higher mechanical properties. The inoculant forms nuclei for separation of the graphite as the cast metal solidifies, resulting in fine and well distributed graphite instead of the larger and weakening graphite flakes in the more common cast irons.

Nodular iron—also called "ductile iron," is produced by the addition of magnesium and/or cerium. These alloying elements cause the carbon to precipitate as tiny balls or spheres of graphite within a matrix that is basically pearlite, although usually some ferrite and some free cementite are also present. These higher-priced irons possess higher tensile strength and greater ductility than the plain gray cast irons. They also have excellent machinability, shock resistance, thermal shock resistance, and rigidity.

White cast iron—is so called because the fracture has a light color (gray cast iron has a dark fracture resulting from the free graphite). White cast iron has no free graphite; all of its carbon is combined as cementite or as pearlite, a laminated structure of cementite and ferrite. Because it has no free carbon, white cast iron is hard, brittle, very difficult to machine, and impractical to weld.

A low silicon content and rapid cooling together prevent the formation of graphite. Both white iron and chilled iron are used to a limited extent where high abrasion or wear resistance is essential.

Chilled iron—has a chemical composition very similar to gray iron, but a lower silicon content. It is made by casting against a chilled iron surface, which quickly freezes the outer molten metal and creates a thick surface zone of extremely hard white iron free from graphitic

---

*ASTM is the abbreviation for American Society for Testing Materials.

carbon. To the inside of this zone, the casting has a typical gray iron structure. The contact surfaces of mine car wheels, for instance, may have a ½ in. of white iron for wear resistance with the rest of the wheel being of less-brittle gray iron structure. The chill zone can be narrowed, when necessary, by a slight increase in silicon content.

Malleable iron—is made by heating white cast iron for a long time below the critical temperature. The cementite (iron carbide) then decomposes, leaving a structure of ferrite and nodules of graphite. The impact strength of malleable iron is low, but higher than that of white or gray cast iron. Other mechanical properties approach those of some low-carbon steels. Tensile strength is typically 30,000 to 53,000 psi. When welded, malleable iron tends to develop a very brittle layer of carbon-free iron.

The normal base structure of malleable iron is ferrite, which is why this metal is sometimes called "ferritic malleable iron." By a variation in the processing, but with the same chemical composition, an appreciable amount of combined carbon can be developed in the form of pearlite, martensite, and spherical carbides distributed through the ferrite. Since pearlite is the dominant constituent in this type of malleable iron, the term "pearlitic malleable iron" is used. The tensile strength of this material ranges from 60,000 to 100,000 psi.

This leads us to a generalized statement of fact: the structures of cast irons of the same chemical composition may vary greatly. A specific carbon-iron-silicon alloy can be either white cast iron, intermediate (malleable) iron, or gray cast iron, depending on the rate of cooling. As an example, if the carbon is 3% and the silicon 2%, all

Table 14-1. Changes in Cast Iron Caused by Varying Heat Cycle
(Same chemical composition: 3% C, 2% Si)

COOLING RATE	KIND OF IRON	STRUCTURE	PROPERTIES
Fast	White iron	Pearlite	Hard and brittle, too hard to machine
Moderately fast	Mottled iron (mixed white and gray)	Pearlite Cementite Graphite	Stronger than white iron, hard to machine
Moderate	Gray iron (fine graphite)	Pearlite Graphite	Best high strength irons, machinable
Moderately slow	Medium gray iron	Pearlite Ferrite Graphite	Fair strength, easy machining, fair finish
Slow	Gray iron (coarse graphite)	Ferrite Graphite	Low strength, open grain, machines soft

cast iron types listed in Table 14-1 are possible, even though the range of typical chemical composition within each cast iron classification is significantly different.

Welding Cast Iron

When iron castings break, they can often be repaired . . . usually by welding. The specific structure and properties of cast iron depend greatly on the heat-cooling cycle. It is important to first know what kind of cast iron is to be welded before selecting an appropriate welding procedure.

Basically, the welding procedures for cast iron are designed to restrict penetration to the minimum required for fusion. They prevent or minimize the transformation of parent metal into an undesirable structure. Preheating of the base metal must be employed when possible, followed by controlled cooling. All welding of cast iron requires the addition of filler metal to accomplish a strong joint. Most of the manual welding processes that deposit filler metal can be used in welding cast iron. See Table 14-2 for summary of process application.

If preheating can be used, the preheat temperature for shielded-arc welding should be held between 500 and 1200 F; however, any amount of preheat is better than none at all. When oxyacetylene welding, a higher preheat temperature is required, usually 900-1200 F. The critical temperature of most cast irons, the point at which changes occur leading to excessive cracking, is about 1450 F. For this reason, the preheat temperature must never be allowed to reach 1400 F and any heat from the welding operation exceeding this should be limited to as narrow a zone as possible.

The preheat should be applied uniformly to the entire part and maintained as well as possible until the weld metal has cooled to that temperature. Then, the entire structure should be cooled slowly to room temperature. With malleable iron and ductile iron, it may be necessary to slow up the cooling by covering the welded casting with asbestos or other insulating materials.

If preheating is not used, the welding procedure must keep the casting as cool as possible. For all practical purposes, only shielded metal-arc welding with steel electrodes can be used when gray iron castings cannot be preheated. A high percentage of all repair jobs on heavy machinery falls into this category. Multi-bead welds are usually employed on cast iron and are essential when the work is not preheated.

Weld groove preparation has a role in the successful welding of cast iron. The method selected must not generate sufficient heat to transform the cast iron; at least not for any appreciable depth. This eliminates the use of flame cutting, which is difficult to do on cast iron anyway and leaves a ragged edge. The use of grinding for groove preparation is limited because on graphitic iron structures it tends to smear the graphite. Thus, machining, chipping or sawing is preferred.

The "open" structure of cast iron allows it to soak up liquids. The surfaces to be welded can be cleaned with a suitable solvent. However, preheating drives out oil and water and most contaminants. Some cast irons are gassy, and the preheating causes some of the gas to escape thereby improving the weld.

Table 14-2. Cast-Iron Welding Procedures Summary

CAST-IRON TYPE	PROCEDURE	TREATMENT	PROPERTIES
Gray iron	Weld with cast iron	Preheat and cool slowly	Same as original
Gray iron	Braze weld	Preheat and cool slowly	Weld better; heat-affected zone as good as original
Gray iron	Braze weld	No preheat	Weld better; parent metal hardened
Gray iron	Weld with steel	Preheat if at all possible	Weld better; parent metal may be too hard to machine; if not preheated, needs to be welded intermittently to avoid cracking
Gray iron	Weld with steel around studs in joint	No preheat	Joint as strong as original
Gray iron	Weld with nickel	Preheat preferred	Joint as strong as original; thin hardened zone; machinable
Malleable iron	Weld with cast iron	Preheat, and postheat to repeat malleableizing treatment	Good weld, but slow and costly
Malleable iron	Weld with bronze	Preheat	As strong, but heat-affected zone not as ductile as original
White cast iron	Welding not recommended		
Nodular iron	Weld with nickel	Preheat preferred; postheat preferred	Joint strong and ductile, but some loss of original properties; machinable; all qualities lower in absence of preheat and/or postheat

Welding Gray Iron with Cast-Iron Filler

Gray cast iron is produced by allowing the molten iron to cool slowly in the molds. This offers a useful hint for the welding procedure: allow the welded assembly to cool slowly. Welds duplicating the properties of the parent metal can be made by preheating the gray iron casting (or castings), depositing molten cast iron in the groove, and then allowing the assembly to cool slowly.

The cast-iron filler metal can be deposited from welding rods using the oxyacetylene process, or from coated electrodes using the shielded metal-arc process. Welding with cast-iron filler is substantially a recasting process and is capable of high quality welds. However, it is expensive and time-consuming. A higher preheat (to 1350 F) is advisable so that the cast-iron weld metal can be cooled slowly through a wider temperature range.

Slow cooling is required to obtain a soft graphitic cast-iron weld. Fast cooling produces white cast iron which, once formed, cannot be transformed except by remelting. When making long, heavy welds, elaborate preparations are necessary (1) to obtain sufficient preheating to reduce stresses caused by contraction of the weld metal, and (2) to ensure the weldment's cooling at a slow enough rate.

The welding rods or electrodes must be high in silicon in order to produce a deposit of graphite and ferrite that will be readily machinable. Oxyacetylene welding of cast iron requires a neutral or slightly carburizing flame. The flux is usually applied by dip coating the welding rod.

Fig. 14-2. A shielded metal-arc weld made on a cast iron cylinder head.

Welding Gray Iron with Steel Electrodes

Good, ductile welds can be made with a coated mild steel electrode (ESt), using the shielded metal-arc process. See Fig. 14-2. The electrode designed especially for welding cast iron gives a very low carbon deposit. The electrode coating allows the use of low welding current, thereby minimizing the penetration needed when welding cast iron.

The weld metal resulting from use of this type electrode is dense, tough, and stronger than the casting itself. Its machinability is poor; therefore, when the final weldment is to be machined, a nickel-based electrode should be used.

When preheating the entire casting to over 500 F, arc welding with the steel electrode is quick, economical, and produces good results. The previously-mentioned pointers on groove preparation and preheating should be followed. The joint is filled by making straight, continuous, parallel stringer beads.

Fig. 14-3. When a large iron casting cannot be preheated, shielded-arc welding may be used to successfully repair the casting.

When impractical to preheat the entire casting because of size, location or other reason, the welding procedure must be modified to ensure good welds. See Fig. 14-3. Preheating only the joint area of an iron casting causes severe internal stresses and is poor practice. Where the entire casting cannot be preheated, the recommended welding procedure keeps the base metal as cool as possible. (That is, close to room temperature.) It is especially important to make certain that surfaces to be welded are well cleaned. This can be done by heating the surfaces with a torch to about 500 F and then allowing them to cool completely before welding.

When hot molten steel is deposited on a large cold casting, the steel shrinks more than the (only locally-heated) cast iron during cooling. This causes a residual stress in both the weld metal and the base metal. Sooner or later, something has to give, particularly when weld beads are long. Since the cast iron is weaker, the tendency is for the casting to crack or fracture just back of the line of fusion.

Remember, gray iron is rich in carbon in the form of graphite. During welding, the metal deposited on the cast iron picks up carbon from it. The weld metal can thus end up being high-carbon steel, which is extremely hard when cooled quickly. Cracking of this hardened weld metal is a natural result. As a second result of this carbon pick-up, there is less carbon near the surface of the base metal. Some of the remaining carbon goes into solution or is combined, while some of the iron forms martensite.

As explained in Chapter 8, martensite is the hardest constituent of a ferrous material and its formation is dependent on a rapid rate of cooling. Martensite forms at about 300 F during a rapid fall of temperature. When the casting is not preheated, the cold mass of metal outside of the immediate welding area draws off the heat and thereby has a quenching effect.

Excessive martensite and excessive tensile stresses resulting from shrinkage of long heavy weld beads provide a situation very susceptible to cracking and fracture. However, this is not as hopeless as it may sound. Successful welds can be made. But care is needed to keep to a minimum the (a) stresses from contraction of the weld metal

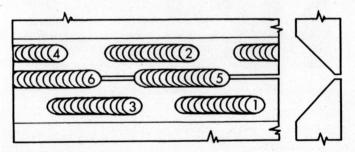

Fig. 14-4. A sequence of short weld beads will help avoid excessive cumulative stresses. When cool, beads in line should be joined by welding in same direction, ending the connecting bead on top of the start of a previous bead.

as it cools, (b) pick-up of carbon by the weld metal, and (c) rate of cooling.

One way to reduce the cumulative effect of the stresses from shrinkage of weld metal is to deposit narrow beads in short lengths (about 3 in.). Each length of bead should be allowed to cool for 3 to 5 minutes, or until it can be touched by bare hand, before another deposit is made within the area heated by the first bead. While one bead is cooling, others are deposited at scattered points throughout the joint (Fig. 14-4). All weld craters must be filled. Whenever possible, this is facilitated through ending a bead by blending its crater into the start of a previously deposited bead. All beads should be deposited in the same direction. Ends of adjacent parallel beads should not line up with each other.

Another method is to lightly peen a deposited bead of weld metal while it is still hot. This stretches the weld metal so as to help compensate for the shrinkage that occurs during cooling. The peened metal is then allowed to cool before another bead is deposited near it.

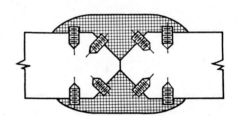

Fig. 14-5. Cross-section through a typical stud-reinforced joint when welding where preheat is impractical and maximum strength is required across the weld.

By using a low welding current, minimum peneration, and a small-diameter electrode and depositing multiple narrow beads, only the lower layer of weld metal has a very high carbon content. It is very hard, tends to be brittle, and has poor machinability. Subsequent layers of weld metal tend to temper and reduce hardness of this first layer but the weldment should be annealed if it must be machined.

Studding the joint provides additional tensile strength when needed (Fig. 14-5). This practice is followed only in cases where preheating is impractical and where the heavy cast members being welded are completely restrained from moving as the weld metal contracts.

The first requirement is to open a wide V along the crack or line of intersecting surfaces to be welded. The casting is thus drilled and tapped along the V so that studs may be screwed into the casting to a depth equal to their diameter. The studs should project about $\frac{3}{16}$ to ¼ in. above the surface into which they are mounted. The cross-sectional area of the studs is usually 25 to 35% of the weld surface area in order to be effective.

One or two beads are first deposited around each stud, providing fusion with both steel stud and iron casting. The complete groove is then filled, following the procedure previously described for gray iron when preheating is impractical.

The repair of the fractured cast iron end frame of a large bending brake is a typical application for repair by shielded metal-arc welding, using steel electrode and the studding procedure. This is illustrated by Figs. 14-6, 7 and 8.

Fig. 14-6. Badly-cracked cast iron end frame of a heavy bending brake.

Fig. 14-7. Here the crack has been V'd out, drilled and tapped and some studs are in place.

Fig. 14-8. Welding with a steel electrode designed for cast iron has completed the repair of the press brake.

Fig. 14-9. Cast iron repairs with non-ferrous electrodes permit easy drilling and tapping of finished welds.

Welding with Nickel Electrodes

The use of non-ferrous electrodes solves one of the metallurgical problems involved in welding cast iron. Non-ferrous alloys do not harden appreciably when deposited on cast-iron base metal, because they do not pick up carbon from the casting. The welds are therefore machinable. However, there is some hardening of the cast iron adjacent to the line of fusion, just as when welding with steel electrode. This results from the quenching effect of the surrounding mass of metal which is at a much lower temperature. Preheating to above 500 F will help to reduce the problem.

One of the non-ferrous electrodes widely used is a coated nickel and iron electrode for shielded-arc welding. Because of its soft, machinable welds and light penetration, it is used extensively for correcting machining errors, filling up defects and repairing cast iron parts which must be drilled, tapped or machined. See Fig. 14-9. Two or more layers of weld metal are desirable.

The hardened base metal at the fusion zone is usually machinable. Some softening of this zone is possible by tempering. Welding is sometimes used to accomplish this tempering. After the weld is completed, the part should be cooled to below 200 F so that the austenite will have time to transform. Then another layer of weld metal is applied on the non-ferrous deposit, keeping away from the cast iron. This will temper any hardened metal close enough to the surface to be encountered during machining.

Braze Welding Gray Cast Iron

Gray iron castings are also braze welded, using either bronze filler rods or coated bronze electrodes. Arc welding can be used; but, if arc welding equipment is available, the preference is usually given to steel or nickel electrodes. Most braze welding is done by the oxyacetylene process. Preheating should be used when possible, and especially if the weld is to be later machined.

The amount of preheat does not need to be up to a dull red as when cast-iron filler metal is deposited. Neither does the weld need to cool as slowly, for it does not hurt the bronze to cool fast. A preheat of about 900 F is best, even though the bronze filler metal has a low melting point. If the casting's temperature is too low, the filler metal does not flow properly through the joint. If temperature of the casting is too high, the bronze filler collects in globules, which are blown out by the flame or arc. Since bronze melts at a much lower temperature than cast iron, the parent metal will not require the extreme slow cooling to render it machinable. However, this does not mean it can be cooled quickly.

When you braze weld gray cast iron, guard against overheating or melting the parent metal. In oxyacetylene welding, use flux and direct the flame against the cast iron just long enough to get the bronze to flow over or "tin" the surface. In metal-arc welding, start the arc on deposited bronze and let it play on the parent metal just long enough to get the bronze to adhere. Penetration is not necessary; surface adhesion is adequate.

If the bronze fails to "tin" the cast iron, the joint has not been properly prepared. Joint surfaces on carbon steels are commonly prepared by grinding. But grinding a gray cast iron tends to smear the graphite over the metal surface. This graphite interferes with brazing; the graphite layer must be broken through or removed to allow the bronze to adhere to the metallic portion of the iron (the ferrite). When the iron doesn't tin, sandblast the ground surfaces or prepare by chipping.

The braze weld in gray iron is usually stronger and is more ductile than the parent metal. Welds tested in tension should fail at the junction of the bronze and the iron, at a stress equal to the tensile strength of the iron.

A braze weld does not make a good color match with the cast iron. In some applications, this is a real disadvantage. Gray cast iron that will be exposed to service temperatures of 500 F or higher should not be braze welded. Also, if the casting is oil-soaked or is badly burned as the result of service conditions or flame cutting, braze welding should not be used.

Welding Malleable Iron

Malleable iron will revert to white iron if it is heated above the transformation temperature. The graphite, which separated during the long, low-temperature heating, will dissolve above the critical temperature and will produce the brittle cementite as the metal cools to room temperature. Any type of welding that melts the parent metal will produce a brittle zone. Preheating is required; but, if too high a preheat is used, the brittle zone will be wide.

The malleable iron part may be welded with a cast-iron welding rod, followed by an annealing and prolonged cooling to restore the original malleable structure. This is called a *malleablizing* treatment. An easier way is to braze weld. Bronze melts at such a low temperature that the iron is not heated enough or long enough to form much cementite. The casting should be preheated to 900 F.

Metal-arc welding with coated bronze electrodes is one arc-welding method recommended for malleable iron. The mild-steel and nickel-base electrodes that are used to weld gray iron melt at a higher temperature than the bronze and would result in appreciable embrittlement of the parent metal. Whether you arc or gas weld, avoid melting of the base metal. Work the bronze up to the side of the joint, allowing it to "sweat" onto the iron.

Welding White Cast Iron

Fortunately, white cast irons seldom require welding. For one reason, they are normally used where the stresses are low. They may be welded with a white-iron welding rod when necessary, but any other welding is not advisable. White iron is a metal with very poor weldability.

Iron castings with chilled or white-iron surfaces are equally difficult to weld. A chilled iron roll can be built up by metal-arc welding, using a coated steel electrode. The first layer will be cracked and porous and the second layer not much better; the holes and cracks will have disappeared in the third and fourth layers. However, the result will be a shrunk-on steel ring or cylinder, not a surfacing truly welded to the chilled iron roll.

How to Weld Nodular Iron

Careful procedures can produce strong, ductile welded joints in nodular (ductile) cast iron, although a simpler weld will frequently be sufficient even though it doesn't have the same properties. The ductility of a nodular iron depends largely on the rate of cooling and any after-casting heat treatment to which it is subjected. The term "ductile iron" therefore refers more to a capability of the particular alloy than to the actual property under all conditions of application. A nodular iron, as applied, may have a relatively low ductility.

As in any welding operation, the base metal should be prepared by cleaning off oil, grease and other foreign materials. Also, the casting "skin" should be removed by grinding or other suitable means.

If maximum strength and ductility are desired after welding, it is desirable that the welding be done on fully annealed metal. However, this is not always necessary.

The heat of welding results in a zone in the base metal containing hard, brittle crystals of martensite and large carbide crystals. These lower both machinability and ductility of the casting. There is an associated tendency to the development of cracks along the fusion line. The speed of depositing metal and the minimum penetration obtainable with metal-arc welding help to limit the width of this critical zone.

Nodular iron of a low manganese and low nickel content is less likely to crack along the fusion line than highly alloyed nodular iron. The less-common pearlitic nodular irons transform more readily into martensite and hard carbides, cracking more frequently during the welding process. Fortunately these alloys are seldom used in applications that necessitate welding.

Preheating to 500-600 F when arc welding, or 900-1000 F when gas welding, decreases the cooling rate, limits the formation of martensite, and helps eliminate underbead cracking. The entire casting should be preheated, and this heat maintained during welding.

Shielded metal-arc welding, using a coated electrode of approximately 60% nickel and 40% iron, is the most satisfactory way to weld nodular iron. When starting to weld ductile iron, it is helpful to "butter" the casting surfaces before starting to lay the beads. The welding current should be as low as possible, yet sufficient to produce a good bead contour when welding in the flat position. For welding in other positions or when a high preheat is used, the welding current should be reduced.

When castings are not preheated, intermittent welding to distribute the heat is advisable. Peening of the bead while still hot will help to reduce tensile stresses. Refer back to previous suggestions for welding gray cast iron with steel electrodes when preheating is impractical.

After welding, care should be taken to insure slow cooling of the casting.

Postheat annealing at 1000-1200 F transforms the martensite into non-brittle constituents. It also reduces the hard carbides, but not to the point of restoring full machinability or full ductility. Higher annealing temperatures transform more of the carbides into graphite, but the nodules formed are very small and do not provide the degree of ductility being sought.

Definitions of New Words

Carbon equivalent (as used in ferrous metallurgy). The relationship of carbon, sulphur and phosphorus content as to the combined effect of these alloying elements on certain properties of the material. In the United States, this is considered to be the total carbon, plus one-third of sulphur and phosphorus content by percentage of weight. NOT to be confused with:

Carbon equivalent (as used in welding only). The relationship of carbon and various alloying elements as to their effect on the cracking of weldments by the formation of hardness zones.

Combined carbon. This is the percentage of carbon that is combined with metal atoms in a crystal constituent of an alloy, as in the iron-carbide cementite commonly found in steels or cast irons.

Free carbon. This is the percentage of carbon that is not combined and usually exists as free atoms at grain boundaries, or in the form of pure carbon flakes of graphite.

Inoculants. Alloying combinations added to a cast iron for the purpose of modifying its microstructure, and therefore its mechanical and physical properties. Usually function in gray iron by forming nuclei (when added just before casting), thereby accelerating the separation of carbon and fine distribution of the resulting graphite flakes.

Malleablizing. The process of annealing and cooling white cast iron so as to transform some of the combined carbon to graphite. Also used to describe the heat treatment after welding or other operations for restoring the original malleable structure.

Precipitate. The change, during transformation, that constitutes a separating and gathering of atoms of a particular element.

Wormholing. The forming of an irregular cavity as a result of internal shrinkage during solidification of a cast material. If the casting is broken open, the cavity can readily be seen by naked eye.

Review Questions

1. Name some reasons why cast iron is used.
2. Why are steel weldments being used for more and more applications where iron castings had been used for many years?
3. What chemical element in cast iron promotes the formation of flake graphite?
4. What is the principal factor in determining whether an alloy is gray cast iron, malleable iron, or white iron?
5. What electrode can be economically used for welding gray cast iron when machinability is not required? What electrode is more suitable for gray cast iron when the weld is to be machined?
6. What happens to malleable iron if it is heated above the transportation point?
7. What preheat temperature should be used for metal-arc welding gray cast iron? For oxyacetylene welding of gray iron?

CHAPTER 15

STAINLESS STEELS AND HIGH-CHROMIUM ALLOYS

Stainless steel was first introduced to the world by Harry Bread-
ley of Sheffield, England. He produced a line of stainless steel cutlery between 1910 and 1915. Since that time, many "stainless" steel
alloys have been developed to resist most types of corrosion, to resist
oxidation caused by hot gases, or to maintain high strength at elevated temperatures. All of these alloys have an iron-carbon-chro-
mium base, while some are additionally alloyed with nickel or with
nickel and manganese.

Stainless steels are designated by means of a three-digit numerical
classification system established by the American Iron and Steel Institute. The AISI specifications are accepted by nearly all engineering
groups in this country. See Table 15-1.

Table 15-1. Numerical Designation of AISI Stainless Steels

SERIES*	MAJOR ALLOYING ELEMENTS	CHARACTERISTICS
2xx	Chromium-Nickel-Manganese	Non-hardenable Austenitic
3xx	Chromium-Nickel	Non-hardenable Austenitic
4xx	Chromium	(1) Hardenable Martensitic (2) Non-hardenable Ferritic
5xx	Chromium (4 to 6%)	Air-hardenable Martensitic

*Second and third digits in number identify specific alloy type.
Letter suffix identifies modification of original grade.

As shown by Table 15-1, the AISI alloys include the 500 series
in which the chromium content is much lower than other types.
However, their "low-chromium" content of 4 to 6% is still considerably above that of the SAE 5000 series of chromium steels, for example, in which chromium does not normally exceed 1.15%. Figure
15-1 shows the general relationship of various steels with respect to
their carbon-chromium content. Any general statements made about
stainless steel will not necessarily be true for members of the 500

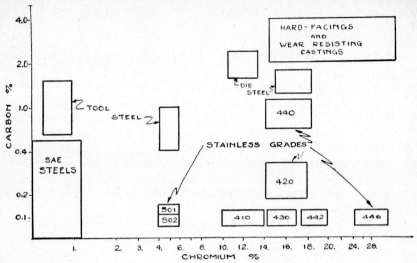

Fig. 15-1. Comparison of the carbon-chromium range of some alloy steels.

series, although the welding of these steels will be discussed later in this chapter.

Because of the high alloy content of the stainless steels, they have many valuable properties. A high percentage of chromium makes the steel stronger at both low and high temperatures, and gives it excellent resistance to corrosion and scaling. Some of the chromium and carbon combine to form chromium carbide, which imparts additional strength, hardness, and resistance to wear. Nickel content also gives excellent resistance to corrosion as well as superior high-temperature properties, and high toughness and strength at very low temperatures. In a few alloys, manganese is substituted for some of the nickel which is higher in cost and, in wartime, is in great demand.

Steels with a high chromium content (over 10%) are commonly referred to as martensitic, ferritic, or austenitic, although some of the alloys may have one or another crystal structure at room temperature, depending upon the specific heat treatment.

The martensitic steels behave like an alloy steel with a very high hardenability. When they are heated, austenite is formed, and during rapid cooling the austenite is transformed to martensite. If a martensitic steel is annealed, a machinable structure of ferrite and pearlite is formed, replacing the martensite. Some of the 400 series of alloys are martensitic when heat treated. (The 500 series of alloys also are martensitic.)

The ferritic steels do not respond well to heat treatment. These alloys have the crystal structure of iron at room temperature (body-centered cubic structure). There is no transformation, recrystallization, or formation of austenite when these alloys are heated. The ferritic stainless steels have a much higher ratio of chromium to carbon content than the martensitic alloys. Some of the 400 series of alloys are ferritic.

The austenitic alloys are alloyed with nickel, which slows up transformation to such an extent that the austenite structure is highly stable at room temperature. As the austenite does not transform when the steel is cooled, these steels cannot be hardened by quenching. An austenitic stainless steel (one containing 6% or more of nickel) is, in fact, softer when quenched than when slowly cooled from a high temperature. The 200 series and 300 series of alloys are austenitic.

Stainless steels possess many properties that differ from those of carbon and other steels. Let us compare them with the properties of low-carbon steel:

1. Their thermal conductivity is much lower. Hence, stainless steels are more susceptible to local overheating and to distortion when they are welded.

2. Their thermal expansion is higher. This tends to increase distortion and also results in higher stresses on the welds during cooling.

3. They are more resistant to certain types of corrosion than carbon steel and are both stronger and more resistant to oxidation at high temperatures. Most are unaffected by many acids, including nitric acid, although they are readily attacked by hydrochloric and a few other acids.

4. They resist oxidation until heated to temperatures near or above their melting point in the presence of air. Then a very *refractory* chromium oxide is formed. This oxide prevents these alloys from being cut with an ordinary oxyacetylene cutting torch. A special powder-cutting process, using an iron powder blown into the flame by compressed air, is needed to flame-cut stainless steels. In welding, the molten metal must be well protected from the air.

5. Some of the martensitic alloys have a very high hardenability. Some become brittle when heated and cooled, due to excessive grain growth at high temperatures. Still others suffer a loss in their corrosion resistance if there is appreciable carbon in the base or weld metal.

6. The austenitic grades are non-magnetic.

Naturally, the properties mentioned above will depend upon the analysis of the steel. As a general rule, the higher the chromium content, the more pronounced these properties become.

Table 15-2 lists the more common grades of AISI-classified stainless steel and their chemical compositions. Many other varieties of high-chromium alloys are available from one or more suppliers.

Metals and How to Weld Them

Table 15-2. Chemical Ranges of Stainless and Heat-Resisting Steels

Group	TYPE	CARBON	MANGANESE	SILICON	PHOSPHORUS	SULPHUR	CHROMIUM	NICKEL	OTHER ELEMENTS
AUSTENITIC	301	0.15 max.	2.00 max.	1.00 max.	0.045 max.	0.030 max.	16.00/18.00	6.00/8.00	
AUSTENITIC	302	0.15 max.	2.00 max.	1.00 max.	0.045 max.	0.030 max.	17.00/19.00	8.00/10.00	
AUSTENITIC	302B	0.15 max.	2.00 max.	2.00/3.00	0.045 max.	0.030 max.	17.00/19.00	8.00/10.00	
AUSTENITIC	303	0.15 max.	2.00 max.	1.00 max.	0.20 max.	0.15 max.	17.00/19.00	8.00/10.00	Mo or Zr — 0.60 max., optional
AUSTENITIC	303Se	0.15 max.	2.00 max.	1.00 max.	0.20 max.	0.06 max.	17.00/19.00	8.00/10.00	Se — 0.15 min.
AUSTENITIC	304	0.08 max.	2.00 max.	1.00 max.	0.045 max.	0.030 max.	18.00/20.00	8.00/12.00	
AUSTENITIC	304L	0.03 max.	2.00 max.	1.00 max.	0.045 max.	0.030 max.	18.00/20.00	8.00/12.00	
AUSTENITIC	305	0.12 max.	2.00 max.	1.00 max.	0.045 max.	0.030 max.	17.00/19.00	10.00/13.00	
AUSTENITIC	308	0.08 max.	2.00 max.	1.00 max.	0.045 max.	0.030 max.	19.00/21.00	10.00/12.00	
AUSTENITIC	309	0.20 max.	2.00 max.	1.00 max.	0.045 max.	0.030 max.	22.00/24.00	12.00/15.00	
AUSTENITIC	309S	0.08 max.	2.00 max.	1.00 max.	0.045 max.	0.030 max.	22.00/24.00	12.00/15.00	
AUSTENITIC	310	0.25 max.	2.00 max.	1.50 max.	0.045 max.	0.030 max.	24.00/26.00	19.00/22.00	
AUSTENITIC	310S	0.08 max.	2.00 max.	1.50 max.	0.045 max.	0.030 max.	24.00/26.00	19.00/22.00	
AUSTENITIC	314	0.25 max.	2.00 max.	1.50/3.00	0.045 max.	0.030 max.	23.00/26.00	19.00/22.00	
AUSTENITIC	316	0.08 max.	2.00 max.	1.00 max.	0.045 max.	0.030 max.	16.00/18.00	10.00/14.00	Mo — 2.00/3.00
AUSTENITIC	316L	0.03 max.	2.00 max.	1.00 max.	0.045 max.	0.030 max.	16.00/18.00	10.00/14.00	Mo — 2.00/3.00
AUSTENITIC	317	0.08 max.	2.00 max.	1.00 max.	0.045 max.	0.030 max.	18.00/20.00	11.00/15.00	Mo — 3.00/4.00
AUSTENITIC	321	0.08 max.	2.00 max.	1.00 max.	0.045 max.	0.030 max.	17.00/19.00	9.00/12.00	Ti — 5xC min.
AUSTENITIC	347	0.08 max.	2.00 max.	1.00 max.	0.045 max.	0.030 max.	17.00/19.00	9.00/13.00	Cb-Ta — 10xC min.
MARTENSITIC	403	0.15 max.	1.00 max.	0.50 max.	0.040 max.	0.030 max.	11.50/13.00		
MARTENSITIC	410	0.15 max.	1.00 max.	1.00 max.	0.040 max.	0.030 max.	11.50/13.50		
MARTENSITIC	414	0.15 max.	1.00 max.	1.00 max.	0.040 max.	0.030 max.	11.50/13.50	1.25/2.50	
MARTENSITIC	416	0.15 max.	1.25 max.	1.00 max.	0.06 max.	0.15 min.	12.00/14.00		Mo or Zr — 0.60 max., optional
MARTENSITIC	416Se	0.15 max.	1.25 max.	1.00 max.	0.06 max.	0.06 max.	12.00/14.00		Se — 0.15 min.
MARTENSITIC	420	0.15	1.00 max.	1.00 max.	0.040 max.	0.030 max.	12.00/14.00		
MARTENSITIC	431	0.20 max.	1.00 max.	1.00 max.	0.040 max.	0.030 max.	15.00/17.00	1.25/2.50	
MARTENSITIC	440A	0.60/0.75	1.00 max.	1.00 max.	0.040 max.	0.030 max.	16.00/18.00		Mo — 0.75 max.
MARTENSITIC	440B	0.75/0.95	1.00 max.	1.00 max.	0.040 max.	0.030 max.	16.00/18.00		Mo — 0.75 max.
MARTENSITIC	440C	0.95/1.20	1.00 max.	1.00 max.	0.040 max.	0.030 max.	16.00/18.00		Mo — 0.75 max.
MARTENSITIC	501	0.10	1.00 max.	1.00 max.	0.040 max.	0.030 max.	4.00/6.00		Mo — 0.40/0.65
MARTENSITIC	502	0.10 max.	1.00 max.	1.00 max.	0.040 max.	0.030 max.	4.00/6.00		Mo — 0.40/0.65
FERRITIC	405	0.08 max.	1.00 max.	1.00 max.	0.040 max.	0.030 max.	11.50/14.50		Al — 0.10/0.30
FERRITIC	430	0.12 max.	1.00 max.	1.00 max.	0.040 max.	0.030 max.	14.00/18.00		
FERRITIC	430F	0.12 max.	1.25 max.	1.00 max.	0.06 max.	0.015 min.	14.00/18.00		Mo or Zr — 0.60 max., optional
FERRITIC	430FSe	0.12 max.	1.25 max.	1.00 max.	0.06 max.	0.06 max.	14.00/18.00		Se — 0.15 min.
FERRITIC	446	0.20 max.	1.00 max.	1.00 max.	0.040 max.	0.030 max.	23.00/27.00		N — 0.25 max.

Adapted from Steel Products Manual, Section: Stainless and Heat-Resisting Steels, American Iron and Steel Institute

4 to 6% Chromium Steels

These steels (AISI 501 and 502) are not stainless steels. They are, however, classified as such by many people. This is probably because such steels possess a resistance to sulphide corrosion of 4 to 10 times that of ordinary mild steel and 3 times the resistance to oxidation at 1000 F. These steels are therefore suitable and are used extensively for furnace tubing, cracking stills, hot oil transfer lines, heat exchangers, bubble tower caps, return bends, valves, etc.

The most noticeable property of the 500 series alloys is their intense *air-hardening*, which is proportional to both the carbon and chromium contents. The resulting structure is a brittle martensitic formation, the stresses in which must be relieved in order to avoid cracking. After welding, the metal must be immediately annealed or stress relieved so that weld cracking and underbead cracking in the heat-affected parent metal will not occur.

Fully annealed 501 or 502 alloy has properties similar to those of mild steels and therefore is suitable for equipment where severe cold work is applied during fabrication. Cold work operations include rolling, bending, flanging, bulging, and drawing.

AISI type 501 contains 4.00 to 6.00% chromium, with more than 0.10% carbon. Type 502 contains the same amount of chromium, but with carbon not exceeding 0.10%.

The carbon content of these steels has an appreciable effect on the yield point and ultimate tensile strength, especially on the soft annealed material. In applications where an alloy of this group is to be used for high temperature service, such as cracking still tubes and condenser tubes, and where severe cold working operations are required, only soft annealed material should be employed. Exposure of semi-annealed material for long periods at temperatures between 800-1200 F gradually produces the effect of a soft anneal.

Additional alloying content of about 0.5% molybdenum does not appreciably affect the physical properties of these steels at room temperatures, but it does substantially increase the strength of these steels at elevated temperatures. This increase in strength at higher temperatures is known as an increase in *creep strength*. Molybdenum, also increases resistance to certain types of corrosion, especially at high temperatures.

The addition of 1% tungsten would have somewhat the same effect but would also slightly increase the tensile strength at room temperature. Tungsten, being a relatively scarce metal however, usually increases the cost and has been seldom used in recent years.

The base metal should be in the annealed condition when welded. Bearing in mind the general characteristics of 4-6% chromium steel and its air-hardening qualities in particular, considerable care should be taken to keep the work material warm during welding and to

Table 15-3. Type 501, Typical Mechanical Properties

PROPERTY	WELD METAL ANNEALED	STRESS-RELIEVED WELD METAL
Ultimate tensile strength	65,000-70,000 psi	80,000-90,000 psi
Yield point	30,000-40,000 psi	55,000-65,000 psi
Ductility, elongation in 2 in.	28-35%	24-30%
Reduction of area	65-75%	60-70%
Hardness (Brinell)	160	155-175
Modulus of elasticity in tension	29 million psi	
Thermal conductivity		
Btu/hr/sq. ft/ft/°F, at 212 F	21.2	
at 932 F	19.5	
Coefficient of thermal expansion,		
32 to 212 F	6.2 x 16⁻⁸/°F	
32 to 1200 F	7.3 x 10⁻⁸/°F	
Melting point	2700-2800 F	

AISI 501 oil-quenched from 1650 F, tempered at 1000 F, develops 175,000 psi ultimate tensile strength; 135,000 psi yield strength; 370 Brinell hardness; but has ductility reduced to 15% elongation.

anneal it afterwards. If this is not done, the welds and, more importantly, the parent metal adjacent to the weld will be quite brittle and will withstand very little stress, especially bending stress.

The 4-6% chromium steels can be successfully welded by the shielded-arc process, using an electrode (E-502) developed particularly for them. This electrode contains 4-6% chromium and 0.45 to 0.65% molybdenum. The weld deposit is thus similar in analysis to the parent metal and possesses high creep strength and other desirable properties. In welding with this electrode, reverse polarity is used (electrode positive, work negative). Welding currents and voltages are somewhat lower than those employed in welding other steels by the shielded-arc process.

The parts to be welded should be preheated to 400-500 F in order to prevent cracking during welding. In no event should preheating be less than 200 F. The work should not be allowed to fall below this temperature at any time.

Before the work has time to cool after welding, it should be placed in an annealing furnace. Anneal at 1550-1600 F and cool slowly. Temperature of the work should not drop over 50 F per hour. When the temperature has dropped to 1200 F, the work may be taken out of the furnace and allowed to cool in air.

When annealed, the weld metal will possess mechanical properties approximating those given in Table 15-3.

Although full annealing is recommended, it is sometimes impracticable. Instead, the base metal near the weld is stress relieved. The metal is heated to 1325-1375 F, held at temperature for four hours, and then cooled uniformly in air. Welds are stress relieved in the field by means of resistance or induction coils, or a gas-fired furnace built around the weld.

When stress relieved, the weld metal will have mechanical properties as given in Table 15-3.

When proper preheating and/or postheating is not feasible, one solution is to use an electrode of 25% chromium and 20% nickel content (E-310). This produces weld metal that is largely austenitic and compares favorably in ductility with the original annealed base metal. This technique should be used with caution, however, since there will still be some embrittlement of the heat-affected parent metal below the fusion line.

The preferred alternative, when the recommended preheating is impossible or impractical, is to weld by the submerged-arc process. However, while this permits doing without preheat, at least 200 F even here would assure a better weld. The use of submerged-arc

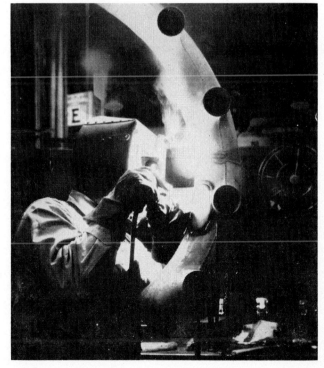

Fig. 15-2. Shielded-arc welding is used extensively in making strong, ductile joints in most grades of stainless steel.

welding on high chromium steels will be discussed later in this chapter.

Very high yield points and tensile strengths result from air hardening and tempering the 500 series alloy, when welded with filler metal of similar analysis. This treatment is quite as effective as the quenching of ordinary steels in liquid media. Combined with high tensile strength, the hardened and tempered alloys also exhibit good ductility (about 15%) and impact toughness. The impact properties and elongation of these alloys are superior to those of some structural alloy steels, when heat treated to the same yield point and tensile strength. Hardening requires heating to 1600 to 1700, cooling rapidly to near room temperature, and then tempering at 400 to 1400 F.

Martensitic Stainless Steels

The alloys making up this group have 11.5 to 18% chromium and 0.15 to 1.20% carbon. Both the martensitic and the ferritic stainless steels are referred to as "straight chromium" types because they do not have any appreciable nickel or manganese content. Together, the martensitic and ferritic stainless steels comprise the AISI 400 series.

Table 15-4.   Martensitic Stainless Steels, Typical Properties*

PROPERTY	410	414	431
Ult. tensile strength	70,000 psi	115,000 psi	125,000 psi
	195,000 psi	200,000 psi	205,000 psi
Yield point	35,000 psi	90,000 psi	45,000 psi
	150,000 psi	150,000 psi	155,000 psi
Elongation in 2 in.	30%	20%	20%
	17%	16%	15%
Hardness (Brinell)	150	235	260
	410	415	415

*The first value stated for each property applies to the metal in full-annealed condition. The value immediately below applies to the metal in maximum hardened and tempered condition.

All martensitic stainless steels are hardenable by heat treatment. When heated over 1500 F, austenite is formed. During rapid cooling in air, this austenite transforms into hard and brittle martensite. The martensitic structure is toughened by tempering, or by stress relieving if the hardening is local—along a weld, for instance.

All alloys in this group are resistant to atmospheric corrosion and are used where the higher strength and wear resistance obtainable by heat treatment is an advantage. Typical properties of these alloys are listed in Table 15-4.

The hardness of martensitic stainless steels increases as the carbon content increases. As hardness increases, the tendency for cracking as the weld cools also increases. In welding these alloys, the necessity for preheating and postheating increases with the carbon content.

Any of the martensitic stainless steels that are to be postheated—annealed, stress-relieved, or used under extreme temperature service conditions—should be welded with a straight-chromium stainless steel electrode of the E-400 series. Such welds, when annealed, have good ductility. The weldment can be hardened by heat treatment to develop maximum strength and corrosion resistance.

Any of these alloys that can not or will not be exposed to postheating should be welded with an austenitic chromium-nickel electrode of the E-300 series. Even though the heat-affected parent metal next to the weld bead is subjected to embrittlement, the ductile bead performs better against impact and deformation than if the entire weld area were brittle.

The thermal expansion is not the same for all of the stainless steels. The rate of expansion for straight-chromium alloys (400 series) varies considerably but averages slightly greater than that of carbon steel. In contrast, the rate of expansion for chromium-nickel alloys (300 series) is about 50% greater than that of carbon steel. If the welded member is to be subjected to repeated heating and cooling, the weld metal and the parent metal should have approximately the same coefficients of thermal expansion. The use of the E-300 series electrodes in welding the AISI 400 series alloys is largely limited to weldments that will be used near room temperature or within a narrow constant-temperature range.

AISI Types 403, 410, 414 and 416 have a low carbon content (0.15% max.) and not more than 14% chromium. The AWS E-410 electrode is suitable for welding all of these alloys. However, the sulphur and selenium content of AISI 416 and 416Se promote porosity and make production welding of these steels inadvisable. The E-410 electrode deposits weld metal of 11-14% chromium, 12% carbon, and 0.60% nickel. The welding procedure outlined for the 4-6% chromium steels should be followed. When the recommended preheating or postheating cannot be used, first choice should be submerged-arc welding with filler metal of analysis similar to that of the parent metal. The alternative is shielded-arc welding with an E-308 electrode (18% chromium, 8% nickel) or one of higher alloy content such as E-309 or E-310.

AISI Types 420 and 431 are intermediate grades of the martensitic stainless steels. These have medium carbon content (0.15-0.20%) and chromium content of 12-17%. They may be welded with either the E-410 electrode or the higher-chromium E-430. If either preheating or postheating cannot be employed, the weld can be made with one of the austenitic chromium-nickel electrodes of the E-300 series (E-308, 309 or 310). Stainless steels of medium-carbon content require both higher preheating and slower cooling than the chromium steels of lower carbon content. Multi-pass welding with a small-diameter electrode, low current and stringer beads will help reduce the build-up of stresses and will minimize embrittlement of the parent metal.

AISI stainless steel Types 440A, B and C have much higher carbon content (0.60-1.20%) and chromium content to 18%. These alloys have poor weldability. Their structure contains free complex chromium carbides. These steels can be welded with the E-430 electrodes, but the precise welding and heat treating technique required to produce welds having properties equal to the original steel is not always practicable. Where equal strength is not essential, one of the E-300 series of austenitic electrodes is more likely to produce a satisfactory weld.

Ferritic Stainless Steels

The alloys in this group, like the martensitic steels, are straight chromium; that is, they have little or no nickel content. The normally ferritic structure of these steels at room temperature is due to the low carbon content relative to the chromium content. The ferritic steels are essentially non-hardenable by heat treatment. Properties of these alloys are listed in Table 15-5.

Table 15-5. Ferritic Stainless Steels, Typical Properties

PROPERTY	405 Annealed	430 Annealed	446 Annealed
Ult. tensile strength	65,000 psi	75,000 psi	85,000 psi
Yield point	40,000 psi	40,000 psi	55,000 psi
Elongation in 2 in.	30%	30%	25%
Hardness (Brinell)	150	160	170

The 14 to 18% chromium steel (AISI 430) is on the borderline between the martensitic and the ferritic steels. This alloy may be welded with an AWS E-430 electrode, which provides weld metal of similar analysis. With a carbon content of 0.12% max., AISI 430 does not have the high hardenability of the higher carbon stainless steels. A local preheat to 300 F should be sufficient and should not be appreciably exceeded. This alloy loses its ductility (due to grain growth) when given a high preheat for a long time. If this happens, ductility may be restored by an anneal at 1400-1450 F for four hours or more depending upon section thickness. The weldment is cooled rapidly from the annealing temperature.

In an alloy of this chromium content, a reduction in corrosion resistance along grain boundaries is associated with excessive grain growth. One variation of AISI 430 has titanium added to its alloying content for better ductility and may appear to eliminate the need for annealing. However, this addition of titanium in this type alloy lowers the resistance to intergranular corrosive attack in the weld zone. This effect is minimized if the weldment is annealed as usual.

If annealing of welded AISI 430 is impractical and the member is to be used as-welded, one of the austenitic stainless steel electrodes (E-308, 309 or 310) can be used. The use of these electrodes is not advisable where corrosion conditions to be encountered in service are especially severe.

The ferritic AISI 405 has an even lower carbon content (0.08%) than AISI 430, and has a low chromium content (11.5-14%). This alloy retains more of its ductility when welded than does AISI 430; however, annealing is still desirable for maximum corrosion resistance. It can be welded with the E-430 electrode, or with one of the more ductile E-300 series electrodes if annealing is impractical.

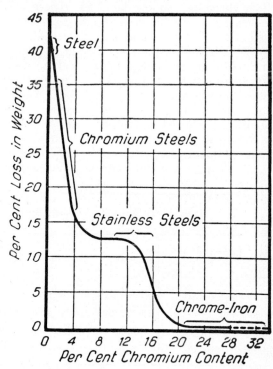

Fig. 15-3. This graph shows how ½ in. cubes of stainless steel and other metals compare in loss of weight by oxidation when exposed to atmosphere at 1832 F for 48 hours.

The straight chromium steels with higher chromium are sometimes called "chrome-irons". AISI 446 (chromium 23-27%, carbon 0.20%) is in this group. The chromium is dissolved in the ferritic iron structure, and the ferrite grains do not transform or recrystallize when heated. The steel has a low impact strength at room temperature. When heated, the ferrite grains grow larger, resulting in a still lower impact strength when the steel is cold. Hot forging is the only way to reduce the grain size, although the brittleness may be reduced by annealing. This steel is used for its excellent resistance to oxidation at elevated temperatures. See Fig. 15-3.

Since the chrome-irons, such as Type 446, have very low impact strength as-cast, we should not expect very much from the welds. If metal of the same analysis as the parent metal is deposited and the assembly is then hot forged or rolled, the coarse grain structure will be broken up and the finer grained steel and its weld will have properties equalling the original material. Type 446 has an elongation in 2 in. of 20-30%, but a Charpy impact value of less than 10 ft-lb, which is very low. Stainless steels 416 and 430 can be heat treated to give the same elongation but Charpy strengths are between 30 and 50 ft-lb.

When a weld made on AISI 446 is required to have a chromium content similar to the parent metal, electrodes that deposit extra-high chromium should be used. These include the austenitic AWS E-309, 310 and 312 types. High preheating is not recommended because the parent metal and the weld are so susceptible to grain growth; however, the steel should be heated to about 300 F to keep it ductile enough to eliminate cracking during cooling after welding. Even with the best procedure, the weld and the parent metal will have large grains when cooled, and the weld may fail if subjected to a sudden heavy load. A decrease in corrosion resistance also is associated with excessive grain growth.

The 446 electrodes contain a small percentage of nitrogen that reduces this tendency toward grain growth. Welds of good quality on AISI 446 parent metal may be produced by using a high-chromium,

Table 15-6. Austenitic Stainless Steels, Typical Properties

PROPERTY	302 Annealed	308 Annealed	310 Annealed	316L Annealed	347 Annealed
Ult. tensile strength	90,000 psi	85,000 psi	95,000 psi	75,000 psi	90,000 psi
Yield point	35,000 psi	30,000 psi	45,000 psi	32,000 psi	35,000 psi
Elongation in 2 in.	60%	55%	50%	50%	50%
Hardness (Brinell)	150	150	170	145	160

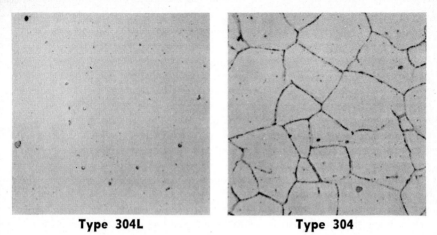

Type 304L   **Type 304**

Fig. 15-4. Photomicrographs (500x) of parent metal in zone next to the weld where temperatures of 800-1400 F were experienced. No carbide precipitation is visible in the ELC specimen, whereas the ordinary Type 304 shows carbides along the grain boundaries.

austenitic electrode such as E-310 (25% chromium, 20% nickel) for the body of the weld and the 446 electrode at surfaces to be protected from corrosion.

Austenitic Chromium-Nickel Steels

The austenitic stainless steels are the AISI 300 series. They range in analysis from 16 to 26% chromium, 6 to 22% nickel, and 0.03 to 0.25% carbon maximum. These steels are all non-magnetic and hence can readily be distinguished from the other stainless steels and chrome-irons, which are all magnetic.

Steels with 18% chromium and 8% nickel, called 18-8 stainless (AISI 302 and 304), are by far the most popular. In 1960, about 35% of all the stainless steel manufactured was of the 18-8 type.

The austenitic stainless steels have many excellent properties, including high strength and resistance to scaling at elevated temperatures. Some of their most important properties are given in Table 15-6. Additional properties of the general-purpose 18-8 steel are given in Table 15-7.

Except for the few free-machining types (which have high sulphur, phosphorus or selenium content), these steels have excellent weldability relative to other high-alloy steels. They require no preheating and no annealing after welding, when used under normal atmospheric or mildly corrosive conditions.

The austenitic stainless steels do not harden by heat treatment but can be cold worked to a high hardness. Annealing may be required after rolling, drawing or such manufacturing processes and may be accomplished by heating the steel to 1900-2050 F, followed by quenching. When treated in this manner, the steel is in the best condition to resist corrosion.

The 300 series steels all have a low heat conductivity and a high coefficient of thermal expansion. As a result, these steels may present some distortion problems unless the usual design and welding practices for controlling distortion are observed. Copper chill bars can be placed under weld areas to draw off the heat more quickly. Use of welding fixtures can prevent movement of base plates that would result in angular misalignment. A multi-pass weld is made with a small-diameter electrode and short bead lengths will minimize the possibility of serious distortion.

Ordinary austenitic stainless steel alloys present a problem when heated in the range of 800 to 1500 F. The steel undergoes a migration of chromium that lowers its resistance to corrosion. This is due to the precipitation at grain boundaries of very fine films of chromium-rich carbides containing as much as 90% chromium. Since the chromium is taken from the layer of metal immediately adjacent to the grain boundary, the metal there may have its resistance to corrosion seriously lowered. This phenomenon is called *carbide precipitation,* and the type of corrosion that is likely to occur is known as *intergranular corrosion.*

Table 15-7.   18-8 Typical Physical Properties

(Annealed Metal)

Ult. tensile strength	85,000-95,000 psi
Yield point	30,000-40,000 psi
Elongation in 2 in.	55-60%
Reduction of area	60-70%
Hardness	135-180 Brinell
Izod impact	80-120 ft-lb
Endurance limit	Usually 40% of ultimate strength. Work hardening will increase ultimate.
Density	0.29 lb/cu in.
Thermal conductivity	.33 times that of low-carbon steel
Electrical resistance	6.4 times that of low-carbon steel
Thermal expansion	1.45 times that of low-carbon steel
Modulus of elasticity in tension	28,000,000-30,000,000
Melting point range	2550-2590 F
Approx. scaling temperature	1,650 F (average, in air)

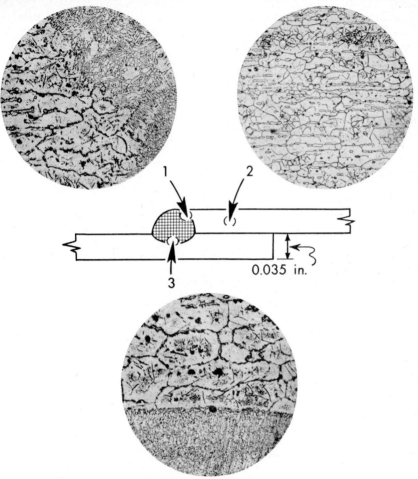

Fig. 15-5. A lap joint made on AISI 321 titanium stabilized stainless steel. Photomicrographs at positions 1 and 3 were made of metal taken from the fusion line. The photomicrograph at position 2 shows unaffected parent metal.

When welding these steels, some of the base metal adjacent to the fusion line reaches the temperature range (800-1500 F), within which the carbide precipitation occurs. This was more fully described and illustrated in Chapter 9, Fig. 9-3. (A similar problem would exist when using these alloys in our welding filler materials.)

An obvious remedy is to reduce the carbon content of the alloy to such a low value that no carbide can be precipitated. There are commercially available extra-low-carbon steels (ELC) that have a carbon content of only 0.03% maximum as compared to the 0.08% maximum carbon for the regular AISA 304 and 316 stainless steels (Fig. 15-4).

Another way to prevent loss of chromium to grain boundaries is by addition of an alloying element, such as titanium or columbium or tantalum, that has a greater affinity for carbon than chromium has. AISI 321 is such an alloy steel, titanium being the stabilizing element (Fig. 15-5). Although effective in the base metal in preventing carbide precipitation in heat-affected zone adjacent to the weld, titanium does not perform its function very well when added to the welding electrode or other filler material. Most of the titanium used in this way is lost during welding.

AISI 347 and its counterpart welding electrode, AWS E-347, have columbium as the stabilizing element. Since columbium is not lost in the welding operation, freedom from intergranular corrosion in the weld metal and in the base metal along the line of fusion is possible by use of an electrode that contains this element in suitable proportions.

When welding chromium-nickel alloys that are neither stabilized nor ELC types, the control of carbide precipitation (and, thus, intergranular corrosion) depends more on our welding procedure. One objective then is to limit the depth of base metal reaching the temperature range of 800-1500 F and to limit the time factor. The longer any of the base metal is held at such temperatures, the more precipitation will occur. Annealing the weldment will remove the effects of carbide precipitation but this is usually an unnecessary expense.

Shielded-metal-arc welding with coated electrodes is the most widely used method of joining these steels. The electrodes have a carbon-free coating and a stainless-steel core wire containing slightly higher chromium and nickel than are required in the deposit. Special alloying elements such as columbium and tantalum, and/or molybdenum may be included in either the coating or the core wire.

Most stainless steel electrodes are designed to give best results with reverse polarity (electrode positive). Some may also be welded with AC.

The welding procedure is similar to that used for welding low-carbon steels, but stainless steel has a much lower electrical conductivity than plain-carbon and alloy steels. Lower welding currents and shorter electrodes will reduce the possibility of overheating the last few inches of the electrode.

AISI 301, 302, 304, 305 and 308 steels may be welded with an AWS E-308 stainless steel electrode. The high alloy content of this electrode minimizes the effect of carbide precipitation. The E-308 electrode is commonly referred to as an 18-8 electrode because it provides weld metal of comparable properties. Stainless steel Types 301 and 302 all have higher carbon content than do 304 or 308, and thus are more subject to carbide precipitation. Faster welding speeds will result in less carbide formation. Type 305 has a tendency toward cracking when cooled.

AISI 302B has a high silicon content (2-3%) to improve its scaling resistance. To match the scaling resistance of the base metal, the higher alloy content of the AWS E-309-Cb electrode is needed. This electrode is also used in welding AISI 309.

AISI 310 is a 25-20 steel; that is, it has 25% chromium and 20% nickel. It should be welded with an AWS E-310 electrode.

AISI 316 and 317 all have molybdenum content of 2% or more for extra corrosion resistance to certain chemicals. Because these alloys are used in highly corrosive situations, welds are usually made with the AWS E-318 electrode. This electrode has columbium plus tantalum added for stabilizing purposes.

Free-machining type steels, AISI 303 and 303Se, are not suitable for production welding. If necessary to repair weld them, E-309 electrode may be used.

The usefulness of austenitic stainless-steel electrodes is not confined to the welding of base metal of similar analysis. The high strength of the austenitic stainless steel weld metal, its minimum tendency for admixture with the base metal, and the low-hydrogen type of coating which minimizes or eliminates underbead cracking, are valuable advantages in the welding of high-carbon and high-alloy steels. (See the chapters on High-Carbon Steel, Austenitic Manganese Steel, and Tool and Die Steels.)

These electrodes are also used in surfacing carbon steels to produce a corrosion-resistant layer or to serve as a base for additional layers of other hardsurfacing alloys.

The 18-8 type electrode (E-308) is usually adequate for the special uses mentioned above. The 25-20 type electrode (E-310) can stand more parent metal dilution on these applications and still give an austenitic deposit.

Welding ELC Stainless Steels

The extra-low-carbon stainless steels do a very good job of preventing carbide precipitation, provided the service temperatures do not go over 800 F for any sustained period of time. While a special technique is not required in the welding of ELC stainless steels, preference is given to electrodes that are equally low in carbon or have stabilizing elements in their analysis. ELC steels are indicated in the AISI numerical designation by the letter suffix "L". These alloys usually have 0.03% maximum carbon content. The suffix "S" also indicates a lower than usual carbon content, but alloys so designated usually have 0.08% maximum carbon.

For AISI 304L, welding with the AWS E-347 stainless steel electrode usually gives the best results. The chromium-nickel E-347 electrode is a stabilized type, having columbium added in its analysis. Although the E-347 electrode has 0.08% max. carbon as compared to the AISI 304L's 0.03% max. carbon, it gives superior resistance to carbide precipitation and, therefore, to intergranular corrosion. When joining 304L stainless to carbon steel, the AWS E-309-Cb electrode may be used for the root bead. The joint can then be filled with the E-347 electrode. The E-309-Cb electrode is stabilized by the addition of columbium, but the properties of metal deposited by it better match those of the carbon steel admixtured by it and those of the E-347 metal deposited over it.

AISI 316L is an alloy that contains molybdenum for high corrosion resistance against certain chemicals. It is effective in combatting pitting-type corrosion. In many cases, welding with E-318 electrode will give satisfactory results. This electrode contains molybdenum as well as the stabilizing element columbium, and should be used when possible. If necessary, maximum corrosion resistance is obtainable by stress-relieving the welded joint by heating at 1600 F and then cooling rapidly. When the weldment will be exposed to hot oxidizing acids, welds should be made with the E-309-Cb electrode. For welding AISI 316 to carbon steel, it is preferable to use E-310-Mo electrode containing molybdenum.

The 0.08% carbon AISI 309S may be welded with the E-309-Cb electrode.

In welding the ELC stainless steels, however, you will seldom go wrong by using an electrode that provides weld metal matching in analysis the steel being welded.

Welding Stabilized Stainless Steels

The stabilized grades of chromium-nickel stainless steels have excellent weldability. These grades are seldom used except for continuous service under severe corrosive conditions at normal or at elevated temperatures where the ELC grades are unsuitable. Since ELC weld metal will not resist carbide precipitation under the same service conditions, ELC type electrodes should never be used to weld a stabilized type base metal. Only a stabilized weld metal will give satisfactory service. In other respects, the electrode selected is usually of a composition comparable to that of the base metal.

Welds in AISI 347 steel should be made with AWS E-347 electrode. AISI 321 includes titanium in its composition. Since titanium is not successfully deposited from an electrode, this alloy also should be welded with the E-347 electrode. AISI 318 should be welded with the E-318 electrode, and AISI 309Cb with the E-309-Cb electrode.

High-Manganese Stainless Steels

Stainless steels in the AISI 200 series are equivalent to chromium-nickel grades of the 300 series, except for a higher manganese and lower nickel content. They were developed primarily for substitute use during periods of critical nickel shortage.

These steels are welded with the same procedure and electrodes as their counterpart 300 series grades. For example, AISI 201 is welded just like AISI 301. And AISI 202 is welded just like AISI 302.

Processes for Welding Stainless Steels

Up to this point, our discussion of the welding of high-chromium alloy steels has been related directly to the use of manual coated electrodes by the shielded-arc process. Other processes used include oxyacetylene welding, inert-gas-arc welding with consumable or non-consumable electrodes, resistance welding, and submerged-arc welding. Silver brazing is also employed in the joining of stainless steels.

Oxyacetylene welding has limited application. In general, it is too slow for use on the high-chromium alloys. The flame must be carefully adjusted for slightly excess acetylene in order to prevent carbon pick-up from the base metal.

The low rate of heat transfer through the stainless steel parent metal plus the slow heating which is characteristic of this process results in a greater volume of parent metal being overheated before melting occurs in the fusion zone. This produces more distortion, grain growth, and carbide precipitation if the alloy is an austenitic

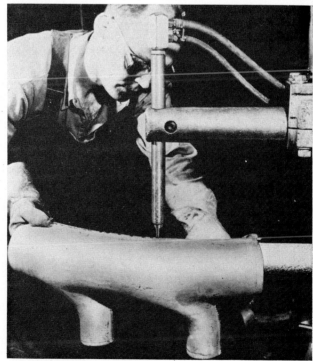

Fig. 15-6. Resistance welding is commonly used in production joining of work-hardened stainless steel sheet metal.

type. Overheating must be avoided in order to prevent the formation of the refractory chromium oxide. This oxide will form if the molten puddle is even momentarily exposed to the air. Welding an oxidized surface presents difficulties, because the metal under the scale will melt even though the oxide does not melt. It remains spread over the surface until it is blown away, scraped away or dissolved by a flux. If any oxyacetylene welding is done, a copper back-up plate should be used below the weld area to draw off excess heat and limit the possibility of oxidation occurring on the underside of the weld.

Because of this tendency for a surface oxide to form, oxyacetylene torch cutting is inadvisable for preparing grooves for welding. However, the intense heat of shielded-arc welding is sufficient to instantaneously melt through this oxide or scale. The oxide is then dissolved by flux materials deposited from the electrode coating.

Inert-gas-arc welding is widely used and has become the preferred method for production welding stainless steels in the plants of aircraft engine builders and other manufacturers of high-requirement products (Fig. 15-6). The inert gas shield prevents any appreciable alloy loss, and the filler metal can be substantially the same as the base metal in analysis. For example, titanium used as a stabilizing element

Fig. 15-7. Silver brazing can be employed in the joining of stainless steels for light service conditions.

can be transferred readily across the arc without any appreciable loss. This means that AISI 321 can be welded with Type 321 filler metal in the welding rod or electrode and thus have more uniform corrosion resistance and mechanical properties.

The use of tungsten electrode with inert-gas shielding (the TIG process) is especially suited for joining thin-gage stainless steel sheets. The highly concentrated heat and fast speeds possible minimize the problems of distortion, grain growth, and carbide precipitation. Filler metal may be omitted for some applications. Fusion welds are often made at the root of a joint. The TIG process is generally limited to not more than three passes. Joints requiring additional passes are often finished by the MIG process, using a consumable metal electrode. The MIG process is often used in making the complete weld on sections over ¼ in. thick.

Resistance spot or seam welding often has advantages in fabricating the austenitic stainless steels. These processes are especially good where the parent metal has been work-hardened by previous operations and this maximum strength is desired in the finished product. The work-hardened stainless steel is easily joined by resistance welding without need for annealing. Only a stabilized stainless alloy should be used for sheets over ⅛ in. thick in order to avoid harmful carbide precipitation.

When the hardenable stainless steels are spot welded, the weld should be given an immediate second pulse of current for tempering purposes.

Soldering and brazing of the stainless steels are generally limited to sealing applications, where the main holding force is provided by spot welds, partial fusion welds, mechanical fasteners, or other means (Fig. 15-7). Silver (hard) braze alloys are most commonly used. These give better appearance, strength and corrosion resistance than the soft solders (70% tin, 30% lead) although not matching the properties of stainless steel welds. Some hard solders also are alloys of zinc or copper, but these should not be used in joining stainless steel because of electrolytic action and reduced corrosion resistance.

Submerged-arc welding can produce joints of excellent quality on any of the chromium-nickel stainless steels and on many of the other types. It is a fast, automatic or semi-automatic process that minimizes the problems associated with overheating of the parent metal. The electrode wire is usually a little higher in alloy content than the base metal, and the flux is either a standard neutral type as used on carbon steel or is a special type developed for stainless steel welding.

An austenitic 18-8 electrode wire is most widely used in conjunction with agglomerated flux formulated to meet the needs of the specific application. In many cases, this will be a neutral flux, plus extra chromium to replace any that may be lost from base metal or filler metal during melting. The slag is largely self-removing and does not adhere to the weld bead in small slivers. The chromium or other alloy content of the flux is modified to balance that of the electrode in order to provide weld metal suitable for the specific steel being welded.

Both the submerged-arc welding and shielded-arc welding are extensively used for hardsurfacing carbon steel with a corrosion-resistant stainless steel alloy. The subject of hardsurfacing is discussed separately in a later chapter.

Definitions of New Words

Air-hardening. Characteristic of a steel that becomes partially or fully hardened (martensitic) when cooled in air from above its critical point. Not necessarily applicable when the object to be hardened has considerable thickness.

Carbide precipitation. As a result of prolonged heating or of slow cooling after partial or full transformation, atoms of carbon and a metallic element migrate to the grain boundaries. The atoms here gather and combine as carbides. In high chromium alloys, the affinity (attraction) of chromium and carbon for each other lead to the formation of a thin intergranular layer of chromium carbide.

Creep strength. The resistance of a material to slow deformation under continuous load at elevated temperatures.

Intergranular corrosion. As a result of carbide precipitation, the loss of chromium from the austenite crystals adjacent to grain boundaries weakens the material's resistance to corrosion.

Refractory. The quality of resistance to the effects of high temperatures, especially the ability of a material to maintain its hardness and shape. A "refractory" material has an exceptionally high melting point, in contrast to a "fusible" material which has an exceptionally low melting point.

Review Questions

1. When comparing 18-8 stainless steel and low-carbon steel, which steel has:
    a. The higher melting point?
    b. The higher electrical conductivity?
    c. The higher thermal conductivity?
    d. The greater amount of expansion when heated to 1000 F?
2. How do the properties of chromium oxide differ from those of iron oxide? What effect do the properties of chromium oxide have on the fabrication of stainless steels?
3. Why is each of the following elements used in some stainless steels: Carbon, molybdenum, columbium, selenium, and nitrogen?
4. Which one of the stainless steels is probably the least expensive, per pound?
5. Which of the following steels should always be in the annealed condition when welded: AISI 302, 304L, 501, or 347?

CHAPTER 16

AUSTENITIC MANGANESE STEEL

Back in the year 1882, an Englishman named Sir Robert Hadfield made an important discovery. He found that a steel having high percentages of both manganese and carbon thrives on bad treatment. The more you batter it, hammer it or otherwise subject it to impact, the harder and stronger it becomes. This remarkable alloy is known as austenitic manganese steel or sometimes, after its inventor, Hadfield manganese steel.

Austenitic manganese steel has around 10-14% manganese and 1.0-1.4% carbon. These are the two most effective elements for increasing the strength and hardness of heat-treated steel. However, when both are present in the approximate ratio of 10 to 1, they produce an alloy that cannot be successfully hardened by heat treatment.

The reheating of austenitic manganese steel to above 800 F causes it to become embrittled. This is a rather low temperature to induce metallurgical changes and prevents use of the steel under elevated temperatures. Even use under sustained temperatures of 500 to 800 F may have bad results. To be safe, this alloy is not allowed to be heated above 500 F either during use or fabrication. Any exception to this necessitates following with a toughening treatment, which will be described later.

Austenitic manganese steel comes from the mill in either cast or wrought shapes. When properly heat treated during its manufacture, the as-cast or as-rolled alloy is relatively soft—typically 187 Brinell or 10 Rockwell C. Any further cold working such as hammering or press-forming increases both its hardness and strength. This surface hardening frequently reaches a maximum of about 550 Brinell. The depth of hardness depends on the amount of applied stress.

Austenitic manganese steel stands up longer than any other known material under constant impact, and still has excellent resistance to wear by abrasion. It wears, of course, but as the work-hardened layer is worn away, additional metal is hardened. Beneath the work-hardened layer, the steel remains ductile. Other steels that are carburized or case-hardened likewise combine a ductile core with a hard surface, but the depth of hardness is fixed. Any removal of surface metal by wear subtracts from this dimension, which does not keep renewing itself as happens with austenitic manganese steel.

Some popular and very logical uses of austenitic manganese steel include power shovel dipper teeth and lips; crusher jaws and mantles; and railroad frogs, switches and crossings. The latter have to take a terrific battering from the wheels of railroad trains. An austenitic manganese rail section deforms slightly as the wheels pound its surface; the pounding and the deformation cause surface hardening, and this hardened and toughened surface resists future yielding. The body of the rail remains ductile.

Properties of Austenitic Manganese Steel

A number of the properties of Hadfield manganese steel are quite different from those of carbon steel:

Thermal expansion—when heated, austenitic manganese steel expands about 50% more than carbon steel (1½ times as much).

Thermal conductivity—is about $\frac{1}{7}$ that of carbon steel.

Electrical conductivity—is about $\frac{1}{7}$ that of carbon steel.

Melting point—is 2450 F.

Austenitic manganese steel is non-magnetic; it is not attracted by a magnet. Severe cold working will make the surface layer slightly magnetic.

Austenitic manganese steel is not much more resistant to the abrasion caused by fine sand than is mild steel; it is not as resistant to such abrasion as a hardened steel. When the wear involves impact, however, and the surface is gouged, scraped, pounded or otherwise mistreated, manganese steel will last up to 10 times as long as mild steel and very much longer than hardened carbon steel, alloy steel, or cast iron.

Effect of Manganese Content

The manganese content of a steel delays transformation of the austenite during cooling. An oil-hardening tool steel of 0.95% carbon and 1.75% manganese can be forged, and has sufficient ductility to

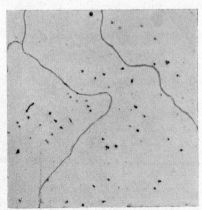

Fig. 16-1. The microstructure of heat-treated austenitic manganese steel shows only austenite grains, with no more than a thin film of carbides at the grain boundaries.

Fig. 16-2. The microstructure of untoughened "as cast" manganese steel is characterized by needle-like carbide formations, and frequently pearlite and other constituents.

withstand heavy forces as a die steel. As the manganese content is increased in high-carbon steel, the ductility decreases in the quenched or forged state. High-carbon steels with 3 to 4% manganese are air-hardening. Without other alloying elements, they are ordinarily brittle, for the austenite transformation has been delayed too long; martensite forming at room temperature is highly stressed, contains microcracks, and is brittle.

Let us now increase the manganese content to 10-14%. Transformation of the austenite is delayed to such an extent that there is no transformation; after quenching, the steel stays as austenite. The microstructure of this austenitic manganese steel is shown in Fig. 16-1. There is only one constituent—austenite. The structure is identical to that of austenitic stainless steel, or of a carbon steel at a temperature above the transformation point.

The composition of Hadfield or austenitic manganese steel as usually produced lies within the limits given in Table 16-1. The usual analysis will be in the middle of the carbon and manganese ranges: carbon at 1.2%, and manganese at 12-13%.

Table 16-1. Analysis, Austenitic Manganese Steel

Carbon	1.00 to 1.40%
Manganese	10.00 to 14.00%
Silicon	0.30 to 1.00%
Sulphur	0.60%, maximum
Phosphorus	0.10%, maximum
Iron, plus impurities	83.90 to 87.90%

High-manganese steel is expensive to machine. Most parts made of it are cast to shape and finished by grinding. As-cast manganese steel that has not been heat treated is quite brittle because a network of carbides surrounds the austenite grains, Fig. 16-2. The standard toughening treatment used at the mill or foundry consists of slowly heating the steel to 1850-1950 F and then quenching it in water to preserve the full austenite structure. This keeps the carbon and manganese dissolved in the austenite, giving the alloy its high strength and toughness. If any later fabricating process should raise the temperature of the alloy above 500 F, the toughening treatment is repeated.

In addition to having the highest work-hardening properties, manganese steel is probably our toughest material. A tough material is one that combines high strength and ductility. The stress-strain diagrams in Fig. 16-3 compare the elongation of high-manganese steel with that of high-carbon alloy steel having the same tensile

strength. The percentages of elongation are: 45% for austenitic manganese, and 15% for the high-carbon alloy. The basic strength-ductil-
ity properties of the austenitic manganese steel are maintained very
well in extreme cold weather.

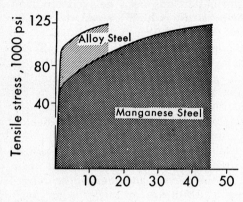

Fig. 16-3. A comparison of the
physical properties of austenitic
manganese and high-carbon alloy
steels, having identical ultimate
tensile strength.

Effect of Heating

Tempering makes carbon steels more ductile, but austenitic manganese steels lose their ductility when tempered. Reason: the austenite is supersaturated with carbon and manganese atoms that precipitate during heating—first as carbide needles in the austenite grains
and after prolonged heating as a network at the austenite grain
boundaries. They may even form an envelope encasing the individual austenite grains. The amount of ductility loss or embrittlement depends on the following:

1. The amount of carbon. A 1.4% carbon steel forms carbides
   more quickly than a 1.0% carbon steel.
2. The amount of manganese. Higher manganese decreases the
   tendency toward carbide precipitation.
3. The temperature, and the length of time the metal is held at
   temperature. Heating to 800 F or higher damages manganese
   steel. Even low-carbon, high-manganese steel heated to 800 F
   for 48 hrs will be embrittled.
4. The rate of cooling after heating within the range between
   800 and 1300 F. Some carbon will migrate from the austenite
   during such heating. Quenching prevents further carbide
   precipitation, while slow cooling causes additional loss of carbon to the grain boundaries.

Heating to 1200 F substantially reduces the toughness of the metal.
However, there will be more embrittlement if the steel is slowly
cooled and less if it is water-quenched.

At 1200 F, the austenite holds only 0.5% carbon in solution; at
1650 F, it dissolves 1.0% carbon. See Fig. 16-4. A 1% carbon steel

heated to 1650 F and then quenched would have no free carbides, but a steel containing 1.4% carbon given the same treatment would have 0.4% carbon in excess of the amount soluble in the austenite. This excess carbon would be present in the form of carbides.

Heating an austenitic manganese steel to over 2190 F permanently weakens it. Water quenching from this temperature does not restore the toughness. A complete toughening treatment following exposure to this very high temperature only partially restores the strength and toughness.

Other Manganese Steels

So far, our discussion has been largely confined to steels with 10 to 14% manganese and 1.0 to 1.4% carbon content. A steel with a manganese content of 12 to 14% and carbon in the lower range of 0.60 to 0.90% is more resistant to embrittlement when heated than is the ordinary austenitic manganese steel. The diagram, Fig. 16-4, explains why. First, note that manganese steel with 0.60% and even 0.70% carbon is all austenite (no free carbon) when at 1400 F. Increase the carbon to 1.2%, however, and you have to heat the steel to over 1800 F to dissolve all the carbon in the austenite. Steel with the lower carbon percentage can be heated to 1500 F without any carbon precipitation, and thin sections of it will air-cool through the embrittling zone (1300-800 F) so fast that there won't be time for appreciable loss of carbon from solution in the austenite.

Despite their obvious advantages for welding, the pure lower

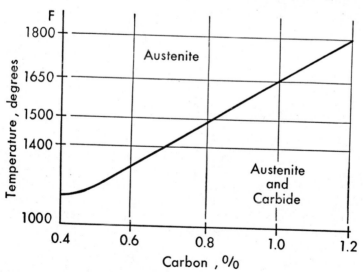

Fig. 16-4. The solubility of carbon in 12.5% manganese steel increases as the tempera-ture increases.

carbon manganese steels are not generally used. They cost more to manufacture; and, an even greater drawback, the alloy is not as resistant to abrasion as the standard product.

Effect of Alloying Elements

Let us now see what the effects are of adding other alloying elements to the standard austenitic manganese steel and to the manganese welding electrodes and fluxes.

Nickel—results in higher elastic elongation but does not change the yield strength. Quenching is still necessary to get the maximum toughness, though the rate of quenching is probably less critical. Additions of nickel may stabilize the high-manganese steels in the same way that stainless steels are stabilized by the addition of titanium or columbium. This means that there will be less carbon available for carbide precipitation.

A group of manganese steels with 0.60 to 0.90% carbon and about 3% nickel has become popular for welding rods and electrodes, wrought products and, occasionally, castings. These alloys surpass the standard grade in resistance to embrittlement caused by reheating.

Copper—is used instead of nickel in some high-manganese steel electrodes. The addition of 1-3% copper reduces the carbide precipitation in the weld deposit.

Molybdenum—ranging from 0.2 to 0.8% in high-manganese steel electrodes will give a "stiffer" deposit; that is, one that will deform less under a given load. The deposit also has a higher hardness after cold working and hence more resistance to abrasion. Molybdenum compensates for the slight loss of toughness due to lower carbon content.

Vanadium—when present in the base metal along with some combination of molybdenum, nickel or chromium, produces a precipitation-hardening grade of austenitic manganese steel.

Chromium—up to 6% in the austenitic manganese steel increases the corrosion resistance of the alloy and decreases its susceptibility to embrittlement during reheating.

Welding High-Manganese Steel

There are two kinds of welds made in austenitic manganese steel: (1) welds to build up worn surfaces, and (2) strength welds to join two parts together. Building up the surface of a bucket lip or a manganese steel rail are examples of the first type. The repair of a cracked bucket, the addition of a new tip to a dipper tooth, or the production joining of two manganese steel members are examples of strength welds.

Only arc welding is recommended. Welding with coated or bare electrode or submerged-arc welding with an agglomerated alloy flux are the processes most successfully used. Oxyacetylene welding is usually considered too expensive and keeps the metal at high temperature for a longer period, with greater possibility of embrittlement.

Electrodes depositing 11-14% manganese steel are available in both bare and coated types. Manganese-steel electrodes are among the few types of bare electrodes that have not been entirely replaced by shielded-arc electrodes.

Bare electrodes are made from rolled or drawn manganese steel and also from mild-steel tubes containing powdered metals and ferroalloys. The shielded-arc electrodes may be coated manganese-steel rods, tube-type rods or carbon-steel core wires containing the alloying metals in the coating.

In using the bare electrodes, the manganese and carbon keep the deposited metal free from harmful oxides. To allow this scavenging action to take place, the electrode is advanced slowly with a weaving motion, puddling the deposit. This gives time for the gases formed from reactions with the oxides to escape. A weld deposited without this lateral motion and slow advance will be full of gas pockets. The bare electrodes are preferred for some applications because of the high build-up obtained with one pass, and because there is no slag to clean off. These electrodes are fed into the arc manually or by a mechanical wire-feeding mechanism which semi-automates the process (a weldor still holds and manipulates the welding gun).

Coated electrodes deposit flat beads, and the surface is smoother than that obtained with bare electrodes. See Fig. 16-5. The shielding acts as a protection against magnetic arc blow and enables the electrodes to be used with alternating current. Today, there are commercially available coated electrode types that contain powdered iron in their coating to increase the deposition rate and improve

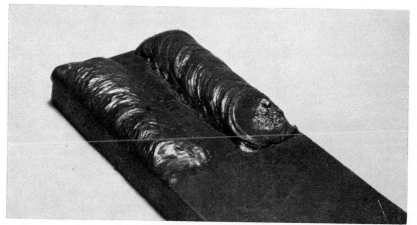

Fig. 16-5. Beads of high-manganese steel. Left, made with shielded-arc coated electrode; right, with bare metal electrode.

electrode performance.

Many of the electrodes for depositing high-manganese steel contain 3-4% nickel or 1-3% copper as alloying agents and are of the lower carbon type. Where greater resistance to impact and abrasion is required, higher carbon electrodes containing molybdenum and copper are recommended.

Bare high-manganese electrodes containing molybdenum and copper are often preferred for fast build-up of a tough, impact-resistant surface on worn high-manganese steel. When service conditions cannot be expected to provide sufficient impact or other pressures sufficient to work-harden the deposit properly, maximum resistance to abrasive wear may be obtained by using a coated, semi-austenitic, high-carbon chromium electrode for the top layer of deposited metal.

Shielded high-manganese electrodes containing molybdenum and copper are available with low-hydrogen coating and iron-powder construction. These are preferred for strength welds—joining manganese steel to either manganese steel or straight carbon steel. Coated electrodes should always be used, rather than bare electrodes, when welding dissimilar metals. These electrodes permit fast deposition without danger of underbead cracking. They also are used effectively in the low-cost hardsurfacing of carbon steel.

When a large amount of build-up is needed, welding time can be reduced by using applicator bars of manganese steel. These are made in a number of sizes and shapes. They are placed on the work and welded on each side with a manganese-steel electrode. Here a coated electrode is used, for it will penetrate into the narrow groove between the bar and the workpiece more satisfactorily than a bare electrode will. After the first pass, there will be room to fill in with the bare electrode.

Peening is not necessary when building up a few layers of weld on a heavy section like the body of a dipper tooth. Proper peening, however, will control warping and eliminate cracking. Peening of the last layer smooths and shapes the deposit, reducing the grinding on jobs that must be finished to size. Peening work-hardens a deposit, making it keep its shape longer. We previously discussed the slight deformation that occurs on a rail crossover when the first train passes over it. Deformation was necessary to the work-hardening. This would not be true of a deposit peened and then ground to shape and size, for this prehardened surface would resist further deformation when first loaded in service.

When building up carbon steel with deposits of manganese steel, care is needed. It isn't a good idea to build up a long, continuous area, such as a rail. Manganese steel contracts 50% more than does carbon steel, and this difference sets up shrinkage stresses. Admixture of the deposited metal and the rail steel forms weld metal that may be low in manganese and very brittle. The brittleness, of course, depends on the amount of penetration and the percentage of admixture.

For a hard deposited surface that will not tend to pull or peel off, carbon steel may be built up with manganese steel in this manner; the first weld layer should be applied with minimum penetration of the base metal. If the work is tilted and welding is done down-hill, it will help to reduce the melting of the base metal. Oxyacetylene welding may be used since we are not concerned about heating the parent metal, but care must be taken to not overheat the deposited metal.

When necessary to build up large surfaces, a better method is to deposit a layer of austenitic stainless (18-8) by arc welding before the manganese steel is applied. The stainless makes a good bond with both the manganese-steel deposit and the base metal, whether it is low-carbon, high-carbon or alloy steel. Also, the layer of stainless steel has enough ductility to act as a cushion to absorb the stresses resulting from the difference in contraction and expansion of the two alloys it is sandwiched between.

Where maximum abrasion resistance is desired on austenitic manganese steel, hard surfacing with a tube-type electrode having about 5% carbon and 20-23% chromium is appropriate. A similar electrode with higher manganese content (4-6%) sacrifices the abrasion resistance slightly in favor of increased toughness. With both electrodes, admixture must be kept to a minimum in order to retain the greatest abrasion resistance possible; however, increasing the penetration of parent metal will increase the toughness of the weld metal.

A better way to get good abrasion resistance with good toughness is to deposit a semi-austenitic surface, using a coated electrode having about 2% carbon and about 7% chromium. In using this electrode to hardsurface austenitic manganese steel, somewhat higher currents are used in depositing the first layer to achieve greater penetration. The admixture in this case produces a better bond.

In most cases, build-up of worn surfaces on high-manganese steels is best achieved by hardsurfacing with the bare high-manganese electrodes previously described. This provides a surface with toughness comparable to the parent metal. If increased abrasion resistance is needed, the high-manganese deposit can be faced over the top with metal deposited from one of the high-chromium electrodes.

When making strength welds in austenitic manganese steel, the following rules are important:

1. Practically all manganese-steel castings and rolled parts are high in carbon (over 1.0%). Prolonged or excessive overheating by welding will embrittle the parent metal. Therefore, low welding current and fast deposit rate are normal requirements. Use a coated high-manganese electrode that has molybdenum and copper content.

2. An optional way to obtain maximum strength and safety is to use 18-8 stainless steel electrodes. Unlike the manganese steel, the stainless-steel weld cannot be cut with an ordinary oxyacetylene torch. It can, however, be cut by powder cutting.

3. Use manganese-steel electrodes for all of the weld only when you have established a standard procedure that will produce the desired performance. In welding with high-manganese electrodes:
   (a) Make wide, short deposits.
   (b) When about ready to stop, move electrode to make crater off to one side or away from the root. Fill the crater to eliminate crater cracks.
   (c) Allow work to cool after the electrode or half the electrode has been deposited.
   (d) Peen the weld while hot, especially on multi-layer welds. Peening will reduce distortion and control cracking.
   (e) The work may be kept cool with water. Quenching the weld itself, however, is not recommended.

Automatic Arc Welding

The work-hardening property of high-manganese material makes its production into continuous electrode wire for automatic welding both uneconomical and impractical for most applications. For years, the only practical way to deposit high-manganese material was by manual arc welding. This is no longer the case.

Automatic and semi-automatic, low-cost deposition of high-quality manganese steel can be substituted for the expensive manual deposition of stainless steel or manganese steel. This result is achieved by submerged-arc welding, using a general purpose low-carbon steel electrode wire and an agglomerated alloy flux that give a deposit of medium-carbon, nickel-manganese content. It is less subject to carbide precipitation than the Hadfield manganese steel parent metal. In fact, hardness and abrasion resistance of the weld metal show little effect from welding procedure or cooling rate.

The nickel-manganese flux has a wide range of application, being used for the joining of manganese steel to manganese steel or to carbon steel, or for the building up of worn parts of manganese steel or of carbon steel. Use of pre-shaped manganese steel applicator bars is here again most economical for major repairs, with the nickel-manganese flux used in the joining of bar to structural member. In such applications, a 100% weld usually requires multiple beads and best results are attained by depositing the first bead at a rate considerably faster than the normal welding speed.

The normal deposition rates are up to 50% faster than with other submerged-arc welding combinations. The nickel-manganese flux produces a well-shaped bead that builds up rapidly with a smooth surface from which slag is easily removed. Deposits on parts that contact a mating surface tend to smooth out and take the form of the mating part. The alloy's high ductility provides even distribution of stresses across the surface, while progressive work-hardening develops good abrasion resistance.

The weld metal resulting from use of nickel-manganese flux is machinable as welded, with a Rockwell C hardness of 11 to 19. Work-hardening raises the Rockwell C values to 48 to 53. Yield strength of the weld metal is about 66,000 psi, and ultimate tensile strength about 107,000 psi. Elongation is about 35% within 2 in.

To achieve satisfactory results, work must be clean, properly fitted and positioned for down-hand welding. In the case of rigid structures, parts being welded must be preheated to expand the metal and reduce any residual shrinkage stresses. When welding austenitic manganese steel, preheat of 150-200 F is sufficient. In order to avoid carbide precipitation and embrittlement in the heat-affected zone of the manganese base metal, preheating and temperature build-up between beads must not be allowed to exceed 500 F. Skip welding and peening are advisable.

Dilution of the nickel-manganese deposit by carbon steel base metal should be kept to a minimum by control of arc penetration. The permissible high welding speeds facilitate this control.

Review Questions

1. Of the two chief austenitic steels, high manganese and 18-8 stainless,
   (a) Which has the greater hardness after surface pounding?
   (b) Which has the higher tensile strength?
   (c) Which has the greater resistance to pure abrasion? To abrasion and impact?
   (d) Which has the higher strength at elevated temperatures?

2. What are the advantages of using high-manganese electrodes for welding new tips on worn dipper teeth?

3. Why is gas welding rarely used for welding austenitic manganese steel?

4. Compare high-manganese steel with carbon steel, as to:
   (a) Contraction when cooling, and expansion when heating.
   (b) Heat conductivity.
   (c) Magnetic properties.

5. Assume that a toughened high-manganese steel casting is reheated for two hours and then quenched in water. What happens to its toughness if the temperature of reheating is: 500 F?   1200 F?   1600 F?   1900 F?

6. Outline the proper procedure for building up a surface of high-manganese steel on a carbon-steel base metal.

7. A bar of carbon steel must be welded to a bar of austenitic manganese steel. The only two electrodes available are a coated stainless steel type and a bare high-manganese electrode. Which will make the best weld? Why?

8. Why do manganese-steel electrodes usually deposit less than 1.0% carbon while austenitic manganese castings contain 1.0% carbon or more?

9. What are the advantages of high-manganese steel electrodes containing copper or nickel?

10. When would it be desirable to weld austenitic manganese steel by the submerged-arc process, using a mild-steel electrode and nickel-manganese flux?

CHAPTER 17

WELDING NON-FERROUS METALS

Most non-ferrous metals and their alloys are not hardened by quenching but by cold working, which results in a finer grain structure. Though some alloys may be heat treated to increase their hardness and strength, heating will generally cause the grain to grow and reduce the hardness.

Non-ferrous metals and alloys are welded by melting the filler metal and the base metal, protecting them from the atmosphere and from gases that result in porosity. The metal must be allowed to contract upon cooling without overstresses to cause cracking. No hard zones are formed by welding. If the parent metal has been heat treated for hardness (as in certain aluminum alloys), it will be softened by welding.

The hardness of a few of the non-ferrous alloys is increased by heating and quenching. In general, however, the alloys of carbon and iron are the only ones that are hardened by quenching and not all of them are. The austenitic manganese steels and the austenitic stainless steels are not heat hardenable. Pure iron is hardened by cold working and softened again by heating above the critical temperature. It is not hardened by quenching.

The other ductile metals are also hardened by cold working and then are softened when they are heated to the recrystallizing temperature. Microscopic examination of a metal that has been hammered shows that the original grains have been severely distorted. The individual grains have been stressed, resulting in hardening of the metal. If the work-hardened or strain-hardened metal is heated high enough and long enough, recrystallization occurs, resulting in new grains that are not stressed and are similar to the grains in the original material. Continued heating results in crystal growth.

Temperatures for the recrystallization of certain metals after severe cold plastic deformation are given in Table 17-1.

Lead and tin do not harden when they are pounded at room temperature, for the distorted crystals are immediately replaced by new and unstrained grains. This recrystallization of cold-worked metals must not be confused with the complete recrystallization that takes place when iron is heated to the transformation temperature and there is a change in the atomic structure.

Precipitation Hardening

The heat-treatable aluminum alloys, beryllium copper and some other alloys are made stronger and harder by a phenomenon called

Table 17-1. Recrystallization Temperatures

APPROXIMATE LOWEST RECRYSTALLIZATION TEMPERATURE, DEG F

Iron	840	Tantalum	1830
Nickel	1110	Tungsten	2190
Gold	390	Molybdenum	1650
Silver*	390	Zinc	Room temperature
Copper	390	Lead	Below room temperature
Aluminum	300	Tin	Below room temperature
Platinum	840	Cadmium	About room temperature
Magnesium	300		

*Under certain conditions, silver may recrystallize at lower temperatures.

Jeffries and Archer, "The Science of Metals," p. 86.

precipitation hardening or age hardening. The alloy is first heated to allow the hardening element to be uniformly distributed in solid solution (in the case of an aluminum-copper alloy, it becomes a compound of aluminum and copper) and then quenched in water. Most of the alloys so treated are dead soft after quenching and if refrigerated will remain soft. The metal is hardened by keeping it at room temperature for a few days (naturally aged) or by heating at a suitable temperature (artificially aged).

During aging, the hardening constituent separates from the solid solution as very fine particles throughout the metal grains. These particles act as keys, making it more difficult for the grains to yield when they are stressed, just as sand grains will keep cards from slipping easily.

Precipitation at higher but sub-critical temperatures may give entirely unsatisfactory results. Depending upon the specific time-temperature conditions and the composition of the alloy, intergranular corrosion and subsequent cracking may result.

Annealing

Heat-treatable alloys are softened by heating them to a point below the temperature needed for solid solution of the ingredients, followed by a slow or fast cooling depending on what properties are required in the material.

The metals and alloys that do not harden by precipitation but are hardened by cold working can be annealed by heating them for a sufficient time above the recrystallization temperature. They are then either slowly cooled or are quenched. It is a popular belief that copper must be quenched in order to obtain the maximum softness. Copper is just as soft after a slow cooling, but quenching saves time and also causes the scale to pop off and leave the surface clean.

The welds on annealed or as-cast non-ferrous metals and alloys have practically the same properties as the parent metal. Age-hardening alloys will be harder in the weld and in the heat-affected zone, depending on the length of time that the metal was held at the temperature necessary for solid solution and on the rate of cooling. To reduce or eliminate any appreciable hardening, a welding process should be used that will keep the metal at a high temperature for a minimum length of time. Usually it is not objectionable to have the weld and adjacent metal a little stronger and harder than the original material.

Non-ferrous metals that have been hardened by heat treatment or by strain-hardening (cold working) are softened by welding. The welding heat lowers the strength of the parent metal in the area near the weld, although the metal is not fully annealed by the welding operation. The strength of the weld and the heat-affected zone is somewhere between the annealed strength and the hardened strength. The properties of the weld can be varied by the choice of the filler metal, and the parent metal can be strengthened by heat treatment or by strain hardening.

Aluminum and Its Alloys

Aluminum is one of the most weldable of all our metals. Some training, however, is necessary before a weldor can turn out con-

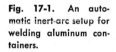

Fig. 17-1. An automatic inert-arc setup for welding aluminum containers.

sistently reliable results when working with aluminum. The weldor works with not only high purity aluminum but also the entire family of aluminum alloys both wrought and cast. With the equipment available today and the procedures which have been developed, aluminum may be welded as easily as any other metal. The important thing to remember when welding aluminum is that it has individual characteristics. Pure aluminum, for example, melts at 1215 F while its alloys melt at lower temperatures, even as low as 900 F.

The oxidation of aluminum is one of the biggest problems in welding. Aluminum oxides form a film or coating on all exposed surfaces. This must be removed before welding. Since aluminum exhibits no change in color prior to melting, it is necessary for the weldor to watch for the "wet" appearance of the surface to indicate surface melting.

To understand the nature of the particular alloy involved is a first essential in obtaining successful results when welding. Alloys of aluminum have been developed to provide the most suitable material for machining, forming, oxide coating or other requirements. Likewise, the alloys intended for welded applications do not have constituents that make welding difficult or costly.

There are so many aluminum alloys that it has been necessary to label them. The wrought alloys are identified as to composition

Table 17-2. Numerical Designation of Wrought Aluminum Alloys

NUMBER SERIES	MAJOR ALLOYING ELEMENT
1xxx	None (99.0% minimum aluminum)
2xxx	Copper
3xxx	Manganese
4xxx	Silicon
5xxx	Magnesium
6xxx	Magnesium-silicon
7xxx	Zinc
8xxx	Other major alloying elements

Notes: (a) In the 1xxx series, the last two digits indicate the specific minimum content of aluminum in hundredths of 1%. Example: 1075 would have 99.75% minimum aluminum. The second digit indicates the number of individual impurities subject to rigid control.

(b) In all other series, the last two digits are assigned to specific alloys and the second digit merely indicates modifications of the alloy.

(c) The letter x before the number indicates it is an experimental alloy not yet accepted as a permanent addition to the aluminum family.

Table 17-3. Interpretation of Letter Suffix
to Aluminum Alloy Number Designation

SUFFIX	SIGNIFICANCE
—F	As-fabricated, or as-cast (seldom used except for nonheat-treatable cast alloys)
—0	Annealed, recrystallized (wrought products only)
—H	Strain-hardened (only wrought products not heat-treatable). —H1 Strain-hardened only —H2 Strain-hardened and then partially annealed —H3 Strain-hardened and then stabilized (applies only to alloys containing magnesium; these would otherwise age-soften at room temperature) The second digit following the H indicates the temper or degree of hardening: Recognizing zero as full annealed and 8 as full hard, 2 is quarter-hard, 4 is half-hard, etc.; 9 means extra hard.
—W	Solution heat-treated, unstable temper. Alloy has been heated and quenched to obtain a solid solution, and no artificial aging treatment has been given. Material is in a condition of unstable temper, for it is slowly aging and becoming stronger at room temperature.
—T	Treated to produce stable temper (other than —F, —0, or —H). The T is usually followed by a number to indicate how the temper was achieved: —T2 Annealed (cast products only) —T3 Solution heat-treated, then cold-worked (wrought products only) —T4 Solution heat-treated, then naturally aged to stabilize it —T5 Artificially aged only —T6 Solution heat-treated, then artificially aged —T7 Solution heat-treated, then stabilized —T8 Solution heat-treated, cold-worked, then artificially aged (wrought products only) —T9 Solution heat-treated, artificially aged, then cold-worked (wrought products only) —T10 Artificially aged, then cold-worked (wrought products only)

by a four-digit numbering system adopted by the Aluminum Association. Table 17-2 shows how to identify the alloy by its number.

The 2000, 4000, 6000 and 7000 series of wrought aluminum alloys are heat-treatable because of the copper, silicon or zinc alloying additions. The 1000, 3000 and 5000 series are nonheat-treatable but are hardenable by cold working (strain hardening).

The cast alloys of aluminum do not have a comparable group-numbering system. Each alloy of specific chemical composition has an assigned number, usually of two or three digits, but two alloys of similar composition may be widely separated numerically. A letter before the number designation for a cast alloy merely indicates it is a modification of that alloy.

Additional letters or numbers that follow the numerical designation of the alloy indicate the condition of the alloy. Specific property values pertain only to the alloy when in the condition stated. Thus, this suffix can serve to indicate the strength of the alloy, and the way in which the strengthening was obtained. The general scheme of this system is presented in Table 17-3.

Let's now look at a few examples: Alloy 3003-O is a wrought aluminum alloyed with manganese and is in the soft annealed state. Alloy 3003-H12 is the same material that has been strain-hardened or cold-worked to produce a small amount of strengthening equivalent to one-quarter the full-hardened condition. Alloy 3003-H18 is the same material that has been fully hardened by cold working.

Table 17-4 shows relative properties of typical wrought alloys in various conditions.

Welding Aluminum and Aluminum Alloys

Most of the welding processes are employed in welding aluminum and its alloys, although some alloys and applications require careful selection of process and procedure. See Table 17-5.

In the welding of wrought alloys, the weld metal is cast and has less ductility than the wrought parent metal of similar chemical composition. Although the heat of welding tends to soften or anneal the parent metal, restoration of strength in the heat-affected zone

Table 17-4. Typical Properties of Wrought Aluminum Alloys

ALUMINUM ALLOY	TEMPER	YIELD STRENGTH psi	ULTIMATE STRENGTH psi	ELONGA- TION[1] % in 2%	BRINELL HARDNESS[2]
1100 (aluminum)	—0 (Soft)	5,000	13,000	35	23
	—H14 (½ Hard)	17,000	18,000	9	32
	—H18 (Full Hard)	22,000	24,000	5	44
3003 (aluminum with 1.25% manganese)	—0 (Soft)	6,000	16,000	30	28
	—H14 (½ Hard)	21,000	22,000	8	40
	—H18 (Full Hard)	27,000	29,000	4	55
5052 (aluminum with 2.5% magnesium and 0.25% chromium)	—0 (Soft)	13,000	28,000	25	47
	—H34 (½ Hard)	31,000	38,000	10	68
	—H38 (Full Hard)	37,000	42,000	7	77
6061 (aluminum with 0.6% solicon, 1.0% magnesium and 0.25% chromium)	—0 (Soft)	8,000	18,000	25	30
	—T4	21,000	35,000	22	65
	—T6	40,000	45,000	12	95
6063 (aluminum with 0.4% silicon and 0.7% magnesium)	—0 (Soft)	7,000	13,000	25	25
	—T4	13,000	25,000	22	65
	—T6	31,000	35,000	12	73

[1]Sheet specimen 1/16 in. thick.
[2]500 kg.—10 mm. ball.

Table 17-5. Process Chart for Welding Typical Aluminum Alloys

| METAL OR ALLOY | GAS | ARC | RESISTANCE | |
			SPOT	SEAM
High-purity aluminum	A	A	A	A
Commercially pure aluminum (1100)	A	A	A	A
Aluminum-manganese alloy (3003)	A	A	A	A
Aluminum-magnesium-chromium alloy (5052)	A	A	B	B
Aluminum-silicon-magnesium alloys (6053, 6061, 6063)	A	A	A	A
Aluminum-copper-magnesium-manganese alloys (2014, 2017, 2024)	No	B	B	B
Alclad 2014 and Alclad 2024	No	B	A	A

A—Welds can be applied generally on a commercial basis.
B—Commercial welding depends on design or special technique.
No—Commercial welding is not feasible.

by strain-hardening or heat-treating means that any tensile failure of the weldment would probably occur through the less-ductile weld metal. The cast weld metal, however, withstands higher temperatures better than the wrought metal and their properties are often comparable in the neighborhood of 500 F.

In welding the nonheat-treatable wrought alloys (1000, 3000 and 5000 series), the heat of welding removes some of the material's strength acquired by means of cold working—rolling, extrusion, hammering, drawing or forming. In no case will the strength be lowered below that of the material in its fully annealed condition (indicated on handbook tables of properties by the letter O after the alloy number). Welding procedure should confine the heat and loss of properties to the narrowest possible zone.

Commercially pure aluminum (1000 series) and aluminum-manganese alloys (3000 series) have good weldability, using gas, shielded-arc, inert-arc, resistance or pressure welding. However, these alloys in the annealed state may present some difficulty when resistance welded. Aluminum-magnesium alloys (5000 series) cover a wide range of properties. Those with more than 2.5% magnesium are extensively used in welded construction because of their high tensile strength in the full-annealed condition. Thus, they have the least susceptibility to weakening effects from the heat of welding. While these alloys are generally weldable, those with highest magnesium content should not be acetylene, arc or pressure welded and may present some difficulty when resistance welded in the annealed state. The inert-gas (TIG or MIG) welding process are preferred for these alloys as well as for most welded aluminum applications.

Most of the heat-treatable alloys (2000, 4000, 6000 and 7000 series) show considerable increase in properties as a result of heat treating and therefore are most susceptible to loss of strength and other damage from welding. The aluminum-magnesium-silicon alloy group (6000 series) have good weldability. Except for pressure welding, any of the processes suited to aluminum can be used for the 6000 alloys. Alloys that can be solution heat treated (such as 6053 and 6061) permit partial or full restoration of their strength by heat treatment after welding, depending upon the application. Other heat-treatable alloy groups (2000, 4000 and 7000) present the greatest difficulties in welding. Higher welding temperatures are required to penetrate these alloys and this virtually excludes acetylene welding, pressure welding, brazing and soldering. Arc welding is possible under controlled conditions, but resistance welding is generally preferred.

It is desirable, when welding any aluminum alloy, to restrict the effect of heat on the parent metal as much as is practical. High speed welding processes are therefore preferred. Shielded-arc welding is used on repair operations, but on these and production welding applications inert-gas-arc welding is often the most suitable process. Resistance welding is most universally acceptable from a strength standpoint, but where appearance is important (as is often the case) it may be ruled out because of surface distortion or discoloration.

Preweld cleanliness—is of paramount importance. Moisture, grease and the thick oxide film that is characteristic of aluminum surfaces must be removed. Since this oxide film has a melting point of about

Fig. 17-2. Vertical welding aluminum by the semi-automatic inert-arc consumable electrode (MIG) process.

Fig. 17-3. Oxyacetylene welding of an aluminum casting.

3700 F, it is generally impractical to consider removing it during the welding operation. If it isn't removed before welding, the aluminum melts beneath it and may only partially break it. The result is poor fusion and entrapped oxides that lower the weld ductility and provide a serious notch effect.

Wire brushing, scraping, or sanding may be used to remove the oxide film on aluminum surfaces. Chemical removal is also possible and is usually preferred when the aluminum has an anodized finish. Welding should follow immediately after the cleaning operation.

Preheating—of the aluminum alloys is desirable and often necessary in order to prevent high stresses and distortion when welding and to minimize cracking. Preheating should never be omitted when oxyacetylene welding. When arc welding with coated electrodes, preheating assures most satisfactory results. It is not normally required when arc welding under an inert-gas shield, but it does facilitate the control of the arc when TIG welding (using a tungsten electrode) heavy plate. Better fusion of thick plates is obtained by preheating, but the uniform preheating of large members especially on fabricated structures may be impractical.

Preheating of the wrought alloys is usually within the range of 300-500 F. Because of the low melting points of the aluminum alloys, care must be taken not to overheat. Also, preheating should be uniform. This means that heating by torch presents some hazard if done by inexperienced workers.

Distortion is best controlled by using a close fit of plates being welded and by avoidance of heavy weld deposits. No greater penetration of the base metal than is necessary for a good bond should be permitted.

Precipitation—The heat-treatable alloys are subject to considerable precipitation of alloying elements as a result of welding heat. Their migration to grain boundaries is especially pronounced in the heat-affected zone of the parent metal parallel with the weld seam. Some of these alloys (particularly 6061, 6062 and 6063) are widely used in architectural and furniture construction. For such applications, they are often given an anodizing treatment for corrosion-resistant and/or decorative purposes after welding. The precipitation resulting from welding tends to cause a distinct difference in color adjacent to the weld. This can be minimized by solution heat treating after welding and before anodizing, in order to redissolve the precipitated elements.

On many applications, a nonheat-treatable wrought alloy can be substituted and will show little color difference. Arc welding is fast and results in a narrow heat-affected zone. Flux that is not completely removed from the aluminum will result in severe pitting. The flux can also mix with the anodizing solution and contaminate it. Inert-gas welding eliminates this problem and produces the least color difference.

In all welding of aluminum alloys where appearance is a factor, it should be remembered that the cast weld metal may have a different texture than the wrought alloy being welded. Using filler metal of the same composition as the parent metal would seem to minimize this but may result in cracking. Admixture of the parent metal is accompanied by additional migration of alloying elements into the weld metal. The loss of these elements weakens the parent metal under the weld and leads to crack formation. The general solution is to use filler metal of higher alloy content than the metal being welded. An aluminum electrode with 5% silicon has the greatest range of application.

In welding aluminum castings—filler metal of the same composition as the metal being welded usually gives the best results. Cast-

Fig. 17-4. This spot weld of 10 aluminum sheets demonstrates the strength of resistance welds made in aluminum alloys.

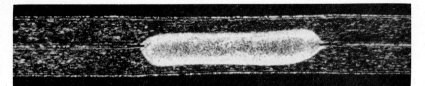

Fig. 17-5. Photomicrograph of aluminum spot weld, showing satisfactory grain structure free from cracks, blowholes, etc.

ings present essentially the same problems as wrought materials. There is even greater possibility of overheating causing cracks due to poor stress distribution across the joint. Preheating is best applied to the entire casting. The heat should not exceed 700 F, and care should be taken during welding to not go above this temperature very far, for very long, or over any appreciable area. Some alloys do permit higher preheat because of their higher melting point, but unless the melting point has been established it is best to use caution. Arc welding permits concentration of the heat and fast welding speeds. An aluminum electrode with 5% silicon melts at a low temperature, has good fluidity, is resistant to hot-short cracking, and has good strength and color. On all welding applications, slag must be carefully removed from each bead, including the final deposit.

Magnesium and Magnesium Alloys

Magnesium is the lightest of the commercial metals. It is about 2/3 the weight of aluminum which in turn is about 1/3 the weight of steel. Magnesium therefore is about 2/9 the weight of steel.

Some comparative values of the properties of pure magnesium and other metals are given in the Table 17-16. The magnesium alloys have much lower thermal conductivity. The alloy Mazlo AM260, Dowmetal C (9% aluminum, 2% zinc and 0.1% manganese) has a thermal conductivity about the same as carbon steel. Magnesium and

Table 17-6. Comparative Properties of Magnesium and Other Metals

	APPROX. MELT. PT.	WEIGHT (LB./CU. IN.)	WEIGHT (LB./CU. FT.)	APPROXIMATE RATIOS, MAGNESIUM = 1.		
				WEIGHT RATIO	THERMAL CONDUCTIVITY RATIO	EXPANSION RATIO
Magnesium	1,204	.063	109	1.0	1.0	1.0
Aluminum	1,215	.098	170	1.55	1.4	0.9
Copper	1,980	.323	560	5.1	2.5	0.62
Steel	2,700	.284	490	4.5	0.5	0.45
18-8 Stainless	2,600	.286	495	4.56	0.17	0.63
Nickel	2,646	.322	560	5.1	0.38	0.52

magnesium alloys, like the aluminum alloys, have low melting points and high thermal expansion and contraction.

The tensile strength of sand-cast magnesium is 12,000 psi and that of hard-rolled magnesium about 37,000 psi. Specific alloys have much higher strengths.

Tensile strengths as high as 53,000 psi are given for the alloy Dowmetal 0-1, Mazlo AM-C58S (8.5% aluminum, 0.5% zinc, and 0.15% manganese) in the heat-treated condition. This alloy hardens after extrusion and aging at 350 F (precipitation hardening) to give the high tensile strength.

All the magnesium alloys may be welded with the tungsten-inert-gas-shielded arc process, commonly abbreviated as TIG. The arc is maintained between the work and a single tungsten electrode in a special holder arranged with an outlet for helium or argon gas around the electrode. The inert gas enshrouds the arc and protects the molten magnesium from oxidation by the air. Abutting edges of the parent metal are melted together, or a magnesium-alloy filler rod of the same composition as the metal being welded is used.

The arc melts the metal so quickly that the metal is solid again before the heat has penetrated very far into the work. This reduces the contracting stresses during cooling and hence the possibility of cracking due to overstressing.

The alloys containing over 1.0% zinc and over 5% aluminum are susceptible to cracking if the weld is restrained from free contraction as it cools.

Magnesium and its alloys that contain only a small amount of alloying elements are weldable with oxyacetylene and with oxygen and carbohydrogen (any of the hydrocarbon fuel gases). Allowance

Fig. 17-6. Inert-arc welding of magnesium plate, with non-consumable electrode and filler rod (TIG process).

must be made for the contraction after welding. Since fluxes are required for gas welding, only butt welds are recommended. With lap welds, welding flux will remain between the parts and will cause corrosion.

The magnesium alloys may be joined by the various resistance welding processes such as, spot, seam, and butt welding. Resistance welding of magnesium offers the advantages of speed, economy and freedom from corrosion. This welding process is not recommended, however, for heavily stressed members, as the welds cannot be adequately inspected and erratic results are occasionally experienced. For advantageous use and economical applications of resistance welding, the part must be designed to permit easy access to the welding location. Magnesium alloys cannot be resistance welded to steel, aluminum or other metals.

To insure success in the spot welding of magnesium, the weldor must be provided with synchronous electric timing devices. If this feature is available, welding machines used for the welding of steel or aluminum will produce satisfactory results.

In the resistance welding of magnesium and magnesium alloys, it is extremely important that the surfaces of the material and the electrodes are clean. This cleaning operation may be done with steel wool, emery cloth or wire brushes. This will materially reduce the alloying of magnesium to the electrode. The alloying of copper from the electrode to the magnesium alloy materially reduces the corrosion resisting qualities of the magnesium.

Magnesium alloys may only be welded to each other and to similar magnesium alloys. Attempts to weld magnesium to aluminum and other metals are "inadvisable," says the Dow Chemical Co., due to the formation of brittle intermetallic compounds and the possibility of producing corrosion-promoting combinations.

As in the case with aluminum, magnesium welds do not have the tensile strength of cold-worked or heat-treated material, but the welds are stronger than the same alloy as-cast.

Welding Pure Copper

Copper, as it is usually made and sold, is one of the purest metals used commercially. The metal is one of the best conductors of heat and electricity and possesses both strength and ductility.

Ordinary copper (tough-pitch and electrolytic copper) is 99.9% pure. A small, a very small amount (about 0.05%) of oxygen is distributed throughout the metal in the form of tiny particles of copper oxide. The copper oxide has a slightly lower melting point than copper, and during welding it tends to migrate to the grain boundaries of the copper, resulting in a loss of ductility.

Copper absorbs carbon monoxide and hydrogen readily at temperatures above 1300 F. If oxygen-bearing copper absorbs these gases, they will react with the copper oxide and release gases (carbon dioxide or water vapor) which are not soluble in the copper. These gases are released between the grains and will exert enough pressure to cause internal cracking and embrittlement.

Because of oxide embrittlement, gas welding is not recommended for ordinary copper. Satisfactory welds are made with the carbon-arc and with the metal-arc, using a high welding current and a high travel speed so that there will not be time for serious embrittlement.

Copper containing a small percentage of silicon, phosphorus or other deoxidizer is designated as deoxidized copper to distinguish it from commercial or electrolytic copper. Presence of the deoxidizer inhibits the formation of copper oxide at the grain boundaries of the copper and thus makes feasible fusion strength of 30,000 to 35,000 psi. Use of deoxidized filler rod is desirable, of course, to assure a weld having the characteristics of the deoxidized base metal.

Deoxidized copper should be specified for all weldments that are to be subjected to severe service. Since this copper is not embrittled by hydrogen, either acetylene, inert-gas or shielded-arc methods of welding may be used. There is an oxygen-free copper produced, but the deoxidized copper produces better welds. Some copper oxide is always formed during welding and the deoxidized copper has enough extra silicon or phosphorus to react with this oxide and prevent any accumulation in the solidifying metal.

Compared to steel, copper has some characteristics that are considered undesirable for welding:

1. Copper has a thermal conductivity (rate of heat transfer) about five times that of steel. Copper melts at 1980 F and steel at about 2775 F; nevertheless, the surface of a 1-in. thick piece of steel can be melted very quickly with the electric arc and in a short time with an oxyacetylene torch, but it takes much longer to melt a pot of copper. The balance of the copper "sucks" the heat away from the heated spot almost as fast as it is put into the metal. It is not until the entire block of copper has been well preheated that we can get the spot to melt. This high thermal conductivity usually makes preheating necessary for welding operations.

2. Molten copper absorbs carbon monoxide and hydrogen readily. These gases are released as the metal solidifies. To prevent porosity, freezing must be from the bottom up to the surface; the torch is manipulated to allow the surface to freeze last, preventing a crust from forming over the molten metal.

3. Copper expands and contracts during heating and cooling more than steel does. In addition, the tensile strength of copper decreases very rapidly at temperatures from 500 F and up. The high contraction and the low hot strength together increase the possibility of the weld cracking during cooling.

Fig. 17-7. Oxyacetylene welding of a copper pressure vessel.

Cold-rolled copper has a tensile strength of 50,000 to 55,000 psi. After welding, however, the weld and the parent metal that has recrystallized will have the tensile strength of annealed copper: 30,000 to 35,000 psi. Cold hammering can be used in some cases to raise the strength of the weld and the heat-affected parent metal. The ductility of welds in oxygen-bearing copper is increased by hammering the weld while it is hot and then reheating. The working breaks up the embrittling film of copper oxide from around the grains, and the reheating relieves the strains and raises the ductility.

Welding Copper Alloys

There are literally hundreds of copper alloys. These include the copper-lead, copper-zinc (brasses), the copper-tins (bronzes), copper-silicon, cupro-nickel, aluminum bronzes, beryllium copper, etc. All of these alloys are weldable, though some are more readily welded

Fig. 17-8. Welded Everdur (nickel alloy) tanks for handling hot dilute sulphuric acid solutions.

than others.

The copper-lead alloys have the poorest welding properties. When this alloy is heated, the lead melts at a relatively low temperature and may be oxidized or volatilized before the copper melts. For this reason, the alloy becomes weak and brittle above the melting temperature of the lead. In welding this material, inert-gas, carbon-arc or shielded-metal-arc welding techniques are recommended and the weldor is warned against breathing lead fumes.

Copper alloys high in zinc are weldable but offer the disadvantage of giving off obnoxious zinc fumes. This tends to make arc welding difficult. Adequate ventilation should be provided in the welding of any of the copper alloys and particularly so when welding copper-zinc alloys. In the acetylene welding of this material, a flux is necessary.

The copper-tin alloys are the most weldable of the various copper alloys. Tin acts as a hardening and strengthening agent for the copper and while tin oxidizes readily with copper, it does not do so suf-

Table 17-7. Typical Nickel Alloys

NAME	COMPOSITION
Nickel	99+ % nickel
Monel	67% nickel, 30% copper, 1.5% iron, 1% manganese
"K" Monel	66% nickel, 30% copper, 3% aluminum
"Z" Nickel	94% nickel, 4.5% aluminum
Inconel	80% nickel, 15% chromium, 5% iron
Hastelloy A	56% nickel, 22% molybdenum, 6% iron

Table 17-8. Properties of the Nickel Alloys

MATERIAL	TENSILE STRENGTH psi	MAGNETIC AT ROOM TEMPERATURE	AGE HARDENING	REMARKS
Nickel	60,000 to 165,000	Strong		
Monel	60,000 to 175,000	Mild		
"K" Monel	90,000 to 200,000	No	Yes	
"Z" Nickel	30,000 to 150,000	Slightly when age hardened	Yes	
Inconel	80,000 to 185,000	No		Resists scaling at elevated temperatures
Hastelloy A, B & C	70,000 to 140,000	Slightly	Yes	Resistant to hydrochloric and sulphuric acids

ficiently to act as a deoxidizer. Phosphorus is generally used as a deoxidizer of the copper tin alloys. As a result, most tin bronzes are referred to as phosphor bronze.

The addition of tin to copper tends to strengthen the alloy and increase its hardness. In fact, when the tin content is increased to more than 12%, the alloy becomes so hard it can only be cast to shape.

Beryllium copper is one of the few copper alloys which may be hardened by heat treatment. A typical analysis is beryllium 1 to 2½%, nickel 0 to 1%, and remainder copper. In its hardened condition, beryllium copper may have a tensile strength as high as 180,000 psi. It is hardened by precipitation heat treatment in the same manner as the heat-treatable aluminum alloys, namely, by heating to obtain a solid solution of all of the alloying elements, quenching and then reheating to a lower temperature. This procedure causes the hardening ingredients to separate from the solid solution. Beryllium copper may be welded with the carbon arc, using a beryllium copper filler rod.

Aluminum bronzes may run as high as 5 to 10% aluminum with varying amounts of magnesium, iron and nickel, plus copper. These copper alloys are generally welded with the carbon arc or with coated electrodes by the shielded-arc process. When attempts are made to weld them, using the acetylene welding process, it is difficult to prevent the formation of film or aluminum oxide. This oxide film is readily entrapped in the weld since there is no available suitable fluxing material to prevent this action.

Table 17-9. Welding Processes for Nickel Alloys

WIDELY USED PROCESSES	LESS WIDELY USED PROCESSES
Inert-gas-arc	Oxyacetylene gas
Shielded-metal-arc	Carbon-arc
Submerged-arc	Furnace brazing
Resistance	Brass brazing
Silver brazing (silver soldering)	
Soft soldering	

Nickel and High-Nickel Alloys

Nickel and high-nickel alloys offer superior resistance to certain types of corrosion. The best known alloys and their compositions are shown in Table 17-7. Properties of these materials are listed in Table 17-8.

Nickel, Monel and Inconel are not hardened by heat treatment. The high tensile strengths are obtained as they are with copper; namely, by rolling, drawing and other types of cold working. The metals are softened by heating to allow crystallization. The rate of cooling from the annealing temperature has no effect upon the hardness.

Monel, Nickel and Inconel are welded as readily as low-carbon steel by the processes listed in Table 17-9.

Welds made with filler metal of the same analysis as the parent metal have mechanical properties equivalent to those of the annealed metal. The heat of welding has no appreciable effect on the properties of the base metal adjacent to the weld.

Age-Hardening Nickel Alloys

The nickel alloys "K" Monel, "Z" Nickel and the Hastelloy group contain aluminum or molybdenum. These alloys are hardened by heating to within the range of 1100 to 1600 F and then cooling slowly. A prior quenching treatment is not necessary, as is required for the hardening of the aluminum alloys.

The age-hardening nickel alloys are welded by inert-arc, shielded-metal-arc, or gas. The shielded-arc process is preferred in some cases to reduce age hardening of the parent metal. Annealing after welding will secure uniform hardness and give the weld and the heat-affected parent metal the maximum resistance to corrosion.

Joining Dissimilar Metals

The nickel-alloy electrodes are very useful for joining dissimilar metals. Monel electrodes may be used for metal-arc welding copper to carbon steel or carbon steel to nickel. Inconel or 18-8 stainless steel electrodes may be used for welding nickel to 18-8 stainless steel.

Review Questions

1. What is the only method for hardening a pure metal?
2. The following three metals are heated to about 1000 F and quenched in cold water: hardened 0.50% carbon steel, annealed copper, hardened 2017 aluminum alloy. What will be the hardness (harder or softer) of each immediately after quenching? After 24 hours?
3. What is meant by age-hardening? Name an alloy that will age-harden. What procedure is used to cause a metal alloy to age-harden? How are some alloys made to age-harden more quickly?
4. Electrolytic or tough-pitch copper may be over 99.9% pure and yet contain an element that will lower the ductility or even embrittle the weld metal and the parent metal near the weld. What is the element and what chemical compound does it form?
5. What procedure may be used to make the embrittled copper weld mentioned in question No. 4 less brittle?
6. Name some of the properties of aluminum that require the use of different welding procedures than are used for steel welding.
7. Which of the following combinations of dissimilar metals can be welded together and how?

   Aluminum to magnesium   Nickel to 18-8 stainless steel
   Copper to carbon steel   Magnesium to cast iron
8. A small amount of phosphorus is a desirable element in copper that is to be welded. Why?
9. What is objectionable about welding copper alloys containing appreciable amounts of lead or zinc?

CHAPTER 18

HARDSURFACING

Back in the stone age, Man knew that neither an all-wood arrow nor an all-stone arrow were as satisfactory as a wooden shaft with a flint arrowhead. The stone age passed into the bronze age, and the bronze age faded gradually into the age of iron. As he worked with this new metal, Man learned that a steel sword blade could be hardened by holding it in an open wood fire. The outer surface of the blade would be carburized to give a wear-resistant surface, while the interior retained its ductility and shock resistance. The armorers who wrought that miracle had learned the first principle of what we today call hardsurfacing.

As the craft of metalworking further improved, blacksmiths found they could impart a very hard surface to a steel plow point by melting a bit of cast iron on the point, hammering it into an even layer, and then quenching and later tempering the point. The layer of white cast iron made the plow point hold its edge much longer, while the steel underneath retained its ductility and strength.

With the advent of electric arc welding, hardsurfacing really came into its own. Equipment is now surfaced by welding to give resistance to corrosion, to protect against high temperatures or sudden temperature changes, and to resist wear resulting from abrasion, erosion, friction, or impact. Providing a wear-resistant surface is probably the most important of these applications. After welded hardsurfacing had proved its value in repair and maintenance work, new products were introduced with hardsurfacing applied at the factory.

The petroleum industry has long been a leader in this field. For many years, rock bits, drag bits, tool joints, and numerous special tools have been furnished with hardsurfacing materials factory-applied on key wearing areas.

Let's see now just what we mean by "wear."

If we exclude heat and chemical corrosion, and erosion, wear may be considered as the result of abrasion, friction, or impact, or a com-

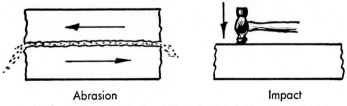

Abrasion   Impact

Fig. 18-1. Most wear results from either abrasion (left) or impact (right).

287

bination of these. Abrasive wear is encountered when one material scratches another, and impact wear when one material hits another (Fig. 18-1). Wear by friction results from the sliding, rolling or rubbing of one metal against another.

We would not make much headway trying to drill a hole in quartz rock (or hard sandstone) with a rotating steel drill, for quartz has a higher scratch hardness than steel, and our drill would be worn by abrasion. So we pound a steel star drill against the rock, and the quartz wears away by impact. The steel has a high enough compressive strength to crack the quartz. But were we to use a rotary diamond drill, it would readily scratch its way through the softer quartz.

A steel star-type dresser for rotary grinding wheels further explains the difference between impact and abrasive wear. If the dresser is used in the normal way, it will quickly wear down a small grinding wheel. The scratch hardness of the particles of aluminum oxide in the wheel is much higher than the hardness of the steel, but the impact of the rotating stars will pound the wheel away. Let us turn the dresser 90 degrees so that the stars will not rotate; the wheel will grind the steel stars at a fast rate and in turn will suffer little wear. The abrasive action of the wheel wears the steel away by millions of tiny scratches.

We can always reduce wear by using a surface material of higher scratch hardness than the substance causing the abrasive wear. Some metals have a lower scratch hardness than sand, which wears them away at a fast rate. A metal harder than sand will last a long time under the same conditions. A white-iron sand-blast nozzle will last for an hour or two, but a cast tungsten carbide nozzle will last 500 hours or more. The cast iron is made up of cementite, which is harder than the sand, and pearlite, which is softer; all constituents in the cast tungsten carbide are harder than the sand.

The Brinell hardness or the Rockwell hardness of an alloy is not a reliable indicator of its resistance to abrasion. Many hardsurfacing alloys with a Rockwell C hardness around 50 are more resistant to wear by sand than is a steel hardened to 60 Rockwell. The alloys with only 50 Rockwell C hardness contain crystals harder than the sand and large enough to stop the sand scratch. The 60 Rockwell steel may be tungsten high-speed steel containing very hard tungsten carbide particles; these particles, however, are so much smaller than the sand grain that they offer no appreciable resistance to the sand scratch. An extreme example would be a mixture of tar and fine sand and one of tar and gravel. The first would cut readily with a knife while the second would be impossible to cut.

A scratch hardness test gives a fair indication of the metal's abrasion resistance, but for really detailed information, study its microstructure and know the hardness of each constituent. Only if two metals are of the same type and have the same kind of *microconstituents* is it true that the metal with the higher Rockwell hardness will be the more resistant to abrasive wear.

Metal-to-Metal Wear

Properly lubricated metal parts wear very slowly, for a film of the lubricant keeps the metals from actually touching. Inadequate lubrication or excessive pressure will allow metal to make contact, and then a gall or *cold weld* may result as one part slides over the other in frictional wear.

Two pieces of aluminum may be cold welded by power brushing the surfaces and then pressing or rolling the prepared surfaces together. In a similar manner, a steel part that slides over another steel member may rub off the separating film. With high enough contact pressure, the iron atoms of each surface may get close enough to each other to exert their powerful atomic forces of attraction. Frequently, the little weld thus formed is strong enough to hold and pull out some of the parent metal. This bit of metal will plow into the surface of the other member, picking up more metal, and soon the parts will be keyed or frozen together. If this does not happen, they will certainly be chewed up to the extent that they must be replaced.

Certain combinations of metals gall less readily than others: steel does not gall when working with brass or bronze. In general, hard metals gall less readily than soft ones.

Impact Wear

Abrasive wear depends upon the surface properties of a metal, but impact wear is related to the properties under the surface. A piece of copper can be scratched easily by a needle, but if we try to drive the needle across the copper too deeply, the point of the needle will break. The scratch is wear by abrasion, the deeper penetration is a form of impact wear. The copper has caused failure of the needle by imposing stresses above the strength of the needle. This failure is due to impact wear at a low velocity but with a high force.

Impact wear results from pounding, hammering, battering, or any overstressing of the metal by localized high loads applied at low rates. Abrasive wear occurs when the *abradant* moves parallel to the surface of the abrasive, but impact wear occurs when the impact-producing material presses more or less perpendicularly against the surface of the wearing member. Abrasion removes metal by scratching; impact removes metal by crushing, pulverizing, cracking, spalling, chipping and flaking. Impact or high loading will also cause metal to flow, to upset, to bend or to otherwise deform.

Sand flowing through a sandblast nozzle wears the nozzle by abrasion; however, the metal that is sandblasted is worn by impact.

A material with a high scratch hardness is needed to make a long-lasting sandblast nozzle; toughness is not important. It becomes very important, however, when we want to choose a metal to resist the sand stream. The hard, brittle metal that made the best nozzle will wear away faster than a material not as hard but tougher.

To resist impact wear, either one of the two following procedures may be used:

1. Use a tough material, which will absorb the impact by yielding to distribute the load. Rubber is superior to some metals for resisting impact wear. The rubber cushions the blow, absorbing the energy, and the final unit load is low enough to cause no damage to the rubber. When a ductile metal receives a blow or a concentrated load, the metal deforms, increasing the area of contact. This reduces the unit stress so that the ultimate strength in compression is not exceeded.

2. The second procedure is the brute force method. The part is made stronger than the abrading material, so that the abrading material will fail when the two come in contact. This procedure is not always possible, and when it is possible it may be more expensive than the first method.

There are over 300 different kinds of surfacing electrodes and materials sold in this country. Each manufacturer blends his own alloys and coating since there are no standard specifications for these welding materials. Nor are there any standard procedures for testing hardsurfacing alloys to determine their resistance to abrasion and their resistance to impact. There are, however, a number of laboratory tests to evaluate hardsurfacing materials for certain specific conditions of wear. A few of these tests will be described.

Abrasion Tests

One type of test drags the specimen over a copper slab in a mixture of quartz sand and water; the abrasion factor is the loss of weight of the specimen compared to the loss of weight of a standard annealed SAE 1020 steel specimen. A material that loses the same weight as the SAE 1020 steel will have an abrasion factor of 1.00. The ideal material would not lose any weight and would have a factor of 0.00.

Another test presses the specimen against a notched rubber wheel, which is rotated in a slurry of sand and water; the loss of weight is taken as the abrasion value.

A preferred method is the use of a grinding wheel of aluminum oxide as the abradant. The amount of wheel that is ground away to remove a standard weight of the hardsurfacing material is taken as the abrasion index. This test is excellent for evaluating the hardsurfacing materials used to dig earth, such as the tungsten carbides.

The loss of weight of the specimen when run against the wheel at standard conditions is taken as the abrasion value for the materials when they are to be used for wear-resistant purposes. It is important to have both values, for the material that shows the least loss of weight may not be the best one on, say, a rotary well drilling bit. In general, a material that will wear smooth is better to resist wear. For earth cutting, however, the best surfacing is one that will wear to give rough, jagged, sharp cutting edges.

The grinding wheel test is preferred to the wet sand tests because the wet sand results do not show as much difference in hardsurfacing materials as is usually found in the field. The grinding wheel method gives a very large difference in weight loss: 0.02 gram loss for a hard grade of sintered tungsten carbide and about 10.0 grams loss for mild steel—a ratio of 1 to 500. It should be noted that the different methods list various materials in about the same order, with the exception of the work-hardening alloys such as high-manganese steel.

The abrasion values are not directly applicable to field service. Some of the variables that can change the order of abrasion resist-

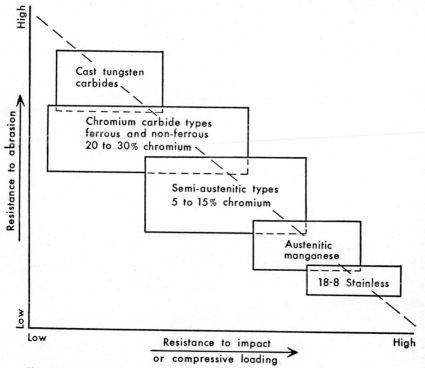

Fig. 18-2. Relationship of the abrasion resistance and impact qualities of various hardsurfacing materials. In general, resistance to impact decreases as resistance to abrasion increases.

ance of hardsurfacing are: temperature, size, hardness and other properties of the abradant, the amount of impact, etc.

Impact Tests

Impact tests have been made on the commercial hardsurfacing materials by pounding weld deposits against each other and against standards. The materials are then arranged according to their resistance to cracking, chipping or spalling.

The results of various impact and abrasion tests are shown in Fig. 18-2. This chart shows diagrammatically the type of the results obtained from the tests of a number of commercial hardsurfacing materials and experimental alloys.

The resistance to abrasion was determined from the loss in weight of the deposit in a given time run under controlled abrasive conditions.

The resistance to cracking under impact was determined by comparative tests of the deposits, using a pounding machine built for this test.

Some highly alloyed and expensive welding rods and electrodes give less wear resistance than rods and electrodes made of lower priced materials. The proper proportioning of the ingredients counts more than the amount and cost of the alloys.

Let's now define the chief types of hardsurfacing alloys:
1. Tungsten carbides—Particles of crushed cast tungsten carbide in steel tubes.
2. Chromium carbides—Cast rods or steel tubes containing ferrous alloys that form a deposit high in chromium carbides. Some of the cast rods in this group are non-ferrous, containing chromium, carbon, cobalt and tungsten, but no iron. Chromium carbide powder may be applied directly to thin surfaces with arc torch or carbon arc.
3. Semi-austenitic—Electrodes depositing high-carbon alloys containing over 80% iron. The deposits are either hard as deposited or become hard after battering. Deposits also are hardenable by heat treating.
4. Austenitic manganese—Electrodes depositing 11 to 14% manganese steel, affording a work-hardenable surface.
5. Stainless steel—Electrodes depositing 18-8 steel (18% chromium and 8% nickel) and other austenitic stainless steels with higher contents of chromium and nickel.

Most of the heat-treatable hardsurfacing alloys are not listed on the abrasion and impact resistance chart (Fig. 18-2) because their properties depend on the rate at which the deposits cool after welding and also on any subsequent heat treatment. Some of these materials will be discussed later in this chapter, and some in the chapter on welding tool and die steels.

Some other hardsurfacing materials that do not fall in the above classifications are cast irons, and alloys containing chromium boride or tantalum carbide as the hard ingredient.

Tungsten Carbide Group

The cast tungsten carbides are not to be confused with the sintered (or cemented) carbides used for metal cutting tools. The sintered carbides are made by pressing a mixture of finely powdered tungsten carbide and cobalt in a mold at a very high pressure, and then heating the mold hot enough to cause the cobalt to bond the powdered carbide. The heating is called sintering because the ingredients are not melted. The sintered carbides have wonderful mechanical properties but they cannot be fusion welded, for if they are heated to the melting point of cobalt, the cobalt and the tungsten carbide will alloy and the superior properties of the tungsten carbide will be lost.

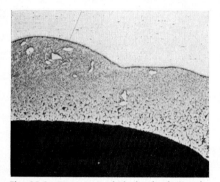

Fig. 18-3. Tungsten carbide hardsurfacing deposit viewed at 10X.

Fig. 18-4. Tungsten carbide hardsurfacing deposit viewed at 1000X.

In a cast tungsten carbide, crystals of very hard tungsten carbide are embedded in a matrix of a relatively tough tungsten and carbon alloy (Figs. 18-3 and 18-4). This alloy melts at about 4600 F, a melting point so high that the material is deposited by the torch or the arc without melting. Though it does not melt, the cast carbide will disintegrate if it is kept in contact with molten steel.

For hardsurfacing, the cast tungsten carbide is crushed, screened to size and the particles placed in steel tubes. During deposition, the mild-steel tube dissolves some carbon and tungsten from the tungsten carbide particles, resulting in a strong bonding alloy. The coarse material is used on equipment for cutting earth or some of the highly abrasive rock formations. The fine material is best suited for abrasion resistance applications requiring a deposit that will wear fairly smooth. In either case the facing has a pebbled surface as deposited and is unmachinable.

Tungsten carbide particles have the highest scratch hardness of all known materials that can be deposited by welding. A deposit of

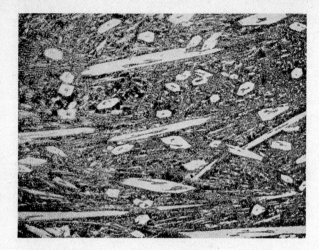

Fig. 18-5. Structure of a cast chromium carbide alloy, containing 3.50% C and 27% Cr (100X).

tungsten carbide is one of the most abrasion resistant of all hard-surfacing materials. There are three main constituents in this deposit:

1. The tiny tungsten carbide crystals, brittle but very hard.
2. The hard tungsten alloy that holds the carbide crystals.
3. The strong iron alloy holding the cast carbide granules.

Chromium Carbide Types

Most of the hardsurfacing alloys in this group contain from 3.5 to 5% carbon and 20 to 30% chromium. Usually one or more of the following elements are present: iron, manganese, molybdenum, vanadium, or zirconium. Carbides that form as the alloys solidify are not changed by any subsequent heat treatment. These needlelike crystals (Fig. 18-5) have a hexagonal cross-section. It is interesting to watch them form on the surface. If a weld deposit is suddenly turned upside down just before solidification is complete, the matrix metal will run away leaving a mass of the chromium carbide crystals piled up like a stack of jackstraws.

The chromium carbides are harder and more abrasion-resistant than iron carbide (cementite), but they are relatively brittle. The toughness of the alloys in this group depends upon the properties of the metal used to bond the carbides.

There are dozens of hardsurfacing alloys, ferrous and non-ferrous, in the group, and some of them offer a very good combination of abrasion resistance and toughness. In general, they are non-magnetic, are not affected by heat treatment, and will resist corrosion. As they wear, their surface becomes very smooth.

The ferrous chromium carbide alloys are too hard to be machined and have excellent resistance to wear by abrasion and friction. They also have high hardness at elevated temperatures. See Fig. 18-6, which gives the *instant hardness* of several materials at various temperatures.

The non-ferrous chromium carbides are commonly called "Stellites" from a proprietary trade name. They are alloys of chromium, 1-2% carbon, plus cobalt and tungsten. In some cases, they are used for the same types of service as the ferrous chromium carbides but cost more. However, the non-ferrous chromium carbides usually are machinable. Although they are not as resistant to abrasion as some of the ferrous chromium carbides, they are superior in resistance to certain types of corrosion. Because of their finer grain structure, they are also superior when a material is required that will maintain a smooth, uniform and sharp cutting edge.

The non-ferrous chromium carbide alloys also are known for their properties of red-hardness (hardness at high temperatures). Some of the ferrous types, however, have still higher hardness at red heat. Figure 18-6 shows this relationship, and also shows the relative hardness of other heat-resistant hardsurfacing alloys at various temperatures.

Semi-Austenitic Alloys

This group includes iron-base hardsurfacing materials with less than 20% alloying elements. The popular alloys contain 1 to 2%

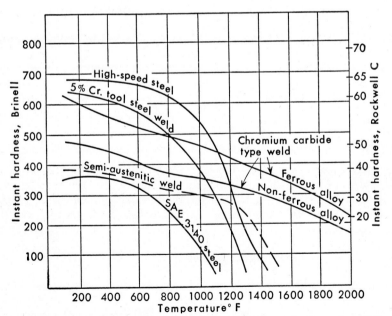

Fig. 18-6. Curve showing change in relationship of the instant hardness of common hardsurfacing materials at various temperatures.

carbon, 5 to 12% chromium, and smaller amounts of other elements. These deposits retain austenite as they solidify; there is not enough carbon and chromium for chromium carbide to crystallize. As the austenite cools, a variety of structures are possible, depending on the analysis and the cooling rate.

The semi-austenitic surfacing materials are so called because not all of the austenite remains as such when the deposit cools. The deposits having a large percentage of austenite are very tough and not very hard as welded. They are, however, work-hardenable; that is, the surface becomes hard after abrading or pounding. One alloy that is 30 Rockwell C as deposited becomes over 50 Rockwell C after moderate peening. The materials with appreciable amounts of martensite are hard as deposited.

The properties of the deposit may be varied by the welding procedure. If the weld metal cools quickly—small electrode, short beads and base metal cold before welding—the deposit will be predominately austenitic: softer, tougher and less resistant to pure abrasion but will work harden.

If the weld metal cools slowly—large electrode, continuous welding or preheated base metal—most of the austenite has time to transform to martensite. This gives a harder, less ductile deposit but one that is more resistant to pure abrasion. Both types of deposit will work harden to the same final value.

The austenitic content of this group of hardsurfacing material gives them a very high resistance to impact, and their hardness (original hardness of that obtained by work hardening) gives them good resistance to abrasion.

The semi-austenitic deposits are machinable with tungsten carbide tools after a long anneal at high temperature. Some of them can be hot forged. This group of alloys combines low cost with excellent resistance to impact and good abrasion resistance. No wonder it is the most popular group of hardsurfacing materials!

12 to 14% Manganese Steel

High-manganese steel deposits are tougher but not so abrasion-resistant as those made with the semi-austenitic electrodes. It is, however, a popular practice to build up worn manganese-steel parts nearly to size with austenitic manganese-steel electrodes and then to finish the deposit with one or two layers of semi-austenitic rod. See Chapter 16, Austenitic Manganese Steel.

Stainless Steels

The austenitic stainless steels are classified with hardsurfacing materials because they are just one step below manganese steel in their ability to work-harden. Moreover, they will stand more pounding without cracking. The stainless deposits are especially advantageous for high impact service under corrosive conditions.

Stainless deposits are sometimes used as base layers for other hard-surfacing materials. High-manganese steel deposits form a brittle bond with carbon steel unless dilution with carbon is minimized. The bond between the semi-austenitic deposits and carbon steel is neither ductile enough nor strong enough to keep a multi-layer deposit from pulling off. The answer is an initial layer of stainless because it bonds well to both base metal and hardsurfacing.

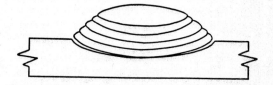

Fig. 18-7. A bond failure between a semi-austenitic hard-surfacing alloy and carbon steel.

Figure 18-7 shows five layers (not recommended) of semi-austenitic hardsurfacing on carbon steel. The bond between the weld and the carbon steel failed, due to shrinkage of the high-strength deposit. The layer of the semi-austenitic deposit on carbon steel is so diluted with the base metal the weld is at least partly martensitic and does not have the ductility of austenite. A layer of 25% chromium, 20% nickel stainless steel would be ductile enough to allow the weld metal to contract without setting up the high stresses. The austenitic stainless contains enough chromium and nickel to remain austenitic and ductile after dilution with the carbon steel.

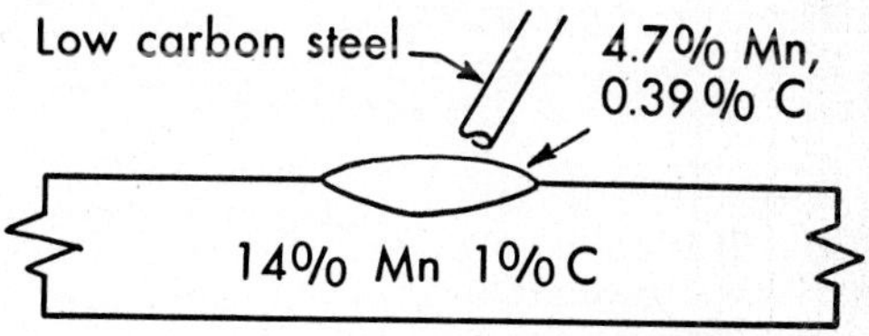

Fig. 18-8. A brittle alloy is formed when low-carbon steel is deposited on manganese steel.

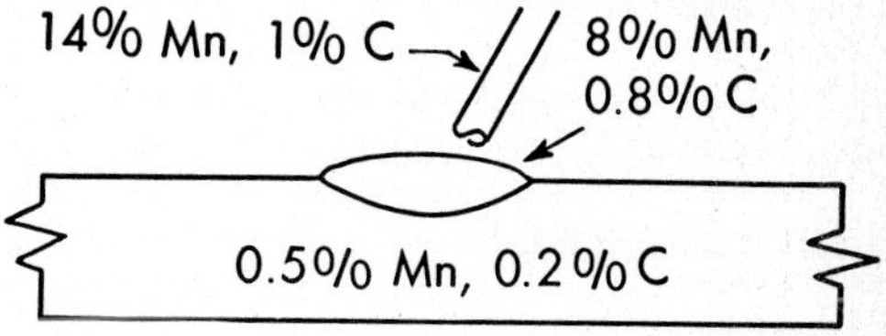

Low carbon steel — 4.7% Mn, 0.39% C

14% Mn 1% C

Fig. 18-9. A less brittle alloy is formed when high manganese steel is welded on carbon steel.

14% Mn, 1% C — 8% Mn, 0.8% C

0.5% Mn, 0.2% C

Though in some cases an 18-8 alloy is all right for bonding purposes, for maximum ductility stainless steels with higher chromium and nickel content should be used. When the analysis of the electrode is not the same as that of the base metal, we do not have a gradual change in composition from the base metal to that of the top of the deposit. In a one-layer deposit the metal that has been melted is of a practically uniform analysis. At the fusion line, there is a layer of grains of intermediate composition as a result of diffusion of carbon in the solid state. The microscope shows that at the fusion line one grain will be like the parent metal and the adjoining grain similar to the weld metal.

Knowing the analysis of the materials involved and the approximate amount of the penetration, the weld metal analysis may be estimated. Assuming that the penetration results in weld metal made up of ⅓ base metal and ⅔ deposited metal, we can see that welding high-manganese steel with a mild-steel electrode is not good practice (Fig. 18-8). In this case, the weld metal will pick up manganese and carbon from the parent metal. If the base metal is 14% manganese, the weld will have one-third of that or 4.7% manganese—a very brittle steel. A much better alloy is obtained when high-manganese is welded on mild steel (Fig. 18-9). Then, if the manganese content of the electrode metal is 12%, the analysis of the weld will be ⅔ of 12%, or 8% manganese. This alloy will be partially austenite and have a fair degree of toughness.

In Fig. 18-10, two layers of semi-austenitic steel are welded on carbon steel that has been prepared by surfacing it with a layer of stainless.

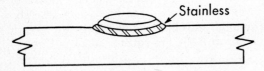

← Stainless

Fig. 18-10. An intermediate layer of stainless steel provides the ductility to successfully bond a manganese deposit to carbon steel.

Heat-Treatable Hardsurfacing Alloys

The heat-treatable deposits are all martensitic types. They form hard deposits if the weld metal cools fast enough, and they may be softened by annealing. There are four chief types:

1. High-carbon steel
2. Medium-carbon steel with alloying elements
3. Tool and die steels
4. High-speed steels

High-Carbon Steel

The cooling rate of a high-carbon steel deposit must be controlled in order to make the surfacing hard and abrasion-resistant. A bead from a small-diameter 1.0% carbon electrode on cold steel will be file-hard and have an abrasion resistance in the class with the semi-austenitic deposits, but the high carbon steel will be low in impact resistance. Larger diameter 1.0% carbon electrodes, welded at high current on preheated base metal, will produce softer deposits, though hard enough to be abrasion-resistant. As the metal passes through the arc, a 1.0% carbon electrode loses carbon; so the deposit has only from 0.8 to 0.6% carbon.

Carbon steel electrodes containing 0.50 to 0.60% carbon are used for deposits that are to be machined without tempering or annealing, provided the deposit can be cooled slowly.

Medium- and high-carbon steel deposits are used for surfacing applications where high-carbon steel properties are desired and also for preliminary build-up prior to the application of other hard-surfacing alloys.

Some charts show the hardness range of various hardsurfacing alloys. These hardness figures are usually for multi-layer manually applied weld deposits. The hardness of single-layer welds, being influenced more by admixture with the base metal, may be higher or lower than that of multi-layer deposits. This depends of course on the hardenability of the weld metal. A low-carbon electrode deposited on high-carbon steel will give a medium-carbon weld metal.

It is possible to have a combination of analyses that will give a very hard deposit. For example, a low-carbon but high-alloy base metal, when surfaced with a high-carbon electrode, will give a weld metal that is high in carbon and has picked up enough alloy to give it a higher hardenability than either a multi-layer high-carbon de-

Fig. 18-11. Hardness increases with carbon content, but preheating to improve impact properties tends to lessen the rise in hardness.

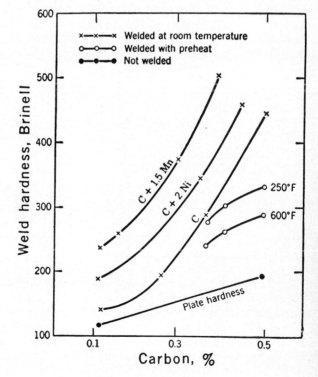

posit or the high-alloy base metal.

The abrasion resistance of high-carbon weld deposits increases with the hardness. The maximum ductility (impact resistance) for a given hardness is obtained by quenching and tempering. Heat-treated properties may be approached by welding alone. To achieve such results, use minimum preheat and apply a small bead or a thin layer, allow time for the high-carbon weld to transform to martensite, and then deposit the next bead or layer. Thus, all of the weld with the exception of the last layer will be quickly cooled (quenched) and tempered.

Medium-Carbon Steel with Alloying Elements

Chemical analyses in this group range from 0.15% carbon with a total of 2.0% chromium, manganese, molybdenum, silicon, etc., on up to 0.50% carbon with 5.0% alloying elements. The alloy content increases the hardenability, giving a higher as-welded hardness on preheated work than is obtainable with high-carbon deposits. The lower carbon limits the maximum hardness obtainable (see Fig. 18-11) but greatly increases the resistance to impact. The metal-arc deposits are air-hardening and in the as-welded condition have good resistance to abrasion and high toughness.

Electrodes in this class are popular for building up carbon-steel rail ends. By using a controlled preheat and welding procedure, a hardness gradient is obtained in the weld and parent metal that gives longer service than the original rail ends.

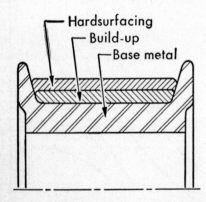

Hardsurfacing
Build-up
Base metal

Fig. 18-12. In many cases, a lower-cost and ductile material is used to build up a worn part before depositing the final layer of metal having the surface properties needed.

In addition to many applications for resisting metal-to-metal wear, these electrodes are valuable for building up steels before they are surfaced with the chromium-carbide, tungsten-carbide or other higher alloys (Fig. 18-12).

The tool-steel and die-steel deposits will be discussed in the chapter on the welding of tool and die steels.

Evaluating Hardness and Abrasion Resistance

The big problem in selection of a hardsurfacing material is that the best is rarely good enough. Figure 18-13 gives the results of a few grinding-abrasion and hardness tests made on various hardsurfacing deposits and on steels. These are plotted on semi-logarithmic paper in order to show values for low and high abrasion-resistant materials.

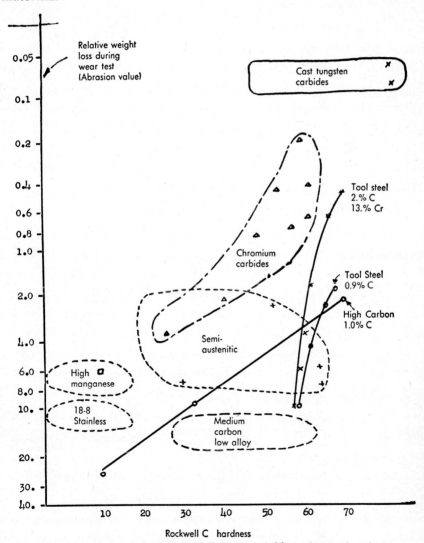

Fig. 18-13. An increase in hardness is usually accompanied by an increase in resistance to abrasion, as measured by weight loss during wear test by grinding wheel.

Tungsten carbide—materials have the highest abrasion resistance and are shown as an area for which the Rockwell C hardness of the deposit cannot be given a definite value. The bonding alloy has a relatively low hardness and the tungsten carbide particles, of course, a very high hardness. Metallurgists use a different procedure in evaluating the hardness of such materials, and hardness values when given are according to the Rockwell A scale. The surface generally has a sandpaper finish.

Chromium carbide—deposits range in hardness from 40 to 63 Rockwell C. In general, the harder alloys are more abrasion-resistant, and they will crack and chip away more easily under impact. The better alloys for any given resistance to impact have a lower hardness. For each material, there is a combination of carbon and alloy (chromium, molybdenum, etc.) content that will give both abrasion resistance and impact strength. An off-balance material, however, may have low resistance to abrasion and also be brittle. Some electrodes are designed to produce good hardsurfacing deposits when diluted with steel, that is, a one-layer deposit that will be resistant to abrasion and to cracking. The best non-ferrous chromium carbide electrodes deposit metal that features high hardness (54-63 Rockwell C), very high abrasion resistance, and the characteristic of cross checking to relieve cooling stresses. This cross checking does not lower the efficiency of the facing.

Semi-austenitic alloys—There is a wide range in hardness in this group, for some of the materials are of the work-hardening type and others are hard as deposited. They do not show a wide variation in abrasion resistance. It is interesting to note that the alloys that are hard as deposited are not as resistant to grinding abrasion as some of those having a much lower hardness. The alloys that work harden are also superior for service involving a combination of impact and abrasion.

High-manganese steel—In the tests recorded on Fig. 18-13, there was not much variation in the hardness or the abrasion resistance of austenitic manganese deposits. The highest abrasion-resistant deposits contained carbon about 1.0% and some molybdenum. Those of lower abrasion resistance are of a lower carbon and nickel content. High-manganese deposits are not recommended for resistance to grinding abrasion but they are superior for resistance to a combination of severe impact and abrasion.

Stainless steel—Only a few tests were run on stainless steel deposits. The abrasion resistance and hardness were both low, but the deposits were more abrasion resistant than those of high-carbon steel at the same hardness. The 18-8 stainless deposits work-harden but not nearly to the extent of the high-manganese steels.

Tool steels—Numerous tests were made on tool and die steel rolled samples after hardening and tempering. The tempering treatments did not change the hardness much but changed the amount of wear by a ratio of 20 to 1. Deposits of tool and die steel types and high-speed steel types gave values in the same range as those shown by the two tool steel curves. At a certain hardness, the deposit with the higher carbon had the higher abrasion resistance.

High-carbon steel—Drill rods were quenched in brine and tempered. The hardness and abrasion resistance of these rods gave a straight line (when plotted on the semi-logarithmic paper), and the weld deposits gave the same type results. Low-carbon deposits lost more weight during the test than high-carbon deposits of the same hardness.

Medium-carbon low-alloy steel—Deposits occupy the lower positions on the chart. But remember that they are not designed for resistance to grinding abrasion. They are resistant to metal-to-metal wear and have a good hardness as deposited and a high toughness. Some of these alloys are outstanding for their high tensile strength and ductility. They resist deformation and cracking when subjected to high impact service.

Analyzing the Job

An analysis of the service that is required will be of assistance. In all instances of wear, there are two members or materials that contact and there is relative motion between them. Considering these two members in terms of required service, there are three things (Table 18-1) that we may wish to do:

Table 18-1. Wear Service Classification

SERVICE CLASS	FIRST MEMBER	SECOND MEMBER	SERVICE
A	Protect (shear blade)	Cut or wear (steel sheet)	A cutting edge is to be maintained Case 1. Wear of edge effects the efficiency —shear blade Case 2. Sharp edge important but wear secondary earth cutting tool
B	Protect (valve gate)	Protect (valve seat)	Two surfaces in contact—both to be protected. Chain links—valve gates and seats
C	Protect (ore chute)	Do not care (ore)	Protect one of the members; wear of the other is of little or no importance. Screw conveyor

A. A cutting edge is to be maintained. We wish to keep the wear of one member to a minimum, but cut or wear the other member.

B. Two surfaces are in contact, both of which must be protected.

C. One surface is to be protected. We do not care what happens to the other member.

One of the two "members" in a wear relationship may be a material such as rock, earth, coal or ore.

To Maintain a Cutting Edge

In Group A applications requiring a cutting edge to be maintained, there are two possibilities to consider: when wear of the cutting edge affects the efficiency, and when wear of the edge does not affect the efficiency of the tool.

(1) *When wear of the edge affects efficiency:*

Shear blades, punches and metal-cutting tools must not only stay sharp, but they must hold their original size and shape to operate satisfactorily. Failure of these parts is by upsetting, chipping, spalling or galling due to high compressive loads, and the flow of the metal being cut. High-velocity impact and scratching abrasion are seldom problems.

Tool-steel and high-speed-steel facings are recommended for service requiring the maintenance of an edge for metal cutting. When wear resistance at high temperature is not needed, tool-steel welding electrodes are used as they are less expensive. The deposits of tool steel and high-speed steel are homogeneous and very fine-grained, which allows grinding to form a sharp thin edge. Because of the steel's high mechanical properties, the edges resist turning over or chipping.

(2) *When wear of the edge does not affect efficiency:*

On earth-cutting tools, blades of rotary drilling bits, ensilage knives, shredder blades, etc., the one requirement is that the edge must stay sharp. These tools are intentionally surfaced with wear-resisting material on the advancing edge so that metal on the back face will wear away and keep a fresh-sharp edge of the hardsurfacing exposed.

Figure 18-14 shows the hardsurfacing procedure to secure this self-sharpening effect. When hardsurfacing carbon steel with a semi-austenitic, chromium carbide or tungsten carbide alloy, an intermedi-

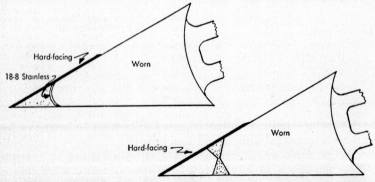

Fig. 18-14. The proper hardsurfacing procedure to secure a self-sharpening effect on earth-moving tool. Slow wear action along bottom provides relief under cutting edge, maintaining a sharpness for high cutting efficiency.

ate layer of stainless steel is required. If a tool tip is broken off or dulled excessively, a new tip can be welded on, and the hardsurfacing then applied. If the tool body is a carbon steel, stainless steel is used to join the new tip. If the base metal is austenitic manganese steel, an austenitic manganese electrode should be used for joining.

Figure 18-15 shows an earth-scraping tool surfaced on both the front and back. From the sketches, one can see that a high force downward is required to make this tool penetrate and cut the earth formation. If the surfacing on the front chips, the tool will slide over the formation.

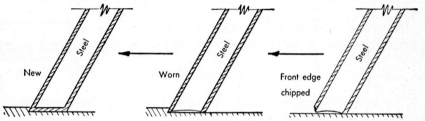

Fig. 18-15. How a rooter tooth wears when hardsurfaced on both front and back faces.

In Figure 18-16, the earth-scraping tool was surfaced on the front only. The backing metal soon wears away, leaving the hardsurfacing in relief. The scraper will penetrate deeper and cut faster.

Rate of wear on a cutting edge is directly proportional to the thickness of the deposit. A thin hardsurfacing layer will give a fast cutting tool, but the tool will wear faster (Fig. 18-17). A heavy deposit of hardsurfacing will reduce the rate of cutting because of the thicker cutting edge (Fig. 18-18).

For example, we will assume that a rotary well drilling bit with a thin layer of hardsurfacing is worn out after drilling 30 feet in one hour. A layer of surfacing three times as thick might drill a total of 90 ft but at only 10 ft per hr, requiring 9 hrs to drill the 90 ft. In some cases, the first drill would be more economical to use and in other cases the second, depending partly on the time to replace the drill bit and partly on the cost of reconditioning it.

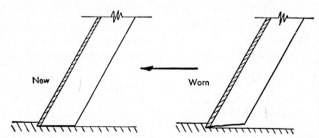

Fig. 18-16. Hardsurfacing only the front face makes the rooter tooth self-sharpening.

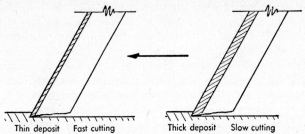

Fig. 18-17. A thin deposit results in fast cutting and a short life.

Fig. 18-18. Slow cutting and a long life will be obtained from a thick deposit.

Materials most resistant to abrasion are used for such applications as drilling bits. Coarse particles of tungsten carbide applied in a mild-steel tube will give the longest life to earth-cutting tools used in sandy formations; as the bonding metal wears, it leaves a rough, fast cutting edge.

Coarse-carbide deposits give an edge that may be likened to a fine toothed rake, while the fine carbide deposit gives a smooth, uniform edge like a hoe. The fine particles are so close together that there is no room for wear to take place between them.

There are applications for both types of edges. The fine carbide surfacing is recommended for bean knives, since the service is highly abrasive and a smooth, thin self-sharpening edge is needed. An edge to resist impact or high-unit loads had better be of another type.

The chromium carbides are used on cutting edges in which the abrasive conditions are not so severe or when a lower cost material is desired. These hardsurfacings will also form a self-sharpening edge and will wear to give smoother surfaces and lower friction than are obtainable with the tungsten carbides.

When the impact service is high, the austenitic manganese semi-austenitic group of hardsurfacing materials will give the longest life to cutting edges. Edges protected by one of these materials are generally not self-sharpening but wear to a rounded contour that will withstand high loads and impact. The tungsten carbide and the chromium carbide deposits will chip off from dipper teeth handling large rock. The austenitic manganese or semi-austenitic deposits will work harden on the surface to become more resistant to abrasion, and the impact or high-pressure loads are cushioned by the softer and lower yield strength metal that lies underneath the surface.

To Protect Two Surfaces in Contact

Group B applications involve metal-to-metal wear (such as bearings) under various combinations of abrasion, impact, friction and corrosion. The surfacing must wear smooth, have a low coefficient of friction, and be free from a tendency to seize or gall. The tungsten carbides are *not* recommended; even the fine tungsten carbide deposit does not wear smooth enough for bearing-type service. However, there are other types of materials that will combat this kind of wear.

Often it is desired to give one of the two contacting members more protection than the other; this can be done by surfacing one member with bronze so that this part will take the brunt of the wear and the non-surfaced member will be protected.

High-carbon electrodes are used to build up shafts that will operate with lubrication. The high-carbon deposit when machined or ground gives a smoother surface than is readily obtainable with a mild-steel electrode deposit.

Bearings operating at elevated temperatures are surfaced with the chromium carbides, the stainless steels and the high-chromium and nickel alloys.

Parts operating under corrosive conditions are protected by surfacing them with the chromium carbides and some of the stainless steels.

Chromium carbide facings give good service on parts that operate in the presence of sand or mud. Rubber is a good-wearing material for journals and bushings used underwater. Steel shafts give long service when they run in rubber bearings and are lubricated with water to keep out sand and mud.

Galling is the major problem to combat when confronted with non-lubricated metal-to-metal contact. Two like alloys are more prone to seize or gall than two different materials. It is probably because the materials are alike in chemical analysis or in surface condition. As an example of problems encountered, one pair of alloys gave good service underwater and fair service in sandy mud, but the parts soon chewed each other up when they were run dry. Soft iron alloys are

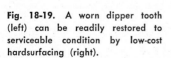

Fig. 18-19. A worn dipper tooth (left) can be readily restored to serviceable condition by low-cost hardsurfacing (right).

more likely to gall than harder ones, and rough surfaces will gall more readily than smooth ones.

A running-in period with some kind of lubricant is an assurance against galling, for freshly machined or ground surfaces have surface irregularities that intermesh with each other and the tears that then result make ideal seizing areas.

To Protect Only One Surface

Group C covers cases where we protect only one of the two contacting materials; the wear of the other material is of little or no importance. It may be desirable to have a low-friction surface that will polish (a plowshare or moldboard for example) or a rough, high-friction surface as in the case of dredge stud clamps. Some typical applications, and the recommended welding electrode are given in Table 18-2.

This service group is made up of the greatest number of hard-surfacing applications. Since wear of the second member or material can be disregarded in many cases, we can freely choose the surfacing material that will provide maximum life.

Table 18-2. Group C Hardsurfacing Applications

APPLICATION	SERVICE CONDITION	HARDSURFACING
Ore chute	Ore slides down the chute; abrasion high, impact low	Chromium carbide
Ore chute	Material falls onto chute; impact high	Manganese steel or semi-austenitic
Tool joints, oil drilling	Abrasion high caused by tool joint rubbing against the wall of the hole during drilling	Tungsten carbide or chromium carbide
Screw conveyors	Abrasion	Chromium carbide or fine tungsten carbide
Water turbine blades	Water hammer impact (cavitation) and corrosion	Stainless steel
Forging dies	Hot-metal abrasion, impact, high stresses	Hot-work die steel
Hot ingot tong tips	Strength and abrasion resistance at elevated temperatures	Stainless steel foundation with chromium carbide facing

Selecting the Best Hardsurfacing Material

Most of the hardsurfacing materials are available as alloy electrodes, welding rods, or agglomerated fluxes. So, in general, the choice of hardsurfacing material can be made on the basis of service requirements. The process to be used does not affect the selection of material to any great extent. The exceptions to this will be mentioned later.

In analyzing the service required, the first step is to determine the class of application—whether a cutting edge is to be maintained, a single surface must be protected, or two contacting surfaces must both be protected.

Secondly, the type of wear and other service conditions must be identified. It is necessary to find out whether wear of the part is caused by: (1) deformation from heat, (2) chemical corrosion, (3) erosion, (4) abrasion, (5) friction, or (6) impact, or by some combination of these.

Examination of a part that is completely worn out is not adequate for diagnosis since it fails to reveal the progress of the wear. When the surfacing is all gone, there is no way to tell whether it was worn off by abrasion or by chipping. First determine the nature of the wear. The hardsurfacing procedure can then be changed to use a tougher deposit if chipping occurred, to use more metal in some places, or to use a material higher in abrasion resistance in other areas.

The rate of wear frequently increases as the total wear increases. In these instances, it is economical to resurface the part before the part is appreciably worn. A scratch on a new dipper tooth may be only ½ in. long, but the same rock that scratched it would put a 2-in. scratch on a worn tooth and remove four times as much metal (Fig. 18-20). The dull tooth not only loses metal faster but also requires more force to take a bite. Find the point of balance between the cost of rebuilding the tooth, and the operating efficiency.

Figure 18-21 shows graphically the most common hardsurfacing alloys available and their relative properties and characteristics. Each of these alloys has a wide field of application dependent upon how its specific combination of qualities matches the various conditions and service requirements of a specific hardsurfacing job.

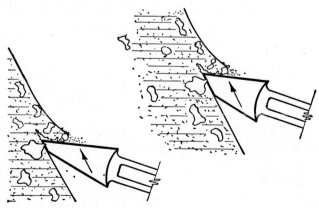

Fig. 18-20. A worn dipper tooth wears faster than a new tooth because more wearing surface is exposed to the abrading action of earth flow.

Fig. 18-21. Characteristics and Properties of Various Types of Hardsurfacing

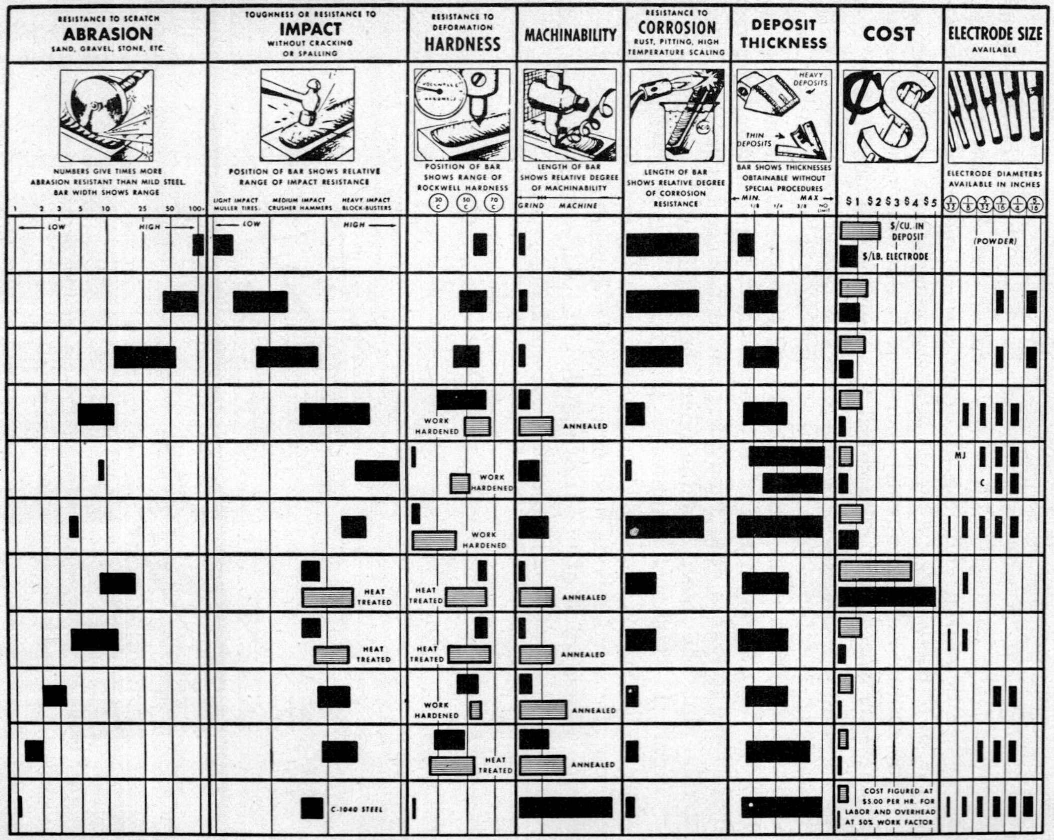

Description of HARDSURFACE Weld Deposit

CHROMIUM CARBIDE. Deposit of chromium carbide crystals held in fairly hard matrix. Both crystals and matrix have high abrasion resistance.

CHROMIUM CARBIDE. Deposit of chromium carbide crystals held in fairly hard matrix. Both crystals and matrix have high abrasion resistance.

CHROMIUM CARBIDE. Deposit of chromium carbide crystals held in tough hard matrix. Has good abrasive resistance and good toughness.

SEMI-AUSTENITIC as welded. High-carbon chromium alloy. Has good abrasion resistance, moderate toughness, and excellent hot forging properties.

AUSTENITIC MANGANESE. Deposit is 11-14% Mn. Has extreme toughness and develops maximum surface hardness by cold working.

AUSTENITIC STAINLESS. Chromium nickel types, 18-8 to 25-20, have excellent corrosion resistance, ductility, toughness, and work hardenability.

HIGH SPEED TOOL STEEL. Martensitic molybdenum type deposit maintains high hardness at high temperatures. May be tempered or hardened.

AIR-OIL HARDENING TOOL STEEL. Martensitic 5% chromium type has excellent properties. Unsatisfactory for high temperature applications.

MEDIUM CARBON & ALLOY STEEL. Chromium-manganese alloy partly martensitic and ferritic as welded.

MEDIUM TO HIGH CARBON STEEL. Chromium-manganese alloy of higher carbon content. Deposit is heat treated to give martensitic properties.

MILD STEEL. Conventional low-carbon ferritic deposit sometimes used for preliminary build-up prior to deposit of surface layer of alloy material.

For each characteristic listed on the chart, Fig. 18-21, the position of the bar indicates how good the electrode is in that respect. The further the bar is to the right in its column, the better the electrode is. The width of the bar indicates the degree to which welding procedures and techniques affect the deposit. The wider the bar, the greater the effect.

In using this chart to select an electrode, start with the characteristic that is most important from standpoint of meeting the primary wear condition that will be encountered. If this is abrasion for instance, then check the one or more electrodes that are high in abrasion resistance for other considerations that may be of secondary importance, such as impact. Finding the electrode or electrodes that have the right balance of properties to meet the service requirements, check through the remaining columns to determine its machinability, relative cost, etc.

The hardsurfacing job may have restrictions that narrow the field of possible surfacing materials. Here are several examples:

(a) The deposit must be machinable as welded. This eliminates all the materials except the medium-carbon, low-alloy types. The machinability of a medium-carbon deposit depends on the rate of cooling; preheating must be used on large members in order to finish with a deposit that is readily machinable. Deposits of austenitic manganese steel, chromium carbide and stainless steel can be finished by grinding. The possibility of using an alloy that will require grinding should always be considered, for the increased life may more than offset the higher finishing costs.

(b) The deposit is to be machined, but it may be annealed after welding and then hardened after finishing. This increases the number of electrodes that may be used. Possible surfacing materials are high-carbon tool steel, and some of the low-carbon, low-alloy types. Materials that shouldn't be used include stainless steel, semi-austenitic, chromium carbides, tungsten carbides, and high-manganese steel.

(c) The part and the deposit are to be hot forged. This requirement eliminates the tungsten carbides and the chromium carbides. The high-carbon and medium-carbon deposits are not only forgeable at red heat, but they are also ductile enough to be straightened and forged to some extent after quenching for hardening. These steels form the hard martensite when quenched, but the transformation does not take place until the work has cooled to 300 or 200 F. The part may be taken from the quenching bath at 400-500 F and then straightened or forged a small amount while it is still in the ductile austenitic state. If then cooled in air or in the quenching bath, it will be just as hard as if it had been given a complete quench. It may also be tougher, for the martensite was given more time to form.

(d) A cutting edge is required for cutting or turning steel. This specification necessitates the use of a material with high hardness,

Fig. 18-22. Hardsurfacing of large areas is done speedily and economically using modern submerged-arc welding techniques, with agglomerated alloy flux selected for the specific application.

high red hardness, and a high edge strength. The field is limited to one of the high-speed tool steels.

(e) The deposit must have maximum resistance to grinding abrasion. One of the tungsten carbides or chromium carbides should meet this requirement. If, in addition, cost of deposited material is a factor, the chromium carbides are the obvious choice.

If there is no past experience to rely on for the specification of hardsurfacing material, one of the tougher types is recommended; it is much better for the facing to be scratched off than to be broken off. Start with one of the electrodes in the semi-austenitic group; if it is found that the impact service is not too severe, one of the tougher chromium carbides may be used on the next trial. To secure still greater resistance to abrasion, use a thicker chromium carbide deposit or try a chromium carbide type of higher abrasion resistance. Caution: As the resistance to abrasion increases, the resistance to impact decreases.

There are so many hardsurfacing alloys and possibilities of application that there is plenty of room left for experimenting. Enormous savings on wearing parts are often obtained by a change in surfacing material or a different method of application. Reports of surfacings that last two, three times or even five times as long are not unusual. Additional savings should be possible by redesigning the wearing member for hardsurfacing so that the ideal amount of surfacing is deposited.

Welding Methods for Hardsurfacing

Although the oxyacetylene torch is still used with welding rod for depositing hardsurfacing materials on some applications, the metal-arc processes are in general preferred for reasons of speed and economy. In addition to the conventional manual metal-arc method of hardsurfacing with bare or coated electrode, the following methods have considerable application:

1. Submerged-arc welding, using a low-carbon steel electrode and an agglomerated alloy flux that adds elements to the deposit to form a hardsurfacing alloy (Fig. 18-22). The wide variety of commercially available alloy fluxes are capable of duplicating the various types of manual metal-arc hardsurfacing deposits already described.

2. Semi-automatic open-arc welding, which mechanically feeds bare electrode through a welding gun. The gun is manually supported and manipulated by the weldor.

3. Carbon-arc welding, using an alloy rod fed into the DC arc; or welding powdered surfacings with the DC or AC carbon arc. The two-carbon arc torch is also used for powdered hardsurfacings.

4. Surfacing with a shielded-metal-arc electrode while feeding in a filler rod ("two-tone" welding). Either or both rods may be a hardsurfacing type.

5. Inert-arc welding, with the surfacing alloy rod fed into a tungsten-electrode arc shielded with helium or argon gas.

The metal-arc (shielded-arc; bare-electrode; submerged-arc) processes should be used for surfacing austenitic manganese steel or for depositing manganese steel, in order to prevent overheating and embrittlement of the parent metal or the deposit. The use of these materials has been thoroughly discussed in Chapter 16.

Other steels and other surfacing materials may be hardsurfaced by oxyacetylene, TIG (tungsten-inert-gas), shielded-arc and submerged-arc processes.

The oxyacetylene and the carbon-arc processes are used for small, delicate parts and when only a very thin layer of surfacing is to be applied. Coal cutter bits, for example, often are hardsurfaced by oxyacetylene welding.

Either the oxyacetylene or the carbon-arc process is recommended to deposit the non-ferrous chromium carbide alloys in cases where the surfacing must be iron-free. By careful manipulation, the alloy may be sweated to the steel base metal and welded without penetration or alloying with the steel. The corrosion resistance and abrasion resistance are both lowered when these alloys are diluted with iron.

The advantages of manual or automatic metal-arc hardsurfacing are lower cost per pound of hardsurfacing material deposited, faster application and localized heating. Deeper penetration, however, is a factor to be considered: the more of the base metal that is melted, the greater the alloying of the deposit with the base metal. Deep penetration is usually a disadvantage since it increases the thickness of the hardsurfaced deposit. The total amount of hardsurfacing is the build-up from the surface plus the penetration below. If the amount of build-up is limited, then deep penetration may be a necessity.

In most cases, the first layer of surfacing has a lower abrasion resistance but more resistance to impact than the undiluted alloy. This gives a gradual change from the base metal to the hardsurface. There are a few instances of diluted surfacing that result in brittle alloys; mention has already been made that care must be taken if carbon steel is deposited on austenitic manganese steel.

Hardsurfacing alloys containing boron should be deposited with oxyacetylene torch, and care must be taken to prevent the formation of the brittle iron-boride crystals.

Manual hardsurfacing for repair or renewal of worn surfaces is usually done by metal-arc welding, using coated or bare electrode suited to producing the hardsurfacing characteristics desired. Production hardsurfacing techniques are often needed due to large volume requirements or for protection of large contact areas, such as caterpillar type tractor idler rolls, or where composite hardsurfacings must be provided on new equipment. For purposes such as these, both the semi-automatic and full-automatic submerged-arc processes previously described can be readily used. The higher deposition rate of this technique will reduce costs, but volume production is needed to justify usually large capital outlay needed for the fixtures and equipment.

Definitions of New Words

Abradant. A substance which causes abrasive wear, i.e. displacement or removal of surface material by a scratching action.

Cold welding. The microscopic fusion of high spots on two metallic surfaces in contact under great pressure. Often a factor in the wear of two sliding members, where the heat from friction or resistance to movement caused by surface irregularities promotes such fusion and further movement causes the weaker member to rupture locally in the form of "galling." Cold welding is also a method of permanently joining certain metals, especially aluminum.

Instant hardness. The hardness of a metal at an elevated temperature as determined by removing the metal sample from the heat and instantly punching it with a standard indentation point and load, then measuring the indentation after cooling to get the hardness value.

Microconstituents. Structural components of a metallic body that are not continuous but appear as crystalline members of a larger mass when viewed through a microscope.

Review Questions

1. Arrange the following hardsurfacing materials in the order of their resistance to grinding abrasion: Chromium carbide, austenitic manganese, semi-austenitic, austenitic stainless steel, cast tungsten carbide.

2. State what material and what hardsurfacing you would use for dipper teeth to handle:
   Quartz rocks about a foot in diameter
   Quartz gravel about an inch in diameter
   Quartz sand
   Very fine quartz sand called silica flour
   Note: Teeth are not needed on a dipper to handle sand, but assume that they are used.

3. Should calks on a horseshoe be surfaced with a fine or coarse mesh tungsten carbide? Which of these tungsten carbides is best for a screw conveyor handling sand? What less expensive surfacing would also be good for surfacing this screw?

4. In a pneumatic star drill, the end of the piston pounds on the head of the drill. The end of the piston was surfaced with a chromium carbide. After a few hundred feet of rock had been drilled, the surfacing cracked and crumbled off. A semi-austenitic type of surfacing was tried, and it upset, making the part too large to work freely in the guides. What surfacing would you recommend? Remember that it must be hard enough to resist upsetting, yet tough enough not to crack and chip.

5. Silicon carbide (carborundum), aluminum oxide (alumina) and diamonds all have very high scratch hardness and are used for grinding wheels. Why are they not used for hardsurfacing?

6. To which of the three classifications of wear do the following belong:
   A drag line chain
   An airplane tail skid
   A horseshoe
   The mold board of a turning plow and the point

7. Of hardsurfacing deposits of the martensitic, the austenitic and the carbide types:
   Which would make the best razor?
   Which would make the best surfacing for a machinist's hammer?
   Which is best for the jaws of a rock crusher?

8. Sintered tungsten carbides are used for metal-cutting tools and for resisting metal-to-metal wear and abrasive wear. Why is cast tungsten carbide unsuited for metal cutting, either as a solid casting or as a deposit of tungsten carbide particles?

CHAPTER 19

WELDING TOOL AND DIE STEELS

The tool and die steels are about the last word in hardenability. Practically all of them have a high-carbon content, some as high as 2.50%. Most of them are highly alloyed with one or more other elements, principally chromium, molybdenum, tungsten, vanadium, cobalt, and manganese. The total content of such alloying elements exceeds 30% in a few grades.

Although the weldability of these steels is poor, as compared with mild steel, the ingenuity of experienced weldors has shown that tool and die steels can be welded to give satisfactory service.

Most of the tool steels have virtually no ductility, hence the conventional method of evaluating yield and ultimate tensile strength of materials cannot be used with any accuracy on this class of steels. In the hardened condition, hot-work tool steels are known to have extremely high tensile strengths. Some exceed 300,000 psi and are used in aircraft structural parts. The compressive strength of hardened high-speed steel of the 18-4-1 type (18% chromium, 4% tungsten, 1% vanadium) is about 400,000 psi.

Although both the tensile strength and compressive strength of a tool steel are very high, there is evidence that they do not vary at the same rate during heating and cooling. This results in greater internal stresses, particularly since martensite—the hard constituent of the tool steels—occupies more room than austenite. Since not all of the austenite transforms at one time, there is an unbalanced condition during heating and cooling. This is one of the factors deserving special consideration in welding.

Since the steels used in tooling construction cover such a broad range of alloys, there is frequently considerable difference in the hardness, strength and coefficient of thermal expansion between two materials to be joined by welding. This may require a ductile filler metal

Fig. 19-1. Chipped and broken dies are among the many types of tools salvaged by repair welding and remachining.

317

in the joint so as to prevent extreme stresses from developing.

Because of their high-alloy content, the tool steels require more time for carbides to be dissolved in the austenite at elevated temperatures. Solution of the carbides would permit formation of hard martensite upon cooling. When welding these steels in the annealed condition, the heat-affected zone is above the critical temperature for such a short time that there cannot be complete solution of the carbides. Thus, the metal under the weld does not necessarily have any appreciable depth of extreme hardness and brittleness that accompanies conventional quenching. Other facts to keep in mind are that a relatively high preheat can better graduate the thermal effects of welding, and that the low thermal conductivity of high-alloy steel does not dissipate the heat as rapidly; therefore, there is less quenching effect on the weld.

Not all tool and die materials are tool and die steels. Consequently, there is much room for application of welding in the construction and repair of tooling aside from the welding of tool steels.

Why Weld Tools

A full discussion of tool-steel welding necessitates a review of the ways in which welding can be used in construction and repair of tooling. These include:

1. The assembly of various jig, fixture or die components into a complete tool.
2. The fabrication of a composite tool, for example by depositing tool-steel weld metal on the cutting edge or wear surface of a carbon-steel base.
3. The rebuilding of a worn surface or edge.
4. The alteration of a tool to meet a change in design of the product being manufactured, or to suit a change in characteristics of a sheet metal being formed or drawn.
5. The repair of broken tools. Tool breakage may result from improper heat-treat, from unexpected stresses in service, or from production wrecks—as when a clamp loosens up resulting in a mis-hit.

The first requirement in welding tool materials is a recognition that a great variety of materials is employed in the fabrication of cutting tools, tool holders, jigs, fixtures, dies and molds. The second requirement is that knowledge of the specific material, the method of heat treating it, and the service required of it is necessary for selection of the welding process and procedures.

Tank or boiler plate and machine steel (hot-rolled SAE 1020) are commonly used for fixture bases, die shoes, large fixture bodies, and other less-critical parts. These materials are easily welded by following suggestions made in Chapter 10 on the low-carbon steels.

Cold-rolled steel, often SAE 1020, is also used in jig and fixture bodies, work rests, stock-guides, other secondary components, and in

Continental and comparable short-run dies. Cold-rolled mild steel has good weldability, although precautions are advisable to prevent distortion.

Low-cost machine steel often permits building tooling that is far more economical than all-tool steel construction. Joining the various machine steel components by shielded-arc welding eliminates much expensive surface grinding and precision hole operation, which must be done on costly machine tools. With a drill jig, for example, frequently only the bushing plate requires such precise hole location and parallelism as to justify work on the jig borer. The addition of adjustable jig feet and work rest buttons made of a more wear-resistant material completes the low-cost assembly.

Surface hardening nearly equivalent to that of some tool steels is often achieved by less-expensive mild steel that is carburized or nitrided. This practice is most frequently followed in the case of press-tool punches or other small intricate tools that are easily machined from the mild steel. After hardening, the tools are finish-ground to size.

Cutting edges and other wear points and surfaces on many short-run dies made of a medium or high-carbon steel are flame-hardened, and welding used in initial construction or repair usually has no effect on the edges. If a fracture crosses the cutting edge, the initial prop-

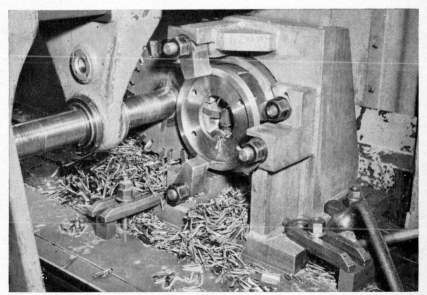

Fig. 19-2. Many jigs, fixtures and dies can be constructed quickly and at low cost by use of metal-arc welding. This milling machine fixture required only a small amount of welding to hold the steel fixture elements together with the rigidity necessary for heavy machining cuts.

erties are easily restored by grinding the weld back to the original contour and then rehardening the edges so that it will be uniform.

Classes of Tool Steel

Tool and die steels are often classified primarily according to the way in which they are normally hardened: water-hardening, oil-hardening, or air-hardening. In general, the cost, maximum hardness, wear-resistance, depth of hardening, and dimensional stability increase in the same order, with the water-hardening steels being low and the air-hardening steels being high. The weldability of these materials progress in reverse order, with the air-hardening steels requiring the greatest care when welding.

Continued development of new steels and the need for standardizing on specific types have resulted in a classification system adopted by the American Iron and Steel Institute and the Society of Automotive Engineers. The AISI-SAE designation includes a letter symbol for the main group followed by a numeral to denote specific chemical composition. In practice, many of the tool steels offered by their producers do not match the chemical analysis exactly but are equivalent in performance characteristics.

Water-hardening carbon tool steels (W group)—differ from conventional carbon steels mainly in the controls exercised in producing them. The composition may be the same, yet the carbon tool steels exhibit a carefully controlled grain size, low porosity and other qualities that ensure their excellent performance in critical tooling applications.

The carbon tool steels are available in a carbon content range from 0.50-1.40%. Some grades are straight carbon; others have small additions of chromium or vanadium. The chromium adds some resistance to heat and corrosion. The vanadium helps refine grain structure, resist grain growth during heating, and improve fatigue resistance. Steels in this group are shallow hardening when water-quenched from above the critical range.

These steels, when heat treated, have the characteristic known as *differential hardening*—a hard, wear resistant surface or case, and a softer, shock-resistant core. This combination of properties is especially valuable on percussion and impact tools such as cold header dies, coining and re-strike dies, and shear blades.

The carbon tool steels are suitable only for cold work applications, since they have low red hardness. They are widely used, despite the disadvantage of their strong tendency to distort during heat-treat. Their good machinability, good weldability (relative to other tool steels), and lower initial cost are advantages. Distortion is kept to a minimum by flame-hardening only along cutting or forming edges to develop a good resistance to wear.

The carbon tool steels are often sub-classified merely by *temper,*

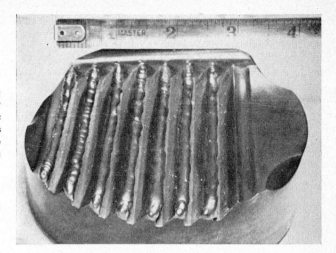

Fig. 19-3. Building up with tool steel alloy deposited by arc welding simplifies change of die shape for plastic molding radio grills.

which indicates carbon content. Although these steels come in tempers ranging from 5 (0.50% carbon) to 14 (1.40% carbon), the greatest use is for tempers 9 through 11 (0.90-1.10% carbon). In this latter range, they are used for trimming dies, blanking dies and press brake forming tools. At the lower end of the carbon range, they are useful in tools such as forge dies where toughness and shock-resistance are more important than abrasion-resistance. At the upper limit of the carbon range, they are used where hardness, resistance to abrasion, or edge strength are required; small form cutters and engraving tools for example.

In the soft or annealed condition, the structure of carbon tool steels is ferrite and an iron-carbide constituent. During heating, transformation to austenite begins at about 1335 F. The upper critical temperature varies according to carbon content. The extent of transformation depends on the temperature attained and the time the piece is held at temperature. If cooling from above the critical range is slow enough, there is a substantial transformation of the austenite to ferrite and pearlite within the range of 1300-1000 F, and from austenite to ferrite and *bainite* below 1000 F. Any untransformed austenite reaching 450 F transforms to martensite.

In tooling applications, the application of water-quenching after heating to above the critical range cools the surface metal swiftly, with most of the austenite being untransformed at 450 F. As it cools below this point, it converts to the martensite essential for good hardness and wear-resistance. This shell of quickly-formed martensite insulates the rest of the piece and delays cooling sufficiently for the tough ferrite-pearlite-bainite structure to form. The lower the carbon content, the deeper will be the case hardness.

Oil-hardening tool steels (0 group)—are alloyed with 0.90-1.45%

carbon; usually 1.00-1.60% manganese; with small percentages of chromium, tungsten or molybdenum in some grades. These steels have medium-deep hardening characteristics when oil-quenched.

Immersed in oil for quenching after heating to above the critical range, these steels can be full-hardened although cooled at a slow enough rate to not develop excessive stresses. Thus, oil-hardening steels are suitable for die sections and other tools having sharp corners and abrupt mass and section changes. Expansion and contraction during heating and cooling induce internal stresses, complicated by the presence of any stress raisers. Tempering after quenching relieves such stresses. Since piece size before and after heat-treat is appreciably unchanged, these steels can be finished to size before hardening.

Because of their alloying elements, annealed oil-hardening steels have a machinability 10 to 35% lower than the water-hardening steels. Although full hardening is achieved, permitting unlimited regrinds, the oil-hardening steels do not have shock-resistant cores and are actually low in impact strength. These steels have low red hardness and are limited to cold-work applications.

The structure of annealed oil-hardening tool steels is essentially ferrite, plus carbides. There is virtually no carbon in solution. During heating, transformation to austenite begins at about 1370 F. With further heating, more carbon goes into solid solution but grain coarsening begins to take place. In normal practice, heating to about 1450 F allows good solution of the carbon without appreciable grain coarsening. Since high-alloy steels require more time for transformation, oil-hardening steels need not be quenched as quickly as water-hardening steels through the range of 1350-900 F in order to trap the austenite without precipitation of the carbon. Untransformed austenite reaching 500 F during cooling will, at that point, begin to transform to martensite.

Assuming that the ideal condition is not achieved, martensite occupies more room than the other products of transformation or untransformed austenite, and high internal stresses develop. The as-quenched martensite must be tempered to relieve the stresses; otherwise, the locked-up stresses may burst the workpiece. If the piece is transferred too soon from the quench medium to the tempering furnace, subsequent cooling will cause retained austenite to transform to untempered martensite. This creates the danger of cracking.

Air-hardening tool steels (A group)—are non-deforming tool steels for applications where minimum size change is needed. These applications include gages, blanking and forming punches and dies, forming rolls, and roll-threading dies. These steels have 1.00% carbon, 1.00-5.00% chromium, and 1.00% molybdenum. One type has about 3% manganese, which gives it medium impact strength. The grade with 5% chromium has medium red hardness, permitting its use in plastic molds.

Steels of this class will uniformly deep harden with quenching only in air. They have no tendency to distort during heat-treat. Annealed, their machinability is 60-65% that of water-hardening tool steels.

The more-difficult-to-work, high-carbon, high-chromium steels have been separated out of this group. The A steels thus have lower hardening temperature, machine more easily, are tougher, and cost less. They are not as prone to cracking as the D-group steels.

High-carbon, high-chromium die steels (D group)—are used in the most critical applications where precision, dimensional stability, outstanding wear resistance, and long life are required. These uses include lamination dies and gages. These steels have 1.00-2.25% carbon and 12.00% chromium; most grades have 0.80-1.00% molybdenum; others have 0.90-1.00% vanadium, and one grade has 4.00%.

Some of these steels full harden in air, others in oil. In general they harden from higher temperatures (1800-1850F), require longer soaking at heat, harden more slowly, and do not deform throughout heat-treat. Thus, they are widely used on pieces of intricate design. Nevertheless, their martensitic structure is a highly-stressed one. Consequently, the D steels have low impact strength and are subject to thermal cracking, especially if stress raisers are present.

The D steels are difficult to machine in the annealed condition, (40-50% the machinability of water-hardening tool steels) and are unmachinable when hardened because of the hard carbide crystals in their structure. Even grinding must be done carefully, since the steel's abrasion resistance causes high heat generation. This results in localized expansion and formation of cracks. Localized high heating of the cutting edge lowers hardness and results in poor life.

As with the high-carbon stainless steels, the high-carbon, high-chromium die steels are subject to carbide precipitation during heating such as when welding.

Fig. 19-4. Welding technique effectively reclaimed this worn die for further service.

High-speed steels (M and T groups)—having high red hardness are widely used in metal-cutting tools that become hot in service: lathe tools, drills, taps, reamers, milling cutters, and others. Tools made of high-speed steel maintain a sharp cutting edge at high rates of metal removal. Such tools need the delicate balance of high red hardness, abrasion resistance, and toughness—resistance to shock and vibration —that are characteristic of M and T steels.

Although these steels are tough in the sense that they stand up well under cutting forces, they have low impact strength and are notch sensitive. In these respects, they are low compared with other tool steels but are far superior to the cemented carbides with which they compete in cutting tool applications. When an insert of cemented carbide is used at the cutting edge, the tool shank or boring bar is frequently made of high-speed steel.

These steels are characterized by a composite structure of hard wear-resistant carbides held in a tough heat-resistant matrix.

The high-speed steels are deep hardening. There is little or no distortion during heat-treat. Most grades are oil-quenched, although some offer the option of air-quenching. The molybdenum-type steels all have this feature.

Composition of the tungsten-type high-speed steels (T group) includes 0.70-1.50% carbon, 12.00-18.00% tungsten, 4.00-4.75% chromium, and 1.00-5.00% vanadium. Cobalt's presence in a few grades in the range of 5.00-8.00% gives a super red hardness, but at the sacrifice of some toughness. Molybdenum also may be present in relatively small amounts, 0.75-1.00%.

Composition of the molybdenum-type high-speed steels (M group) includes 0.80-1.15% carbon, 4.50-8.50% molybdenum, 4.00-4.25% chromium, and 1.00-5.00% vanadium. Tungsten also is usually present, up to 6.50%. Cobalt, 5.00-12.00%, is present in some grades and not at all in others.

The molybdenum-type steels (M group) are lower in cost than the tungsten grades. However, they are more sensitive to heat treatment and overheat easily. The non-cobalt M grades are somewhat tougher than the cobalt-alloyed T steels. Annealed, the M steels have 45-55% the machinability of water-hardening steels, whereas the T steels have only 40-50% machinability.

All tool steels are somewhat susceptible to *decarburization*—the loss of carbon from surfaces because of its reaction with elements in the atmosphere at high temperatures. Grades having significant amounts of molybdenum, cobalt or silicon are more seriously subject to this loss of carbon, which results in lower surface hardness and wear-resistance. Decarburization is largely a function of time, and usually is significant only when the tool is soaked for long periods at a high temperature (over 1400 F). On high-speed and shock-resistant steels, decarburization must be considered by the weldor.

Hot-work die steels (H group)—have medium to high impact strength, medium-high to high red hardness, and other properties that are ideal for hot-work tooling applications. There are three important sub-groups.

Chromium-type grades have 0.35-0.45% carbon, 5.00-7.00% chromium, 1.50-5.00% molybdenum or 1.50-7.00% tungsten, and sometimes 0.40-1.00% vanadium. Nickel may replace some of the chromium content. These steels are air-hardening. They are used on high-impact and other high-stress applications where temperatures do not exceed 600 F, except for short periods of time. Forging dies represent a major field of application, also mandrels and hot shears. One grade used for aircraft structural parts resists softening during continuous temperatures up to 1000 F. These steels have good weldability.

Tungsten-type grades have 0.25-0.50% carbon, 9.00-18.00% tungsten, and 2.00-4.00% chromium. The chromium content of one grade is 12%. These steels have high resistance to softening and deformation at high temperature, although they do not withstand as high impact forces as the chromium-type grade. They withstand temperatures up to 1100 F and are extensively used in extrusion and casting dies, shear blades, and punches. Deep hardening is achieved by either air- or oil-quenching, although they tend to scale in air. A major disadvantage of this group is that they are subject to cracking from thermal shock. The steels cannot be safely water-cooled during service. They are normally preheated before use at elevated temperature.

Molybdenum-type grades have 0.55-0.65% carbon, 5.00-8.00% molybdenum, 4.00% chromium, up to 6.00% tungsten, and 1.00-2.00% vanadium. They cost less than the tungsten-type steels but require greater control of hardening temperature because of their tendency to decarburize. Otherwise they have characteristics and service performance similar to the tungsten grades.

Some other tool steels have higher impact strength at room temperature, but the hot-work steels surpass these and have superior toughness at elevated temperatures. Annealed steels in this group have 60-70% machinability of water-hardening steels.

Shock-resisting tool steels (S group)—have high impact strength and are used in riveting tools, impact hammers and chisels, rock tools, and similar applications. They harden to a medium depth when quenched from above the critical range. Some grades are quenched in water, most in oil.

S-group steels have 0.50-0.60% carbon plus other alloying elements, often 0.12-0.25% vanadium. Some of these steels have 0.70-0.85% manganese, 1.00-2.00% silicon, and 0.25-0.50% molybdenum. Other grades include over 1% chromium and over 2% tungsten; these are oil-hardening types.

The shock-resisting steels are subject to considerable distortion during heat-treat, but this condition usually does not mean much on the class of tools to which they are applied. They have low to medium red hardness. Grades having silicon and molybdenum are especially subject to decarburization at high temperatures. However, the softening at the surface that results from loss of carbon is not likely to be serious on the class of service in which these tools are used. Machinability of these steels, when annealed, is 80-85% that of water-hardening tool steels.

Low-alloy tool steels (L group)—with 0.50-1.20% carbon and not more than 2% additional alloying content, are frequently substituted for the higher-cost and more-difficult-to-machine tool steels. Some of these steels for general-purpose application have 1.00-1.50% chromium. Others have up to 1.00% manganese, 0.45% molybdenum, or 0.20% vanadium.

In addition to these more common groups of tool and die steels, there are other special application steels. Many mavericks do not fall under the industry-wide standardization systems, even though they have excellent performance records.

Graphitic tool steels—are proprietary quality steels, not as universally available as other tool steel types. They are produced in various compositions paralleling other tool steels ranging from the low-alloy steels to the high-carbon high-chromium types. Regardless of the analysis, they all have considerable free graphite.

Controlled graphite content gives these compositions good machinability in the annealed condition, excellent resistance to abrasive wear after hardening, excellent resistance to wear by friction together with anti-galling properties, good resistance to stress cracking, and better weldability than conventional steels for the comparable service. The graphitic tool steels include water-hardening, oil-hardening and air-hardening types.

The segregated graphite in these steels has a low yield point and serves to relieve internal stresses during the heating and cooling associated with welding and heat-treating.

A number of the conventional tool steels are available from their producers in free-machining versions, through the use of graphite, free sulphur, aluminum or other special additives.

Major Problems in Welding Tool Steel

The metallurgy of tool steels may be summarized by these important facts: (1) they cover a wide range of analyses and properties; (2) all have a high-carbon content, good hardenability, and very low ductility; (3) all require considerable time at high temperature for the carbides to go into solution; and (4) they are notch-sensitive and, being susceptible to formation of cracks from various causes, they fail by brittle fracture after cracks do occur.

In welding the tool steels, problems to be guarded against include weld cracking, underbead cracking, decarburization, and the introduction of impurities by atmospheric contamination or otherwise. These problems demand further study.

Weld cracking—results from too rapid a rate of cooling. Stresses develop as the weld metal shrinks in relation to the adjacent base metal. These stresses tend to cause cracks through the weld metal, usually in the longitudinal direction. On multiple-pass welds, weld cracks may be limited initially to the root bead but will travel through the succeeding beads when subjected to service stresses. This has been discussed at considerable length in Chapter 12 on Welding High-Carbon Steel.

Cracking is especially pronounced in welding tool and die steels. Carbon content of the simplest water-hardening grades usually ranges from 0.90 to 1.10% but may run to 1.40%. Carbon content of the other tool steels range to 2.50%, in addition to the presence of multiple carbide-forming alloying elements. Compared to alloy steels, tool steels have very rigid structures and develop internal stresses when hardened.

Carbon pick-up in the weld deposit, particularly in the first bead or layer, can not be avoided because of the base metal's high carbon content. This complicates the stresses developing during weld cooling. The amount of carbon pick-up by the weld metal, when welding a high-carbon tool steel with a mild steel electrode, may seriously lower its ductility and increase its crack sensitivity despite preventive measures.

There are four ways to avoid weld cracking, in addition to those already mentioned in Chapter 12. These approaches require (1) preheating the base metal, (2) depositing a ductile weld metal, (3) limiting excessive carbon pick-up to the first bead or layer, and (4) immediately stress-relieving the joint.

Underbead cracking—in the base metal may occur whether the tool steel is annealed or hardened. Consider the worst condition: welding on cold base metal.

If the cold tool steel is in the annealed condition when welded, it has a quenching effect on the overheated base metal adjacent to the weld. As cooling progresses, a transformation to hard martensite along the fusion line occurs. Base metal in this zone expands and remains expanded when transformed into martensite, while the massive untransformed adjacent base metal shrinks to its original volume. This produces locked-up tensile and compressive stresses that tend to crack the brittle crystals of martensite in the narrow hardening zone.

If the cold tool steel is in the hardened condition when welded, welding anneals the base metal immediately outside the transition zone. The result is a zone of untempered martensite parallel to the fusion line. This weakened structure may produce immediate microcracks. In any case this brittle structure will be susceptible to fracture during service. If the alloy is a complex of multiple carbides, the danger of micro-cracks and early fatigue failure is greatly increased.

Micro-cracks, once formed, can be corrected by reheating the metal to the melting point; however, this is a highly impractical process.

Underbead cracking can be avoided or minimized by (1) preheating the base metal, (2) limiting heat input during welding to the minimum required to produce sufficient penetration for good fusion, (3) cooling the entire weldment slowly and uniformly, and (4) immediately stress-relieving the joint.

Decarburization—or loss of carbon, is a frequent cause of surface softening or worse. Standard practice when machining tool components, especially with tool steels most subject to decarburization, is to leave a grind allowance. This permits removal of scale and/or decarburized surfaces after heat-treating, and also permits dimensional correction for any minor warpage or size change that may occur. For these reasons, the opportune time to weld is during initial construction of a tool before this final over-all grinding is performed.

When edge and surface properties are of vital importance, tools already finished to size should be heated in a controlled-atmosphere furnace or oil bath, or protected in some other manner. Coating the surface with powdered borax is one satisfactory means of protection. Blanketing the tool in cast iron chips is also effective.

High-speed steels and hot-work steels, especially, should be protected against decarburization. If the steel is held for any length of time at a red heat or above, sprinkle exposed surfaces with powdered borax. When welding, the weld bead and exposed surfaces of the base metal within the heat-affected zone can be so protected immediately after the weld is deposited.

The high carbon in tool steels has a tendency to react at high temperatures with other elements to form gases. The molten steel easily absorbs these gases, which contribute to porosity and underbead cracking.

Decarburization and its effects are avoided or minimized by (1) not overheating the base metal, (2) not soaking it at high temperature any longer than necessary, (3) using low-hydrogen or inert-gas shielding in welding, or welding in a protective atmosphere, and (4) carrying out hardening and annealing, when required, in a protective atmosphere and with the tool blanketed by an inert or carbonaceous material.

Impurities—frequently factors in weld cracking and underbead cracking, are seldom found in the tool steels as supplied by the mill. These steels are produced under extremely rigid controls. Incorrect heat-treatment or other processing during manufacture of the tool may introduce oxygen, hydrogen or other undesirable elements. Also, surfaces of tools taken from service for repair or edge renewal may be contaminated from coolants, greases, or protective coatings on the work materials processed through the tooling.

No welding of a tool steel should be attempted unless surfaces are perfectly clean and dry. In cleaning such surfaces, use care to not produce any brush or tool marks that will later function as stress raisers and weaken the structure. Notch sensitivity is especially acute in the high-hardness tool steels.

In tool and die welding, processes that provide the means for scavenging any undesirable elements from the weld metal are preferred. The electrode must not be a source of such elements. Electrodes must be thoroughly dry and preferably have a low-hydrogen type coating. In addition to hydrogen contamination of the weld, low-hydrogen electrodes have good deoxidizing and scavenging characteristics that remove undesirable elements and compounds from the weld deposit.

Heat Treatment of Tool Steel

The weldor who wants to work successfully with tool and die steels must adhere to the heat-treat requirements of the specific alloy being welded. Some generalities can be discussed for rough guidance, but the steel supplier usually makes specific recommendations available for each grade. He may not make welding recommendations, but the weldor who understands heat-treating can interpret the heat-treat recommendations to help establish a welding procedure.

A weldor who is not working daily with tool steels can do well to work cooperatively with an experienced tool steel heat-treater. The heat-treater, familiar with his specialized furnaces, protective atmospheres, and the idiosyncrasies of specific grades of tool steel, can help the weldor develop the complete procedure and then relieve the weldor of much of the non-welding activity.

Annealing—of the tool steel is accomplished by heating slowly to a point slightly above the critical range, holding at that temperature long enough for heat to penetrate through the entire piece, and then cooling very slowly. A typical maximum cooling rate for high-speed steel is 50 F per hour, down to 1000 F (to a point within or below the tempering range). Further cooling usually occurs at a faster rate, in still air. The cooling rate must be adjusted to suit tool size; small pieces can be cooled at faster rates.

Packing to prevent decarburization or scaling is not usually required when annealing in a protective atmosphere. However, procedures recommend that high-speed steel be packed in clean charcoal or other carburizing material mixed with dry ashes, lime or sand. This is called *pack annealing* and is accomplished in a controlled temperature, atmospheric furnace. Graphitic tool steels should always be pack annealed.

We've already learned that the water-hardening steels tend to distort and change size during heat-treatment. And, because of internal stresses developed during water quenching, they are easily cracked if used on tool components with design features such as sharp corners and abrupt section changes that constitute stress raisers. These stresses may cause initial breakage during quenching. For this reason, shallow hardening is often achieved more safely by use of a fine water spray. Remember that the hardenability of these steels increases in relation to the carbon content. Where submersion in a bath is required, because of piece size for example, a saline (salt-saturated) bath gives less distortion than a straight water bath.

Stress-relieving—releases residual or locked-up internal stresses set up by machining or by the cooling of weld metal on annealed base metal. Stress-relieving is done below the critical range, usually at 1100-1300 F, and is sometimes called *subcritical annealing*. A clean, open fire can be used, but tools most susceptible to decarburization and scaling should be packed. Cooling is held to a slow rate. Do not stress relieve a weld on hardened tool steel at this high temperature or you will upset the necessary balance of hardness and toughness achieved by the prior tempering. Follow the same slow heating and slow cooling cycle used for annealing.

With annealed base metal, the common procedure is to preheat, weld, stress relieve, finish machine, stress relieve, and grind; then harden and temper. If the base metal is already finished to size, preheat, weld, stress relieve, and grind weld flush.

Hardening—of the tool steel is accomplished by slowly heating to a point above the critical range, holding at this heat long enough to allow complete solution of the carbides, then cooling rapidly. Small units may be heated more quickly than large ones. The rate of heating—and of cooling—is inversely proportionate to alloy content. The higher alloy steels are normally heated very slowly to the upper critical temperature and then raised quickly to the hardening range, which may be several hundred degrees higher.

Steels hardening over 1600 F scale badly in an oxidizing atmosphere. This also promotes decarburization. Such steels should be heated in a protective atmosphere while packed in an inert or slightly carburizing material. Steels hardening under 1600 F do not scale heavily and thus need less protection against oxidation. Excessive soaking of the tool steel at a high temperature causes decarburization, scaling, and grain coarsening.

Quenching—from the hardening temperature can involve rapid cooling down to somewhere below the upper limit of the tempering range. This is known as *interrupted quenching*. High-speed steels, for example, can be bath-quenched down to 900-1100 F, and then air-cooled to 150 F before tempering. Some steels are cooled all the way in the quench-bath to the lowest permissible temperature before tempering.

Tempering—follows immediately after quenching to relieve the hardening stresses, to prevent cracking, and to toughen the alloy's hardened structure. In most cases, the tool steel is not allowed to return to room temperature between quenching and tempering. Liquid-quenched tools are removed from the bath at 150-200 F and tempered immediately. Air-quenched tools are cooled to 100-150 F, depending on alloy content, and then tempered.

Within the recommended tempering range for the specific steel grade, a higher temper gives greater toughness at some sacrifice of hardness. Tempering at the low end of the range gives maximum hardness and wear-resistance but lowers the toughness.

Tempering above the recommended range may result in loss of toughness without any improvement in hardness. At several hundred degrees above the tempering range, some steels attain considerable toughness but sustain considerable loss of hardness.

Good heat treatment always includes tempering after quench-hardening, but tempering is sometimes omitted when service conditions indicate that little toughness is required. CAUTION: Welding on hardened but untempered tool steel will probably crack or burst the piece.

*   *   *   *

The major points to remember are these:

• Fast heating of the tool steels is hazardous. Sudden localized heating of hardened tool steel may cause the highly-stressed cold plate to crack. Even annealed tools may crack under such conditions, and the lower alloy steels will distort badly if they don't crack.

• Quenching, while needed for hardening a tool steel, implies fast

Fig. 19-5. Draw die for producing bottom caps for steel piling, in portable horizontal press, wore excessively from abrasive action of the 3/16-in. boiler plate work material until refaced with semi-austenitic high-carbon chromium weld deposit.

cooling. The rate of cooling that is best for one grade of steel may be much too fast for another. Heat-treaters follow supplier-recommended cooling rates for each tool steel; the weldor should do the same.

• Remember that a specific grade may vary greatly from other members of the same group in its behavior at high temperatures.

• The temperatures required in welding the tool steels—preheating before welding, stress-relieving after welding, hardening the weldment, tempering—are all keyed to the basic heat-treat recommendations for the specific grade.

• One more fact to remember: Don't get too many irons in the fire! If the steel is at that point in its heating or cooling cycle when something else should be done to or with it, that something else MUST be done or you'll be in trouble. For example: Letting the steel soak too long at a high temperature will dangerously weaken its structure.

Preheating Tool Steels for Welding

Preheating of tool steels before welding is necessary for a number of reasons, primarily these: (1) to minimize the possibility of thermal shock damaging the steel as the welding arc is applied; (2) to slow up the cooling and prevent the formation of an excessively hard fusion zone; (3) to prevent excessive hardness in the weld itself; and (4) to help equalize the cooling of weld and base metal and thereby minimize the possibility of shrinkage cracks.

Tool steel to be welded must be preheated whether it is in an annealed or hardened condition. There should be no exception to this. The use of low-hydrogen electrodes, a graphitic tool steel, and other measures may make success less dependent on preheating but do not make preheating unnecessary. Welding cold tool steel is very likely to result in the weld falling out as soon as the tool is put to use.

CAUTION: The preheat temperatures for welding must not be confused with the preheat temperatures normally included in the steel supplier's heat-treat recommendations. The latter show the temperatures at which the soft steel should be preheated before subjecting it to the hardening medium and temperatures.

When preheating hardened tool steels—for welding, be careful not to exceed the temperature at which the tool was last tempered or drawn. If this is unknown, preheat into the lower half of the steel supplier's recommended tempering range for the specific steel. (On small parts, do not exceed the low limit. On large parts, do not exceed the midpoint of the tempering range.) If the specific grade of tool steel cannot be identified, preheat only to the lower limit of the tempering range typical for the general class of steel.

When preheating annealed tool steels—for welding, preheat to the upper limit of the steel supplier's recommended tempering range for the specific steel. Higher preheat temperatures (1100 to 1300 F) are often used, but are seldom necessary and usually require too much time. In some cases, a high temperature will slow up the cooling of the weld metal through the critical range to such an extent that excessive grain coarsening and carbide precipitation will occur in the heat-affected zone of the base metal.

*   *   *   *

Tool steels should be heated slowly to the preheat temperature, in order to ensure full heat penetration and a uniform increase in temperature throughout the piece. As the alloy content increases, the rate of temperature increase should be slower.

Preheating tool steels is preferably performed in a brine or oil bath brought to temperature slowly, or in a furnace with variable temperature control. These methods ensure better distribution of the applied heat around the piece. Small sections are often heated on a hot plate over an open fire, but the temperature is more difficult to control. The hot surface beneath the steel block and the cold air above create a condition of severe internal stresses.

The entire piece must be preheated. Using an oxyacetylene torch is hazardous, particularly on the higher alloys. Even on the water-hardening steels, the non-uniform heat distribution of torch heating may cause distortion.

The amount of base metal preheat should be maintained as constant

Fig. 19-6. Cone for steel mill uncoiler is economically resurfaced with air and oil hardening tool steel weld metal for longer life than was obtained with all tool steel. Cone is preheated before hardsurfacing.

as possible throughout the welding operation. Metal beyond the weld zone can be insulated with asbestos to retain the heat. The welding technique should further limit heat input by low penetration, use of the smallest diameter electrode that will fill the gap adequately, intermittent welding, and depositing stringer beads instead of weaving. Every effort must be made to hold temperature in the heat-affected zone of hardened base metal below the upper limit of its tempering range. Higher heat input will weaken the base metal structure and may draw its hardness excessively. Interpass temperature should be checked and time taken to permit it to drop back to the original level.

If any of the preheat is lost during the welding operation, reheat the base metal to the original level before continuing welding.

Selection of Electrodes

As discussed in the welding of alloy steels, Chapter 13, it is not practicable to match the chemical analysis of the base metal with that of the deposited metal.

In the first place, some tool steel analyses do not make satisfactory welding rods or electrodes. Some, for example, may have a variable deposition efficiency that depends on arc length and other welding variables. It is better to use an electrode with known welding characteristics and deposit analysis that can be depended upon.

Secondly, the numerous electrodes and welding rods that would be necessary for the great variety of tool steels used in a typical plant would result in increased costs and confusion in purchasing, stocking and use. It is much more satisfactory to have only a few general-purpose electrodes. In addition, some of the alloys would be costly to produce in electrode form in relatively small quantities.

In either repair welding of broken tools or in the build-up of a worn cutting edge or forming surface, it is unnecessary and usually inadvisable to match the base metal exactly. For instance, some properties of the metal used in a blanking die block are required only to provide maximum wear life of the cutting edge. The same hardenability, fine grain size, and edge strength are not needed in repair of a fracture across an outside corner of the block. Likewise, a built-up cutting edge on a worn tool does not need the depth of hardening of the base metal.

The following electrodes have the greatest range of application in the welding of tool and die steels:

Low-hydrogen ferrous electrodes—can be used broadly in the repair of broken tools, and in their initial construction. They are especially applicable to the water-hardening carbon tool steels (W group), to the low-alloy tool steels (L group), and with care to lower-alloy steels of other groups. On the higher-alloy steels, they can be used to fill a weld after first buttering sides of the bevelled groove with an austenitic stainless steel.

Electrode E-11018-G deposits an alloyed filler metal of high tensile strength as-welded. Electrode E-9018-G has a lower strength but offers better ductility and impact resistance. Although these electrodes give desirable welds on hardened tool steels without further heat-treatment, their maximum hardness and tensile strength are developed by oil and water quenching.

These electrodes give a weld deposit that are practically free of hydrogen, reducing the possibility of micro-cracks and underbead cracks. They have excellent deposition characteristics. In using them to weld tool steels, penetration must be kept to a minimum, to avoid excessive carbon pick-up from the base metal.

Because of the low-carbon content of the low-hydrogen electrodes, weld deposits do not have high hardness and should not be used for wear-resistant purposes. Also they should not be used under high heat service conditions.

On any weld, before using low-hydrogen, high-tensile electrodes it is preferable to (1) butter with austenitic 25-20 stainless steel, or (2) make a root pass with the austenitic, or with a lower-carbon, more ductile low-hydrogen electrode.

When depositing dissimilar metals in a multiple-layer weld or pad, it is advisable that the lowest layer have the highest draw temperature. Thus, deposit of additional layers is less likely to affect properties of the one at the bottom.

Austenitic stainless-steel electrodes—of 25% chromium, 20% nickel content can be used where a ductile joint is needed: welding many broken tools, fabricating a tool from two or more tool steel parts, welding dissimilar metals such as tool steel to mild steel, and in depositing the bottom layer for hardsurfacing with tool-steel electrodes.

Fig. 19-7. Draw punch and ring used in production of automotive front door panel were fabricated quickly by using metal-arc welding. Tools cost much less than would conventional cast die.

This type electrode (E-310-15) does not deposit hard metal. If the fracture crosses a cutting edge or forming surface, finish off the working surface with an air-hardening electrode or high-speed steel electrode as required. The high-alloy content of the E-310-15 austenitic electrode discourages excessive admixture of base metal.

To weld a broken tool or die, make a bevel groove along the line of fracture and fill with a stainless-steel electrode. On heavy welds, or where greater strength is needed, butter the groove surfaces with the stainless steel, then complete the weld with a low-hydrogen high-tensile ferrous electrode such as E-11018-G.

Although the austenitic alloys have good ductility, their rate of shrinkage during cooling will be greater than that of the hardened tool steel base metal. If the austenitic alloy is a single layer there's no danger, but better assurance of success is had on heavier welds by making additional layers of high-tensile, low-hydrogen electrode (E-11018-G). A heavy mass of austenitic alloy may exert too much stress on the base metal and cause underbead cracking along the fusion line.

High-carbon steel electrodes—depositing 0.70% or higher carbon are used on many strength-weld applications. Their main advantage is the limited pick-up of carbon from the base metal. However, a disadvantage in their use on hardened steel is that the low ductility of the deposit may develop excessive stresses between the rigid structures of base metal and weld bead, producing cracks.

Tool-steel electrodes—of composition comparable to each main group of tool steels are sometimes used for repair welding or initial construction of tooling. In general, they are premium priced due to the high cost of fabricating them into rod form. Because of their

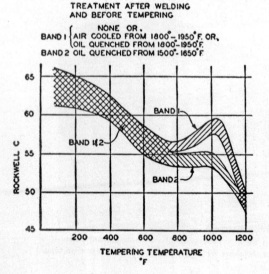

Fig. 19-8. Effect of tempering on hardness of general-purpose air- and oil-hardening tool steel weld deposit.

Fig. 19-9. Long-life chromium carbide hardsurfacing is deposited on large die ring worn from severe abrasion and moderate impact.

composition, some require high welding current or have other undesirable deposition characteristics.

Air-hardening electrodes—of high-carbon, 5% chromium content for hardsurfacing and build-up of forming and cutting tool edges give a martensitic deposit when cooled rapidly from above their critical temperature (1600 F). Alloyed deposits are hard as-welded, but properties are improved by heat-treat. They are air or oil hardening. These general-purpose tool-steel electrodes give deposits having excellent toughness, impact strength, and edge strength. They are used extensively on all kinds of tool applications at temperatures up to about 600 F.

High-speed steel electrodes—for hardsurfacing and build-up of cutting tool edges give a martensitic high-molybdenum deposit. Weld metal retains full hardness to temperatures above 1000 F. Deposits are used as-welded, or properties may be improved by heat-treat.

*   *   *   *

Deposits made by these last two electrode types are non-machinable as-welded, but can be ground to size. Deposits may be annealed for machining. Both electrodes give metal with high edge strength.

Other hardsurfacing electrodes—can be used for special-purpose tooling requiring unusual properties. The most commonly used are the chromium-carbide types and the austenitic manganese steel types. See Chapter 18.

Repair of Broken Tools

Tool steels are relatively expensive. Their initial cost per pound in log, bar or other mill form or as pre-ground flats and rounds, is higher than that of most other steels. When fabricated into an intricate die, for example, after many precision machine, bench and heat-treat operations, the total investment in a single component may run into the hundreds of dollars. If this component is fractured, the choice may be to repair-weld or to scrap the part at a considerable loss.

Breakage of tools may be the result of (1) production wrecks or accidents, (2) fatigue failure occurring after the tool has been in service for a commendable length of time, or (3) early failure from additive residual and service stresses. In the latter case, there is often a fatigue factor involved. If the failure occurs early after the tool has been placed in service and provided there was no faulty setup or mis-alignment or excessive vibration in the machine, the fault may have been incorrect design, use of wrong steel, or improper heat-treat. The best welding technique used in repair of the component is unlikely to prevent a repeated failure if incorrect design or the wrong steel caused the first failure.

We can therefore limit ourselves to considering welding for the repair of production wrecks, fatigue failures, or early failures due to improper heat treatment. Fractures resulting from accident may occur anywhere in the tool. Fracture resulting from fatigue or heat-treat usually occurs along a stress line or at some other point conducive to high stress concentration. A ductile weld metal along the line of fracture may prevent any recurrence of the failure, since fracture itself relieved the high localized stresses.

It is necessary to determine just what properties are needed at the point of welding. On many tool components, the steel's high tensile strength is not needed at all to withstand high service stresses but is a byproduct of the method by which the needed wear-resistance and dimensional stability are attained.

A major problem in repairing tools is frequently that of maintaining dimensions on the broken tool components. For example, on a pro-gressive-die plate where center distances of dowel holes and die open-ings must be held to a fraction of 0.001 in., weld repair may be im-practical if not impossible. For the greatest possibility of success in a case like this, weld without annealing the base metal. Depending on where the fracture lies, brazing may be applicable here. Or, welding with an austenitic alloy may be the answer.

In welding steels with 1.00% carbon or more, the penetration needed for a sound weld raises the carbon content of the weld metal to a point where it no longer is sufficiently ductile to withstand shrink-age stresses. When welding such steels use a 25% chromium, 20% nickel (25-20 stainless) electrode (E-310-15). If a large weld, butter with the stainless and complete with a high-tensile low-hydrogen elec-trode.

There are few exceptions that can be made to the general rule that welding should not be attempted while the tool is mounted in the pro-duction machine. For that matter, the broken component should be disassembled for welding so that it can be uniformly preheated without disturbing other components of the tool.

Decision: Anneal or Weld Hard?—When the situation permits, repair-weld tool steel while in the hardened and tempered condition in order to eliminate the full annealing and complete hardening cycle, and to avoid possible necessity of costly correction of changed dimensions (not a factor on all tools, such as a boring bar). If the base metal was previously hardened but not tempered, it cannot be safely welded and annealing will be necessary.

When repairing tool steel in the annealed condition, remember that low-melting alloys will not stand hardening temperatures. Also, the welding electrode used must give a weld deposit that is responsive to heat treatment.

When repairing tool steel in the hardened condition, a greater choice of welding methods and filler metals is permitted.

The basic procedures available are:

1. Anneal, preheat, weld, stress relieve, machine, harden, and temper.
2. Preheat, weld with austenitic stainless electrode, and temper.
3. Preheat, butter with austenitic stainless electrode, fill with multiple layer of high-strength electrode metal, and temper.

In either an annealed or hardened condition, tool steel should not be oxyacetylene welded. The slowness of this process introduces too much heat to the base metal. This causes distortion, excessive softening of hardened metal or excessive embrittlement of annealed metal, and cracking. Nearly all repair of the tool and die steels is by shielded-arc welding.

Preparing for welding—is relatively simple. If the tool is to be annealed for welding, clean and dry all surfaces thoroughly, and anneal. Assemble the pieces together very closely and anchor in position. Unless the joint can and will be brazed, bevel out the fracture in a single V if the plate is thin. Usually a double V will be required, depositing weld metal on both sides. Use extra care in ensuring that the groove is of uniform width for the full length of the weld. The root gap should not be more than $\frac{1}{16}$ inch.

If the tool has been annealed, the groove can be cut by torch or by grinding. If hardened, the groove should be cut by grinding or arc-air gouging. Be especially careful in grinding thin plate. The usual wheel speeds are 5000-6000 sfpm. Do not apply too much pressure and use a clean, sharpened wheel. Glazing or discoloration of hardened steel indicates damage to the steel. The presence of vanadium in the steel greatly increases the possibility of damage by grinding. Preheating before grinding or flame cutting will lessen the possibility of damage.

Be sure that all cracks are eliminated from the surfaces to be welded. Be sure that all surfaces of the pieces are perfectly clean and smooth.

When welding—a combination of good practices is needed. Always preheat. Use the smallest diameter electrode that will satisfactorily fill the gap. On multiple-pass welds, it is best to continue with a ⅛-inch electrode unless the plate is very thick. Weld flat, or better yet weld slightly uphill so that slag rolls back covering the weld, thereby limiting decarburization and oxidation. Do not strike arc on tool steel outside of weld zone. Strike the arc on a carbon block or piece of copper lying adjacent to the weld.

Peening each bead will reduce the formation of shrinkage cracks. Peen only while weld metal is at high heat. Otherwise, weld-cracking may result.

Build up weld metal slightly. Maintain required preheat temperature between passes. If the groove is long, blanketing the hot weld with inert insulating material will slow up the cooling rate so that entire weldment can later be cooled uniformly.

Stress relieving the weld—should be done immediately after the weld cools. The weld should be cooled slowly to the preheat temperature, and then the entire structure cooled to about 100-150 F. At this point, the tool can barely be held in the hand. Temper immediately to relieve hardening stresses, to prevent cracking, and to increase toughness.

Relieve stresses by tempering at the preheat temperature. If welding was done on annealed stock, stress relieve at a higher temperature (usually 1100-1300 F), especially if the weld is to be exposed to any post-weld machining. Always temper in favor of the base metal except after hardsurfacing.

After stress relieving and the structure has returned to room temperature, let it sit for awhile to stabilize. Then grind back the weld flush with the tool steel surface in order to eliminate any stress-raiser effect. Take the same precautions as when preparing the groove. Remember that grinding must get under any scale with a single pass. Check to make certain there are no toe cracks.

Brazing and Braze-Welding

These methods are often used successfully in repair of the hardened high-speed steels (T and M groups), air-hardening steels (H group), and even high-carbon, high-chromium steels (D group). These steels are usually tempered in the neighborhood of 1000 F for maximum wear-resistance. If heated briefly to 1200 F during brazing, their hardness will not be appreciably reduced.

Low-melting copper-based alloys are used. (Silver-brazing type alloys are preferred because tool steels containing chromium develop a film of chromic acid when in hot contact with copper alloys. Chromic oxide then prevents a good wetting of surfaces to be joined.) Because braze alloys melt at a low temperature, no further heat treatment of the tool is possible. Neither can these alloys be used where service temperatures in the weld area will exceed about 500 F.

Nor can they be used successfully where high stresses are experienced at frequencies conducive to fatigue.

On most repair jobs where a brazing alloy can be used, this procedure may be followed:

1. Fit the pieces of the broken part together and check to make certain no fragments have been lost from the fractured surfaces. Brazing should be used only for closely mated surfaces. Separate the pieces to be welded.

2. Preheat the broken parts uniformly at lower end of tempering range.

3. Coat the fractured surfaces with a brazing flux.

4. Again, fit the pieces together as snugly as possible and clamp or wire them together.

5. With the brazing wire held along the fracture, apply heat along the joint to about 1200 F. An oxyacetylene torch with neutral flame may be used, but avoid thermal shock from sudden direct impact of flame on the cold steel. The wire will melt, the braze alloy being "sucked" into the joint by capillary action. Be careful not to overheat, especially on the A and D group steels.

6. Allow the brazed tool to cool slowly.

Brazing alloys are available in flat strip, rod or wire forms. In initial construction, lap and butt joints are frequently made by sandwiching the flux and braze alloy cut from strip stock between the hardened steel parts. A stronger bond, and more ductile joint for dissimilar tool steels can be obtained by using a commercially prepared bimetal "sandwich." Production brazing with silver-braze alloys

Fig. 19-10. Low-hydrogen electrode is used effectively in correcting machining errors in tire curing mold made from free machining steel having high sulphur content.

is best done by induction heating, and with straight copper alloys in an atmosphere controlled furnace.

If the pieces cannot be fitted together snugly, cut a groove along the fracture and braze-weld the part. Copper alloys yield readily during cooling and thus contribute little to development of residual stresses along the joint.

Welding Hot-Work Steels

Because of the thermal service conditions under which hot-work steels are used, a constant metallurgical structure is usually required throughout the tool. Most of these tools, such as forging dies, are large and heavy. Being exposed to high temperatures, such die blocks must expand and contract uniformly and to do so must have an identical coefficient of thermal expansion over the entire member.

The intermittent heating and cooling to which many of these tools are exposed in service, make conventional welding of doubtful value. If welded, the weld metal should have the same transformation-temperature-time characteristics as the base metal, and the heat-affected zone should be as thin as possible. Ordinarily, a hot-work tool steel is most satisfactorily welded by use of a filler metal having the same composition. The producers of the hot-work tool steel to be welded may be able to supply an electrode or welding rod that deposits the same or comparable metal.

Fig. 19-11. Cutting edges of this angle shear die were built up with tool steel deposit, providing long life without cost of solid tool steel construction.

To weld, preheat slowly to above the upper critical point (about 1500 F); continue to preheat but rapidly to the yellow temperature range (1900-2000 F); weld using filler metal of same composition; normalize above the lower critical point (at about 1450 F); and cool slowly in air or under a neutral insulator such as lime. Then harden and temper.

Shock-resistant tools are handled in the same way, although a lower-strength low-hydrogen electrode (E-7018) is sometimes used.

Usually fracture of high-speed steel results in fracture at a point where resistance to shock, vibration, or torsional stress is far more important than red hardness. However, high heat transfer through a tool body or other exposure to high red heat may necessitate special weld considerations. In this case, preheat as for the hot-work steels; weld with high-speed electrode; before weld cools below red heat take it back up for annealing at 1600-1650 F; cool slowly in furnace with tool packed in lime or other inert material. Then harden and temper.

Building Composite Tools and Dies

The high-alloy tool steels are expensive. Substantial savings can be obtained by composite fabrication of tooling. The tools are made by using low-cost, machinable metal such as mild steel for the main body of the tool and building up on this base the cutting or forming edges of hard tool steel. These edges are laid by hardsurfacing with weld metal deposited from a standard tool-steel arc-welding electrode. Although such tools are low in cost they often have longer life than tools made by more conventional methods.

In selecting a base metal for a composite tool, choose the least expensive and most readily available material that will function adequately. This may be a mild steel. However, some tools require specific properties in the tool body that are not available in mild steel. The right material may be a cast iron, a medium-carbon steel, or a high-tensile low-alloy steel. Composite fabrication enables you to build a tool with exceptional edge strength and wear-resistance, together with a base or tool body with the impact strength, machinability, ductility, or whatever else you need.

Blanking dies, trimming dies, forming dies, drop-hammer dies, shear blades, lathe tools, planer tools, woodworking tools, milling cutters, and many other types of tools have been made successfully by these methods.

The two general-purpose electrodes that fit most needs in building up working edges and surfaces on composite tools are (1) the chromium-type, air and oil hardening tool-steel electrode, and (2) the molybdenum-type, high-speed steel electrode. The first is used on all applications except where high red hardness is needed. The second type is used on cutting tools and other applications where full hardness is needed at temperatures as high as 1000 F.

Deposits provided by both electrodes are hard as-welded, although they may be heat treated. Edges may be ground to sharp corner or smoothly radiused, in either case retaining the contour under severe metal-to-metal impact loading. Both electrodes provide metal that can be finished very smooth, that have a low coefficient of friction, and that resist micro-welding and galling.

Additional hot strength for a mild steel or low-alloy base metal can be provided by depositing a layer of 25-20 stainless steel prior to the tool-steel surfacing. Other hardsurfacing electrodes are available to provide special properties as needed to tool surfaces (see Chapter 18).

Tool-steel surfaces should be deposited in multiple layers with minimum current consistent with adequate fusion. With multiple-layer deposits, admixture of the base metal is largely limited to the bottom layer, and the undiluted outer working surface will have maximum desired properties. At least three layers of the tool steel should be deposited to achieve this effect.

In determining the size of the weld, allowance should be made for later redressing or sharpening of the tool. However, excessive thickness of the surfacing material only increases the cost and may also reduce the impact strength somewhat.

In most cases, the tool-steel surfacing material will be deposited on annealed or soft base metal. Preheat the base metal to 400-500 F, and maintain this temperature between passes.

The preheat and interpass temperatures must be high enough to prevent underbead cracking. However, if the tool-steel surface is to be used as-welded and will not be further heat-treated, the preheat and interpass temperatures must be low enough for the weld deposit to be quenched quickly to form martensite. If the interpass temperature is too high, either pearlite or untempered martensite will form, neither of which will have good wear-resistance. By keeping down the interpass temperature, the weld metal will transform to hard, wear-resistant martensite. This metal will be tempered when the next layer is deposited. The last layer may be tempered by depositing an extra layer and then grinding it off, or by postheating with an oxyacetylene torch.

Composite tools are often furnace tempered at 1025 F to relieve weld stresses and to ensure more uniform properties than are obtainable by tempering with an extra layer of deposited metal or by torch heating. Before tempering, the completed weld should be allowed to cool long enough to give the austenite time to transform to martensite. Any untransformed austenite will, during tempering, transform at high temperature to a different type of martensite. This has lower hardness and wear-resistance than the martensite formed at the lower temperature during initial rapid cooling of the weld.

Hardened tool steels to be hardsurfaced can be preheated to a higher temperature, but never above the temperature at which they were last tempered. During hardsurfacing, care must be taken to prevent the heating of more than a local area and then for as short a time as possible.

Building Up Worn Tools and Dies

Worn edges or surfaces of tools and dies can be easily restored by using tool-steel electrodes and hardsurfacing techniques as for making composite tools. Similarly, product engineering changes that usually demand retooling or at least expensive alteration hard steel tools can often be accommodated with little time delay and minimum cost.

To restore a cutting or forming edge, first grind back the surface to provide a shelf of adequate uniform depth (at least ⅛ inch) below original surface line. The weld deposit must be at least this thick after it has been ground down. A cutting edge should have somewhat greater depth, depending on tool size and cutting forces involved.

Be certain that all surfaces to be faced are clean of scale and oxide, and that all cracks are removed. Cracks in the ground surface may be detected by rubbing in kerosene or a light oil, wiping off the oil, and then brushing on a talc or chalk powder. The oil in any cracks will ooze out and darken the powder in a few minutes. One crack-detection process calls for inspection of the surface with ultra-violet light. The cracks show up as bright lines, for the oil used is fluorescent. Magnetic-particle inspection also reveals cracks.

Do not expect to melt to the bottom of a crack with the arc. All too often the crack remains and later progresses right up through deposited weld metal. Cracks should be completely removed by grinding before any welding is done.

After the built-up surface or cutting edge has been ground back to size, check carefully to make certain that there are no weld cracks, nor toe cracks at edge of deposit.

Definitions of New Words

Bainite. An aggregate of needle-like ferrite and carbide particles. It is tougher than martensite and harder than austenite or pearlite.

Decarburization. The loss of carbon from a ferrous alloy in a reactive atmosphere at high temperatures.

Differential hardening. (1) The characteristic of certain steels to develop high surface or case hardness and to retain a tough, soft core. (2) Any hardening procedure designed to produce only localized or superficial hardness.

Interrupted quenching. Any quenching procedure that cools the metal part way in one medium or at one rate, and then completes the cooling in another medium or at another rate. Term is usually applied only where the temperature of interruption is in the critical or immediately sub-critical range, and where the metal is held for a definite period at the temperature of interruption.

Pack annealing. Any annealing in which the object is surrounded by inert material to prevent reaction at high temperatures. Usually this packing is done in a box-like container. Similarly, we have "pack hardening" and "pack carburizing" in which packing is done with a carbonaceous material; at high temperature the surface of the metal picks up carbon from this surrounding material and develops a hard case when cooled at a fast rate.

Subcritical annealing. Heating of a metal to a point below the critical or transformation range, in order to relieve internal stresses.

Temper. (1) The amount of carbon present in a steel: 10 temper is 1.00% carbon. (2) The degree of hardness left in a steel after quench-hardening and tempering. (3) The degree of hardness that an alloy has after heat treatment or cold-working, viz. the aluminum alloys.

Review Questions

1. Name the elements that give high-temperature hardness to high-speed tool steels.
2. What is the primary reason for using a low-carbon, ductile filler metal when making a repair weld of a tool steel?
3. Two pieces of hardened high-carbon, high-chromium die steel are heat treated. One is heated quickly to 1700 F and quenched in oil. What will be the difference in the hardness and in the micro-structures?
4. Improper grinding by using too much pressure or the wrong type of wheel may overheat or burn the surface of tool steel. In what way does this injure the tool?
5. Why should certain tool-steel deposits be cooled to 200 F or lower after welding or during quenching before the deposit is heated for tempering?
6. Why should tool steel be preheated for welding, whether the steel is in an annealed or hardened condition?
7. Which die, a simple or an intricate one, can be more suitably made from water-hardening steel? From air-hardening steel?
8. What steps can be taken to prevent excessive decarburization when welding across a wear-resistant surface?
9. Explain why it is not necessary to match the analysis of the parent metal when welding a tool or die.
10. Give a typical procedure for welding a tool and die steel to achieve: (a) High strength in the joint. (b) A wear-resistant die draw radius. (c) A cutting edge of high red hardness.

CHAPTER 20

WELDING THE EXOTIC METALS

Our entry into the space age has necessitated the introduction of newer metals to be fabricated—metals to meet the demand for light-weight structures having high strength at high temperatures. Matching Man's progress into space, stride for stride, has been the extensive development of nuclear energy applications in defense and in public power generation. This has created the need for metals with extremely high resistance to corrosion and erosion from new powerful chemicals and from hot liquid metals, and metals capable of high absorption of gamma rays.

For many years, we had known of metals having these needed properties. But these were "exotic" metals—laboratory curiosities that behaved strangely in contrast to other metals better known to engineers and weldors. They were difficult and costly to extract from their ores, and difficult to work with because of their great affinity for elements common to the atmosphere and for elements used in most refractory materials. In small percentages the exotic metals have long been important as alloying elements in ferrous and other metallurgical products. Now, however, these exotic metals are also available for commercial application in pure and alloyed form.

Among such metals are titanium, zirconium, tantalum, columbium, vanadium and molybdenum. These metals possess a combination of unique characteristics—high corrosion resistance, high strength at high temperatures, and good physical properties in general—characteristics that make them the modern design engineer's dream-come-true. The proven and potential value these hold for Man so excite our engineers and challenge their ingenuity that, for many people, these elements are truly the exotic metals.

Unfortunately, these materials cannot be manufactured or fabricated without difficulties. Stringent precautions must be applied to avoid embrittlement by absorption of oxygen, nitrogen or hydrogen at elevated temperatures. Thus, the fabrication of these materials presents two problem periods: during the initial production of the metal, and during any subsequent hot working, welding or brazing that must be performed to produce a finished product. For this reason, all of these operations must be performed under an inert atmosphere or vacuum with complete freedom from grease or other foreign materials. Many of the alloys of these exotic metals work-harden readily during rolling and comparable mill operations, requiring frequent annealing under an inert atmosphere.

Working under such conditions naturally increases production costs, but these increased costs are often outweighed by the ability of these metals to give service and application where more common metals would not be usable. It must be stressed, however, that economic use of titanium or any of the newer expensive metals depends on careful design and fabrication that use fully their special properties while utilizing a minimum quantity of material consistent with strength requirements. Consequently, most items fabricated from these metals are relatively light gage and small in size.

Since the prevention of embrittlement is the prime consideration when fusion welding these metals, conventional oxyacetylene or metal-arc welding processes are unsuitable. In some instances resistance welding can be employed, but here again precautions must be exercised. Generally, techniques involving use of the TIG process have proved most satisfactory. Most sections of these high-cost metals are within the preferred thickness range for resistance welding and TIG welding.

Welding is complicated by the need to protect not only the molten weld pool but all parts of the component being welded as well. Thus, it is necessary to create an inert-gas shield that will give a far greater than normal coverage of the workpiece and of the weld deposit.

Cleanliness is of the utmost importance. Any grease or oxidation products on the sheet's surface prior to welding will provide another source of contamination. Mechanical cleaning methods and normal degreasing treatments should be carried out, but care must be exercised in using chemical cleaning agents since some of them may form explosive compounds with the exotic metal being welded.

Probably the most popular of the newer metals, and one in which the greatest amount of experience has been gained in fabrication, is titanium.

Titanium and Its Alloys

Titanium is a silvery-gray metal that weighs about ½ as much as steel. Pure titanium is soft and has a low ultimate tensile strength (45,000 psi). Many references to its use as a structural material actually apply to its alloys. The more extensively used alloys incorporate rather high percentages of chromium and iron; chromium and aluminum; manganese; or manganese and aluminum. Zirconium and vanadium are also used as alloying agents.

The very good corrosion resistance of titanium and its alloys has broadened its use into the marine field and into chemical processing equipment. Its primary application, though, remains in aircraft structural and engine components. Commercially-pure titanium is used extensively for aluminum anodizing racks and in unfired pressure vessels.

Alloyed titanium has a remarkable high strength-weight ratio, retaining its strength and corrosion resistance at sustained temperatures up to about 800 F. When uncontaminated, it has exceptional fatigue life. Hardened alloys have an ultimate tensile strength ranging as high as 200,000 psi, and relatively low ductility. Therefore, welding is usually done on the annealed metal. Some of the alloys, however, are not hardenable by heat-treatment.

Titanium has a normal closely-packed hexagonal crystal structure at room temperature. This alpha phase transforms at 1625 F to the beta phase—a body-centered cubic structure. Alloying elements influence the alpha-to-beta transformation. The addition of aluminum stabilizes the alpha phase and raises the transformation point. In contrast, chromium, iron, vanadium or zirconium additions slow up the transformation from beta to alpha during cooling and stabilize the beta phase at lower temperatures. The result is a grouping of the titanium alloys according to the crystal structure that exists at room temperature and throughout their useful range of temperature application.

With the rigid observance of good practices, the commercially-pure titanium and the alpha alloys can be MIG or TIG fusion welded with joints having properties equivalent to the parent metal. Resistance spot and seam welding, electron-beam welding in a vacuum, and brazing have also been used successfully. The mixed alpha-beta alloys are sensitive to micro changes caused by heating and cooling above 1500 F, and are subject to embrittlement by welding. A few of these

Fig. 20-1. Best known of all exotic metals is titanium. Sheets of a titanium alloy are here being resistance welded for a space capsule bulkhead.

alloys have been successfully fusion welded in production under rigidly controlled conditions. Attempts to weld the low-ductility beta alloys have been discouraging. All three types have been spot welded in production, with good tension-shear strength but usually poor cross-tension strength.

In many respects, the titanium alloys have physical properties, fabricating and heat-treat characteristics comparable to the high-nickel alloys such as Inconel. However, the high chemical activity and the sensitivity of titanium to embrittlement impose limitations and require special welding procedures. In addition to its high reactivity with the gaseous elements mentioned (oxygen, hydrogen and nitrogen), titanium at high temperatures readily absorbs carbon and its compounds which also have adverse effects. Even a minute amount of one of these elements may have a drastic influence on properties of the metal.

Hot titanium + air, moisture, dirt, grease = contamination.

Although simple, this equation is at the heart of the most basic consideration in welding titanium: the elimination of contamination. And, it's equally applicable when welding any of the other reactive metals.

TIG Welding of Titanium

Considerable effort has been expended to develop satisfactory techniques for fusion welding titanium. TIG welding has become generally accepted as the standard process to use.

Joint designs for titanium are about the same as those for other metals. With the TIG process, butt welds may be made with or without filler rod, depending on the thickness of the joint and the fit-up. If fit-up is good, filler rod is not required; if poor, filler metal is added to obtain full-thickness joints. The filler metal usually is of the same chemical analysis as the parent metal.

When welding material up to 0.062-in. thick, good welds can be made with no filler metal using a square-butt joint with tight fit-up. If a thicker material is welded (up to about 0.125 in.), square-butt joints with clearance of ½ to 1 times the base metal thickness are recommended. Filler rod should be used.

When a single-V butt joint is used on thickness above 0.125 in., the first pass should be made without filler, and the fusion zone should be kept to about ½ the plate thickness. The second pass is then made with filler in the conventional way.

Because of molten titanium's extreme chemical reactivity, thorough cleaning and drying of joints and filler material before welding is very important.

For scale-free material, a simple degreasing operation is sufficient to remove dirt and oil, followed by light wire-brushing. For materials with large amounts of light oxide scale, acid pickling treatments are generally used.

The most effective and practical titanium cleaning method is a good, thorough wire-brushing. A clean, stainless-steel brush is preferred. A new, clean steel brush is adequate if surfaces are wiped free of any brush-deposited rust. Sandblasting is recommended for any heavy or difficult-to-remove scale.

Since hot titanium has the usual property of dissolving even its own oxide, all cleaning should be done just prior to welding, covering a surface distance from the weld joint of about 10 times the base metal thickness. Surface should be antiseptically clean; even a finger-print smudge may cause some weld embrittlement.

Whenever the hot metal (above 800 F) comes in contact with air, contamination occurs. When welding, therefore, inert-gas shielding is most essential and must be adequate in all directions. In some cases, an auxiliary trailing shield will be sufficient to keep the weld zone blanketed with inert gas until it has cooled below 800 F. Back-up bars should be provided to protect the underside of the weld.

Starting and stopping the arc should be done with the aid of an amperage-varying control unit. This will avoid burn-through, since lower amperage can be used when starting and stopping, and will also allow the torch to be held in place until the weld has cooled. If a variable-amperage control unit is not available, starting and finishing tabs should be used to take up the burning and contamination.

Good ductility and the color of the weld are both functions of proper shielding. Therefore, weld quality may be estimated by its color, but only if the colors are very distinguishable.

For example, if the surface of the weld is a metallic silver color, shielding was excellent, and the weld has good ductility. A light straw color ranging to a light blue color indicates the weld was not protected at low temperature, but ductility is probably good.

On the other hand, if the weld color ranges from dark straw to dark blue, the weld was not adequately shielded and poor ductility is the result. Should the weld be dark blue, gray or yellowish, or if

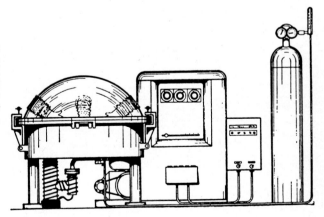

Fig. 20-2. Welding chamber that can be purged of air and filled with inert gas, is typical of those used for joining tantalum, and other highly reactive metals.

deposits have little or no lustre, the shielding was extremely poor and the welds are very brittle.

The keynote to successful titanium welding is adequate gas shielding.

Similar precautions must be observed in connection with any heat-treatment of titanium and its alloys. Welds on commercially-pure titanium may be stress-relieved at 1000 F, and air cooled. Welds on the alpha alloys require 2 hours at 1000-1200 F for full stress-relief.

Welding Tantalum

Tantalum has many electrical applications and is used in chemical equipment for its high resistance to acids and in anatomical components for its corrosion resistance and non-irritation of living tissues.

Strong, ductile welds can be made on tantalum by using the TIG welding process and taking into consideration this metal's melting point and great reactivity at high temperatures. Electron-beam welding and copper brazing in a vacuum, and resistance seam and spot welding are also employed.

Tantalum has an extremely high melting point of 5,425 F, as compared to approximately 2,700 F for most steels. Also, at elevated temperatures (570 F and higher) tantalum combines with oxygen, nitrogen and hydrogen; in fact, it combines with all but the inert gases. When welding tantalum, all undesired gases must be kept away from the weld area.

Other points must also be kept in mind: the thermal conductivity of tantalum is somewhat lower than that of steel; the thermal coefficient of expansion is about half that of steel. Aside from these points, the physical properties of tantalum and mild steel are similar.

Because of its relatively low work-hardening rate, it is not usually necessary to anneal tantalum before welding. However, if tantalum has been deliberately hardened by cold working, its ductility will be extremely low compared with the normally excellent ductility of this metal.

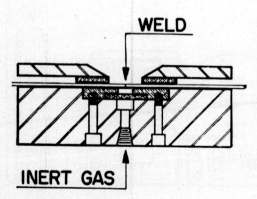

WELD

INERT GAS

Fig. 20-3. Fixtures for longitudinal TIG welds on tantalum feature porous metal back-up plate, or copper back-up plate grooved and drilled for flow of inert gas to protect underside of joint from reactance with atmospheric elements.

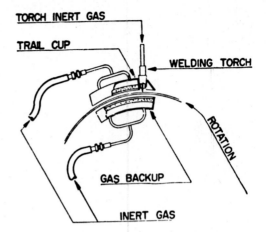

Fig. 20-4. Fixture for making circular butt-welds on tantalum. Inert gas back-up and trailing cup cover the entire heated area with inert gas until it has cooled.

Thorough cleaning of the metal is required. Tantalum is shipped cleaned and ready to use. If, during unpacking or prior in-plant operations the material picks up dirt and oil, cleaning by degreasing will be satisfactory before welding.

After cleaning, the tantalum must be wiped dry or dried in a warm air draft. Immediately prior to welding, a final cleaning with a cloth saturated with alcohol is recommended to remove surface dust and finger marks in the weld area.

It is necessary that the weld and heat-affected zone be flooded with an inert gas to exclude all gaseous contaminants that could reduce the ductility of the weldment. Helium, argon or a mixture of the two can create an atmosphere to which tantalum is inert at all temperatures. And, when the purity of the gas is maintained at a high level, the weld and heat-affected zones exhibit ductility similar to the parent metal.

Where a perfectly ductile weld zone is required, a welding chamber that can be purged of air and filled with inert gas is desirable. Essentially, a welding chamber (Fig. 20-2) provides a perfectly sealed enclosure which allows a wide visual range; arm holes or a remote control device to manipulate the weldment; a vacuum system to evacuate the air where purging is not considered satisfactory; a pure inert gas supply; a welding system including power supply, torch and ground cable.

Provisions in the fixture design must allow clearance for inert gas flow around all heated surfaces. If back-up plates are used, they must have deep, wide grooves open to the inert-gas atmosphere.

To weld a sealed assembly, provisions must be made to either assemble after purging or add weep holes for gas circulation during welding.

In many cases, the use of a welding chamber is impractical because of the weldment's size or shape. In such cases, the heated surfaces

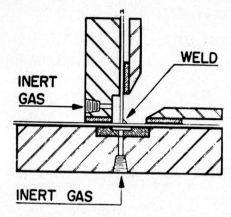

Fig. 20-5. Fillet welding fixture performs the triple functions of holding alignment, chilling, and inert gas back-up of heated area.

can be protected by proper gas-backed fixturing (Figs. 20-3, 4 and 5). This usually serves three purposes:

1. To hold the work in proper alignment.
2. To chill the work in order to limit the heat-affected area.
3. To act as a seal to exclude the outside air and to conduct the inert gas to the heated areas.

The welding power source most desirable for TIG welding tantalum is a DC welder capable of maintaining an arc at 10 to 300 amp.

Accessory equipment should include a remote control foot switch with a contactor relay switch to extinguish the arc at the conclusion of a weld pass. Solenoid control of torch, trail and back-up gas with purge and post-weld gas flow timing intervals is a desirable feature to ensure controllable gas coverage without gas waste. High-frequency arc starting is mandatory to avoid tungsten pick-up in the fusion zone.

A motor generator set with the necessary accessories will be adequate for most welding operations.

The welding torch nozzle size should be as large as is feasible to provide maximum inert gas coverage over the molten puddle with low gas velocity. The electrode size depends on the welding current. Thoriated tungsten electrodes are recommended because of their excellent arc initiation and arc stability characteristics.

The choice of helium or argon for welding tantalum is dependent on many factors. The most important consideration is their individual arc characteristics. Normal TIG welding voltages are from 10 to 12 volts DC straight polarity in an argon atmosphere and 16 to 20 volts in helium. These values are for similar arc lengths.

Where back-up cups or large diameter expanding fixtures are used, the low density of helium relative to air is a desirable factor. The lighter helium forces the air down and away from the back side of the weld joint. Conversely, argon is more desirable on the top surface because of its greater density relative to air.

Welding Columbium

Columbium is used primarily for its resistance to corrosion by most water-based liquids and by various liquid metals. Alloyed with 1% zirconium, it is used in nuclear equipment.

Most of the statements referring to the welding of tantalum, apply equally well to the welding of columbium (also known as niobium). The principal difference between the two metals is that the melting point of columbium (4,379 F) is somewhat lower than that of tantalum. It oxidizes rapidly above 750 F, and absorbs hydrogen within the range of 500 to 1750 F; both with adverse effect on the metal's ductility at room temperature.

Welding Zirconium

Alloys of zirconium are employed in nuclear applications, in chemical equipment, and in anatomical components for surgical purposes.

Zirconium and the zirconium alloys (Zircaloy-2 and Zircaloy-3) possess excellent weldability; but, like titanium, they readily absorb and alloy with oxygen, nitrogen and hydrogen when heated to high temperatures.

To combat the detrimental effects these elements have on mechanical and corrosion properties, arc welding must be conducted in a high-purity inert atmosphere. When welding is exceptionally critical, a dry-box should be used.

The dry-box is a chamber in which the work, torch, fixtures and

Fig. 20-6. Columbium is another of the highly reactive metals that can be welded safely. Here TIG welding of tubing protects hot weld and base metal from atmosphere.

power leads can be installed, and which can be evacuated to about 0.1 to 5 microns and then refilled with helium or argon at atmospheric pressure.

When zirconium and Zircaloy were first welded for nuclear reactor applications, the chambers were evacuated to 0.03 microns for at least 12 hours, then back-filled with helium. With the purity of today's zirconium, however, any slight contamination that may occur through relaxed standards for dry-box welding can be accommodated.

The dry-box atmosphere can be further purified of residual air (due to insufficient pump-down or leakage during refilling) by holding an arc on scrap zirconium for several minutes. The operation is then halted when discoloration-free weld beads are obtained.

Welding zirconium outside a dry-box will satisfy many nuclear applications, and almost all non-nuclear applications, if Grade A helium or argon of guaranteed high purity is employed.

Precautions, however, must be taken when designing the shielding equipment to be used when inert-gas arc welding. Proper shielding will exclude all trace of air from the weld metal and heat-affected zone until the metal has cooled to below 700 F. Rapid cooling can be promoted by using copper back-up plates and hold-down clamps.

Inert-gas shielding of the weld bead's underside, plus a trailing shield, are absolutely essential if zirconium is to be welded outside a dry-box. The trailing shields must be designed to meet the weldment's contours.

Shielding lines should be designed and assembled to permit uniform movement of inert gas. A dead-end pocket in the shielding gas flow line, such as a Y or T fitting, cannot be purged of all air, which will then continue to bleed into the shielding gas during welding. Indications of air or moisture in the shielding lines can often be recognized by discoloration of the electrode's end. In TIG or MIG welding, the electrode tip should be shiny-bright after welding has been completed.

Shielding lines should be grease- and oil-free, and preferably made of a metal such as annealed copper, or of a high-grade plastic such as Teflon or Tygon.

Prior to welding, the shielding lines, nozzles and back-up plates should be thoroughly purged, using about 10 times the volume of the shielding passage. After completion of the weld, the shielding gas should continue to protect the weld and heat-affected zone until it has cooled to below 700 F.

When using the MIG welding process, the welding wire should be hard-drawn and coiled to have a "cast" (diameter of an unimpeded coil) of about 20 in. or less to ensure good electrical contact at the guide tube. The wire should be shiny-bright, and the MIG torch should have provisions for gas purging at the point of wire entry to prevent drag of air into the torch with the wire.

Annealing should be avoided unless the weld has been cold-worked.

It may cause additional grain growth, if time or temperature is high enough, thus further reducing weld ductility. Short time heating below transformation temperature will not change weld structure or heat-affected zone, but will relieve stresses already caused by welding.

The corrosion resistance of the weld metal and heat-affected zone is comparable to wrought material, providing the weld is free from contamination. Frequently, the surface of the heat-affected zone will show poorer corrosion resistance than the fused weld metal. This is due to the concentration of any contaminants in the shielding gas at the surface of the heat-affected zone, whereas in the weld they are distributed throughout.

Welding Molybdenum

Molybdenum-based alloys and arc-cast molybdenum are best for welding. The most common of the alloys has 0.5% titanium. The alloys have more high-temperature strength than unalloyed metal, and above 1700 F are stronger than any metal previously used.

With a melting point of 4,730 F, molybdenum alloy is ideal for use in gas turbines, ramjets and rockets. In sheet form it can supply plate elements for vacuum tubes; in wire form, it is a heating element in electric resistance furnaces.

The three arc-welding methods—TIG, MIG and atomic-hydrogen—

Fig. 20-7. TIG welding of Zircaloy-2 extruded tubes is being performed here in 40-ft. dry-box. Operator views process through porthole of inert-gas welding chamber.

are most effective on relatively heavy parts and sheets more than $\frac{1}{32}$ in. thick. They have also been used on thinner sheets.

Manual arc-welding is possible, but it is not so reliable as automatic welding. Whether MIG or TIG is chosen, oxygen and nitrogen must be carefully controlled since they have a negative effect on ductility. Only purified argon and helium, therefore, can be used. Carbon dioxide cannot be used. Molybdenum alloys also can be brazed or electron-beam welded in a vacuum, or resistance welded.

Oxygen should not exceed 0.005% in the atmosphere, and nitrogen must be held well below 0.1% for maximum ductility. In conventional or careless heat-treatment, the surface may be contaminated by oxygen to a depth of several thousandths of an inch. This surface metal does not recrystallize when reheated and causes unpredictable behavior during forming or later in service. Before welding or heat-treat, surfaces must be absolutely clean. This includes the necessity for removal of surface oxidation.

Preheat for welding is optional; however, when welding complex assemblies, a preheat of 400 F has been found efficient.

Corner and edge welds are more easily made than butt welds, which in turn are less difficult than fillet welds.

Stress-relief is recommended in all cases, but timing and temperature should not be such as to allow metal recrystallization unless considerable forming is to be done. Molybdenum work-hardens in such a way as to cause properties to vary greatly in different directions; therefore, weld beads should not be peened.

Vanadium

Vanadium, used in nuclear and high-temperature applications, readily absorbs oxygen, nitrogen, carbon and their compounds with unfavorable results. Ductility of this metal is fairly good in the annealed condition, but very low when work-hardened. Therefore, any welding should be done with the metal annealed.

Welding recommendations developed for zirconium apply, in general, to vanadium.

Review Questions

1. Why are the exotic metals so difficult to fabricate?
2. What welding process is preferred for most assembly operations on the exotic metals?
3. What is the major extra precaution to be taken in shielding with inert gas?
4. Does the addition of chromium as an alloying element tend to raise or to lower the transformation point of titanium?
5. When making a single-V joint in titanium of 0.1875-in. thickness, how should the first pass be made?

CHAPTER 21

GOOD WELDS AND HOW TO MAKE THEM

The importance of welding was emphasized in the first chapter of this book. Now that the major metallurgical considerations in welding have been discussed, the reasons of why welds are preferred in joining metals will be better understood.

Welding is the only commercial method which can be used for joining metals that is capable of giving full strength to the joint. Welds having yield strength and ultimate tensile strength equal to or greater than the parent metal, are usual rather than the exception. Filler metals in welding rods and electrodes are carefully engineered, their chemical composition is rigidly controlled, and their melting and deposition by electric arc assures higher quality than is normally available in the parent metal (Fig. 21-1).

Tensile strength and toughness are the two most important properties in evaluating how well a joint will perform.

As deposited, the weld metal should have higher yield strength than the parent metal. Thus, any accidental overload of the structure or assembly will produce yield in the parent metal rather than in the weld. Since the parent metal has much greater mass than the weld, failure is less likely to occur.

The higher tensile strength of the weld metal has no adverse effect on the pieces joined by it. Below the yield point, the welded members act as a continuous beam. Table 21-1 compares typical properties of mild steel weld metal (E-60xx electrode) with those of two common structural materials—one a mild steel, the other a low-alloy high-strength steel.

The relative ductility of materials, as measured by standard elongation tests, is not ordinarily of any great significance. No more than

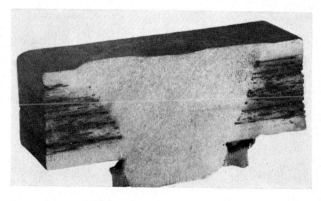

Fig. 21-1. The superior quality of weld metal relative to the parent metal is indicated by this etched section of a plug weld in mild steel plate. The more uniform homogeneous structure of the weld metal is apparent.

Table 21-1. Comparative Properties of Weld Metal

PROPERTIES	ASTM-ASME PLATE METAL		WELD METAL DEPOSITED WITH E-60XX ELECTRODE
	A-7 (Mild Steel)	A-242 (Low Alloy)	
Ult. Tensile Strength, psi	60-72,000	65-75,000	62-90,000
Yield Point, psi	33,000	50-65,000	52-86,000
Elongation, % in 2 in.	28	20-22	17-25

a few percent elongation is made use of during the usual service of a weldment. No appreciable elongation can occur until the yield point of the material has been reached. Since the structure is designed with a large safety factor, the stress is not at all likely to reach the yield point. Thus, comparisons are of little value. If the weld metal has a higher yield point than the parent metal, the possibility of its full ductility ever being needed is very slim.

When materials of very high strength but little ductility are joined in a structure, it is often desirable to weld with an electrode that will furnish weld metal of good ductility so as to minimize shrinkage stresses. But most welding is not in this category.

For lack of a better yardstick, ductility (elongation) is often asked for when toughness is the property actually desired. Toughness is not easily defined, but it is the ability to absorb energy, not only the ability to deform. This toughness is partially the result of ductility, and also is related to tensile strength.

The usual values for tensile strength and elongation are obtained from tests made at room temperature under a slow pulling load. Two metals that test the same for tensile strength and elongation may vary appreciably as the velocity of the applied load increases.

Standard impact tests provide values that represent the metal's toughness under impact but more truthfully reflect the metal's notch sensitivity. The values change radically under different types of impact, and as the size and shape of notches change.

Most failures from shock loading are related to metal fatigue, or occur at low operating temperature. Toughness evaluated at room temperature may be lost at a lower temperature. The important factor in early shock-load failures is the transition temperature of the metal—that point below which the metal fails under shock loads by brittle fracture with little or no apparent absorption of energy.

Properly designed weldments normally will not fail from shock loads, provided the transition temperature of parent metal and weld is lower than the temperature at which the weldment will operate. Where weldments are to be used outdoors or otherwise exposed to low temperatures, electrodes having low transition temperatures are desirable.

Electrode types in order of desirable transition temperatures are as follows: low-hydrogen types E-xx16 or E-xx18 (lowest transition temperature); E-xx24 and E-xx27; E-xx10 and E-xx11; E-xx13; and E-xx12 (gradually increasing to highest transition temperature).

In many cases, the fact that mild steel welds made by metal-arc welding are usually stronger than the base metal is overlooked. The tendency is to seek insurance against weld failures by building up the weld thickness. Where codes exist that cover weld specifications, these provide a safety margin. The designer calculates the required weld size and then adds a bit for good measure. The weld shop foreman looks at the print and decides he'd better increase the specified size to be safe. The job then goes to the weldor who, not knowing the chain of additions, makes the prescribed weld on the heavy side.

In the case of a fillet weld, the ¼ inch weld that becomes ⅜ inch takes twice as much filler metal!—unnecessarily. And, the overwelding may cause distortion and high locked-in stresses that actually reduce the effective yield strength.

Butt welds, too, are often overwelded. Figure 21-2 shows a set of welded tensile specimens, not one of which was welded all the way into the root. Two of these welds were reinforced by build-up, and the others tested after being ground flush with the surface. Each of these test bars failed through the parent metal and not through the

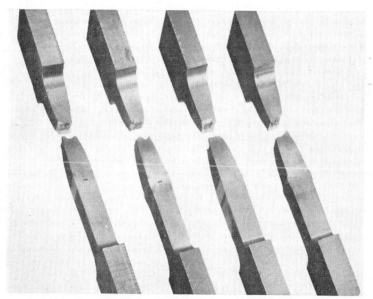

Fig. 21-2. All four butt-welded tensile bars failed in the parent metal even though weld penetration was incomplete in each case. Root opening in specimen at left is over 30% of effective throat; yet the weld held.

weld or the heat-affected zone. 100% penetration should not be specified unless loading demands it.

Welds are stronger than most people realize. Even porosity, undercuts, slag inclusions, and other "defects" have far less influence than is commonly acknowledged. Of course, some jobs must have more rigid control of these defects than others. A rotating shaft, for instance, when ground after welding will have its fatigue strength much reduced by the presence of even minute pores in the weld deposit. Titanium used in a highly stressed wing structure must not be porous.

The weldor can't be expected to investigate all the conditions under which the weldment must give service. A good weld, then, is one which meets the job specifications when they exist. Such specifications usually govern production welding and field construction, and often do not exist in repair welding.

Every Weld a Good Weld

Every weld should be a good weld. Occasionally something goes wrong. The most frequent cause of a poor weld is carelessness on the part of the weldor, generally involving a poor welding technique. "Any job worth doing is worth doing well." This saying is particularly applicable in welding.

Doing a job well does not mean overwelding. It means doing the job properly, depositing sufficient weld metal to meet the structural requirement of the job but not so much as to make it too costly. Care and pride in the work being done would help eliminate some of the defective welds produced.

The weldor should remember that properly made welds will result in products that are stronger, lighter in weight, more pleasing in appearance and generally at less cost. His continued success depends on his making good welds. If careless habits or the lack of knowledge causes him to make poor welds, these faults must be corrected.

The best means of overcoming such difficulties is to determine what causes the defect and how it may be corrected. That is how good welds may be made consistently.

Problem: Appearance of Weld

Probably the most common of welding defects is poor weld appearance. While this is not a defect which is detrimental from a structural standpoint, it most certainly detracts from the finished appearance of the weldment.

Cause—1. Failure to clean finished weld deposit. 2. Improper joint preparation. 3. Poor welding technique. 4. Failure to set current properly or improper electrode manipulation. 5. Use of the electrode in a different position than that for which it was designed.

Cure—1. Be sure to remove all slag, flux and spatter from weld bead and the adjacent base metal. 2. Use proper joint preparation:

get best fit possible. 3. Use the proper technique for the electrode selected. If the electrode is deposited with a weave, keep the motion uniform. Travel along the joint at a constant rate. 4. Do not use excessive welding currents.   5. Select an electrode designed for the position to be welded. If such an electrode is not available, position the work to meet the requirements of the electrode. Electrodes with a stable, soft quiet arc deposit beads of good appearance. Coated electrodes with this arc characteristic usually have powdered iron in their coating.

Problem: Weld Spatter

Weld spatter is an appearance defect of no consequence to the structural function of the weld. Excessive spatter is not necessary, however, and its appearance on a weldment is not pleasing.

Cause—1. Too high a welding current. 2. Wrong electrode. 3. Wrong polarity. 4. Too large an electrode.

Cure—1. Select the proper current setting for the diameter electrode and plate thickness. 2. Be sure that the electrode does not have an inherent spatter producing characteristic. Powdered-iron-coated designs of particular electrode types produce much less weld spatter. 3. Make certain the polarity is correct for the electrode. 4. Use an electrode of the proper diameter for the plate thickness.

Problem: Undercut

Undercut generally is more of an appearance defect than a structural detriment (Fig. 21-3). However, under some service conditions, an undercut may act as a stress raiser and be the start of a fatigue crack. Unfortunately, however, some inspection agencies are against undercut of any type and demand that it be chipped out and the joint rewelded. For these reasons undercut should be avoided.

Cause—1. Welding current too high. 2. Electrode diameter too large. 3. Improper electrode manipulation. 4. Use of the welding electrode in a position other than that for which it was designed.

Cure—1. Use a moderate welding current and do not try to weld too rapidly. 2. Use a smaller diameter electrode. 3. Don't let the molten weld puddle get too large. A uniform weave of the electrode will tend to prevent undercutting when making butt welds. Excessive weaving will cause undercut and should be avoided. Undercut on the vertical plate when making a horizontal fillet weld is caused by the electrode being held too near the vertical plate. 4. Select an electrode suitable for the position required for a specific job.

Problem: Incomplete Penetration

While most of the defects discussed thus far are appearance defects, incomplete penetration may result in structural failure from one of two causes. First of all, with incomplete penetration there may not be sufficient weld metal to withstand the stresses developed in the joint Secondly, incomplete penetration may result in a cracking of the weld The fact that strength can still be maintained even though penetration is incomplete, is demonstrated by Fig. 21-2.

Cause—1. The welding speed is too fast. 2. Improper joint prep· aration. 3. Insufficient welding current. 4. The electrode used is too large.

Cure—1. Do not weld too rapidly. If the speed of travel is too fast insufficient weld metal is deposited. 2. Be sure to allow sufficient gap at the bottom of the weld. Use a back-up bar if possible. Chip or cut out the back of the joint, then deposit a back-up bead. Never expect excessive penetration from an electrode. If the plates are over $\frac{3}{16}$ in thick, play safe and bevel them. 3. Be sure to use sufficient welding current to attain proper penetration. If necessary, switch to an electrode type having deeper penetration characteristics. 4. When welding in narrow grooves, use small diameter electrodes.

Problem: Poor Fusion

Poor fusion is sometimes associated with incomplete penetration and likely it is a structural fault. Often, poor fusion cannot be detected without a radiographic examination of the weld. This difficulty is serious since it may be present in a weld that outwardly appears to be strong and perfect.

Cause—1. Improper current setting. 2. Improper welding technique 3. Failure to prepare joint properly. 4. Wrong size welding electrode

Fig. 21-3. Fillet weld undercuts, up to 15% of plate cross-section in depth, did not cause tensile failure through the weld. Weld undercuts are serious only under extreme fatigue conditions.

Cure—1. Remember heavier plates require more current for a given electrode than small plates. Be sure to use sufficiently high welding current to insure correct deposition of weld metal with a good penetration of the base metal. 2. In connection with welding technique, be sure the weave is wide enough to thoroughly melt the sides of the joint. 3. In preparing the joint, be sure the face of the groove is clean and free of foreign material. 4. Use an electrode sufficiently small to reach the bottom of the groove in making the weld.

Problem: Distortion

When welding on precise work, one of the greatest difficulties confronting the weldor is that of avoiding distortion of the work. In some instances, a distorted weldment is of no value. In others, it means that considerable work must be done to return it to the desired shape. Such problems may be avoided by proper designing and the exercising of due care during welding.

Cause—1. Improper welding sequence. 2. Insufficient control of the welding heat. 3. Shrinkage of deposited weld metal, pulling parts together and changing their relative positions. 4. Failure to maintain proper dimensions by welding parts in a distorted position.

Cure—1. Before attempting to weld a new and difficult weldment, study the structure and develop a definite welding sequence. 2. Exercise care in distributing the welding heat by skip sequence, back stepping, etc., to prevent excessive local heating. Preheat is sometimes desirable to avoid an excess heat condition, particularly on heavy structures. 3. The effects of weld metal shrinkage can be minimized by preforming the parts sufficiently to compensate for weld shrinkage. Clamping or tack welding the parts will also help resist shrinkage. The higher welding currents and speed available with submerged-arc and vapor-shielded arc welding result in minimum weld shrinkage and distortion. 4. Be sure the various parts of the weldment are properly aligned prior to starting welding. Preheating may be helpful prior to welding since it will tend to relieve stresses brought about by rolling or forming.

Problem: Warping

While heavy plates may tend toward distortion, thin plates are very easily warped during a welding application. When working with thin gage material, care must be exercised to avoid warping it. This defect may not structurally weaken the part, but the finished weldment will certainly be less pleasing to the eye. Additionally, the warped weldment may not function properly when put to use. Warping, in some instances, may be removed by flame heating applications. It is best, however, to follow a welding program that will hold warping to a minimum.

Cause—1. Improper preparation of the joints to be welded. 2. The wrong welding procedure. 3. Failure to clamp parts properly. 4. Excessive local heating in the area of a weld. 5. Shrinkage of deposited weld metal.

Cure—1. Be careful of the fit-up when it comes to joint preparation. Do not have excessive space between the parts to be welded. Where there is likely to be shrinkage despite all normal precautions, hammer the joint edges thinner than the rest of the sheet before welding. This will elongate the edges so that weld shrinkage will cause them to pull back to their original shape. 2. To avoid shrinkage use a back step or skip sequence welding procedure. 3. Clamping the parts adjacent to the joint will tend to eliminate shrinkage. If possible use a back-up bar to increase the speed of cooling the weld. 4. In welding thin-gage material, weld as rapidly as possible to prevent excessive local heating in the vicinity of the weld. 5. To avoid shrinkage of the weld metal, use a high speed welding electrode with moderate penetrating characteristics.

Problem: Cracks

Cracks in a weld usually indicate weld failure or at least the start of a condition that may lead to weld failure if it is not corrected. There are many kinds of cracks in welds, some of which are more serious than others. Even so, all types of cracks should be considered as points of weakness and steps taken to eliminate their cause and occurrence.

The most common cracks in and about a weld joint are crater cracks, underbead cracks and longitudinal cracks. Cracks along the edge of the weld are sometimes referred to as toe cracks, then there are also hairline cracks across the weld and micro-cracks.

While these various cracks appear in different parts of the weld and result from different causes, identification and elimination of the basic fault leading to such structural defects will result in crack free welds.

Cause—1. The base metal is not of a weldable grade material. 2. Improper preparation of the weld joints. 3. Wrong welding procedure. 4. The weld joint is too rigid. 5. Welds too small for the size of the parts being joined in the structure.

Cure—1. Avoid trying to weld a high-sulphur, high-phosphorus steel. If necessary to weld this type of base metal, use a low-hydrogen electrode. If the carbon content of the metal being welded is over 0.45% carbon, preheat prior to welding. 2. In preparing joints for welding, space the members uniformly so the gap is even. In some instances this may mean there is a gap in the welding groove while in other instances the parts may be welded closely together. The size of the weldment and the welding problem at hand will determine the gap spacing. Be sure surfaces to be welded are completely free of dirt, oil, moisture or other contamination. 3. Be sure the welding procedure is such as to provide sound welds of good fusion. The welding sequence should allow the open ends of the weldment to move as long as possible. Avoid stringer bead welding if cracking is a problem; use a weaving technique to make a full size weld, doing the job by sections 8 or 10 in. long. Crater cracks may be eliminated by filling the weld crater at the end of each bead. Preheating the parts to be welded is often helpful in avoid cracked welds. If electrodes are of type whose performance is affected by moisture pick up, be sure they are thoroughly dried before using. 4. Be sure the structure to be welded has been designed properly and a welding procedure developed to eliminate rigid joints. 5. Always be sure the weld bead is of sufficient strength to withstand the stresses that might develop from the heat of welding. Do not use too small a weld bead between heavy plates. Be sure to use welds of sufficient size on all joints.

Problem: Porosity

Porosity in welds does not normally present a problem from a strength standpoint, unless the weld is extremely porous. Uniformly distributed porosity that is microscopic in size may be beneficial under some service conditions. Surface holes in the weld bead are undesirable from an appearance standpoint and can be starting points for fatigue cracks or result in other defective weld conditions. Weld imperfections closely related to porosity are blow holes, gas pockets and slag inclusions. These conditions tend to weaken the weld much more than ordinary porosity.

Cause—1. One of the major causes of porosity is poor base metal. 2. Improper welding procedure also results in porosity of weld metal. 3. Porosity may be an inherent defect of the welding electrode being used.

Cure—1. Be sure the base metal is one that will produce a porosity-free weld. High sulphur, phosphorus and silicon steel sometimes produce gaseous combinations which tend to make blow holes and gas pockets. Non-ferrous material high in oxygen also tends to result in porous welds. Base metal containing segregations and impurities contribute to porosity. 2. The welding procedure has much to do with the soundness of finished welds. Do not use excessive currents but be sure that each layer of weld metal is completely free of slag and flux before depositing another layer. Puddle the weld, keeping the metal molten sufficiently long to allow entrapped gases to escape. Use a weaving pass in making the weld since a series of stringer beads is apt to contain minute pin holes. 3. Since some electrodes have a tendency to produce sounder welds than others, try to use such electrodes in making welds. Most low-hydrogen electrodes will be found helpful in eliminating porosity. When using the submerged arc process, be sure the flux is suited to scavanging gaseous elements. When using bare electrodes, thorough drying of them or selection of a type that has a copper flash coating will eliminate oxygen or hydrogen being introduced into the weld from moisture on the surface of the electrode.

Problem: Brittle Welds

Brittleness in a weld is a very undesirable characteristic. This weakness, though generally not readily apparent, might result in a weld failure under conditions of extreme loading or shock. Brittle welds can and must be avoided if the desired life and maximum efficiency are to be obtained from a weld joint. This type of weld is not desirable under any condition even though it may be a type of weld that produces an extremely hard deposit which might seem satisfactory for overcoming abrasive wear.

Cause—1. The most general cause of the brittle weld is the use of excessive welding heat in the making of a weld. 2. Welding high carbon or alloy base metals without proper considerations. 3. Improper joint preparation. 4. Failure to use a satisfactory welding electrode.

Cure—1. Avoid excessive welding heats as they may result in a coarse grain structure and burnt metal which tend to result in a brittle weld. 2. If there is any likelihood of a brittle weld, exercise care in selecting the base metal. It should not be welded until the analysis and welding characteristics are known. In some instances the weld deposit may absorb alloying elements from the base metal to make it hard and brittle; lower welding current and faster electrode travel will decrease penetration and admixture. Multiple layer welds will provide upper layers of less alloy content and greater strength. 3. Improper welding procedure or base metal preparation often results in brittle welds. When welding on medium carbon (above 30% carbon) or certain alloy steels, the weld zone may become hard and brittle as a result of rapid cooling. Avoid this by preheating to 300 to 500 F prior to welding. While a single pass deposit may tend to embrittle, multiple pass welds will result in annealing of the hardened zone to produce a refined structure in the weld deposit that lacks brittleness. Annealing at 1100 to 1200 F after welding will generally reduce hardened areas formed by welding. 4. Use a coated electrode that will deposit metal which when mixed with base metal will provide a weld metal of nonbrittle composition.

Problem: Corrosion

The corrosion of weld deposits on base metal after welding is an undesirable characteristic. While this corroded condition may not be classified as either a structural or appearance defect, it is undesirable and may lead to one or the other of these defects by its persistence. Welds that corrode may eventually fail because of cracks and other defects resulting from corrosion. The light metals are especially susceptible to corrosion as are the unstabilized stainless steels.

Cause—1. Improper weld deposit for the corrosive working conditions. 2. Failure to clean weld deposit and base metal after welding. 3. Metallurgical effects of welding.

Cure—1. Corrosion will be a problem when the weldment incorporates a material that corrodes readily when exposed to corrosive atmosphere. Exercise extreme care in selecting the base and filler metals of weldments to be subjected to corrosive atmosphere. This selection should be based on the best metallurgical knowledge of the material to withstand corrosion. 2. Be sure to completely remove flux and other materials deposited on the base metal which might tend to accelerate corrosion. It is extremely essential that the light metals, such as aluminum and magnesium, be thoroughly cleansed of their fluxes, since the welding flux used on these materials is of a highly corrosive type. 3. When welding stainless steel, use a filler metal equal to or better than the base metal. When the application calls for an austenitic material, an extra-low carbon or stabilized stainless base metal is preferable to avoid corrosion after welding. Otherwise, carbide precipitation in the heat-affected zone of the stainless may result in a loss of the corrosion resisting qualities. These qualities can be restored after welding, however, by annealing the weldment at 1900-2050 F.

Problem: Magnetic Arc Blow

Magnetic arc blow, or *arc blow*, as it is more commonly known, is a difficulty sometimes encountered in welding in tight places using a DC power source. The magnetic field developed causes the arc to jump one way or another from the point at which it is directed. This condition naturally makes welding much more difficult and the appearance of the finished weld less pleasing.

Cause—The magnetic field developed by the DC arc causes the arc to blow away from the point at which it is directed. This difficulty is quite prevalent at the ends of joints and in the corners of weldments.

Cure—Arc blow can frequently be eliminated by proper location of the ground connection on the work. Making the ground connection in the direction the arc blows from the point of welding will often prove helpful in reducing arc blow. Separating the ground into two or more parts also is generally quite helpful. Another means of eliminating arc blow is to weld toward the direction the arc wants to jump. Use a short welding arc. In some instances the placing of a bar across the open end of a weld groove will complete the magnetic circuit to provide a path for the magnetic flux which would otherwise crowd across its arc.

If these suggestions do not eliminate arc blow, switch to AC welding which is arc blow free.

The Good Weld

It is the aim of every weldor to produce good welds. A weld is not satisfactory if it will not perform the function desired of it. Many characteristics are expected of a satisfactory weld! It should be strong, yet have sufficient ductility to withstand the service conditions to which it will be subjected. Usually, a weld is expected to be sufficiently tight to provide a leakproof joint. In some instances, this leakproof characteristic is expected to resist corrosion as well. Wear resistance, likewise, is a quality that is important, so far as welding is concerned. Appearance, likewise, plays an important role in the finished product. In fact, a satisfactory weld usually produces a product that is lighter in weight, stronger, more pleasing in appearance and generally less costly.

How to Reduce Costs

Everyone engaged in manufacturing is interested in reducing costs. Sometimes this desire is motivated by the hope of making a greater unit profit and on other occasions to permit production of lower cost products to promote greater sales. The greater the savings made possible by welded fabrication, the more widespread will be the use of various welding processes.

There are many ways in which welding costs may be reduced. Some are the responsibility of management in directing the activities of the weldor, while in other instances the weldor himself can materially reduce the costs of fabrication by welding.

Management can contribute greatly to the reduction of cost by increasing the effective time the weldor works. This can best be done by setting up a program where the weldor's activities are confined to welding with other people doing the non-welding work in connection with the fabrication. The effective time of the weldor can also be increased by providing him with convenient, comfortable working quarters.

The easiest way to increase actual welding time is to replace manual welding methods by automatic, semi-automatic or manual automatic processes. Of course, such replacing of processes can not be done without careful study to determine whether the replacement is feasible. On many operations, a change to submerged-arc welding will eliminate the cost of joint preparation. Also, such a change often reduces or eliminates preheating. On long joints and highly repetitive work, change to any method utilizing continuously fed electrode wire eliminates time required for changing electrodes and also eliminates the waste of electrode ends.

Good Equipment Essential

In any welding operation, if the weldor is expected to do an efficient job of welding, working at a maximum duty cycle, he must have equipment with which he can work. The welding equipment must be good and in good condition. In arc welding for example, he should have an electrode holder that will stay cool and does not require work stoppage to permit cooling of the holder. He should be provided with efficient welding jigs. If preheat is required, efficient equipment must be provided for this purpose. The welding machine should be located so that current adjustment may be made quickly and easily. Electrodes should be readily available and of a type that may be slagged easily.

It is also essential that the material with which the weldor is to work is clean. A weldor cannot be expected to be efficient and make sound welds if much of his time is spent in trying to weld over rusty or greasy metals or if he has to take time to clean the work before he can start his job. If chipping and peening are required, adequate air tools should be provided to handle such jobs.

On production welding jobs, particularly where the weldor is engaged in the fabrication of repetitive articles, the parts should be pre-assembled in jigs so that the weldor is welding a high percentage of his time. If the job is one that requires multiple-pass deposits, the products being fabricated should be arranged in welding stages so that the weldor can move from one to another, when cooling between deposits is required. In this way, many parts will be in process at one time and little time will be lost waiting for them to cool down.

Increasing Speed Reduces Costs

The cost of nearly any welding operation can be reduced provided the speed of welding is increased. Care must be exercised, however, to be sure that an increase in the speed of welding does not result in a reduction of the weld quality.

Since much of today's production welding is by arc welding methods, there are many ways in which the speed of this process may be increased. Preheating the work always provides a means of increasing welding speed; likewise the use of readily weldable base metals makes possible welding at a high speed.

The use of the highest welding current practical together with the largest practical welding electrode will give a high *melt-off rate*, meaning that more metal is deposited in a given length of time. The type of electrode is also a key to the speed at which it may be deposited. The E-602x series electrodes have a high melt-off rate. The E-6014 and E-6012 are medium high and the E-6013 is medium while the melt-off rate of E-6010 and E-6011 electrodes is low. Vapor-shielded arc welding and submerged-arc welding both permit high deposition rates.

Welding in the flat position or positioning the work so that welding might be done in the flat position offers a means of increasing the speed at which welding is done. Changing the polarity will increase the speed of melt-off on some electrodes but it nearly always is at the sacrifice of some other properties of the electrode. The speed at which weld metal is deposited may also be increased by using the shortest possible arc and if possible by dragging the electrode. Heavily coated electrodes often permit this, whereas bare electrodes don't.

In building up a surface where the highest quality of weld metal is not necessary, applicator bars or similar fill-in bars or rods may be welded in place. Where high quality weld metal is desired on build-up, it is often possible to feed in an additional metal through a second electrode. This electrode is held in the hand and melted into the base metal by the electrode connected to the holder. In this manner twice as much weld metal is deposited in a given period of time. Hardsurfacing can be greatly speeded and costs reduced by using submerged-arc welding.

Decreased Power and Material Costs

Welding costs may be reduced by studying the problem at hand and selecting the least expensive welding procedure that will produce satisfactory results. This can best be done by taking in consideration the first cost of the equipment, its maintenance cost, portability, the availability of power, gases and other materials. Be sure that the material being used on the job is necessary.

Often, costs may be reduced by using less expensive base metal which will produce highly satisfactory results. Likewise, use the least expensive welding electrode or rod that will secure the desired results. If the job is one of arc welding, burn the electrode down to the shortest possible stub. When using expensive electrodes, for example as in hardsurfacing, use the stub by arcing the stub to the end of the new electrode. Using coil-fed continuous electrode eliminates this problem. Also, submerged-arc welding generally permits more economical application of high-alloy materials in the flux rather than in the expensively fabricated electrode.

Placing the arc welding machine power switch in the welding booth enables the weldor to cut the machine off when it will not be needed for a long period of time. With gas welding equipment, use gas-saver equipment to cut down the consumption of welding gases when the torch is not in use.

Reduce Amount of Welding

Another effective way of reducing welding cost is to reduce the amount of welding required on a job. Care must be exercised here to insure that a finished weldment will have adequate strength. In some instances, the amount of welding may be reduced without materially affecting the strength, because the weld is stronger than needed. In these cases intermittent welding might serve as well as the continuous weld specified. Likewise, it is possible to reduce the amount of welding required by redesigning the weld section or by eliminating build-up which rarely gives added strength. When reducing the strength of a weld joint by reducing the amount of welding, always be sure that the safety factor meets the requirements established for the service conditions.

The higher welding currents and speed of submerged-arc welding greatly reduce the amount of filler metal required in a joint. Under certain conditions, inert-arc welding eliminates the need altogether although the cost of the shielding medium must be considered.

The amount of welding can be reduced without lowering the original strength of the weld joint. This is done by using a higher strength welding electrode or rod which will permit a reduction in the amount of weld metal deposited without changing the overall strength of the weld joint. Likewise, a deeper penetrating filler material or deeper penetrating welding procedure will produce similar results. Frequently a weld joint may be redesigned; for example, a small welding groove may be one way to produce a more efficient joint.

Never be guilty of making oversize welds that then necessitate grinding or machining them to the base metal just for the sake of appearance. Weld to size and make them of such pleasing appearance that you and your customer will be happy to see the unfinished weld surface.

Remember, though, that labor and overhead are the most expensive items in welding costs. The cost of the materials of welding are minor when compared to labor and overhead. Quality materials are essential for if they will not do the job for which they are used, it will be necessary to replace them with a resulting loss of labor.

Definitions of New Words

Arc blow. Jumping of the welding arc away from point at which the electrode is directed, a condition sometimes experienced with DC current, resulting from magnetic effects particularly when working in close quarters.

Melt-off rate. The rate at which metal is deposited from a welding electrode or rod, usually stated in terms of weight of electrode or rod consumed per unit of time.

Review Questions

1. Which of the following will tend to increase underbead cracking, which will decrease it and which will have no effect:
    a. Preheating?
    b. Welding with work cold?
    c. Welding with an E-6010, E-6016 or coated 18-8 stainless steel electrode?
    d. High current and slow travel? Medium current and medium travel speed?
    e. Steel containing 0.20% carbon and 0.60% chromium? Steel with 0.60% carbon and 0.20% chromium?
2. Would underbead cracking be more likely in the first part of a continuous bead or in the last part?
3. Can underbead cracking be eliminated by following a weld bead with a second weld bead?
4. How does preheating affect the tensile strength, the ductility, the hardness and the impact strength of a weld?
5. Is it possible to have magnetic arc blow during the welding of nonmagnetic materials, such as 18-8 stainless, high-manganese steel, copper, etc.?

Abradant. A substance which causes abrasive wear, i.e. displacement or removal of surface material by a scratching action.

Admixture. The interchange of filler metal and base metal during welding resulting in weld metal of composition borrowed from both. Limited admixture is necessary to complete metallurgical union across the joint.

Agglomerated flux. A granulated flux for submerged-arc welding to which any alloying elements can be added without loss of individual and physical identity. Thus, during welding no complex chemical compounds in the flux need be broken down before the alloying element is free to enrich the weld metal as intended.

Aging. The recrystallization that occurs over an extended period of time, resulting from austenite or other normally elevated-temperature structure being retained at a temperature and under conditions where it has no permanent stability. The result may be a change in properties or dimension. Under some circumstances, aging can be advantageous.

Air-hardening. Characteristic of a steel that becomes partially or fully hardened (martensitic) when cooled in air from above its critical point. Not necessarily applicable when the object to be hardened has considerable thickness.

Allotropic change. The shifting of atoms relative to one another, resulting in a change in the state or structure of a material. Certain metals are allotropic in that their atoms can rearrange from one crystal structure to another at certain critical temperatures, each structure having distinct properties and stable within definite limits of temperature and pressure.

Alloy. A material having metallic characteristics and made up of two or more elements, one of which is a metal.

Annealing. The process of softening a metal by heating it, usually above the upper critical temperature, and then cooling it at a slow rate.

Arc blow. Jumping of the welding arc away from point at which the electrode is directed, a condition sometimes experienced with DC current, resulting from magnetic effects particularly when working in close quarters.

Atom. The smallest unit of an element which can take part in a chemical reaction.

Austenite. A solid solution of carbon or iron-carbide in face-centered cubic iron.

Automatic welding. Welding with equipment that automatically controls the entire welding operation (including feed, speed, etc.). In arc welding, the electrode or welding rod supplying filler metal is fed automatically into the arc to compensate for its melt-off and thus maintain the correct length of arc. Granulated flux or shielding gas, when called for by the specific process, is also fed automatically through the welding head.

Bainite. An aggregate of needle-like ferrite and carbide particles. It is tougher than martensite and harder than austenite or pearlite.

Base metal. Often called *parent metal,* the metal used in workpieces being joined together.

Blowhole. A defect in metal caused by hot metal cooling too rapidly when excessive gaseous content is present. Specifically, in welding, a gas pocket in the weld metal resulting from the hot metal solidifying without all of the gases having escaped to the surface.

Brittleness. The tendency of a material to fail suddenly by breaking, without any permanent deformation of the material before failure.

Carbide. The chemical combination of carbon with some other element. A metallic carbide takes the form of very hard crystals.

Carbide precipitation. As a result of prolonged heating or of slow cooling after partial or full transformation, atoms of carbon and a metallic element migrate to the grain boundaries. The atoms here gather and combine as carbides. In high chromium alloys, the affinity (attraction) of chromium and carbon for each other leads to the formation of a thin intergranular layer of chromium carbides.

Carbon equivalent (as used in ferrous metallurgy). The relationship of carbon, sulphur and phosphorus content as to the combined effect of these alloying elements on certain properties of the material. In the United States, this is considered to be the total carbon, plus one-third of sulphur and phosphorus content by percentage of weight. NOT to be confused with:

Carbon equivalent (as used in welding only). The relationship of carbon and various alloying elements as to their effect on the cracking of weldments by the formation of hardness zones.

Case. A thin layer of metal below the surface having composition, structure or properties distinctly different from the main body, or core, of the part.

Cementite. Iron carbide (Fe_3C) constituent of steel and cast iron. It is hard and brittle.

Coated electrode. A consumable metal arc-welding electrode having a relatively thick covering around the core of filler metal. As the covering melts off, it stabilizes the arc and provides the chemicals needed for removing impurities from the weld metal.

Cold shortness. The characteristic tendency of a metal toward brittleness at room temperature or lower.

Cold welding. The microscopic fusion of high spots on the metallic surfaces in contact under great pressure. Often a factor in the wear of two sliding members, where the heat from friction or resistance to movement caused by surface irregularities promotes such fusion and further movement causes the weaker member to rupture locally in the form of "galling." Cold welding is also a method of permanently joining certain metals, especially aluminum.

Combined carbon. This is the percentage of carbon that is combined with metal atoms in a crystal constituent of an alloy, as is the iron-carbide cementite commonly found in steels and cast irons.

Composition. The contents of an alloy, in terms of what elements are present and in what amount (by percentage of weight).

Compressive strength. The resistance of a material to a force which is tending to deform or fail it by crushing.

Constituent. A physically and chemically homogeneous portion of a crystal system visible under the microscope. Solid phases in an alloy may be elemental metals, solid solutions or compounds.

Consumable electrode. A metal electrode that establishes the arc and gradually melts away, being carried across the arc (deposited) to provide filler metal into the joint.

Core. The innermost mass of metal having composition, structure or properties distinctly different from the outer or surface metal, known as the case.

Crack propagation. The development, growth, or progress of a crack through a solid.

Crater cracks. Cracks across the weld bead crater, resulting from hot shrinkage.

Creep. The slow deformation (for example, elongation) of a metal under prolonged stress. Not to be confused with that deformation which results immediately upon application of a stress.

Critical cooling rate. A rate of cooling that is fast enough to transform austenite into 100% martensite.

Critical temperature. See "transformation temperature."

Crystal. A solid body whose atoms are arranged in a definite pattern which repeats itself in various directions, corresponding with growth in size of the crystal.

Curie point. The temperature at which a cooling metal (iron, nickel or cobalt or an alloy of these) becomes magnetic. At temperatures above this point, the normally magnetic material is nonmagnetic.

Decarburization. The loss of carbon from a ferrous alloy in a reactive atmosphere at high temperatures.

Deoxidizing. The removal of oxygen from the molten weld metal, usually by chemical combination with other elements forming inorganic compounds that float to the surface of the molten metal to form slag when cooled.

Deposition rate. The speed with which filler metal is added to a weld joint, usually stated in terms of volume of metal deposited per minute.

Differential hardening. (1) The characteristic of certain steels to develop high surface or case hardness and to retain a tough, soft core. (2) Any hardening procedure designed to produce only localized or superficial hardness.

Ductility. The ability of a material to become permanently deformed without failure.

Elastic limit. The maximum stress to which a material can be subjected without permanent deformation or failure by breaking.

Elasticity. The ability of a material to return to original shape and dimensions after a deforming load has been removed.

Element. A substance which can't be broken down into two other substances. Everything on Earth is a combination of such elements, of which there are only 103.

Elongation. The stretching of a material by which any straight-line dimension increases.

Eudurance limit. The maximum stress that a material will support indefinitely under variable and repetitive load conditions.

Eutectoid mixture. A mixture of two or more constituents, formed on cooling from a solid solution, to which state it can return again when heated.

Fatigue failure. The cracking, breaking or other failure of a material as the result of repeated or alternating stressing below the material's ultimate tensile strength.

Fatigue limit. The maximum stress that a material will support indefinitely under variable and repetitive load conditions.

Fatigue strength. The resistance of a material to repeated or alternating stressing, without failure.

Ferrite. Pure iron of body-centered cubic crystal structure. It is soft and ductile.

Ferrous. Descriptive of a metallic material that is dominated by iron in its chemical composition.

Fill welds. Welds in which a filler metal is deposited into the joint from an electrode or welding rod, fusing with the base metal on each side.

Filler metal. The metal which is deposited into the joint from an electrode or welding rod in order to achieve a weld of desired properties.

Flux. A fusible non-metallic material that dissolves and prevents further formation of metallic oxides, nitrides or other undesirable inclusions within the weld.

Forge welding. A process of joining metals by pressure, usually with the assistance of heat but at temperatures below that at which there would be true fusion.

Free carbon. This is the percentage of carbon that is not combined and usually exists as free atoms at grain boundaries, or in the form of pure carbon flakes of graphite.

Freezing. The solidification of a hot liquid metal. In the case of pure iron, this starts and ends at the same temperature. With the addition of carbon, freezing starts at one temperature and ends at a lower temperature.

Fusion. Melting of metal to the liquid state, permitting two contacting or neighboring surfaces to partially exchange their contents with the result that there is a thorough blending of the compositions after cooling.

Fusion line. The junction between the metal that has been melted and the unmelted base metal.

Fusion welds. Welds in which the two metal members to be joined are fused directly to each other, without the addition of filler metal from consumable electrode or welding rod.

Grain. The crystalline body which may be viewed under a microscope as having definable limits.

Grain boundaries. The irregular separations of adjacent crystals that are oriented in different directions and therefore cannot join in a continuation of the basic lattice pattern.

Grain growth. The increase in size of individual crystals as the result of absorption within a crystal of atoms at the grain boundaries, or of the wedding of adjacent similarly-oriented crystals.

Graphitic carbon. Free, uncombined carbon existing in a metallic material, in the form of flakes.

Hard crack. See "underbead crack."

Heat-affected zone. The portion of the base metal, adjacent to a weld, the structure or properties of which have been altered by the heat of welding.

Hot crack. Also known as "auto crack," resulting from stress concentration in relatively thin weld metal that is last to freeze. Both root cracks and crater cracks are forms of hot cracking.

Hot shortness. The characteristic tendency of a material toward brittleness at elevated temperatures.

Hot shrinkage. A condition where the thin weld crater cools rapidly while the remainder of the bead cools more slowly. Since metal contracts or shrinks as it cools, and this shrinkage in the crater area is restrained by the larger bead, the weld metal at the crater is stressed excessively and may crack.

Inert gas. A gas, such as helium or argon, which does not chemically combine with other elements. Such a gas serves as an effective shield of the welding arc and protects the molten weld metal against contamination from the atmosphere until it freezes.

Inoculants. Alloying combinations added to a cast iron for the purpose of modifying its microstructure, and therefore its mechanical and physical properties. Usually functions in gray iron by forming nuclei (when added just before casting), thereby accelerating the separation of carbon and fine distribution of the resulting graphite flakes.

Instant hardness. The hardness of a metal at an elevated temperature as determined by removing the metal sample from the heat and instantly punching it with a standard indentation point and load, then measuring the indentation after cooling to get the hardness value.

Intergranular corrosion. As a result of carbide precipitation, the loss of chromium from the austenite crystals adjacent to grain boundaries weakens the material's resistance to corrosion.

Interpass temperature. When making multiple-pass welds, the lowest temperature of the deposited weld metal at the time the next pass is started.

Interrupted quenching. Any quenching procedure that cools the metal part way in one medium or at one rate, and then completes the cooling in another medium or at another rate. Term is usually applied only where the temperature at point of interruption is in the critical or immediately sub-critical range, and where the metal is held for a definite period at the temperature of interruption.

Lamination. An elongated defect in a finished metal product, resulting from the rolling of a welded or other part containing a blowhole. Actually, the blowhole is stretched out in the direction of rolling.

Load. The amount of a force applied to a material or structure.

Lower critical temperature. The temperature at which an alloy completes its transformation from one solid structure to another, as it cools.

Malleablizing. The process of annealing and cooling white cast iron so as to transform some of the combined carbon to graphite. Also used to describe the heat treatment after welding or other operations for restoring the original malleable structure.

Manual welding. Welding in which the electrode is in fixed position in a holder held by the weldor, who guides it along the joint while maintaining the proper arc gap.

Martensite. A structure resulting from transformation of austenite at temperature considerably below the usual range, achieved by rapid cooling. It is made up of ultra-hard, needle-like crystals that are a supersaturated solid solution of carbon in iron.

Matrix. The principal, physically continuous metallic constituent in which crystals or free atoms of other constituents are embedded. It serves as a binder, holding the entire mass together.

Mechanical property. A material's ability to resist or withstand a particular kind of physical force applied against the material. This ability is measurable by mechanical means.

Melt-off rate. Or deposition rate, the rate at which metal is deposited from a welding electrode or rod usually stated in terms of weight of electrode or rod consumed per unit of time.

Metal. An element that has all or most of these characteristics: solid at room temperature; opaque; conductor of heat and electricity; reflective when polished; expands when heated and contracts when cooled. For all practical purposes, we also use the word metal in speaking of many alloys—materials having metallic characteristics, even though they may contain more than one element including non-metals.

Metallurgy. The science and technology of extracting metals from their ores, refining them, and preparing them for use.

Microconstituents. Structural components of a metallic body that are not continuous but appear as crystalline members of a larger mass when viewed through a microscope.

Micro-cracks. Cracks or fissures in a metallic structure which cannot be seen except with the aid of a microscope.

Microshrinkage. Shrinkage of individual crystals or crystal "trees," that tend to pull away from each other. Such shrinkage is microscopic, as opposed to shrinkage that tends to change the over-all dimensions of the entire body.

Microstructure. The detailed structure of a metal or alloy, as revealed by microscopic examination, showing the various continuous phases as well as any non-metallic inclusions.

Modulus of elasticity. The ratio of tensile stress to the strain it causes, within that range of elasticity where there is a straight-line relationship between stress and strain. The higher the modulus, the lower the degree of elasticity.

Mushy stage. The elevated temperature range during which a metal or alloy is essentially a liquid with a varying content of solid crystals.

Non-consumable electrode. A carbon or tungsten welding electrode that merely establishes the arc and maintains it, without being melted.

Non-ferrous. Lacking iron in sufficient percentage to have any dominating influence on properties of the material.

Ore. The rock or earth in which we find metals in their natural form.

Orientation. The principal direction in which a crystal has developed, relative to polished surface or some other reference plane.

Overheating. Sufficient exposure of a metal to an extremely high temperature for an undesirable coarse grain structure to develop. The structure often can be corrected by suitable heat treatment, cold working or a combination of these.

Pack annealing. Any annealing in which the workpiece is surrounded by inert material to prevent reaction at high temperatures. Usually this packing is done in a box-like container. Similarly, we have "pack hardening" and "pack carburizing" in which packing is done with a carbonaceous material; at high temperature the surface of the metal picks up carbon from this surrounding material and develops a hard case when cooled at a fast rate.

Parent metal. The metal to be welded or otherwise worked upon; also called the base metal.

Pearlite. A continuous granular mixture composed of alternate plates or layers of (pure iron) ferrite and (iron-carbide) cementite.

Penetration. (1) The depth below the surface of the base metal to which welding heat is sufficient for the metal to melt and become liquid or semi-liquid. Also called the depth of fusion. (2) The ability of arc or electrode to reach into the root of the groove between two members being welded.

Photomicrograph. A photograph taken through a microscope, showing a greatly enlarged area and revealing structural details not visible to the naked eye.

Physical metallurgy. That division of metallurgy applying to the changes in structure and properties of metals as a result of shaping, fabricating and treating.

Physical property. An inherent physical characteristic of a material which is not directly an ability to withstand a physical force of any kind.

Pick-up. The absorption of base metal by the weld metal as the result of admixture. Usually used specifically in reference to the migration of carbon or other critical alloying elements from the base metal into the weld metal. Depending upon the materials involved, this can be an asset and not a liability.

Porosity. The scattered presence of gas pockets or inclusions in a metallic solid.

Postheating. Heat applied to the base metal after welding or cutting, for the purpose of tempering, stress-relieving, or annealing.

Precipitates. A result of a solid solution decomposing, usually into another solid solution and the precipitate—one or more elements, atoms of which tend to group together.

Precipitation hardening. The process of heating to a temperature at which certain elements precipitate forming a harder constituent, and usually then cooling at a rate to prevent return to the original structure.

Preheating. The heating of parent metal prior to welding or cutting for the purpose of minimizing thermal shock and of slowing the cooling rate.

Process metallurgy. That division of metallurgy applying to the extracting, refining, and primary shaping of metals into a usable form.

Properties. Those features or characteristics of a metal that make it useful and distinctive from all others.

Proportional elastic limit. The stress point beyond which (1) an increase in stress is no longer proportionate to the increase in strain, and (2) an increase in stress results in permanent deformation.

Radial crack. A crack originating in the fusion zone and extending into the base metal, usually at right angles to the line of fusion. This type of crack is due to the high stresses involved in the cooling of a rigid structure.

Radiographic quality. Soundness of a weld that shows no internal or underbead cracks, voids or inclusions when inspected by x-ray or gamma ray techniques.

Recrystallization. In a metal, the replacement of deformed or dislocated crystals by new unstrained crystals. This process is usually carried out after cold working operations by heating the metal for a sustained period at a suitably high temperature.

Red hardness. The property of a metallic material to retain its hardness at high temperatures.

Refined zone. The base metal zone of fine-grained austenitic structure below the coarse-grained zone, progressing away from the weld. Metal in the refined zone was heated to the transformation temperature just long enough to recrystallize as austenite, and then cooled before the grains had time to grow.

Refractory. The quality of resistance to the effects of high temperatures, especially the ability of a material to maintain its hardness and shape. A "refractory" material has an exceptionally high melting point, in contrast to a "fusible" material which has an exceptionally low melting point.

Residual stresses. Internal stresses that exist in a metal at room temperature as the result of (1) previous non-uniform heating and expansion, or (2) a composite structure composed of a ductile constituent and a brittle one.

Reverse polarity. An arrangement of the leads from a direct current power source whereby the electrode is the positive pole and the workpiece is the negative pole of the arc.

Root. The narrowest point in the gap between two members to be welded, or the point in the gap furthest removed from the electrode. Usually these points are one and the same.

Root crack. A weld crack originating in the root bead, which is usually smaller and of higher carbon content than subsequent beads. Crack is caused by shrinkage of the hot weld metal as it cools, placing the root bead under tension.

Seed crystals. Solitary crystal units, or unit cells (often a single cube), which are formed first as metals cool and which are repetitive in three dimensions. The growth of the crystal extends outward from this original seed crystal.

Segregation. The tendency of alloying elements, under certain heat conditions, to separate from the main crystalline constituent during transformation and to migrate and collect at the grain boundaries. There they often combine into undesirable compounds.

Semi-automatic welding. Welding in which the electrode, welding rod and/or flux is fed automatically but the welding head or gun is held in the hand and guided manually along the joint.

Shielding. Primarily the protection of metal molten by the arc from oxidizing or otherwise reacting with elements in the surrounding air. Usually, the shielding also stabilizes the arc.

Slag. The non-metallic layer that forms on top of molten metal. It is usually a complex of chemicals (oxides, silicates, etc.) that float to the top of the hot molten metal. When a bead of weld metal cools, the slag "cap" on the bead can be readily chipped or ground away. In wrought iron, slag is the iron silicate constituent which is distributed throughout the pure iron in the form of threads, fibres or stringers extending in the direction of rolling.

Slip bands. Bands, visible under a microscope, stretching across a deformed polished surface and caused by numerous closely spaced parallel slip lines.

Slip lines. The parallel lines, visible under a microscope, on a specimen that has been polished and then deformed. Lines show the strain along slip planes which permitted the deformation to take place.

Slip plane. The plane within a crystal along which one layer of atoms slip, under stress, relative to another layer of atoms.

Soaking. Prolonged heating of a metal at a selected temperature.

Solid solution. A continuous crystal in which one metal remains dissolved within another, without interruption of the atomic structure of that metal.

Solution. The state in which atoms of one element are dissolved (uncombined, but held suspended) by crystals of another element.

Solution heat treatment. Heating an alloy to a suitable temperature for a sufficient period of time for one or more alloying constituents to enter into solid solution (to be dissolved by the principal grains), and then cooling rapidly in order to retain the solution at room temperature.

Space lattice. The definite geometric pattern or structure in which atoms arrange themselves, and in which a basic cell is repeated along three-dimensional lines. Each solid crystal (or "grain," if atoms are of a metal element) develops around such a space lattice.

Stabilized stainless steel. A high-chromium steel that does not lose its chromium from solid solution by precipitation, because of the addition of elements that have a greater attraction for carbon than does chromium.

Straight polarity. An arrangement of the leads from a direct current power source whereby the workpiece is the positive pole and the electrode is the negative pole of the arc.

Strain. The physical effect of stress, usually evidenced by stretching or other deformation of the material.

Stress. The load, or amount of a force, applied to a material, tending to deform or break it.

Stress crack. See "radial crack."

Stringer bead. A weld bead deposited along a straight line, without weaving. Term is usually used only when there are a number of such beads deposited parallel to each other.

Stringers. The tendency of segregated atoms of alloying elements or their compounds to attach to one another in thread-like chains.

Subcritical annealing. Heating of a metal to a point below the critical or transformation range, in order to relieve internal stresses.

Supercooled. The condition of a material that has been cooled at such a rate that it is still liquid at a temperature below its normal freezing point. In the case of a metallic material, this effect may also be the result of certain alloying elements.

Temper. (1) The amount of carbon present in the steel: 10 temper is 1.00% carbon. (2) The degree of hardness that an alloy has after heat treatment or cold-working, viz. the aluminum alloys.

Tensile strength. The resistance of a material to a force which is acting to pull it apart.

Toe crack. A crack originating at the junction between the face of the weld and the base metal. It may be any one of three types: (1) radial or stress crack; (2) underbead crack extending through the hardened zone below the fusion line; or (3) the result of poor fusion between the deposited filler metal and the base metal.

Transformation range. Unless otherwise specified, the temperature range during which a metal when cooled is changing from one type of crystal structure to the structure it will have permanently at room temperature.

Transformation rate. The rate of speed at which a metallic material changes from one state (type of physical structure) to another, as temperature of the material increases or decreases. Unless otherwise identified, it applies to the transformation of a heated material into that crystal structure which exists at room temperature.

Transformation temperature. The temperature at which a metal changes from one type of structure to another. This is usually different when heat is being added than when heat is being taken away. And usually, the transformation starts at one temperature and is completed at a slightly higher or lower point.

Transition zone. The base metal zone of mixed structure, below the refined zone, where some grains have transformed to austenite.

Ultimate tensile strength. The maximum pulling force to which the material can be subjected without failure.

Underbead crack. A crack in the hardened base metal just under the fusion line. It usually originates in the coarse-grained zone and is caused by hydrogen released from the austenite as it transforms during cooling. If cooling is rapid, the free hydrogen cannot escape to the surface and exerts tremendous pressure on the hard martensite crystals being formed. Underbead cracks occur parallel to the fusion line.

Upper critical temperature. The temperature at which an alloy begins to transform from one solid structure to another as it cools.

Weld metal. A product of fusion, the metal that was fully melted by the heat of welding.

Welding rod. Filler metal, in wire or rod form, used in the oxy-acetylene welding process and those arc welding processes wherein the electrode does not furnish the metal needed in the weld.

Work hardening. The capacity of a material to harden as the result of cold rolling or other cold working involving deformation of the metal.

Wormholing. The forming of an irregular cavity as a result of internal shrinkage during solidification of a cast material. If the casting is broken open, the cavity can readily be seen by naked eye.

Yield strength. The stress point at which permanent deformation results.

Appendix 2—MELTING POINTS OF SOME ELEMENTS

ELEMENT	CENT.	FAHR.	ELEMENT	CENT.	FAHR.
Hydrogen	—259	—434	Uranium	1,132	2,070
Oxygen	—218	—360	Manganese	1,260	2,300
Nitrogen	—210	—346	Beryllium	1,277	2,332
Phosphorus	44	111	Silicon	1,420	2,588
Sodium	97	207	Nickel	1,452	2,646
Sulphur	113	236	Cobalt	1,480	2,696
Selenium	218	424	Chromium	1,520	2,768
Tin	232	450	Iron	1,530	2,786
Bismuth	271	520	Titanium	1,668	3,035
Cadmium	321	610	Thorium	1,750	3,182
Lead	327	621	Zirconium	1,852	3,366
Zinc	419	787	Vanadium	1,900	3,450
Antimony	630	1,166	Hafnium	2,222	4,032
Magnesium	651	1,204	Boron	2,316	4,200
Aluminum	659	1,218	Columbium (Niobium)	2,468	4,474
Calcium	810	1,490	Molybdenum	2,610	4,730
Barium	850	1,562	Tantalum	2,996	5,425
Silver	960	1,761	Tungsten	3,410	6,170
Copper	1,083	1,981	Carbon	3,828	6,700

Appendix 3—KEY TO CHEMICAL SYMBOLS OF ELEMENTS

SYMBOL	ELEMENT	SYMBOL	ELEMENT
Ag	Silver	N	Nitrogen
Al	Aluminum	Na	Sodium
B	Boron	Ni	Nickel
Ba	Barium	O	Oxygen
Be	Beryllium	P	Phosphorus
Bi	Bismuth	Pb	Lead
C	Carbon	S	Sulphur
Ca	Calcium	Sb	Antimony
Cb	Columbium	Se	Selenium
Cd	Cadmium	Si	Silicon
Co	Cobalt	Sn	Tin
Cr	Chromium	Ta	Tantalum
Cu	Copper	Th	Thorium
Fe	Iron	Ti	Titanium
H	Hydrogen	U	Uranium
Hf	Hafnium	V	Vanadium
Mg	Magnesium	W	Tungsten
Mn	Manganese	Zn	Zinc
Mo	Molybdenum	Zr	Zirconium

Appendix 4—WELDING PROCESSES CHART

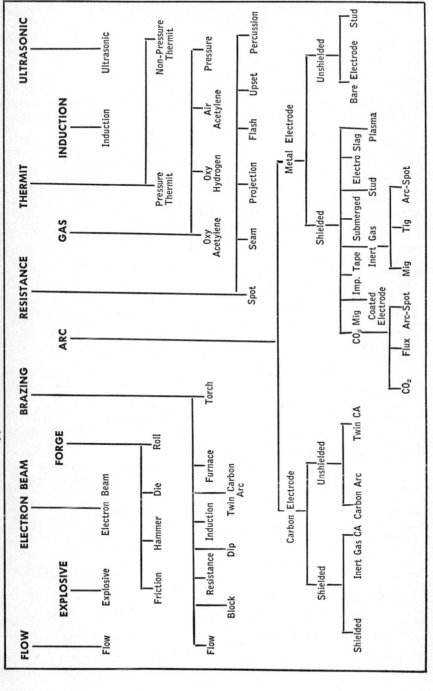

INDEX